EMILY BINGHAM

Irrepressible

Emily Bingham is the great-niece of Henrietta Bingham. She is the author of *Mordecai: An Early American
Family* and the coeditor of *The Southern Agrarians and
the New Deal: Essays After "I'll Take My Stand."* She
holds a Ph.D. from the University of North Carolina
at Chapel Hill and frequently teaches at Centre College.
She lives with her family in Louisville, Kentucky.

Irrepressible

Irrepressible

THE JAZZ AGE LIFE OF
HENRIETTA
BINGHAM

EMILY BINGHAM

FARRAR, STRAUS AND GIROUX

NEW YORK

Farrar, Straus and Giroux
18 West 18th Street, New York 10011

Published in 2015 by Farrar, Straus and Giroux
First paperback edition, 2016

The Library of Congress has cataloged the hardcover edition as follows:
Bingham, Emily.
    Irrepressible : the Jazz Age life of Henrietta Bingham / Emily Bingham. — 1st edition.
        pages   cm
    Includes bibliographical references and index.
    ISBN 978-0-8090-9464-6 (hardcover) — ISBN 978-0-374-71380-5 (e-book)
    1. Bingham, Henrietta Worth, 1901–1968. 2. Bisexual women—United States—Biography. 3. Bingham family. 4. Upper class women—United States—Biography. 5. Socialites—United States—Biography. 6. Lesbians—United States—Biography. 7. Women analysands—United States—Biography. . 8. Women alcoholics—United States—Biography. 9. Louisville Region (Ky.)—Biography. I. Title. II. Title: Jazz Age life of Henrietta Bingham.
HQ74.43.B55 B55 2015
306.76'5082—dc23

                                                                                2014039375

Paperback ISBN: 978-0-374-53619-0

Designed by Abby Kagan

www.fsgbooks.com
www.twitter.com/fsgbooks • www.facebook.com/fsgbooks

1   3   5   7   9   10   8   6   4   2

FOR STEPHEN

Herein lieth hid a Creature
Excellent beyond all nature.
Not save in her could Heaven find
Right lodgings for so fair a mind
I, over-confident before
Eyes like hers had burned me, swore
That poor women (tho' quick-witted,
Tutored, polished) should be pitied,
   All being blind.
   —

But I know one now that moves
Inch by inch my faith, & proves
Never man that walked on ground
Good & wise as she was found.—
—Half as fair again as Cressid,
All I'd give to be the blessed
   Man she loves!
   ÷

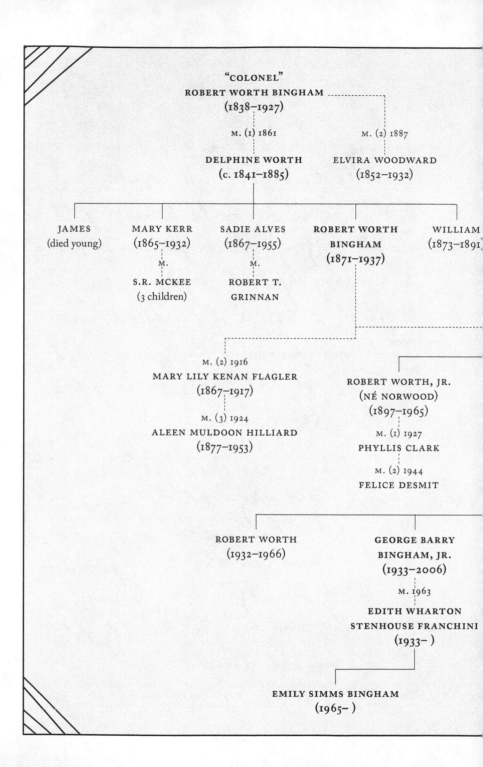

"COLONEL"
ROBERT WORTH BINGHAM
(1838–1927)

M. (1) 1861

DELPHINE WORTH
(c. 1841–1885)

M. (2) 1887

ELVIRA WOODWARD
(1852–1932)

JAMES
(died young)

MARY KERR
(1865–1932)
M.
S.R. MCKEE
(3 children)

SADIE ALVES
(1867–1955)
M.
ROBERT T.
GRINNAN

ROBERT WORTH
BINGHAM
(1871–1937)

WILLIAM
(1873–1891)

M. (2) 1916
MARY LILY KENAN FLAGLER
(1867–1917)

M. (3) 1924
ALEEN MULDOON HILLIARD
(1877–1953)

ROBERT WORTH, JR.
(NÉ NORWOOD)
(1897–1965)

M. (1) 1927
PHYLLIS CLARK

M. (2) 1944
FELICE DESMIT

ROBERT WORTH
(1932–1966)

GEORGE BARRY
BINGHAM, JR.
(1933–2006)

M. 1963
EDITH WHARTON
STENHOUSE FRANCHINI
(1933–)

EMILY SIMMS BINGHAM
(1965–)

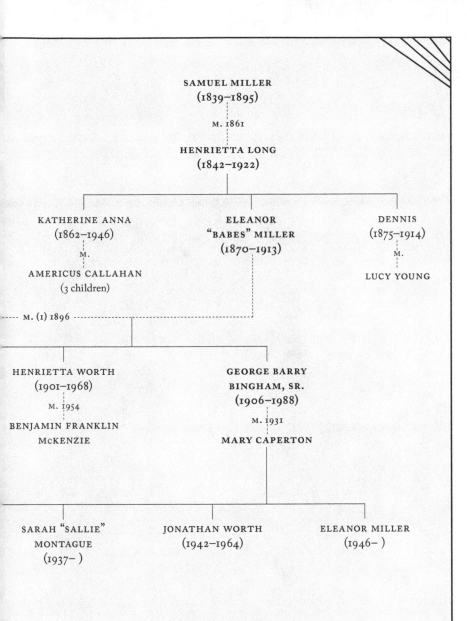

SAMUEL MILLER
(1839–1895)

M. 1861

HENRIETTA LONG
(1842–1922)

KATHERINE ANNA
(1862–1946)
M.
AMERICUS CALLAHAN
(3 children)

ELEANOR
"BABES" MILLER
(1870–1913)

DENNIS
(1875–1914)
M.
LUCY YOUNG

M. (1) 1896

HENRIETTA WORTH
(1901–1968)
M. 1954
BENJAMIN FRANKLIN
McKENZIE

GEORGE BARRY
BINGHAM, SR.
(1906–1988)
M. 1931
MARY CAPERTON

SARAH "SALLIE"
MONTAGUE
(1937–)

JONATHAN WORTH
(1942–1964)

ELEANOR MILLER
(1946–)

Bingham
FAMILY TREE

CONTENTS

PART THREE

Irrepressible

HEREIN LIETH HID A CREATURE

*T*he surest way to make a child curious about an ancestor is never to discuss her. And when it came to Henrietta Bingham, my great-aunt with the most great-aunt-like name, there was much to be curious about. Born in 1901, she came of age amid tragedy and enormous wealth, and spent much of her twenties and thirties ripping through the Jazz Age like a character in an F. Scott Fitzgerald novel. There were parties, music, great quantities of alcohol, and, on both sides of the Atlantic, lovers—lots of them, men and women, but far more women than men. In Henrietta's time, that took courage. Later there would be mental breakdowns, scandals, and a decline no one talked about. Within our family, charity meant silence when it came to Henrietta.

Long-ago forebears who defy propriety and cause wringing of hands can feel as thrilling and dramatic as fairy-tale figures, but even for those who knew Henrietta, she was an almost magical physical presence with a muse-like influence, an irresistible way of being with others.

They talked about her eyes. People had never seen "eyes like Henrietta's," "purple eyes with tangled lashes." In the absence of color photographs, their arresting hue would be lost to history were it not for her lovers' attempts to capture them in language. The actor and producer John Houseman, Orson Welles's collaborator and the winner of an Academy Award, called them "violet-blue." "Brilliantly blue," offered the novelist David Garnett. But it was not just their color. "She looks the memory of her eyes into you," a poet explained. They were "fascinating" with her "coquettish" lashes—"the eyes of a too-wise little girl." Henrietta's hair was jet, her face oval, her skin cream-white, and one companion declared she "should preach, her voice is so divine." The painter Dora Carrington called her a "Giotto Madonna."

One London night in 1923, at a party in the studio of the artist Duncan Grant, twenty-two-year-old Henrietta mixed deliciously unfamiliar cocktails, played the mandolin, and sang. Her voice, soft, low, "faintly husky," moved over "Water Boy"—a chain-gang tune later recorded by Paul Robeson and Odetta—exuding extraordinary warmth.

> There ain't no sweat boy
> That's on this mountain
> That run like mine boy,
> That run like mine.

A lament about exploitation became a seductive performance that helped establish her position as a "Kentucky princess" in the Bloomsbury Group, the high-minded bohemians who coalesced around the novelist Virginia Woolf and her sister, the painter Vanessa Bell. (Henrietta was one of very few Americans to penetrate that elite set, where conventions of marriage, art, and domestic life were often flagrantly disregarded.) Her singing violated cultural, racial, and sexual boundaries, and was just the sort of transgression she delighted in making during the Jazz Age years. But Henrietta did more than assume the accoutrements of 1920s youth culture. The Charleston and the Black Bottom, saxophones, stride piano, whiskey jugs and blues women, all then emerging from marginalized African American communities, were for her points of deep identification, sources of rapture, and proof that genius could overcome discrimination and injustice. This privileged white southern debutante taught herself to play the saxophone and promoted black performers, some of whom became her friends. It is no coincidence that these art forms bristled with eroticized energy, for Henrietta's greatest connection with the spirit of the 1920s and 1930s was the way her youth blazed with sex. The passage of time usually drains the past of desire and its fulfillment, but if Henrietta had an essence, this was it.

Her provocative acts succeeded because they drew on something deep in her, an emotional sweat that showed in the panic attacks and destructive behavior she spent years untangling in the consulting room of an eminent London psychoanalyst, Ernest Jones. Sigmund Freud's pioneering and controversial theory of the unconscious mind revolutionized twentieth-century ideas about the individual and society—and, of course, sex—and undergoing psychoanalysis offered hope of self-understanding and acceptance. At the same time, arousing others distracted Henrietta from her problems. It was deeply satisfying—and she was incredibly good at it, too. That London night in 1923, she blasted into the hearts of Dora Carrington and a sculptor named Stephen Tomlin. Like many before and many after, they couldn't drive her from their minds. They were caught, as I would be nearly a century after them, in her irresistibility.

Henrietta began as a curiosity to me, a historian who had moved home to Kentucky to raise a family. She died in 1968 when I was three—I never knew her. But my husband and I appreciated her unconventionality and liked her unfashionable Victorian name, so we gave it to our newborn daughter. Only then did my startled father tell me that to him Henrietta was a mess, an embarrassment, "a three-dollar bill." His sisters remembered her as fascinating but dangerous. To be like Henrietta, one of them told me, would mean to "never be married, never have children, and be a lesbian." But her name was again among the living and despite such judgments, relatives, family friends, and people I barely knew wanted to talk about the earlier Henrietta. They came forward with photographs, bejeweled cigarette cases, bits of gossip, a few crumbling letters, and hints about where more Henriettiana might be found.

So began my pursuit of one of the countless outsiders who populate the past. If we try hard enough, can we call them back, give them form beyond mere names and dates and whispers? I found Henrietta listed in the indexes of memoirs and biographies and scholarly volumes. Visits to archives across the United States and in England unearthed discoveries, some marginal, some mother lodes. I mined quite a few of these repositories before heeding the advice my father had offered in 2006, shortly before he died.

"You might want to look up in the attic. I think there's an old trunk of Henrietta's."

The attic was in my former home, a Georgian mansion overlooking the Ohio River on the outskirts of Louisville. Henrietta was seventeen when her millionaire father acquired the place with a legacy from America's richest woman, his second wife. An earlier, hasty look in the trunk marked H.W.B. had revealed a hodgepodge of old clothes and shoes. To figure out Henrietta's magnetism, I needed more—primarily letters and diaries—so I wasn't in a hurry to comb through the steamer chest. But on a raw January morning in 2009, I went up to the gable storeroom on the southeast side of the house. Lining the trunk were oranged London newspapers from 1937—she had apparently packed it in England during her father's last months as Franklin D. Roosevelt's ambassador to Britain. I tried on a pair of woven driving gloves and turned over a hand-tinted photograph of the mother who perished when Henrietta was twelve. There were puzzling items of finely made women's underwear marked with the initials H.T.C., and, thrillingly, monogrammed tennis clothes belonging to Helen Jacobs, the Martina Navratilova of the 1930s, with whom Henrietta became, in the parlance of the day, "close friends for a number of years."

Hours passed. The soot was making me cough. I stood up to unscrew the lightbulb hanging overhead. Then, in the garret's dimmest corner, I saw another trunk, scuffed and dented, with peeling Cunard Line stickers. I pulled out a heavy wooden Dreadnought Driver tennis racket, a slender riding whip, a first edition of Virginia Woolf's *The Years*. I was bent over and up to my armpits when my hand struck stacks of well-preserved letters.

They were love letters to Henrietta, nearly two hundred of them, from Stephen Tomlin and John Houseman. Here she was, seen through their besotted eyes. "Dearest Creature"; "Darling"; "My Angel"; "My Beloved." They had been there all my life, almost directly above my childhood bed.

Henrietta's lovers heard her voice, felt her breath on their skin, and knew her touch, but for a biographer, she came with what seemed like insuperable silences. Fewer than two dozen of the thousands of letters she posted over her lifetime have been found. Discretion explains much of this absence: same-sex couples had to protect themselves or be shunned as perverts. All was not lost, however. The following pages are a patchwork of interviews, correspondence, memoirs and novels, sheet music and poems, diaries, calling cards, paintings and newspaper clippings, tennis trophies and linen sheets, snapshots and scrapbooks—many of them from a time before cars had turn signals.

This is emphatically a work of nonfiction. I have not presumed to speak for Henrietta. Text between quotation marks comes from historical sources. Readers may close this book feeling like one of Henrietta's admirers who had the sense of "catching a glimpse of you at the end of the street and not being able to overtake you." True history, true life, is often that way.

Speeding north at night from Greenwich Village to Harlem in 1925, Henrietta counted thirteen blocks before she hit a red light. During her extraordinary and at times exhilarating rush against the ramparts of a dominant culture that did not approve of her, she strove—as we do—to resolve her terrors and to love and be loved in return.

Henrietta would hate to be seen as a victim, and this book is not a rescue operation. It is a story of one complicated person acting on her drives and her desires, finding shelter in enclaves where sexual freedom and same-sex love were tolerated, giving great pleasure and sometimes generating immense emotional distress. Although her charisma attracted powerful and ambitious people who left a mark on their time, Henrietta's sister-in-law considered her "not fundamentally a very serious person." She had a point. But Henrietta knew what it meant to live. Her power and her mystery—and her contribution—lie in the way she asserted herself and affected the hearts of others. Her allure, embodied in her low, drawling voice and piercing cerulean eyes, was her survival strategy. Henrietta, variously characterized as radiant, intoxicating, selfish, and shameful, was suppressed for years. Repressed—never.

Part One

How they are provided for upon the earth, (appearing at
    intervals,)
How dear and dreadful they are to the earth,
How they inure to themselves as much as to any—what a
    paradox appears their age,
How people respond to them, yet know them not,
How there is something relentless in their fate all times,
How all times mischoose the objects of their adulation and
    reward,
And how the same inexorable price must still be paid for the
    same great purchase.
                    —WALT WHITMAN, "BEGINNERS"

Henrietta, Asheville

1

COQUETTING

*E*arly on, a friend warned Robert Worth Bingham that a daughter could make a "fool" of a man. No child sets out to do such a thing. Still, evidence of Henrietta Bingham's extraordinary seductiveness, and the bravado that appealed to so many, can be found early in her life. Someone photographed her in a meadow, costumed as a four-year-old geisha, her raven hair crowned with white blossoms, her expression dead serious. In other pictures, turn-of-the-century sepia tones contrast with assertive, even masculine poses: commanding a tricycle, a look of pure determination on her face; astride a pony, decked out as an Indian princess with fringed chaps and a headdress; posing as a rough rider in a cowboy hat, military jacket, and someone else's boots, a cigarette dangling from her mouth. Almost from the beginning, Henrietta showed little interest in expressly feminine activities. In so doing, she invited gazes and questions.

Born at the outset of a new century, Henrietta Worth Bingham grew up in bustling Louisville, Kentucky. The leading city in what was widely called the northernmost southern state, Louisville's population was double Richmond's and four times Atlanta's. And Louisville literally

Henrietta, Fourth Street, Louisville

glowed. For five summers in the 1880s, this transportation hub in the nation's midsection hosted the Southern Exposition, featuring the world's largest installation of Thomas Edison's new electric lighting. Cement, agricultural implements, whiskey, and tobacco poured out of Louisville, and Frederick Law Olmsted's firm designed an impressive network of parks and connecting parkways.

On her mother's side Henrietta had deep roots in the River City, so-called for its placement on the great interior avenue, the Ohio. An Irish immigrant great-grandfather named Dennis Long amassed a fortune assembling steamboat engines and cast-iron cookstoves in the mid-nineteenth century. Long's heirs adapted the foundries to the municipal water systems being built from Chicago to Birmingham, and the firm became the nation's leading producer of cast-iron pipes. Dennis Long's daughter, Henrietta, married a flour mill manager, Samuel Miller, who eventually headed the Dennis Long & Company. Miller also brought a light heart and a passion for art and literature to the union, though he gave up his political aspirations (the Longs were Republicans and he had been a Democrat). Henrietta's mother, the second and most attractive of Samuel and Henrietta Miller's three children, grew up in an imposing limestone house with a mansard roof and a tower, arguably the city's most opulent residence, once described as "an exclamation in the language of High Victorian Gothic."

Samuel and Henrietta Long Miller House, 1236 Fourth Street, Louisville

Henrietta's mother, Babes, had wavy dark hair that she swept up from her forehead into a soft crown. Her mouth played with smiling even when she didn't want it to, and she had a habit of spontaneously breaking into song. However, when Babes's friends were fielding wedding proposals or starting families, darkness fell on the Miller household. For the better part of a decade, her father had been spearheading the drive to build and finance a railroad bridge over the Ohio River. A series of delays and misfortunes plagued the bridge's construction, however, and on a Saturday in December 1893, a freak gust of wind blew a crane off a span and onto a two-million-pound truss. Forty-one men were laboring on the truss when it collapsed into the frigid waters. More than half of them perished. It was national news. *The Courier-Journal*'s banner headline read ANOTHER APPALLING ACCIDENT ADDED TO THE ALREADY LONG LIST OF HORRORS—for sixteen lives had previously been lost during construction. In the wake of the disaster, Samuel Miller fell into a severe depression. His doctors sent him, with his family, to Asheville for a change of air. In the evenings, the Millers

gathered, with other guests and well-to-do locals, on the broad porch
of the fashionable Battery Park Hotel. Here Bob Bingham, a teacher at
a nearby military academy, met pretty Babes Miller before she and
the family returned to Louisville.

Eighteen months later, Samuel Miller was still battling "acute melancholia" and, accompanied by his son Dennis, had gone back to Asheville for further treatment. Twenty-five-year-old Babes journeyed from
Louisville to visit him, but as her train pulled into the station, her father
"eluded the vigilance of his son, ran between two of the [railroad] cars
and was immediately knocked down and instantly killed, two cars passing over his body." The ghastly scene deeply shocked Babes, and of course
the news raced through the resort town.

Bob Bingham offered his services. "My whole heart throbs for you,"
he told Babes.

For longer than anyone alive in 1895 could remember, the Binghams
had run a school for boys in North Carolina. The academy's history
reached back to the 1780s, when the first member of Henrietta's patro-
nymic line arrived from Scotland, having been recruited to prepare
students for the new state university at Chapel Hill. In 1895, the school
was headed by Bob's father—who fought for the Confederacy, and was
captured, released, and reenlisted in time to witness Lee surrender
at Appomattox. A subsequent honorific from the governor of North
Carolina made Bob's father "Colonel Bingham," a title he embraced to
the end of his days.

Bob Bingham's childhood had ended at fourteen with the death of
his mother. Delphine Worth Bingham, whom Bob idolized as a quin-
tessential selfless southern lady, weathered the hard times of war and
Reconstruction while keeping the (by then) military academy operat-
ing. She bore responsibility for the welfare of cadets marooned in the
school's Spartan atmosphere, and even while she lived Bob, born in
1871, may not have gotten the attention he sought. When she died, two
older sisters doted on him, but his angry bereavement continued into
his twenties, abetted by the fact that Colonel Bingham emerged from

his own catatonic grief as an even more rigid disciplinarian. Bob detested the former schoolteacher his father took as his second wife.

All the Bingham men attended Chapel Hill. Bob enrolled in 1888, but two years into his studies he transferred to the University of Virginia to pursue a course in medicine. The Bingham academy's good reputation was the result of three generations' labor, and Colonel Bingham expected his son to extend that tradition, whereas Bob looked to his mother's father, Dr. John Milton Worth, for professional inspiration. Worth, an M.D., had found a career in state politics and riches as a textile mill owner. When the Colonel refused to pay the Virginia tuition, Bob borrowed against a small legacy of Worth Manufacturing stock left by his mother.

Bob's turn from family duty came at a time when his father had taken out large loans to move the academy from near Chapel Hill west to Asheville. On a mountain overlooking the French Broad River, he erected a state-of-the-art campus—encompassing a pool, gymnasium, and fireproof dormitories—an $80,000 gamble that would take years to pay off, if it ever did. Bob wanted none of it. (Thomas Wolfe later declined an offer to teach at the school for fear of becoming "a sour, dyspeptic small-town pedant.") Bob was perfectly willing for his younger brother, Will, a student at Chapel Hill, to assume the family mantle, but just before the Asheville complex opened, Will died from a burst appendix. In the wake of this tragedy, Bob came home from Charlottesville (sans diploma) to teach Latin alongside his father. He may or may not have admitted that his difficulties in science class had boded ill for a future in medicine.

Bob badly wished himself away from "Bingham Heights" in 1895, and falling in love with Miss Miller of Louisville promised an escape. Though women pursued him, Bob told Babes that his experience with the female sex "had bred a considerable measure of contempt"; Babes, one year his elder, was different. The Millers were obviously rich, and Babes's mother openly questioned Bob's merits and intentions. Her recent family trials reinforced her determination to guard what remained of her social and financial status, and Mrs. Miller felt sure Babes could do better. Bob naturally took offense. He told Babes that if he seemed "distrustful and suspicious . . . that's the only way to save oneself from constant defeat in this so-called 'battle of life,' and I don't take to defeat very kindly." He would soon visit Louisville to explain to her mother "my present position and future prospects from a business standpoint." He lectured Babes that "as I have remarked to you before she has no ground for objection to me on the score of birth, position, character, or prospects, and I do not anticipate any long continued disapproval." Meantime, he took out a subscription to *The Courier-Journal*, the local Democratic paper, to familiarize himself with Louisville's politics, business, and social life. Babes loved him; she was also a smoother-over and devoted to her mother, who, unlike any woman Bingham had contended with, had power over him—and money.

Bob (and love) won the day. The wedding was set for June 1896, the end of the school year. The couple exchanged vows at the Episcopal Church, where Bingham willingly forfeited his family's Presbyterian- ism. The carefully scripted marriage announcement that ran in the newspaper emphasized not the legacy of Bingham educators but the bridegroom's relationship to John M. Worth, "perhaps the richest man" in North Carolina. Babes's mother was said to have signaled her disap- proval by insisting on wearing black sixteen months after her husband's suicide. Dr. Worth extended his grandson $2,500, with a stern warn- ing against indebtedness.

Working his way up in the cast-iron-pipe business that had made Babes's family wealthy was never Bingham's plan. He wanted a more public position in Louisville. Eighteen months after moving to Ken- tucky, he had obtained a law degree from the University of Louisville, passed the bar, opened a practice, and fathered a son, Robert. The young family saved money, indeed would do so for nine years of marriage, by living under "Ma" Miller's Gothic-Victorian roof.

Bob persuaded a Chapel Hill classmate, Texan-born William Watkins Davies, to join his legal practice. The two of them speculated in mining ventures in Kentucky and the West—"Dame nature holds . . . something for us and we will find it yet, by gum!" Davies exclaimed— but more than anything Bob hankered for public office. He pasted articles about state and city politics into ledgers and in time his name began appearing in the papers. Louisville politics were notoriously dirty, however, and he faced an uphill battle. Four years into his marriage, twenty-nine-year-old Bob told Babes he had aborted a run for elected office even though he felt sure that he could defeat his opponent. Bob thought it would require "a great deal of money" and he had no war chest.

Bingham's life wasn't supposed to turn out like this. He took his wife and baby boy to North Carolina to see his failing grandfather, but when John Milton Worth died a few months later the bulk of his estate went to Bob's aunt and her family. Instead of inheriting an even share of $200,000, Bob's old loan was forgiven—a mere 1.25 percent of his grandfather's wealth. One of Bingham's cousins quoted the old man saying, "Bob seems to care more for his old Grandaddy's money than the Grandady [sic] himself."

Wills generated Dickensian drama in Robert Worth Bingham's life. He went to court, claiming that his grandfather had been subject to undue influence. Driven by righteous fury, Bob wrote that to permit this travesty to stand would be "the most contemptible thing in the world."

On January 3, 1901, when Babes delivered their second child, Henrietta Worth—named for her rich great-grandfather and even richer grandmother Miller—Bob was still disputing the will. In the end, he and his sisters won $3,500 each. It was hardly the legacy he sought.

Babes admired her husband's feverish energy, his passion for whatever crossed his path, and his chivalric sense of honor—it was what made him so appealing. But he could also be reckless and exhausting. Besides his legal practice and burgeoning political interests, he joined Confederate veterans groups, fraternal organizations, gentlemen's clubs, and charitable boards. A crack shot and avid angler, he helped establish clubs for the pursuit of quail and largemouth bass. All this frenetic activity was accompanied by physical ailments. Bob suffered from eczema, intestinal problems, headaches, and high blood pressure, and one summer he took an expensive cure in Carlsbad, the Austro-Hungarian spa town. Such luxury was not unusual; other years he made solitary tours of the English countryside seeking out records of prominent ancestral origins.

His self-importance occasionally provoked ridicule. In-laws remembered Bingham's habit of practicing public speaking on the landing at Babes's uncle's Thoroughbred horse farm, holding forth before a full-length mirror like Demosthenes, his mouth full of pebbles the better to train his tongue. Bingham speechified at every opportunity, it seems. By his own admission, he could also be a "badtempered [*sic*] fool," trying his wife "with my pettiness, my little meanness of temper and disposition." His career advanced in fits and starts and he needed constant reassurance that he was in the right. Babes understood and responded generously. When Henrietta was one year old, Babes soothed her husband: "You are so perfect to me and my life with you has been perfect, so don't you forget that I always want you with me."

In 1905, when Henrietta was four, her father's political star was rising. Bingham was serving as Democratic county attorney, a plum post he won in some of the dirtiest balloting ever documented in Kentucky. Mrs. Miller never liked his political maneuvering to start with, and

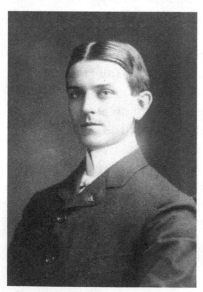

Robert Worth Bingham, circa 1905   Eleanor "Babes" Miller, circa 1905

when a sudden stock market drop left her son-in-law's account exposed, she covered his margin. Ma Miller then seized the opportunity to castigate Bob for his failures as a family man. His poor health, which she blamed on his heavy cigarette smoking, was impacting his legal practice. He had two children and Babes was expecting a third but the young family still lived for free, sharing the Miller house's single bathroom, and depended on Babes's trust fund for income. Bob had been managing the assets and distributions, but her mother announced that henceforth *she* would "invest Babes [*sic*] money for her and give her the interest. I will make no explanation to her except to say that after five years you should be able to take care of your family without her help."

To Henrietta, who came into her conscious years amid these souring relationships, the family conflict would have been difficult to untangle. Her father was the preoccupied and elusive prince; her grandmother the ever-present queen; and her mother a benignant handmaiden to them both. The turreted grandness of her grandmother's house appealed to the child. A grand piano filled a parlor where her mother sang and played. As her grandmother's favored namesake and only female grandchild, Henrietta was told the home might one day be hers.

Henrietta associated the birth of her brother in 1906 (he was named Barry after the Fifth Baron Clanmorris, an Irish peer who shared the Bingham name) with the breakup of her childhood home. Grandma Miller deeded Babes two lots on a hill edging Frederick Law Olmsted's new Cherokee Park along with $50,000. Plans took shape for a Tudor-style house with a garden for Babes and a baronial library for Bob. However, this liberating act of generosity failed to dampen the smoldering conflict between Bob and his mother-in-law. For reasons not known, Mrs. Miller asked Babes to return the deed to her, though she acceded to Bob's desperate request that the change be left out of the official records. In retaliation, perhaps, Babes appointed Sadie Grinnan, Bob's sister, as her children's guardian should she and their father die. During the same period, Bob's judgeship was in jeopardy, as the entire 1905 election was being contested. Unable to get what she needed in the emotional shuffle, Henrietta withdrew. According to her mother, the child almost never cried.

They had just moved into the new home in 1907 when Kentucky's Court of Appeals vacated the 1905 election and the governor appointed Bingham interim mayor of Louisville. A special election was set for November, and he energetically pursued his party's nomination, positioning himself as a reformer who would clean up city hall. Chasing down a relatively minor instance of corruption proved fatal to Bob's hopes, however. The previous mayor—under pressure from Bingham and others to make good on the city money he'd spent on an expensive saddle horse—shot himself. Bingham became politically toxic, an accessory to a popular man's untimely death. (Babes meanwhile spent weeks in Chicago for an unnamed operation—Barry's birth had left her weak and she may have undergone a hysterectomy.) More races followed but all ended in defeat for Bingham. In 1911, the governor appointed him to a vacant circuit court seat; although he declined to stand for election afterward, he remained for the rest of his life "Judge Bingham," and simply "the Judge" to family and friends.

While Henrietta's father sought power and influence through elected office, Henrietta, like many ambitious female children, bid for the part of honorary boy in his eyes. Weighing almost twelve pounds at birth, she was stronger and taller than other girls and many boys, too. Sports and physical activity were exhilarating for Henrietta, and a welcome break from home life. Her physical daring, competitiveness, and accomplishments won public notice. They also attracted the Judge's admiring attention. No longer very robust himself, he prized her athleticism. So Henrietta rode her tricycle like a demon and during visits to relatives roughhoused with the Asheville cadets in their Confederate gray uniforms with braided cuffs and brass buttons. The baseball team made her their mascot, setting her in front for their picture.

No record of what Babes thought of Henrietta's athleticism has survived, but her daughter's sexual precociousness was a concern. When Henrietta and a playmate went missing in Asheville, the mothers hunted high and low until they discovered the long-lashed, tousle-haired six-year-old "coqueting" young Thomas Pearson in a pony cart. Henrietta, it seems, instigated the episode. The adults tore the children from each

Robert and Henrietta with the Bingham School baseball team

other and marched them off. No one was to speak of it. Whether such conduct was part of a pattern or merely an instance of innocent exploration is not certain. Babes may have countenanced Henrietta's flirtatiousness at home as a way of bolstering Bob's spirits, for her husband had never fully recovered from the loss of his mother and depended heavily on women for emotional comfort. In any case the child got a conspicuously early start deploying her charms.

A consolation in moving to the suburbs was keeping a pony, a pinto Henrietta could collar with a rope, and which she liked to ride bareback, feeling its animal warmth. All summer, brown and white hair stuck to her long uncovered legs. Down the hill in the park's Beargrass Creek she hunted crawdaddies and spider bugs. When winter came, she sledded there, losing her stomach on the descent and puffing clouds on the climb back up, feeling roses prickle and bloom in her full cheeks.

Henrietta stood out all the more because Barry, frail from an early age, spent long days in the sick room and Robert had been sent to Asheville to be educated as generations of Bingham boys before him had been. Her tomboy role, encouraged as a sign of fortitude by her father, also set her apart from her mother, who was at home in the gender-

Henrietta, circa 1910

bound world of social visits and women's club work. How this influenced their bond is impossible to say, but it was Barry who trailed happily behind Babes as she gardened, while Henrietta swam competitively and smacked tennis balls with all her might.

In the spring of 1913, early in Henrietta's twelfth year, fate dealt the Binghams a terrific blow. The trees in Cherokee Park wore tender green gowns, Dutchman's britches pirouetted unashamedly throughout the woodland floor, and the dogwood trees sprang cream petals dotted at the center with "the savior's blood." An extended family party packed for a Sunday excursion to Grandma Miller's summer house some twenty miles outside the city. (Robert was at school and Judge Bingham, having a case to argue the next morning in Cincinnati, stayed behind to catch the train.) It was a long drive. Seven-year-old Barry dropped off to sleep in his mother's lap while Uncle Dennis Miller guided the six-cylinder "machine" around the carriages and wagons that still made up most of the traffic in Louisville's outskirts. As they reached a country store, Babes's brother slowed to a stop and took out his handkerchief to wipe his eyeglasses. Just ahead, the road crossed two railroad lines. A commuter train was rumbling down its track. Everyone assumed Dennis was aware of this, but, as reported in the newspaper, he replaced the handkerchief and put the car into gear.

The passengers screamed, but it was too late. The collision threw a Chicago cousin from the car, which broke in two against a telephone pole. Dennis walked away unhurt, but Barry was unconscious and Babes, in silence, bled severely from the head. When Barry came to, his mother was being loaded into a passenger train for transport to the hospital and Henrietta was crying hysterically. At some point the Cincinnati-bound L & N carrying the Judge passed the scene. He was oblivious as he worked on his briefs. Surgeons would remove a piece of crushed skull from Babes's brain, but it was no use. Henrietta never saw her mother alive again.

Bob's sister Sadie brought Robert up from Asheville, and after the burial the sixteen-year-old remained in Louisville. The Asheville family advised against this and urged that Robert complete his studies at the Bingham School. But, having lost the woman he loved and who legitimized him, the Judge could not part with his children. No one survived Babes's death without severe emotional injury. Bingham was simultaneously grieving his spouse and reliving, through his offspring, the memory of losing his own mother at roughly their age. He would never be able to let them stray far from him or lead fully independent lives. Only Robert got away—by crawling into a bottle.

For each child, the Judge ordered a miniature of their mother's wedding portrait with its mischievous closed-mouth smile. In going through her possessions, he put aside a piece of her favorite lace and stowed it in a desk drawer where he could reach it and remember. He stoically pressed ahead, going to work and attending civic meetings, but in the depths of his sadness he would slip away to a movie house around the corner from his law office and sit there alone while a projectionist screened a home movie. He and Babes were in each other's arms at a Louisville ball, waltzing, twirling. She smiled at him once more.

The children struggled, the boys most obviously. Shock rendered Barry nearly mute. By one account, he walked only on tiptoe for months. Unable to bear to see the child this way, Judge Bingham packed him off to Asheville for the mountain air and care of doting aunts. He was kept in bed so long that when he did get up he could scarcely walk. Visits from his family were precious to Barry; he felt particularly drawn to his sister's irreverent humor and posture of cool fortitude.

Robert, the eldest son, tried to please the Judge after Babes died, officially changing his name from Robert Norwood Bingham to Robert Worth Bingham, Jr. But something in the boy seemed broken. He exhibited no emotions at his mother's death and openly resented the mourning period that kept him off the dance floor at parties. On one occasion, he became so frustrated at being sidelined that he leapt on-stage and took over from the drummer. Babes had probably acted as a buffer against paternal expectations for their firstborn. Now, insecure in spite of his movie star looks and formerly respectable marks in Asheville, Robert was a disappointment in class and complained about his teachers. His peers even immortalized his underperformance. Beneath Robert's yearbook picture were inscribed the damning lyrics:

> He came to us for knowledge all athirst
> But his books he has forsaken
> So our faith in him is shaken,
> And oh, we hoped so much for him at first.

Moody, entitled, and increasingly rebellious, he ended his high school career with a bender.

2

PRETTY BOXES

*H*enrietta knew how to read other people—how to listen, when to chatter and distract—and her charm did as much as anything to keep her father from losing his hold on life when grief and depression stalked him. She did not criticize his expenditures, his impracticality, or his presumption. She did not question his morals or his parenting. She was there with a daughter's eagerness to please, a funny story to bolster his spirits, her mother's eyes, and at certain angles Babes's precise profile. In 1914, Bob Bingham sailed first-class with his father to England. Henrietta wrote teasing letters addressed "Dearest Judge." He responded with pictures of stone churches and reclining effigies of crusaders he claimed as forebears—and with endearments. "I am just hungry for the sight of you, my lovely darling." It was confusing to be needed so intensely yet left behind so often.

In his sorrow and loneliness, Bingham blurred the child who needed him and naturally wanted to ease his suffering with the precocious companion whose reactivity roused him from grief. Henrietta had learned how to turn heads and to flirt, skills honed and deployed on her dad. Indeed, father and daughter were similar in needing to be sought after and admired. It amused her (and tickled him) when she called the stiff and formal Judge "Honey." She reported from Asheville that a northern senator vacationing there "yiked my yooks" and had suggested a match with his eldest son. Upon learning Henrietta's surname, the senator's wife exclaimed, "You mean to tell me you are that Prince's daughter? Every woman in North Carolina was at his feet by the time he was 16."

While healthy families seek safety and trust in intimacy, bereavement made Henrietta Bob Bingham's mother, admirer, love object, and emotional center. The father-daughter relationship became a spinning merry-go-round of excitement and disappointment, affection and fear, collusion and guilt, anger and denial, and it sustained such a potent centrifugal force that Henrietta never stopped feeling its pull.

John Mason Brown, 1915

In 1915, Henrietta's spell also fell upon a garrulous and imaginative redhead who grew up around the corner from Mrs. Miller's Fourth Street home. John Mason Brown (always called "John Mason," perhaps to distinguish himself from the famous abolitionist) had also suffered a grave loss. His father had been accused of embezzlement and his parents had divorced—a stunning and mortifying series of events for a respected local family. Over their eighth-grade winter, the children gobbled treats at Miss Jennie Benedict's tearoom, sneaked unchaperoned to a movie, and tobogganed by hitching a sled to her pony. When "phenomenal" "'Retta" cooked him an egg, John Mason swore no food had ever tasted better. Nights, they spent hours conversing on the relatively novel telephone, with playfulness and desire floating through lines the operator might at any moment listen in on. Henrietta dropped John Mason midway through ninth grade, but ten years later, as he launched his career as a New York drama critic, Brown remained in pursuit. Artistic and ambitious, unathletic and emotionally vulnerable—he was the prototype for the men she found attractive in years to come.

Robert was guzzling through his last year of high school and Barry was still under Aunt Sadie Grinnan's care in Asheville when Judge Bingham rented out the house they had shared with Babes and moved with the two elder children into a new apartment building closer to town called the Hiawatha. For Henrietta, it was like playing house. She helped select which carpets, couches, beds, and books could fit into the rooms, and over dinner, they chatted about school and social life, his legal practice, and everlasting city politics. Charlie Chaplin's tramp was waddling across movie house screens, and they followed the grim news from Europe. The Kaiser's lightning advances, the slaughter at the Battle of the Marne, and the subsequent stalemate outraged Bingham, who became an early advocate of American intervention against Germany.

It was a difficult time and Bingham needed all the affirmation he could get. He hoped to keep the reasons for the change of household from Henrietta and Robert, but they surely absorbed the almost hysterical animosity that erupted between their grandmother and their father in the wake of the family's tragedy. These two figures, both of great importance to Henrietta, went at each other with every weapon they could find. Naturally, they used the children to defend their positions.

Mrs. Miller kept a hawk eye on her investments and expenditures and repeatedly revised her last will and testament. She was fiercely devoted to her daughters—often to their dismay, as the flip side of her maternal concern and munificence was suspicion of their spouses. (One friend of Barry's remembered Henrietta Miller as his "lovely mother's horrible mother.") Babes's will gave Bob (so long as he did not remarry) control over her money for the benefit of their children. When he rented out the Cherokee Park house, their grandmother cried foul. As she saw it, Bingham had evicted her grandchildren from the home she had provided for them and to which she held legal title. She was also furious that some $26,000 worth of her stocks was still keeping his brokerage account afloat, having covered his losses from ten years earlier. "I'm getting to be an old woman and I want my securities back," Mrs. Miller declared. His response, that he was "not now in a position to take up these notes," seemed to prove that his finances were wrecked. To protect the children's legacy from their father's creditors, Mrs. Miller demanded that Bob surrender his trusteeship of Babes's estate.

Money, family, and his manhood hung in delicate balance. Bingham stalled, several times offering a compromise co-trusteeship but failing to execute it. He was particularly concerned that no public records suggest he was, as he said, "short or anything of that kind." Tempers rose. Bob's mother-in-law made motions to take him to court, and he told her he would limit his authority over the trust. But Bingham first wanted assurance that he could be buried beside his wife in the Miller plot. When this was not forthcoming, he got his own court order and moved Babes's remains. In a final offer, Mrs. Miller agreed to erase the debt if he "effaced" himself from the trust. Otherwise Bob would meet her in court—under the public eye. Anxiety overtook him and he could not work.

Such was the situation in the summer of 1915, two years after Babes's death. Bingham's friend and former law partner rose to his defense. In a long letter to Mrs. Miller, "W. W. Dave" Davies sketched Bob's "frantic joy" in caring for his children. Did she realize Babes's trust income was utterly insufficient to pay their expenses, which helped explain his renting the house? Had she forgotten that for years her son-in-law devoted "unsparingly and without a cent of fees" nearly half his legal work to her family's business concerns? This was a man who sustained himself on "intense joys and hopes and ambitions." True, Bob had come to Louisville expecting to "go on hastening feet to the attain-

ment of wealth." This had eluded him, but had his speculations succeeded, would his mother-in-law complain? As to paying the note, it
was out of the question.

> I know what I am talking about. I know his finances. I know his phys-
> ical condition . . . It will take every cent that Bob can make to educate
> the children and do the things for them that are necessary. He is not
> physically strong. His recent illness was due entirely to a nervous con-
> dition brought about by his intense worry over this whole condition of
> affairs existing between you and him.

Surely she did not want her grandchildren to wonder what "hidden
trouble in their father's life sent him to a break-down or a death-bed . . .
Good Lord no!"

Under siege, Bingham unwisely focused on Robert, taking him to
Cambridge to sit for entrance examinations at the nation's most prestigious college. Robert's matriculation at Harvard would mark the family's
rising status, but he did so poorly on the exams that the Judge hustled
to Virginia and enrolled him in the university there. The experience
served notice to Henrietta and Barry. To succeed where their brother
failed was paramount if they were to please the Judge. Perhaps if Robert
had gone to Harvard, Henrietta might not have been the object of such
great hopes and lavish attentions.

She watched the unfolding melodramas: her father's misplaced expectations and embarrassment with respect to Robert; the disturbance
of her mother's grave; the Judge's strain and her grandmother's fury as
they self-righteously squabbled over money and the children. Just how
poisonous a mix ambition, money, and family could make was apparent
to Henrietta even before she entered high school.

Talk in Asheville, where she spent the summer of 1915, revolved around
two subjects: first, whether the United States would intervene in the
European war (the German attack on the British liner *Lusitania* killed
more than a hundred Americans), and second, "the wealthiest woman
in the United States." This extraordinary figure and a clutch of her

family members were enjoying the mountain air from Asheville's grand new Grove Park Inn. Everyone in town had heard of Mary Lily Kenan Flagler, but the Binghams knew somewhat more of her than most.

Mary Lily, a native of Wilmington, North Carolina, met Bob's elder sister Sadie when she attended finishing school in Raleigh, where Mary Lily briefly studied music. Her brother, Will, knew Bob from his years at Chapel Hill, and at some point Mary Lily visited Charlottesville and they apparently dated for a time. Though "not heavily endowed with brains," Mary Lily had a pretty voice, petite figure, and vivacious spirit, and these made her a popular belle. Other friends swept her into the world of Gilded Age pleasure spots—Newport, Saratoga, White Sulphur Springs—and introduced her to Henry M. Flagler, Rockefeller's Standard Oil partner and a Florida railroad and real estate magnate. Flagler and his first wife originally visited Florida on the advice of her physicians. Her health never recovered and he remarried, but Flagler's second wife had suffered increasingly disturbed states and was placed in a sanatorium. The sixty-six-year-old millionaire turned to Mary Lily, twenty-nine, for companionship, and in spite of gossip, she appeared with him in Palm Beach at his Royal Poinciana Hotel. The year Henrietta was born, Florida's legislature made incurable insanity grounds for divorce, opening the way for Flagler to remarry. Whitehall, a seventy-five-room Palm Beach Taj Mahal designed by Carrère and Hastings, was Mary Lily's wedding present, and from this base she became a renowned hostess—"so small of stature but so big of heart." Three weeks after Babes's fatal accident, Bob read in the papers that Henry Flagler, too, had died. Mary Lily's estate was said to be worth as much as $100 million.

Mrs. Flagler was no longer petite—her weight was a sensitive point and she sometimes had photographers retouch portraits to reduce her waistline—but she had a sweet nature and treated her North Carolina relatives with generosity. During her stay, the Asheville paper covered Mrs. Flagler's every move. Henrietta wrote to her father in Louisville that her life centered on "a quiet steed . . . riding is my only amusement," but her family members fluttered to Mary Lily's flame. Robert escorted Mary Lily's twenty-year-old niece and announced heir, Louise Wise, to a "Japanese Ball," and Mrs. Flagler gave him an earful about his father, her old flame, whom she called "Rob." Colonel Bingham also moved to establish her acquaintance—he had known her mother in his youth—and press for a major gift to the university in Chapel Hill. Mary Lily complained of receiving dozens of "begging letters" a day, nevertheless she responded positively to the Colonel's idea of attracting top faculty with high-paying Kenan professorships.

The curious and opportunistic swarmed the richest widow in the land, but weeks went by before Henrietta's father called on her. Colonel Bingham said his son feared being accused of "fortune hunting," and if this is true it was perhaps because money and Mrs. Miller's demands were in fact at the top of his troubled mind. In September 1915, Henrietta concluded a letter, "P.S. Have you written to Mary Lily yet?" What exactly transpired isn't known, but by winter Mrs. Flagler and her father were an item, appearing together in her box at the Metropolitan Opera.

That fall of 1915, Henrietta brought nine-year-old Barry home from Asheville with her, and sometime in 1916 they returned to the house by the park, part of a compromise, presumably, with Mrs. Miller. Henrietta got her name in the papers for winning Louisville's Cherokee Ladies Doubles Tennis Tournament and attended suppers and dances with children of the local elite. She entered the ninth grade at the just-opened Louisville Collegiate School for girls, and though she claimed she would as soon count the stars as attack her algebra, she succeeded admirably. As captain of the basketball team, Henrietta won the student-faculty game with a foul shot. She composed athletics notes for the school magazine and was runner-up in the spelling contest. This is especially remarkable because spelling required herculean effort from her—though she may not have told anyone so. The few letters of Henrietta's that have survived are amusing and wonderfully descriptive, but also painstaking. Very possibly she struggled with dyslexia, a condition then scarcely understood or diagnosed, much less treated. The Judge offered constant admiration and encouragement. "Of course you have brains, rather more than anyone else I know, for you have a well-rounded mind—a poise, mental and spiritual which is the finest form of development."

But Bingham was spending much of his time in New York with Mary Lily and this distraction, combined with his determination to get Henrietta admitted at one of the elite women's colleges, prompted him to send her away to school in the fall of 1916. He selected Stuart Hall, an Episcopal boarding school in Staunton, Virginia, where Robert E. Lee's daughters studied half a century earlier. Forty miles away, Robert (Barry called him "a real Virginia playboy") contributed meaningfully to the University of Virginia's tennis team but his grades fell short even of gentleman's Cs. Stuart Hall's standards were a step more rigorous than Collegiate's, and Henrietta repeated the ninth grade. As she settled into life in a grubby southern railroad town, Robert Worth Bingham and Mary Lily Kenan Flagler announced their engagement at the deluxe Greenbriar Hotel in White Sulphur Springs, West Virginia. Bob promised her brother, Will, to renounce any legal claim to Mary Lily's fortune before the November wedding. He did less to reassure his children about the upcoming change. Tellingly, Robert, Henrietta, and Barry were not included in the New York City ceremony—though Mary Lily's niece was. The only Bingham to witness the union was Bob's sister, Sadie, from Asheville.

Henrietta was unprepared for the way the marriage would affect her. Suddenly she was catapulted into the public eye. The very rich naturally attract curiosity, and not only did newspapers everywhere carry the story, but she had to field her schoolmates' awkward questions: Was Mary Lily pretty? Did Henrietta like her? Why wasn't she going to the wedding, and was her father truly in love? Would she spend the winter in Palm Beach? Could they come with her? Henrietta had few answers and, like most fifteen-year-olds, was excruciatingly sensitive to her peers. Her family, however broken and unstable, was in the midst of another collision wholly beyond Henrietta's control. What was to happen to her?

The Judge told reporters that he would remain a Kentuckian, although Mary Lily was planning a home on an entire block of Fifth Avenue and meantime would be keeping her apartment at the Plaza Hotel. The scale of her riches is difficult to convey. The union did bring Henrietta's father immediate relief: a transfer of $26,500 into his

Louisville brokerage account released Henrietta Miller's stocks and erased Bingham's debt.

Henrietta first confronted her new stepmother in Louisville on December 22, 1916, when she came home from Stuart Hall for Christmas. The Cherokee Park house was not up to Mary Lily's standards, so the couple was living in a suite at the Seelbach Hotel, the setting for Daisy Buchanan's wedding party in *The Great Gatsby*. Having done her holiday shopping in New York, Mary Lily prepared to impress the young Binghams—and soothe any bruised feelings over their exclusion from the wedding itself. Wrapped packages for her stepchildren covered the bed and teetered on the dressing table.

Apparently the fact that her role as her father's most intimate companion had been usurped hit Henrietta, because she came into the suite, gazed at the grinning, pudgy, strangely giggly woman, and swept the pretty boxes to the floor. She marched out, leaving her father to sputter apologies. Sophie Preston Hill, a family friend and peer of Robert's, sympathized. "They don't want any of those things," she thought. "They just want to come home." Just where home was and what it meant Henrietta no longer knew. She was frightened and furious.

Mary Lily was appalled. No one treated her this way. The girl's hostility sat between them all like a dare. Invitations had gone out for a lavish New Year's Eve dance at the hotel's grand ballroom in honor of Henrietta's sixteenth birthday. In reality, the Louis XV–themed event, which Mary Lily planned and paid for, was as much the new bride's Louisville debut as Henrietta's. Champagne and favors had been ordered, and the party went ahead (confetti fluttered down upon the dancers as in a "fairy land") but Christmas was ruined. Mary Lily fell ill and was isolated in the hotel suite, where Henrietta's outburst solidified in her mind and became unforgivable.

Henrietta returned to school in January 1917 to more questions from the students of Stuart Hall. Barry remained in Louisville with his father and new stepmother, cared for by servants, and recalled only that Mary Lily took an awful lot of naps. With his financial problems solved, their father contemplated a run for the U.S. Senate, but decided

Henrietta, circa 1916

against the effort. He and Mary Lily moved to Palm Beach for the winter season. Old Colonel Bingham visited and marveled at the way the guests—and money—rolled in.

The Judge sent Henrietta a set of souvenir postcards depicting the "Home of Mrs. H. M. Flagler," couples dancing at the Flagler-owned Breakers Hotel, and bathers bobbing in the waves. "Don't forget I am thinking of you even if I don't write very much," he wrote. "You really can't realize the demand on my time here." The Palm Beach paper announced Henrietta's impending arrival for Easter vacation—she would get one of Whitehall's sixteen guest suites—but she, or perhaps Mary Lily, balked. Henrietta never came, which dealt the new family yet another embarrassment. Stuart Hall's 1917 class notes nevertheless predicted "Bing" would become a "fan" of Palm Beach, with its Vanderbilts and Fricks, tennis tournaments and luxury shops.

Barry did not visit, either, and later claimed his father "found Whitehall oppressive and the society shallow and ostentatious." Still, the winter was a productive one for the Judge: he secured from Mary Lily an allowance of $50,000 per annum. When he objected that this

Mary Lily Kenan Flagler Bingham with Colonel Robert Bingham
and wicker rickshaw driver, Palm Beach, 1917

felt too much like being on her "payroll," his wife signed over to him some $700,000 worth of oil securities, enough to generate $50,000 in income. In gaining what was then called "an independence," Robert Worth Bingham joined the unenviable ranks of the kept man. Henrietta's father would need to manage the marriage and its public image deftly. He and Mary Lily were outfitting a grand Louisville house called Lincliff for their new home, but Mary Lily, who lacked any sense of how to manage her stepchildren, did not want Robert, Henrietta, or Barry there. Bob had spoken of them so gloriously. He had praised his daughter in particular, but to Mary Lily's mind they were horrid, especially Henrietta. As Stuart Hall's term drew to an end, the fundamental question of where she would live remained unresolved.

With the Kaiser moving to ally with Mexico, the United States finally went to war in April 1917. Henrietta's father hoped to honor his family's military tradition by doing battle against the German "menace." But at forty-six, the Judge's eyes were too weak, and even the officer reserve corps turned him away—he was just over the age limit. His college friend and recent best man in New York, Dr. Hugh Young of Johns Hopkins, was headed to Europe as a member of General Pershing's staff, and Bingham went to see Young before his deployment. He left the visit with an introduction to Herbert Hoover, whom Woodrow Wilson had appointed to lead the U.S. Food Administration. Perhaps Hoover could use him in Washington.

Returning to Louisville in late May, Bob and Mary Lily quarreled over the ballooning guest list for an early June 1917 housewarming party—she seemed to want to invite all of Louisville. Her letters to Kenan family members made clear the honeymoon was over. Bob had "misrepresented" his financial status as well as his children's characters. The children scarcely saw their father and were sent to Asheville to keep the peace. Mary Lily welcomed more than six hundred guests to the fete—a seated outdoor dinner with a full orchestra for dancing afterward. Indoors, a silent movie was screened. People walked around with their mouths hanging open. The next day Mary Lily rewarded the caterer with a platinum-and-diamond pin on top of a gratuity that could have paid for a new car.

It probably did not please his wife that immediately after the party Bob traveled to Asheville to visit the children. But he rushed back when news came to Bingham Heights that Mary Lily had fallen ill. Bingham's longtime dermatologist, Dr. Leo Ravitch, attended her, supported by round-the-clock nurses. From Asheville, Barry and Henrietta sent postcards they hand-painted, wishing that their father hadn't had to leave, but failing to mention Mary Lily. While the Judge was in Louisville, his thoughts were somewhat surprisingly taken up with his first wife. He purchased an expensive triple lot in Cave Hill Cemetery and Babes's remains were dug up and moved—again.

In mid-July, Mary Lily felt well enough to go out, but then suffered convulsions and for several hours remained in a coma. The Judge wrote to her family that he was "terribly anxious" about her condition. Her brother, Will, came to visit and her sister, Jessie, came to stay. On July 27, 1917, the second Mrs. Robert Worth Bingham died, aged fifty, and her body was carried by train to North Carolina for burial. There, to the shock of her relatives, Bob produced a codicil to her will, signed June 19 while he was in Asheville and witnessed by Dave Davies and Dr. Ravitch. Contrary to the prenuptial agreement the codicil left Bingham $5 million.

But the Judge and at least some of Mary Lily's relatives were privy to an even deeper secret: her addiction to alcohol and morphine. Just when Henrietta's father found out is not clear, though one Louisville matron said "everybody knew right away she was not all there." Henrietta's pre-Christmas outburst at the Seelbach Hotel prompted a frightening binge; others followed, and by May 1917 Bingham was desperate. His trip to see Hugh Young in Baltimore was in fact a bid for help with this "great trouble." He told Young that Mary Lily shut herself in her rooms for days and consumed vast quantities of gin to the point of stupefaction. Barry remembered hearing that "her habit was to lie in a hot tub and drink brandy, in order for the alcohol to have its maximum effect." Apparently, no one could deter Mary Lily, and she hid behind illness and vague indisposition, for "excessive drinking by a woman was not a matter to be discussed." She refused all treatment, but Bob hoped that if he took a war job in Washington she might be persuaded to discreetly enter a sanatorium. This plan never came off; Bingham claimed that she refused to go and that he and Will Kenan agreed not to force his sister. Not long before she died, Bob wrote to the Flaglers' Palm Beach minister seeking advice. "I know what you are going thru [sic]," the pastor replied. He had witnessed Mary Lily's affliction.

Self-control and moral uprightness were paramount to Judge Bingham, and to lose his esteem was to hear a door slam. Mary Lily's gaiety and generosity had always served her well, and at first she tried to laugh at Bob's severity. When that failed, it stung badly. Each had much to lose if the union failed. He feared driving her (and her goodwill and deep pockets) away, while Mary Lily dreaded the public embarrassment of a separation and what Bob might say about her. Another breakdown had followed the June housewarming party (and Bob's appeal that she seek a cure). It seems likely that Mary Lily was looking for some way to appease her husband while he was in Asheville with the children. A scrawled note in her handwriting, found among a set of his most private papers, reads, mysteriously, "Have kept my promise."

Mary Lily was apparently a willful and troubled patient whose condition remained obscure to her full medical team. In early July 1917 Ravitch wrote to Mary Lily's brother.

My dear Mr. Kenan, I was very sorry I did not feel well when you came here on a visit. I had so much to say and was anxious to have a long talk with you. Your poor sister needs so much help and guidance. Sunday last she had a bad attack with her heart. I had to call in Dr. Boggess, who specializes in diseases of the heart. He found a cardio-vascular dilation, but not knowing your sister's real trouble, gave me little assistance. I watched her very carefully and gave her a long talk. She took it nicely and promised to help me help herself. Let us hope so. Will have Dr. Boggess out again and see if we can help her to lead a more rational life. Am doing all I can. It is true I get tired and impatient, but I soon get over it, knowing your sister needs help and sympathy. Will let you know at intervals her true condition. Sincerely, (sgd) M. L. Ravitch

Mary Lily could have engaged the world's best physicians but preferred to rely on a dermatologist who probably gave her what she asked for, including morphine at two-hour intervals. Her nurse, interviewed afterward, claimed "a great deal of experience" and could tell "from the quickness with which the effect of the morphine wore off Mrs. Bingham that she had [used it] to a considerable extent before I began to wait on her." Two weeks before she died, Dr. Ravitch felt at a loss. He was apparently trying to treat her alcoholism and told her brother, "While the injections of [the stimulant] atrophine have reduced the excessive craving for alcohol, her general condition has not improved materially. Her heart is bad and sometimes I get alarmed."

After Mary Lily suffered yet another attack on July 16, Bob telegraphed Will Kenan to "come immediately," and urged members of her family to converge on Louisville. Kenan arrived from New York and left again, concerned that his sister might never fully recover but satisfied with her "splendid care." Four days before she died, Ravitch reported more "bad spells." In an almost unheard-of treatment, the doctor explained that he had injected "alcohol in her arm, as she was very low. She is doing nicely now."

In the weeks after her death, relatives questioned Mary Lily's treatment and the validity of changes that had been made to the will that summer in Bingham's favor. BINGHAM WILL CONTEST THREATENED; RELATIVES RESENT HUSBAND'S BEQUEST read one local headline. But Kentucky stood to gain a record $135,000 in taxes when the will was filed in court in early September. Bingham (who was taking Henrietta back to school) and Ravitch (said to be on a sorely needed vacation) did not attend the hearing. It would normally be a formality, but not so in this case. Davies testified under oath that Mary Lily was of sound mind when, in the presence of Ravitch and himself, she signed the amendment to her will. That she took this step in her physician's office seemed odd. That she engaged Davies, her husband's closest friend, to draw up the document also fueled suspicions. Under questioning from a lawyer representing the Kenans, Davies said Mary Lily didn't want to be seen meeting with an attorney and that she wanted to keep her decision about the bequest private. Then the Kenans' attorney asked,

> Mr. Davies, did you not know it to be a fact that what Mrs. Bingham termed the improper treatment of herself by Mr. Bingham's children and their lack of appreciation of what she had done for them had given her very great pain and the pain had gone to such an extent in the latter part of her life that she told Judge Bingham that his children could not come into her house?

Bingham's attorney objected. But the question appeared in the proceedings published in the next day's papers. In the public mind, Henrietta and her siblings were entangled in their stepmother's early demise.

Then an "Unseen Witness" sent the Kenan camp an anonymous letter alleging that the codicil was composed "from beginning to end by Dr. Ravitch . . . Mrs. Bingham was hounded to sign." The Kenans and the Judge each hired private detectives. Ravitch's office was broken into, his medical files ransacked, and in late September in a macabre turn, *The Courier-Journal* reported, BODY SECRETLY EXHUMED AND AUTOPSY HELD LAST SATURDAY. Her enormous estate naturally generated copy, but Mary Lily's family digging up her corpse in the middle of the night, aided by "badly scared Negroes," and hired pathologists carrying away her vital organs for laboratory testing made the story irresistible. The *New York Herald* proclaimed, MRS. BINGHAM WAS DRUGGED! Readers across the country were left to infer that Bingham might soon be charged with murder.

"I almost fainted it was so horrible," recalled one of Henrietta's friends. Bob Bingham undeniably stood to gain from Mary Lily's demise. Just that winter, he had gotten her to transfer stocks to his name rather than receive an allowance, and Mary Lily's emotional distress may have exposed her to undue influence. Still, no one could prove that the Judge had pressured her for the $5 million, and if he renounced the legacy, he looked guilty. If he revealed Mary Lily's embarrassing addictions, further doubt would be cast on the will. Bingham wanted the money—badly—but was damned if he took it and damned if he didn't.

Henrietta had faced curious schoolmates when her father married Mary Lily the year before. Now, back in Staunton to start her second year at Stuart Hall, she confronted an adolescent inquisition. Had her father poisoned the millionairess? The Judge was shattered by the innuendo and she knew it. His last bereavement had been one she shared. If he grieved this time, he grieved alone. Sixteen years old now rather than twelve, Henrietta tried to comfort him in a letter. "Dearest Dad . . . I have never had anything to come [*sic*] as near killing me as leaving you did," she wrote after he left her at school and went back to Louisville to face lawyers and reporters, "but then too I have never had such a good time as I did on our drive up." They had shared a "grand dinner" and she would "try to live on that." Her sunny affirmation of the fun they had together was touching. Just as important, any competition for first place in his heart was now removed. She reported that she was playing center on the basketball team, which meant she could call the plays—she wanted him to feel she was fine. Henrietta also dialed into his worries about the Kenan attorneys he met with in New York. "Please honey write me about your trip." When her father was wounded, Henrietta gave him the nurturing response he craved; it was a role she played many times.

In the fall of 1917, citing the damage to his children, Bob vowed to take the Kenans to court for the "criminal slanders perpetrated all over the country." Bingham's attorneys felt the special medical report ordered by Mary Lily's family after her exhumation was a bluff and, indeed, the Kenans never released it. Amid flying correspondence between lawyers, doctors, and private detectives in multiple cities, Bob visited Henrietta at Stuart Hall and found her "showing the effects of strain and responsibility." His "steadfast and manly conduct" concealed his rage. He had been wronged, his honor besmirched, as had happened before at the hands of his Worth relatives and Mrs. Miller.

That November, Judge Robert Worth Bingham lost a bid to reclaim his seat on the circuit court. Republicans swept the 1917 election both nationally and locally as Woodrow Wilson's popularity ebbed. Barry later forgot that his father even ran for office in 1917. The child was a master at repressing unpleasantness; the emotional atmosphere was so freighted and his father so fragile that he pushed away the events of that "terrible episode" from which his father "never recovered."

Just before his first payment was due from the executors, Bingham was told that a second autopsy report showed an overdose of salvarsan had killed Mary Lily. Salvarsan was a drug used to treat syphilis, and thus he was implicated in her death as her spouse. Bingham's lawyer advised that this "monstrous and impossible" allegation was meant to deter him from suing the Kenans for libel. Bingham remained quiet and the money gushed forth. But the great fortune came with "villainous suggestions and innuendoes" of foul play. Within the family, Mary Lily, her death, and the $5 million became subjects to avoid at all costs. Henrietta's confusion about her role in the disaster was never fully cleared up—had she made Mary Lily ill? The situation intensified her sense of responsibility for her father.

Henrietta was "bursting" to come home, anyway. Persecution at the hands of an especially unpleasant teacher provoked a half-joking appeal to Aunt Sadie: "I am afraid I will be forced to kill Miss Howard if I stay much longer." Certainly Henrietta had a temper. She also "crushed" on other girls—which, if taken past the innocent stage, would alarm Stuart Hall's authorities. Given the swirling publicity, the Judge may also have realized that having his children at his side could improve his image. In any case he decided to let her stay in Louisville after Christmas, and Henrietta returned to Collegiate School and her position as center on their basketball team. More important, she was restored to the center of her father's tumultuous life. Henrietta had been here before, helping run his household, delivering comfort and cheer and feminine companionship. But in the years between Babes's and Mary Lily's deaths Henrietta had learned that she could be displaced, that her attachment to her father, perhaps any attachment, could leave her wounded and alone.

When she was home, Judge Bingham spoiled Henrietta with horses, cars, furs, jewelry, shopping sprees. She was a confident and gifted horseback rider who competed successfully, but automobiles represented modernity, speed, freedom, and—not incidentally—masculinity. She seemed to get anything she wanted, provoking her siblings. Even twelve-year-old Barry, who adored her, complained that Henrietta had her own car and "loads and loads of beautiful clothes." When their father brought her a Tiffany diamond-and-sapphire ring from New York, he wrote in his diary, "I would like to have a few nice things now and then."

Henrietta's enthusiasm for music and musical theater kept her father feeling young. He bought her tickets to shows like the curvaceous young Mae West's 1918 revue, *Sometime*, featuring the hit "Ev'rybody Shimmies Now." Henrietta carried home the sheet music (with Mae on the cover) for the hot new dance, picked up from black nightclubs. Such songs evoked danger and sex, and though Jazz was roundly condemned in polite circles as an atrocity, Henrietta loved the rhythm, the way it let her forget herself. She seized every opportunity to hear more and her father indulged her. In early 1919, for a costume party celebrating Barry's thirteenth birthday, she hired a five-man band that included two saxophones. Barry wrote in his diary that he liked the band, but got an even bigger kick from dancing with the boys in his Swiss dirndl.

His millions all but in hand, their father had no clear plans when a family dispute among the owners of *The Courier-Journal* and its afternoon sister, *The Louisville Times*, opened an unlikely door. In 1917, the publisher refused to print one of the anti-German invectives by the famed editor "Marse" Henry Watterson, and two of the publisher's siblings and Watterson himself took over management. The business entered a free fall and they began to look for a buyer. Bingham fully apprehended the power of the press from his years in politics; if he couldn't win office, he could help determine who did. Thus, for just under $1.5 million, he obtained two papers he called "instruments for public service, champions of uprightness in public affairs, [and] advocates of justice and fair-dealing everywhere." Party loyalty was not in question, however, and Bingham made no secret of his Democratic preferences. "I am not myself a trained newspaper man," he admitted, and he never tried to manage everyday operations.

To match his new status, Henrietta's father purchased an estate on a bluff overlooking the Ohio River. Completed in 1911 for a local flour magnate, the imposing brick house with limestone columns and marble porches accorded with Judge Bingham's English taste. (For years,

Melcombe Bingham, 1914

Louisvillians referred to him as "Lord Bing.") For Henrietta, playing house with the Judge now meant playing mansion. A large staff served, cooked, and cared for the small family and its horses, cars, gardens, and hunting dogs. Henrietta competed in local horse shows and honed her skills on the sunken tennis court, dominating city tournaments. Bingham christened the place "Melcombe Bingham" after a sixteenth-century Dorset manor whose ancestral owners he claimed as relations.

Apart from the Kenans, the chief thorn in his side was his eldest son, Robert. He was put on academic probation during his second year; by the fall of his third, amid the worst of the Mary Lily scandal, Robert left college altogether. Bingham, skeptical of his son's account of what had happened in Charlottesville, wrote to the dean for clarification. He learned that Robert, twenty-one, had thankfully not sullied his reputation "as a gentleman," but simply "failed to perform his duties as a student." Robert described for his father the privations of a rustic camp where he had gone in hopes of "redeeming myself in your opinions." He then enrolled in flight training school near Boston in preparation for service in the war, though armistice came before he completed basic training. Lacking both direction and a college degree, Robert enrolled at Tulane and became a quick study of New Orleans's bars and brothels. He never graduated.

Judge Bingham was, if not a teetotaler, a very moderate drinker, yet he tolerated the extravagant entertainments the children put on at Melcombe Bingham. A New Orleans friend who visited them after the war described Henrietta, Robert, and Barry's "strange, fantastic existence." Parties at the brick mansion featured local jug bands and jazz ensembles all the way from the Big Easy, and one morning the Judge had to ask a servant to pick fried chicken out of the piano. Robert's consumption of alcohol increased along with his resentment of a father he seemed unable to please. One night, drunk, he drove his car through the front door into the house. Another time, according to family legend, Robert closed a holiday performance Barry had arranged by stepping onto the stage in the nude and presenting the Judge with a flower box; opening it, his father found only horse manure.

While Robert worried the Judge, Henrietta impressed him as daring

and independent, charming as ever. Before her 1920 high school graduation, she charged a saxophone to her father's account at Louisville's
Krausgill Piano Company. (No lady smoked in public, much less blew
a horn—the associations were too crude.) In spite of her difficulties
with writing, Henrietta took a school medal for best essay and was
admitted to Smith College, the first member of her family to access
an elite northern education. Her potential was clear to all, and she was
fulfilling a dream her father had treasured for as long as she could
remember.

3

DETRIMENT TO COMMUNITY

*S*mith College, located in Northampton, Massachusetts, had a reputation for brainy and well-to-do pupils. In the fall of 1920, just after the last state ratified the Nineteenth Amendment, securing women's suffrage, Henrietta and more than five hundred freshmen sat for the entrance exams. According to college practice, students were not ensured full acceptance until Christmas. She needed to work hard.

Henrietta lodged in Mrs. Sessions's three-story white clapboard boardinghouse across the street from campus. (More than half of Smith's all-female student body lived in approved off-campus houses.) She enrolled in two English courses, one in composition and another surveying early English literature, plus Latin, French, Astronomy, and Hygiene—a required class which, among other things, instructed the young women to refrain from sports during their menstrual periods. Freshmen were ritually inducted with a "Frolic," an all-female dancing party to which each sophomore took a first-year girl. The elder girl played the attentive suitor—bringing her date flowers, escorting her to the decorated gymnasium, filling her dance card, and fetching her drinks until bidding her good night at her boardinghouse window. New girls

Henrietta, Smith College, circa 1920

who made a "hit" received invitations to join exclusive societies or to take part in special outings. In the wider culture, women's colleges like Smith drew criticism for upending traditional gender roles. The word "lesbian" could not be uttered in polite circles, but Vice President Calvin Coolidge accused the Seven Sisters colleges of fomenting "morbid tendencies" in its students, since they married at below "normal" rates. An anonymous mother writing in the October 1913 *Harper's Bazaar* believed adolescent crushes were usually harmless, but cautioned that one in ten involved "moral degenerates" and were clearly "not legitimate."

Among Henrietta's instructors, an onyx-eyed, newly minted composition professor stood out. A member of Smith's class of 1918, twenty-four-year-old Mina Stein Kirstein was nothing like the corseted older women or bewhiskered men who formed the bulk of the faculty. Mina's youth would make her a curiosity to her students, and she was nervous. On the first day, a pigeon flew through an open window into the class, and Mina, who had a terror of birds, fled in search of aid. By the time she returned Henrietta had coaxed it out into the late summer heat. Sometime after this, Henrietta ascended to Miss Kirstein's office on Seelye Hall's third floor, where the autumn light entered through gable windows. Mina heard the low voice, not tentative, just deep, drawn out in its southern tones. Henrietta's face was full and sweet. She wore her short hair curled up at the ends with a flapper's headband over her brow. As they discussed the assigned theme, the keenness of the girl's mind was evident. Then her sapphire eyes filled with tears. Beneath her show of bravado, this unnervingly charming student was also "homesick, frightened, and miserable." Such feelings were common for freshmen, but Mina blamed the strangeness of the New England atmosphere. Henrietta was an outsider and Mina knew all about that.

Henrietta's effect on her teacher was such that Mina Kirstein spent a great part of the next five years admiring, coaxing, petting, corralling, and fretting over the Kentuckian. One of the first students Mina taught, Henrietta would become one of three great loves of her life. And yet Mina felt such a mix of heat and shame toward Henrietta that she scrubbed nearly every suggestion of their relationship from her papers. She considered her pupil to be brilliant, a rebel in whom rare wisdom and unmatched sympathy coexisted with self-destructiveness. She presented an irresistible package to a romantic and ambitious young professor. And Henrietta appealed to Mina's maternal drives—Henrietta badly needed mothering, and Mina was determined to treat these Smith "girls" as her mother had not treated her.

Mina had two younger brothers, Lincoln and George, and grew up first in Rochester, New York, then in Boston, where her father partnered with the Filene brothers in their department store. She recalled first having to confront her heritage when a group of children at a playground shouted, "Go on home, you dirty Jews," to her and little Kay Filene. At Miss Capen's, a boarding school that applied a quota of no more than two Jewish students, olive-skinned Mina avoided the "very

Mina Kirstein, circa 1918

Semitic-looking" other girl; her image of female perfection at the time was a "cornstalk" blonde, the Bostonian Faye Albertson, who married the journalist Walter Lippmann. Mina hoped her looks passed as "czarist" rather than Semitic; indeed, wrapped in furs and with a brimless hat pulled low, she appeared mysterious. Her broad mouth was the tiniest bit crooked.

Mina adored her father, who took her seriously, while Mina and her mother were perpetually at loggerheads. Rose Kirstein complained that her daughter did nothing with her hands, and Mina resented her mother's tantrums, the threat of which kept the household in her thrall. Boarding school relieved her from her mother's running critique of her complexion, clothes, manners, and above all, her insufficient gratitude. Mina thought she understood what drove her mother to make her "as beautiful as possible. If the daughter is not duly grateful then the mother talks about sacrifice," she observed, "and yet the whole performance is primarily catering to her own vanity."

Rose urged Mina to pursue a year of "domestic science and manual training" after Miss Capen's. But Mina had intellectual ambitions. At Smith she studied hard. She also decided to announce rather than conceal her Jewish background to her roommate, who declared, "How interesting! I thought all Jews were peddlers." Mina boycotted the required Christian vespers—and got away with it. She convinced a dozen students to resign from one of Smith's secret honorary societies, which excluded Jews. During junior year, with the world at war, Mina condemned the school's frivolous social clubs, where evening dress was de rigueur and ice cream was served. She put pen to paper and took paper to publication in a small but prestigious New York literary magazine, *The Seven Arts Chronicle.* "Never have I heard anyone say that she came to college," Mina wrote tartly, "because of any true love of culture." Mina took pride in mentioning "subjects that it seems uncivilized to discuss" and that most Smith students were "brought up to consider taboo." Her serious-minded activism won a sympathetic audience with Smith's president, William Allan Neilson, who "combined a strong sympathy for minorities with an exquisite sense of humor."

It was a time of breathless idealism on the left, and Mina, discarding all czarist associations, believed "that salvation and revolution were synonymous." Mina's unfeminine radical politics, critiques of classmates, campus activism, coziness with the college president, Jewish background, and made-to-order clothes made her a ripe target for the class of 1918's graduation-eve lampoon. "How Doth the Busy Bolshevik (An Agitation in 2 Spasms)" satirized "Mina Trotzky Lenine (Perverse Product of Petrograd)," who talked "man to man" and recruited revolutionary "Min-ions" using her automobile as bait. (Mina was the only undergraduate with a car.) The leather-coated, lorgnette-wielding leader roars,

> For everybody's equal
> And everything is wrong!
> Come let's reform society,
> It surely can't take long.

The caricature stung all the more for being well done.

Mina dreaded more than anything being seen as a dilettante. After graduation she did a short stint in military intelligence in Washington, then enrolled in classes at Radcliffe. She met the English political scientist Harold Laski, then teaching at Harvard, and became one of the students Laski and his wife, Frida, regularly invited to their Cambridge home. In 1919 Laski was forced out of the university after he supported Boston's striking police. Writing from England, where Harold had joined the faculty at the London School of Economics, Frida gently ribbed Mina for being a "bloated capitalist."

The Jewish Laskis moved in a highbrow crowd, and through them Mina met the publisher Benjamin Huebsch. This son of a Hungarian immigrant rabbi had published work by Sherwood Anderson, D. H. Lawrence, and James Joyce. In 1920 he also started an influential left-leaning magazine of politics and literature, *The Freeman*. Huebsch, like Mina, felt self-conscious about his heritage—one friend teased that he needed a partner to handle the "Jewish end" of his business so Ben could "go on being a Christian." An affair began, and in part to be near him, Mina transferred to Columbia and began work on her master's thesis about Henry Adams. Adams was perhaps at the peak of his fame at that moment—his *Autobiography* won the 1919 Pulitzer Prize after circulating privately for years. In the stacks of Harvard's library, Mina noticed annotations in Adams's copies of the *North American Review* (which he edited) identifying authors (often Adams himself) of anonymous articles. Mina's thesis traced Adams's dance of privilege, ambition, fame, and modesty, which spoke directly to her own concerns and shaped her intellectual interests for years to come. *The Atlantic Monthly* agreed to publish an essay about the discovery, a notable achievement for such a young scholar, but the triumph was spoiled by the end of her affair with the dazzling Huebsch; their relationship fizzled when he met and married a Swede.

Her master's degree in hand, twenty-three-year-old Mina was hired by Smith's president, William Allan Neilson, to teach freshman composition. Her model was Adams, of course, who had taught history at Harvard in the 1870s and "sought education; he did not sell it." In the fall of 1920, Miss Kirstein pledged to treat students "exactly as though they were my equals in every way, and I shall learn much more about them this way than any other." She expected to find them "excellent company." If students understood Mina's faith in them, they could perform to their limits. She urged them to dig deeply, and *then* write, not only with feeling but with thought. "What I care about in life," Mina declared to her father as classes began, "is to find out the truth, and to follow it wherever it may take me." Two years into her career, an examiner reviewing Smith College singled out for distinction "a young woman . . . named Kirstein, who left a permanent impression on every student who chanced to get her as an instructor."

Henrietta, wounded in spite of her privilege, insecure beneath her striking beauty and aptitude, elicited a strong response in Miss Kirstein. As she nervously assumed a new job and nursed her hurt feelings after Huebsch's rejection, Mina told herself it was "only natural that the company of an understanding, intelligent, mature, sophisticated girl would mean a very great deal to me."

Mina was more than satisfied with Henrietta's performance in English 11; however, in mid-November 1920 the freshman received "a friendly warning" about her grades in two other classes. Her petition to drop Astronomy was not considered before campus emptied for the Christmas recess, and Henrietta packed with a rising sense of panic about the exams she would face in January. She was hardly alone in her difficulties—nearly one in five first-year students would not return. In the interim, an unremitting series of social distractions helped her forget her troubles.

On the way back to Northampton after the holidays, Henrietta stopped in New York with her father and Barry for a few days of theater and shopping. She didn't know how she could pass all her exams. What if she failed out of college and disappointed the Judge as Robert had? Mina met the family at the Waldorf-Astoria Hotel to help deal with the crisis.

One night in the Bingham suite, Henrietta "made love" to her teacher "in such a way" that drove Mina to admit she was "in love with me—and I with her." Henrietta made Mina desire her. Doing so gave

Henrietta a sense of control (in one area of her life, at least) and boosted her shaken confidence. In a pattern she repeated over the years, Henrietta deployed her allure to manage her own fear and anxiety.

Mina had experienced crushes on girls during her teens, and "How Doth the Busy Bolshevik" made unflattering insinuations about her dominating her "minions." But no woman had made her feel this way— she experienced a level of excitement Huebsch had never aroused, and her physical response mixed uneasily with maternal and teacherly impulses.

While fourteen-year-old Barry chattered about the plays they might see in New York, Mina sized up the man some said had murdered Henry Flagler's widow. He considered her, too. Her Adams article was in the new issue of *The Atlantic Monthly*, and though Louisville's elite generally excluded Jews, Bingham had close Jewish colleagues in his law practice and at *The Courier-Journal*. Mina listened to his concerns about Barry's education—he felt the sooner the boy got into a New England preparatory school, the better his chances of admission at Harvard— and offered assistance. Then she explained as calmly as she could to her prim host that Henrietta required his attention. Could he come to Northampton and see the dean?

Barry wandered the cold quadrangle alone while the dean met with the others. Rather than have her sit for exams, the college gave Henrietta the option of withdrawing and petitioning to reenter in the fall. Henrietta left campus shaken, but Barry was "ecstatic" that his sister "was persuaded," as he explained in his diary, to come home. That winter, Bingham took his two younger children to Boca Grande, a non-Flagler Florida resort popular among tycoons and prized for its sportfishing. While wading in the turquoise Gulf of Mexico, Barry learned that rather than enjoy the Kentucky spring with Henrietta, he would transfer mid-semester to Middlesex in Concord, Massachusetts. In New England, homesickness swamped him, and he never quite forgave Mina for her hand in his exile from Kentucky and Henrietta.

Barry's exit made his sister's return to Louisville especially welcome to the Judge. He had missed her far more than he realized. But Mina had no intention of letting her quit college, and Henrietta herself was determined not to follow Robert's feckless course—he was then working in sales at a Louisville car dealership. In the spring of 1921, Smith accepted her for readmission. She would begin anew with a clean record.

Before her return to Northampton, Henrietta and Barry accompanied their father on his annual summer trip to Britain. Mina would be visiting the Laskis and promised to meet the Binghams in London. In New York, before boarding their ship, Bingham discussed American agriculture with the financier and Democratic advisor Bernard Baruch. Tobacco prices, controlled by a handful of manufacturers, had dropped precipitously in 1920 and thousands of Kentucky farmers and their families faced ruin. Growers who sold at bottom rates were threatened with violence by others who wanted a boycott. The Judge perceived in the tobacco crisis a cause with broad implications for Kentucky, the Democratic Party, and perhaps his own career.

As the Binghams sailed for Europe, Zelda and F. Scott Fitzgerald were returning from their continental sojourn. Prohibition laws did not extend to the steamship's deck, thus Henrietta's penciled lines in Barry's travel diary: "Between the claret, the Chartreuse, the Burgundy, the port, and the scotch, I really cannot concentrate on my impressions of this day." But she listened sympathetically to Barry's confidences about the misery of boarding school. Their father worried about his younger son's lack of prowess on the field and what Middlesex's headmaster called his "effeminate" ways; Henrietta found nothing the matter with him.

In London, where the lifting of wartime restrictions created a sense of hope, Mina accompanied the Binghams to see the Ballets Russes perform Sergey Diaghilev's bewitching productions, with their innovative choreography and modernist sets, scored by the likes of Stravinsky and Debussy. They bought the poet Edith Sitwell's *Russian Ballet Gift Book* as a souvenir and convinced the Judge to let them go back for another performance. Mina, obliging her host's infatuation with the powerful, especially if they were titled, introduced the Judge to the department store magnates Sir Woodman Burbidge (of Harrods) and Gordon Selfridge (of Selfridges). While lodging with the Laskis, Mina met George Bernard Shaw and H. G. Wells; the *New Republic* editor Herbert Croly was visiting, too, and Harold Laski was at work on a biographical essay about Marx to be published the following year by the Fabian Society. Thrilling as all that was, Henrietta's allure kept pace. Mina joined the Binghams on their excursion to St. Ives, whose lighthouse mesmerized the young Virginia Woolf.

Laski's wife, Frida, scolded "Poor Old Mina" for not locating a man to replace Huebsch: contemporary Freudian thought informed her advice to Mina to do something about her single state or risk being filled up "with repressions . . . The only alternative is to have your sexual organs removed along with your wisdom teeth." Mina didn't have a man; she had Henrietta. But she could not go into her feelings with the Laskis, who found the Kentucky crew unbearable, due in part to their Confederate genealogy and connection to a region of appalling racial violence. Fifty-nine black Americans died at the hands of lynch mobs in 1921 and a race riot—sparked by an alleged sexual assault—left dozens dead and the black section of Tulsa, Oklahoma, in ashes.

Henrietta wasn't Mina's only troubled student in London that summer. Eleanor Carroll Chilton, an aspiring poet with enormous, heavy-lidded doe eyes and a romantic swirl of fair hair, was another of Mina's acolytes. Her father, a former senator from West Virginia, published *The Charleston Gazette*. Eleanor admired Edna St. Vincent Millay and memorably dressed head-to-toe in violet to give a reading for the school's literary society. Despite shared connections to the South and journalism, the West Virginian and the Kentuckian did not always mix well. One of Chilton's poems suggests why: Eleanor was in love with Mina, who was in turn in love with Henrietta. In "To Mina," Chilton wrote, "I have kissed a thousand things / Hoping that one might kiss like you." Mina did not discourage such effusions; indeed, she welcomed the flattery and the power it conferred.

Henrietta appears in Chilton's verses, too. She sits with Eleanor before Mina's fireplace until "silence bared its teeth, and bade" Chilton depart, "tension at my heel." The girls competed for the professor's attention—and the emotional stakes rose. In a poem from that summer in London, Eleanor referred opaquely to something Henrietta did, something it would take "years to understand." In "To H. W. B.—In Reply," Chilton concluded bitterly,

Eleanor Carroll Chilton

But now, there's nothing on this earth
I can forgive—except the thought
That smiles are always bought
With some one's tears, and hence their worth.

Mina's two southern students returned to college in the fall of 1921, Chilton for her senior year and Henrietta to begin again as a freshman, and may even have traveled by the same train. Henrietta was reportedly "reconciled" to her studies, but she was much more engaged by the Congo Grind and Black Bottom, dances enjoying craze status. Louisville's Episcopal churches barred jazz from their youth gatherings, citing deleterious "jazz manners and jazz morals" spreading among the young. Chaperones were directed to police the parties to prevent "couples retiring to automobiles and remaining there during dances."

At Smith and other women's colleges, the boardinghouse system made monitoring student behavior beyond the classroom difficult, and during Henrietta's time the administration announced plans for expanded campus housing to address the problem. Henrietta and her peers demanded looser regulations for smoking, playing records, and excursions (often with Amherst College boys), which the "unsupervisable automobile" rendered easier than ever. They scored a small victory when Smith abolished its ten o'clock lights-out rule.

Midway through the fall term, Henrietta came down with appendicitis. The timing was particularly bad; she was doing solid academic work, but surgery and recuperation meant weeks of missed classes. In Louisville, her grandmother Miller warned her of the lingering effects of anesthesia on the nerves and worried that traveling to Cuba via New Orleans over the Christmas break would prove too strenuous for "an invalid." "You must not do any walking, and don't be teased into trotting around like you were well and strong." Henrietta was not about to miss a trip that would include the opportunity to hear the likes of young Louis Armstrong, but she tried to reassure her grandmother. Henrietta Long Miller died a few months later. Her $450,000 estate included only small legacies for Babes's children: Grandmother Miller made clear in the will that Babes's share had been advanced during her lifetime. She appointed Henrietta caretaker of the family plot from which the Judge had removed Babes's remains in 1917—and, if her aunt agreed, Henrietta could use the Fourth Street house she had loved as a child.

Judge Bingham was too busy in 1921–1922 to dwell on this final reminder of his previous dependence on Mrs. Miller—and his children obviously didn't need her money. With the day-to-day work of the newspapers in others' hands, he set out, as he told Henrietta, to "get the poor [farmers] to accept their salvation." To advise him on his campaign, Bingham recruited Aaron Sapiro, a San Francisco lawyer with a record of successfully organizing cooperatives for California's vegetable farmers, and Bingham barnstormed through the Burley tobacco belt, giving speeches and winning applause. A majority of growers in the Burley region agreed to pool their crops, and the Judge invested $1.5 million in warehouses where the leaf could wait out low prices. By winter he was the most popular man in Kentucky. Bingham and Sapiro took their show on the road in 1922, preaching the gospel of cooperation to peanut farmers in Georgia and potato farmers in Maine.

Henrietta was making conquests, too, including, apparently, Eleanor Chilton. A January 1922 poem described the intoxication that struck all Henrietta's lovers. "Look at her eyes," it began, "and you will have the most of her." These "coquettish," potent eyes "wonder at you," thoughtful, intense, blue beyond blue.

> If you do not please her
> She stares your gaze away.
> If she likes you
> She looks the memory of her eyes into you . . .
> When she talks
> You only know of her lips

And there was "the quick, magnet-answer / Your body makes to her presence." It was as though her eyes said, "I am trying to find out / What you are really like."

Shining her bright beams upon others, melting them, restored Henrietta's sense of control. Her seemingly effortless ability to attract desire and give pleasure lay at the core of her identity, but once more Henrietta was falling short in her studies. By spring, she couldn't manage physics and was failing in at least one other class, laying waste to Mina's and her father's expectations. The school doctor and class dean allowed her to drop a course. But an accumulation of infractions (leaving campus without permission to ride horseback, drive in cars, or see a movie) came to the dean's attention. In March, she saw the college physician about dropping more classes. Having witnessed Henrietta in the grip of panic attacks, Mina made her an appointment with Dr. Marion Leeper, a local practitioner. Struggling with her coursework and unwilling to button herself in to the school's regulations, the pressure mounted; if the authorities discovered anything amiss in her relationship with Professor Kirstein, dismissal would almost certainly follow—for all involved. Following the 1922 commencement, Smith's Administrative Board cited

Miss Bingham for a shortage of credit hours as well as "Miscellaneous Actions" and "deficiencies." The verdict: "Detriment to Community."

Despite her difficulties at Smith, no one who spent time with Henrietta doubted her intelligence, which was demonstrated less in scholarship than in her razor social awareness and her ability to charm. Her writing was sharp and occasionally wildly humorous, but she probably never admitted how difficult it was to focus on words on a page. While Henrietta's correspondents adored her letters, they uniformly complained that they were too rare or too brief. Reading was laborious—even though she loved literature—and given her likely dyslexia (as well as illness and anxiety), college-level work overwhelmed her. Henrietta's family name was known across the South for its connection to education, and yet her father, her brother, and now she had fallen short academically—a point of shame and yet another subject to avoid at all costs.

Henrietta's abbreviated career at Smith tested desires, revealed powers, and exposed shortcomings. She was there long enough to cultivate a profile as a prototypical flapper, with her cropped hair and ne'er-do-well reputation. Henrietta "cut quite a figure" on campus, frustrating authorities and forming bonds where love met danger. A friend teasingly proposed Mina's epitaph:

> I tried to teach the truth
> To virgins, but forsooth
> All my success in teaching was to see
> My pupils lie with me.

Part Two

"The very substance of the ambitious is merely the shadow of a dream."

—SHAKESPEARE, *HAMLET*, ACT 2, SCENE 2

4

AN AMERICAN GIRL OF TWENTY-ONE

*W*hen the college Administrative Board decided her fate, Henrietta was already in Louisville, but her father seems to have known nothing of the proceedings. In the past, Mina had defended her to Smith's administration, and in 1922 Mina may have prevented a formal expulsion, of which Bingham would have been informed. It is also possible that Henrietta was counted among the students who suffered breakdowns in 1921–1922, girls whom the college physician suggested might return once they outgrew their "period of instability." Though the school year had not been easy, Mina inscribed a gardening book by her Northampton neighbor George W. Cable, "For Henrietta—In Memory of a happy year." Mina believed her favorite could still complete her studies, especially if she received professional help for her emotional problems.

For her part, Henrietta at all costs wanted to keep the news of her suspension from college from her father and remain in the orbit of the woman she adored. Mina arranged a meeting for Henrietta with her old flame, Ben Huebsch. The publisher was so taken with this "spontaneous person" that he asked her to join the business staff of *The Freeman*.

From Manhattan, Henrietta, with Barry in tow, rushed to Boston to discuss the offer with Mina.

Living in New York and working at a radical magazine, while exciting, would not support the illusion Henrietta and Mina were staging for the benefit of Judge Bingham—that her time off from Smith was merely elective. Upon renewing her teaching contract that spring of 1922, Mina requested leave to spend a year "studying and traveling in Europe," which Smith's president approved even though she had completed only two years' service. (One possible explanation for this may have been that the spread of rumors about her involvement with students made time away from campus advisable.) Henrietta's father was going to England for part of the summer, and the two young women seized on the idea of touring France and Italy, then attending classes at the university in London. How much their sexual involvement influenced this arrangement is difficult to say, but they would need to be careful. The proposal fed Lord Bing's Anglophilia but it required his continued confidence in Mina as a force for good in his daughter's education and broader life. If everything went as planned, he would open his pockets for their adventure and meantime Henrietta could get the psychological help Mina felt she needed.

Judge Bingham and his children crossed together, and Professor

Robert Worth Bingham with Robert and Henrietta, London, circa 1922

Kirstein was to sail for England a few weeks later. On their journey, Barry produced a small, leather-bound diary, with PLACES VISITED in gold lettering on the cover and implored Henrietta's help in filling it. She awarded the prize for their favorite fellow passenger to a vaudeville player with a center-parted bob, whom she described going at the piano "like a streak" after the orchestra "boogered off for the evening." "Everyone danced." Barry noted that Robert pursued a girl whose brother "got a terrible crush on Henrietta."

Upon arrival, Henrietta and Barry broke off for long walks around Chelsea, sampling restaurants and scouring bookshops until they were footsore. They hunted for James Joyce's just-published *Ulysses*, banned both in Britain and the United States. (The novel was such hot property that their copy was almost immediately stolen.) Henrietta was Barry's goddess as well as his favorite companion, and they laced their repartee with made-up words and inside jokes. Both adored the theater. She found John Galsworthy's new play, a tale of anti-Semitism among the British upper class, "perfectly wonderful, though harassing from end to end"—a credible reaction from someone in love with a "member of the tribe." One of her diary entries related their beeline to Madame Tussaud's Chamber of Horrors and the "bloody perambulator," which turned their father "as gray as a badger." Barry induced his siblings to make "a triumph of endurance and good spirits"—a sodden pilgrimage of thirty miles from Reading to Oxford. They journeyed by road, river, and foot for two days, until the ancient university's "dreaming spires" gradually came into view.

But Henrietta was on edge. She was in love with a woman—a woman she admired and looked up to as much as she admired and looked up to her father, and a woman who in some ways replaced her dead mother. All children worry what their parents will think of their romantic relationships. For Henrietta, the situation was particularly complicated. She did not feel safe telling Judge Bingham about her feelings for Mina; any intimate alliance might upset their intense bond, and a homosexual one, given the prevailing views about such matters, threatened to alienate him from her entirely. He might even cut her off financially. She badly wanted to be with Mina, but as she awaited her father's ruling on her and Mina's plan during the summer vacation in England, Henrietta grew so agitated about being "found out" that she "could hardly bear to have him touch her." She tried to be reasonable in the face of her quandary, but her problems at school and her involvement with Mina created a wedge between her and the man whose admiration she could not bear to forfeit. He must have been confused by his daughter's behavior; she was near panic.

In the end, Judge Bingham agreed to let her stay on and left for America with Robert and Barry.

Henrietta and Mina were alone and it was divine. One day in early September they stepped off the train at Chartres, an arrival Mina described as "almost as exciting as Jesus' entrance to Jerusalem," except he came on a donkey and they followed one pulling a "rickety cart" piled with luggage. With Henry Adams's *Mont-Saint-Michel and Chartres* in hand, they paced the labyrinth and strained their necks gazing up at the rose windows. The soaring structure emphasized God's infinite glory and man's smallness, but the effect wore off by the time they arrived at their hotel, having walked the town's narrow, hilly streets for hours. Henrietta, always worth more than the trouble she caused, kept Mina in stitches, "howling about the coarseness of her sheets." Mina tried to impress upon the young Kentuckian "how fortunate she is not to have anything more to complain about." There were tender moments; Mina read love poems by Donne and called Henrietta "Petroushka," after the Russian puppet that love and suffering bring to life, made famous by Diaghilev's Ballets Russes.

The poet H.D. and her female lover had traveled this way, too. Outsiders regarded the pair as merely friends—they "were always 'two women alone' or 'two ladies alone,'" H.D. wrote. From Chartres, Mina and Henrietta pointed toward Rome, their route taking shape as they went. With Henrietta behind the wheel, they reached Toulouse and stopped in Marseilles for the boat to Genoa, whose cathedral wore restrained Romanesque stripes rather than dripping Gothic statuary. By late September they were in Carcassonne—booked into a fashionable hotel perched atop the town's medieval wall. The trip was winding down and soon they would be back in England.

Mina felt that Henrietta must obtain psychological treatment if she were to live happily and achieve her remarkable potential. As she contemplated the remainder of her sabbatical, Mina also likely questioned how the women would relate to each other in London and beyond. For a host of reasons, they must not be seen as a couple. Mina felt quite clear that she was not a lesbian and she saw no future for them as lovers. To simply break up with Henrietta, fragile as she was, was impossible. Nor did Mina want to give her up. The more she thought about it, the more it seemed that an expert psychoanalyst, by helping Henrietta overcome her problems, could also get them past their affair.

Leading psychoanalysts, Clark University, 1909. Back row, left to right: A. A. Brill, Ernest Jones, Sándor Ferenczi; front row, left to right: Sigmund Freud, G. Stanley Hall, Carl Jung

So it was that from their room in Carcassonne, Mina composed in her loose, rolling hand a long letter to Dr. Ernest Jones, Harley Street, London. She was given his name by Dr. A. A. Brill, a New York psychiatrist who had been aboard her ship that summer en route to the International Congress of Psychoanalysis in Berlin. Brill had welcomed

Sigmund Freud, Carl Jung, Sándor Ferenczi, and Jones to the United States in 1909 when Freud delivered his famous Clark University lectures. Jones, a Welsh-born physician who came to prominence after Freud's rupture with Jung, was doing more than any other individual to improve the reputation of Freudian analysis. At the time he received Mina's letter, he chaired the British and International Psycho-Analytical Associations and edited the *International Journal of Psycho-Analysis*, and it was not long before he began to oversee the English translation of the complete Standard Edition of Freud's writings.

Psychoanalysis was edgy. Many were talking about the Viennese doctor's theory of the unconscious—the seat of powerful feelings and primal urges—and about the mysterious new treatment he had developed to cure troubled patients. Before and during World War I, Brill's patient, the Greenwich Village salonnière Mabel Dodge, helped seed Freudian ideas among "advanced" American artists and intellectuals who avidly passed around books like *Psychoanalysis: Its History, Theory, and Practice*, which Huebsch published in 1919. The war left people with agonizing questions about how supposedly civilized nations could have permitted the slaughter of millions; Freud offered new ways to think about the individual and society and how they could go astray. Besides, it was liberating to speak openly about repression and the sex drive. But in 1922 barely a handful of Americans had undergone a formal analysis.

It would take many years to build demand for the practice, partly because Freudian theory was widely viewed as obscene. In advancing the notion of an unconscious, where deep and sometimes inappropriate feelings were kept hidden, Freud asserted that a primary inappropriate feeling was sexual attraction to both our parents. We wanted them physically, not just emotionally, and from this desire stemmed all later sexual development. Bookstores routinely refused to stock his writings, and throughout the 1920s Jones appeared on a British Broadcasting Corporation list of speakers "dangerous to the public morality." Earlier that year, Jones's photograph illustrated an article in *Lloyd's Sunday News* headlined PSYCHO-ANALYSIS DANGERS. NEED FOR PROTECTION AGAINST QUACKS WHO EXPLOIT HYSTERICAL WOMEN.

Freud's insight—that human beings are by nature bisexual, that they unconsciously (and consciously) experience same-sex urges—led many "contrary sexuals or inverts" to psychoanalysis. Here was a place to speak openly about sexual experiences the wider culture condemned and to get help managing the shame and painful difficulties arising from their "abnormality." Some analysts touted "adjustment therapy," a process of helping patients accept and take a measure of control over their sexual urges. Nonetheless, even among the Freudians, consensus reigned that heterosexuality was far preferable. The profession was very young; no one could have known how psychiatry, often abetted by psychoanalysis, would pathologize homosexuality, advocate its repression, and perpetrate humiliating and punishing treatments—electroshock, nausea-inducing behavioral conditioning, and lobotomies. Even A. A. Brill, Mina's fellow shipboard passenger in 1922, later revised his sympathetic assessment and ultimately labeled homosexuals as paranoid, impetuous, and unreliable.

Mina dangled her twelve-page history of Henrietta like catnip before Ernest Jones. Whether Henrietta helped with the letter or even knew about it remains obscure, along with whether or not she agreed with her friend's views. Mina described "an active homosexual,"

> an American girl of twenty-one who is at the present time, in a sense, under my care. She is a very attractive person with a keen mind who has suffered from overwhelming attacks of fear ever since she was ten years old or before. Between the ages of ten and twelve she was hysterical a large part of the time, and shortly after her twelfth birthday she was in an automobile accident in which her mother was killed before her eyes. Her younger brother, who is now sixteen[,] was also with her in the accident. Although she has an older brother who is now twenty-five her father depended entirely upon her after her mother's death . . . until two years later when he married again. At that time she went to boarding school and it was here that her homosexual tendency first manifested itself.

Mina tied Henrietta's homosexuality directly to trauma from Babes's death and the corrosive influence of Judge Bingham's unusually strong emotional dependency. Henrietta's early emotional affairs did not develop very far, Mina said; her first full-fledged homosexual experience came in Louisville after Stuart Hall. Aged seventeen or eighteen she

> became very intimate with an extremely beautiful, highly over-sexed woman who was unhappily married. Much against her will in the beginning she finally gave in to an out-and-out sexual relationship with this woman. This woman later left her husband and has now become a rather wealthy prostitute. Henrietta, the girl of whom I am writing you, loved this woman very deeply and had the utmost faith in her own ability to reform her. So that her utter degeneration was as much of a spiritual shock as the homosexual relationship was a physical one.

Mina's surprising account aligned strikingly with Freud's most sustained meditation on lesbian sexuality to date, "The Psychogenesis of a Case of Homosexuality in a Woman" (1920), in which a "beautiful and clever girl of eighteen, belonging to a [Viennese] family of good standing" had fallen in love with an older "society lady." The latter shared a house and had "intimate relations" with a married female friend while offering "bodily favors" to male clients. The girl's parents brought her to Freud to rid her of the embarrassing behavior, and if Henrietta really had suffered a broken heart at the hands of a high-class courtesan it would naturally pique Jones's interest.

Mina explained that Henrietta's lesbian activity further developed during college, involving another (at least somewhat) older woman of independent means—Mina herself. Nevertheless, Miss Kirstein was at pains to make clear, "I am not homosexual, though I love her very much." Mina had "once more come to desire the company of men," inevitably causing tension between the couple and perhaps dealing Henrietta another heartbreak. She hoped her pupil would also leave behind her lesbian activity, and spoke for them both. "It isn't that either one of us is ashamed of our relationship from our own point of view. It has always been an extremely beautiful and honest one," Mina wrote in fine liberal fashion. "But it simply does not seem to be conducive to the fullest and most useful sort of life. And the secrecy it involves is in itself unhealthy."

Few could dispute that the burdens imposed by homophobia were severe, and Mina was sadly correct about the risks of a continued sexual relationship with Henrietta. Teachers like her regularly lost their positions for violating community morals. Moreover, Mina already felt marginalized as a Jew and a left-leaning liberal, and she refused to become a pariah. Mina's letter, which began by presenting a troubled "American girl of twenty-one," ended by pressing for a therapeutic solution to Mina's own entanglement with her. Henrietta's extraordinary combination of charm and vulnerability made Mina susceptible to the Kentuckian's advances, yet Mina yearned for recognition and acceptance in a society where open lesbians were not received. She wanted Henrietta healed and wanted them both redeemed.

Freud's "Psychogenesis of a Case of Homosexuality in a Woman" made clear his misgivings about just the sort of change Mina was asking Jones to effect in Henrietta. A patient's parents had asked Freud to return their daughter to heterosexuality, but the girl did not see anything wrong in her lesbian feelings. The necessary transference never took hold, the parents were disappointed, and the young woman went on to live contentedly with her "perversion." Freud surmised that someone truly motivated to alter her choice of sexual object would come wholly of her own accord, and not under family pressure or fear of societal "disadvantages" like the ones Mina described. He also suggested that rerouting the libido after genuinely felt homosexual desire had been satisfied was nearly impossible. Research on hormones might hold a key, he suggested, but in 1920 Freud concluded that "it is not for psycho-analysis to solve the problem of homosexuality."

It is highly unlikely that Henrietta or even Mina had plumbed Freudian thinking on these matters. But they must have gathered that Freud saw homosexuality as an arrested stage of development and not, as the English sexologist Havelock Ellis argued, congenital and hence irreversible.

Ernest Jones returned from the summer psychoanalytical congress and read Mina's letter. Freud encouraged practitioners to accept that homosexuality was relatively common and conquer their "disgusted" reactions, something Jones was confident of having done. He judged there was plenty to work with—the girl suffered from neurotic symptoms (her irrational attacks of fear), which the talking cure could relieve, and Jones had written that homosexuality and other aberrations *were* "in general amenable" particularly when the patient felt "a strong abhorrence of what he considers as an unnatural but uncontrollable impulse." A full analysis with successful transference—which Freud had not yet achieved with a homosexual woman—could supply important insights about the course of female sexuality. Besides, in 1922 Jones was short on patients, his wife was pregnant with their second child, and money was on his mind. Psychoanalysis was costly, even extravagant, and the doctor noted Mina's explanation that she taught "because I love the work" and that she possessed "a large home of my own." Jones would see Henrietta as soon as she was ready.

In the fall of 1922 the women settled into a furnished flat around the corner from London's Ritz Hotel and Mina began attending university lectures. Mina had a harder time getting Henrietta onto the analyst's couch than persuading Jones to treat her. While Mina foresaw a bleak future for lesbians, Henrietta, a cultural bellwether who waded wholeheartedly into sexual experimentation, seems to have regarded sex more fluidly, more "something that we *do* rather than something *we are*," as the psychotherapist Ann D'Ercole has written. There were realms where lesbian sex, at least as an expression of bisexuality, qualified as radical chic. Harlem divas like Ma Rainey, Bessie Smith, and Gladys Bentley were acting on and sometimes singing about their same-sex attractions. In London the American heiress Betty "Joe" Carstairs, having served in a female ambulance unit in France during the war, opened the X Garage with lesbian mechanics and chauffeurs catering to a fashionable clientele, and that winter, the "pale and ravishing" twenty-one-year-old Alabama-born Tallulah Bankhead appeared on a West End stage, oozing sex appeal that attracted men and women alike. With money and mobility, Henrietta Bingham navigated a bisexual culture where flamboyance and secretiveness often overlapped.

Nonetheless, in late 1922, she climbed the stairs to Ernest Jones's second-floor Harley Street consulting room. Jones wrote to Freud of the young American girl he was treating "both for her inversion and for neurotic symptoms." Henrietta's decision to pursue psychoanalysis does not necessarily mean she rejected her attraction to women. What Henrietta had in mind—whether placating Mina, addressing the anxiety that helped defeat her at Smith, confronting her mother's death or her demanding and suffocatingly dependent father—remains hazy, but the timing of her plunge into psychotherapy is revealing. Ringing in her ears was Judge Bingham's command that she come home at once.

The autumn of 1922 mixed public triumph with private anguish for Robert Worth Bingham. The cooperative agriculture movement consumed almost all of his energy as he and Sapiro helped persuade some sixty thousand tobacco farmers to sign pledges to hold their crops until the large manufacturers met a minimum price. The outcome was never guaranteed, but R. J. Reynolds and other tobacco companies ultimately purchased nearly the whole crop from the pool. By year's end, newspapers (and not just the ones he owned) portrayed Bingham as a Moses pounding his staff on the earth and transforming the tobacco patch into a land of milk and honey. People spoke of him as a likely candidate in the upcoming gubernatorial campaign. *Courier-Journal* employees signed an acclamation hailing his effort as the "greatest piece of public service any Kentuckian has ever done."

At the same time, Henrietta's father concluded that twenty-five-year-old Robert was "well on his way to Hell." Southern Motors either fired him or he quit his sales position, and his father alternated between dangling carrots (a directorship of the Courier-Journal and Times Company and an undemanding management post at a printing concern the Judge purchased for him) and waving sticks (outright banishment). As the publisher was entertaining a group of British notables including the former Lord Mayor of London, Robert came in drunk and disheveled, looking like a "haggard old man." Judge Bingham's embarrassment and alarm reached new levels in October when, at the height of the cooperative organizing, Robert vanished altogether. Bingham and his aides scoured Louisville bars, bathhouses, and brothels. Turning up nothing, search parties fanned out into the state.

He cabled Henrietta to pack immediately. He expected her to take the first ship so she could be on hand "in time for my funeral," or Robert's, or both. Robert was discovered the next day guzzling liquor with a companion in a private room at the nearby River Valley Club, where the laws of Prohibition were studiously ignored. That night, as he prepared to leave for rallies in the western part of the state, the Judge "collapsed completely."

Bingham railed that his own "child stabbed me in the heart at the climax of the fight" and if Henrietta did not return she was guilty of the same. She wired back that she needed to be in London a bit longer. The Judge, believing that she was taking an academic class, understood that Henrietta wanted to complete her "course . . . in psychology." She could remain

> until early in December without injustice to yourself or your family. I do not think you can stay there any longer without the gravest wrong to yourself. However important your intellectual development may be, there are certain other obligations devolving upon you which, in the end, are of greater importance. It will not be possible for you to evade these obligations without great spiritual loss to yourself. I do not mean for a moment that I think you wish to evade them, but I want to give you the benefit of my fixed judgment on the subject, after considering it from every angle.

Five days later, he wrote again: without her he might fail—physically, morally, emotionally, politically, and as a parent to her brother. It was "imperative" that Henrietta come to his side.

> I have made up my mind if he goes on another spree simply to turn him out, and I do not know whether I should be able to withstand the effect

this would have upon me if I were forced to do it. Doubtless I could if you were here; I think I could not if you were not here, or at least on your way. In a crisis of this sort I think it would be up to you to come home at once and do what you could to save something from the wreck.

Bingham's narcissistic attachment helps explain the impossible position Henrietta occupied in the family. Under stress, his need for her ministrations reached hysterical proportions. He laid upon her an extraordinary degree of responsibility for his well-being. Only a parent who subjected his child to intense and unreasonable idealization could expect such things. And a child bonded in such a way was certain to provoke her siblings' jealousy. It was a controlling cycle: without Henrietta he would be lost to the world; a corollary was that shirking her caretaking role meant forsaking her chief purpose in life.

But Henrietta idealized him, too: he was powerful and, in trying to prove that he loved her more than anyone else, he spoiled her. Bob Bingham had favored Henrietta even before Babes died, which left her feeling guilty; she was haunted by the accusations that her behavior drove Mary Lily to drink and to death; now her father was again on the point of losing his grip. Emotional pressure always made Henrietta agitated and confused, but with Mina by her side and Dr. Jones consulting, she stood her ground. Mina wanted her to see that her duty was not to service the Judge, but to be strong for her own sake, her own future.

The reality that Henrietta relied on her father's goodwill for her financial support underpinned everything, however, and after Robert's situation stabilized, she disclosed that childhood wounds had led to difficulties which, with the help of a specialist Mina had found, she was working to surmount. In what proved to be an effective pivot, she showed that if he was distressed and ill, so was she.

"Thank God for Mina," Bingham exclaimed in his next overwrought letter. "I really failed you, my precious girl, but it was a poor, miserable man's stupidity and your own gallant, unselfish effort to save me."

Henrietta succeeded in getting her father's attention when she confessed that she struggled with the effects of what he called a "terrifying accident which marked her" at five as well as Babes's violent death. "Many people would have been mere shattered wrecks for all their lives after such experiences," he wrote, "but you were so steady & so strong it left you only a wound which your own strength will heal—and without even a scar." Hyperbole, exaggerated expectations, shame—these were typical of Judge Bingham's communications with his daughter.

She gained a reprieve until Christmas, when he, Robert, and Barry came to England. Judge Bingham insisted on meeting her specialist, and departed satisfied that "the loveliest daughter God ever gave a father" was making rapid headway. Jones suggested that two months more would complete her treatment and gratified the publisher by saying of Henrietta, "there never was such material to build on!"

5

FREE ASSOCIATIONS

By early 1923, Ernest Jones was treating not only this "actively homosexual girl," but "her female partner," as well. He was thrilled (and ethically untroubled) to have both participants in a sexual relationship under his care and considered it a golden opportunity to excavate lesbian psychology. That Henrietta and Mina could afford treatment was additional cause for celebration; that they were educated and bright was cause for hope, for Jones believed that the young and intelligent were most amenable to analysis. Together, the Americans supplied "specially interesting" work.

Henrietta truly liked him. The analyst Joan Riviere called Jones "irresistible" and noted that he was somehow able to meet the opposite sex "on their own ground." His already-healthy ego doubtless benefited from the transference that was central to a successful analysis—at some level the patient must fall in love with her analyst. At five feet four the forty-three-year-old doctor came up to about Henrietta's nose, but his presence exceeded his size and projected energy and assurance. Penetrating eyes and a dominating forehead, crowned with sandy, smoothly combed hair, gave Dr. Jones a thoughtful look. He was particular about his appearance, favoring three-piece suits with a gold watch in a pocket. Self-righteous zeal, a thin skin, and an autocratic streak characterized the young doctor, but if anything dogged him, particularly early in his career, it was multiple accusations of inappropriate behavior. In 1906, at twenty-seven, he allegedly exposed himself to children at a home for the mentally disabled. Two years later a London hospital dismissed Jones for his interaction with a paralyzed ten-year-old boy. His defense was that he was forthright in discussing sex, and adults overreacted to such directness. Forced to take a job in provincial Toronto, Jones departed in a cloud after it came out that he had paid off an adult patient who had accused him of having intercourse with her.

Back in England after World War I, Jones initiated the London Psycho-Analytical Society, treated D. H. Lawrence's wife, Frieda, and tended to shell-shocked soldiers. As for his "murky reputation," by the time Henrietta and Mina arrived in London, Jones claimed to have achieved in his own life what he wanted to see in his patients—"a richer development of will-power and self-mastery."

During this period, Jones psychoanalyzed Donald Winnicott, later an important theorist and practitioner. Psychoanalysis has been called "The Impossible Profession"—it is so individualized that its process stubbornly resists encapsulation—but Winnicott tried to lay out the "analytical situation": at a regular hour, perhaps five times a week, the analyst would "put himself at the service of the patient," "keep awake and become preoccupied by the patient," seek to understand the patient, and reflect that comprehension in language. "Love and hate were honestly expressed" in the nature of the sessions—the analyst's interest in the patient expressed love; the firm start time, end time, and the payment for the analyst's services were expressions of hate. The analyst is "much more reliable than people are in ordinary life; on the whole punctual, free from temper tantrums, free from compulsive falling in love." The setting—a quiet, comfortably lit room with a couch for the patient— invited regression, a pathway to the unconscious.

How did Henrietta's sessions go? Hackneyed images of traditional analysis with its reclining patient free-associating for long stretches in the presence of an almost silent analyst probably do not capture her experience. H.D. said Freud was "lively, directive, talkative, gossipy, emotional, anxious for news, and often eager to offer advice about people's lives and families." Jones took a similarly warm interest in these "girls" and corresponded with them outside of their therapeutic meetings. Henrietta regularly brought gifts—pheasants, grouse, flowers—and Jones never hesitated to discuss Mina with Henrietta and vice versa. While he sounded biting at times, the doctor's certainty that he could improve the lives of his patients won Henrietta's confidence.

Dreams were key entry points to buried psychological material, and Jones leveraged his patients' emotional strain in the hopes of gaining analytical insight. He viewed homosexuality as "a psychoneurosis" closely connected to narcissism. When Henrietta resisted analysis and clung to a homoerotic "world of phantasy, however pleasurable this may be," it served to confirm her neurotic fixations. If Jones could bolster Henrietta's latent heterosexual feelings he would consider it a triumph.

They doubtless discussed Henrietta's oedipal development. From a Freudian view, the preadolescent girl would have been in competition with her mother for her distracted father's attention, a dynamic that saddled Henrietta with her own particular burden of guilt for Babes's death. Henrietta's unconscious wish to supplant Babes coincided with her mother's actual removal from the family. This was indeed unfortunate, for children easily err when linking cause and effect. Henrietta survived the crash to become the nuclear family's only female member, and she may have felt she owed her father a debt for his loss. But she had been a child. Judge Bingham was an adult, and his emotional reliance on his daughter complicated her oedipal journey. In *The Psycho-Analytic Study of the Family* (1921), Jones's colleague, the London analyst J. C. Flugel, addressed the issue of bereavement. "Widowers . . . frequently display a more than normal degree of attachment to their children," Flugel wrote, "the latter receiving, in addition to the love that would ordinarily fall to their share, the displaced affection which would otherwise find its outlet in the love of the wife."

While Henrietta unpacked history, fears, and "phantasy" with Ernest Jones, her father replaced his hopes for her college education with a collaboration between them that would employ her gifts and keep her close. In 1923, *The Courier-Journal* was turning a profit of almost $1,000 per day, and circulation was expanding throughout the state. He looked forward to having her home, at which point the two of them would read the news together and hold daily conferences to "consider apt subjects for editorials and the proper time for them." In preparation, he sent Walter Lippmann's book *Public Opinion* (1922), which he considered especially "valuable to us newspaper owners." Propaganda and herd mentality had led nations into a brutal war; liberty and democracy might depend on the content of newspapers. In Kentucky, Henrietta could undertake what he called a "true romance," the history of the Burley Tobacco Growers Co-operative Association in which he himself played the hero's part. Bingham was forging a new era for American farmers—"any man should be willing to die" a martyr, he pronounced, "to achieve such a result for humanity." (The cooperative movement was also seeding Democratic votes and boosting his reputation with the national party.) With Henrietta by his side and Robert "straight" (he appeared to be on the wagon), Judge Bingham could "preserve enough vigor to do anything worthwhile." He impatiently folded ship schedules into his letters to London.

But the last thing Henrietta wanted to do was book passage home. She and Mina were pursuing romance and adventure of a different nature in the early months of 1923. Mina had declared to Jones that she wanted to put their erotic relationship behind them. They spent evenings at the Savoy, where the hotel's Orpheans and Havana Band played foxtrots like "You're in Kentucky Sure as You're Born," and where Harry Craddock, a Manhattan bartender and Prohibition refugee, mixed lime rickeys and gin fizzes. Late nights, they moved on to nightclubs like the 43, a fashionable jazz locale. Henrietta, especially, was making a splash. A French *vicomte* and wartime flying ace had married the daughter of London's American-born department store magnate, Gordon Selfridge, whom the Kirsteins knew from their merchandising association. The aviator took to Henrietta, prompting the Judge to warn her to "cut him off entirely" lest she "disturb [the man's] domestic ménage." Still, Bingham appreciated the responses his daughter provoked, and at some level relished the attention she received. During the same winter weeks, he heard of her "disturbing the peace of a crown prince," the dashing blue-eyed Nicholas, heir to the Romanian throne, then serving in the Royal Navy. He didn't want anything to keep her from Kentucky and, he told her, foreigners, the English excepted, were "rotten inside" and incapable of treating a woman honorably. In fact, Bingham added, "the best American is not one hundredth part good enough for you."

A basement bookshop and not a nightclub provided the entrée for Mina and Henrietta's most thrilling and lasting social ties in London. Francis Birrell and David Garnett's bookstore opened soon after the war in the Bloomsbury neighborhood near the British Museum and University of London, and, benefiting from a close association with Leonard and Virginia Woolf's Hogarth Press, became a favorite among the loose band of artists, writers, and intellectuals known as the Bloomsbury Group. Even the tables that held the stock were the work of the Omega Workshop, a prewar art collective including Vanessa Bell, Duncan Grant, and Dora Carrington that produced original decorative items for everyday use.

Manning the store the day Mina came in to do Christmas shopping was Garnett, a twenty-nine-year-old blond with appealingly soft features. He watched closely as a "tall dark American girl" scanned the wares. Wrapping up Mina's stack of volumes, Garnett slipped in his newly published novella, *Lady into Fox*, which he considered "a *reductio ad absurdum* of the problem of fidelity in love." Within days, she was back, having read the tale of a young couple's dilemma when the wife mysteriously transforms into a vixen. She was delighted—but confused. Where had it come from? Was the author the same Garnett whose name was on the sign outside? In the ensuing conversation, David gathered that she was staying in London with a friend who had been her student at a place called Smith College in Massachusetts. David Garnett had a penchant for distinguished outsiders, especially women. (He later published a novel about an African princess and a biography of

Pocahontas.) Miss Kirstein stirred his interest, and he was soon telling his mother about the book she had recommended to him—Henry Adams's *Education*.

Garnett was also something of a hustler, drawn, like Jay Gatsby, by the "inexhaustible charm" and "jingle" of money. Mina and "her friend, Henrietta Bingham, a lovely girl," were clearly "the daughters of very rich men," he wrote. This commonality accentuated their differences. When he came to their service flat for tea, David (whom his Bloomsbury friends always called "Bunny") took immediately to Henrietta as well, nicknaming her "Puppin." He called her a sweetheart, "a pudding," with a striking "oval face of a Buddha." Her voice struck him the most: a deep, evocative, "caressing voice of the South." Henrietta had none of Mina's bluestocking bookishness, but her "strength of personality" lifted her to the center of even the most sophisticated company.

Garnett had stumbled on something exotic and delicious and potentially useful in these two American girls and he relished the complete package. Early on, he gained their confidence and learned of their love affair. It was David who authored the teasing lines about Mina's success in having her students fall in love with her. Irreverent and ribald at times, Garnett was also tender, entertaining, and loyal. Perhaps because he had been lonely as a child, he found pleasure mediating the complicated lives of his friends. Mina and Henrietta themselves were not always on the best terms. "Henrietta is a very great dear," Garnett reminded Mina one day. "You mustn't hurt her, or undervalue her love, or yours for her."

Advice on this point from David Garnett was of particular weight to Mina in the winter of 1923: she was falling in love with him. Garnett possessed unusual charm. He looked on his interlocutors with intensity—a forceps delivery had damaged one eye, leaving David with a disarming sideways gaze. His literary bona fides were lofty enough to win over any young aesthete; his grandfather oversaw the printed books section of the British Museum, his father had played a key role in the publication of D. H. Lawrence's scandalous *Sons and Lovers*, and his mother knew Lenin and had translated the first English editions of Tolstoy, Dostoevsky, and Chekhov.

But Edward and Constance, as David unconventionally called his parents, could not afford to send him to Cambridge or Oxford, and he lacked the cushion of an annual income. Breaking from family tradition, he enrolled in London's Royal College of Science. When war broke out he spent six months in France with the Quaker-led War Victims Relief Mission alongside Francis Birrell. Garnett had befriended Adrian Stephen, the younger brother of Virginia Woolf and Vanessa Bell. Through Adrian he gained entrée to the circle that included these women and their husbands, Leonard Woolf and Clive Bell. Their conversation and way of living—philosophical and modern and irreverent—drew him like "a stray kitten which had firmly made up his mind to be adopted." Garnett spent the latter part of the war at Charleston House, the whimsically hand-decorated East Sussex country home the Bells shared with Duncan Grant, Vanessa's sometime lover. To avoid conscription, David and Duncan performed agricultural labor. Grant (delightful and dead handsome) had been sexually involved with Adrian Stephen and John Maynard Keynes, the economist and a fellow member of Bloomsbury's inner circle. Who seduced whom isn't clear, but Grant and the younger Garnett fell into an affair.

That relationship settled into a close friendship after the war, and Mina probably knew nothing of its earlier phase. But the fluidity of sexual connections in Bloomsbury informed David's unruffled appraisal of Mina and Henrietta. Their preoccupation with psychoanalysis, which he considered a highly suspect path to personal satisfaction, puzzled him, for Garnett saw nothing "wrong or maladjusted with either" of them. In the weeks following their first afternoon tea, the trio met frequently, and David and Mina exchanged playful, increasingly intimate letters. When she was confined to bed with measles David sent a volume of Edward Lear verses, suggested playing darts, and instructed Henrietta to enliven the patient by practicing her saxophone. Then he wrote abruptly, "Did I tell you that my wife presented me with a most delightful boy about a week ago?" Mina had known nothing about David's approaching parenthood—she had not even known he had a wife.

Mina tried to understand David's breach in mores. "Our relationship, from his point of view, had certain limitations," she later wrote.

"He could not understand my Puritanism, as he called it. And wishing to appear sophisticated," Mina could not admit how David's behavior disturbed her "deeply ingrained belief in the sanctity of marriage." Garnett occasionally repented of his wandering eye: "I will not have love affairs with other women without talking to you about it at the time and I will not have any at all if I can help it," he told his wife of one year, the talented and exceedingly shy artist Ray Marshall. But he did not believe in monogamy. He was "a pouncer," and had no intention of letting his formal union deter him from following lightly where love led.

David Garnett, to Mina, 1923

When his new friends managed to extend their time in England through the summer of 1923, David gladly offered to help them find a country retreat. He thought right away of Tidmarsh Mill in Berkshire, home to Lytton Strachey (yet another of Duncan Grant's former lovers), Dora Carrington, and her husband, Ralph Partridge. The wild success of Strachey's *Eminent Victorians*, which he followed in 1921 with *Queen Victoria*, made travel possible, and he was treating the household to a North African adventure. So much the better, David reasoned, if the Americans paid to rent Tidmarsh Mill during their absence.

One early March day, Henrietta steered a shining blue Sunbeam motorcar to the red-roofed house straddling the narrow River Pang. When the brace of "exquisite American girls" arrived, Carrington (she loathed her first name and insisted that her friends not use it) was in her studio putting the finishing touches on a sign for the Spreadeagle, an inn and tavern in neighboring Thame that was favored by the Bloomsbury set.

Carrington was surprised to find the pair so appealing. A few weeks before, she had seen a performance at Covent Garden called *An American Revue*, which she thought "appallingly stupid and vulgar." The costumes created by Duncan Grant were charming, but, she huffed, "Americans must be detestable people." Touring the two women around the house, Carrington thought twenty-six-year-old Mina "lovely," "tall with an olive skin, dark shining eyes like jet beads, and a perfect slim figure, short black curling hair." Henrietta was "my style, pink with a round face, dressed in mannish clothes, with a good natural smile." As they moved down the corridor, Mina surveyed the book-lined study Carrington had decorated for Lytton. Calling Henrietta to a window, she pointed to the yellow blossoms sprinkling the early spring lawn. "Say Henr-ie-t-ta aren't those dog violets just too lovely?" Carrington corrected her: those were celandines. Mina persisted, "We call them dog violets in America." While take-charge Mina did the talking, Henrietta remained cool, catching Carrington's gaze and holding it. Henrietta left Carrington oddly shaken, and she watched the car pull away with regret. Nearing her thirtieth birthday, the painter imagined that these "lovely creatures" took "about as much interest in me as if I'd been the housekeeper." But when they phoned with an offer Strachey refused. He "couldn't bear to have" them living in his home.

Mina and Henrietta regularly confronted such expressions of English superiority. At one party given by David's friend Adrian Stephen, the host addressed Mina in loud, slow tones, as if the professor spoke a foreign language. This kind of snobbery, on top of her self-consciousness of being Jewish, particularly rattled Mina. David took little notice, and, eager to repay Henrietta and Mina's "lavish hospitality," determined to use his upcoming birthday party to formally present them to his circle of friends.

Carrington greeted her third decade with dismay, but David Garnett had cause for celebration. His book *Lady into Fox* had gone into a fourth printing, and he began to feel he might manage to make a living by his pen. An earlier pulp novel written under a pseudonym and featuring cocaine-abusing young Londoners had sold 15,000 copies. He got a publicity photo taken and wrote up a biography underscoring his literary lineage. In the photo, Garnett looked barely old enough to have a beard, but he was hungry for an audience. English readers liked his book—it went on to win the Hawthornden and the James Tait Black Memorial prizes—and if he could tap an American readership his career would be secure. Mina knew important publishers personally. And David told Ray of Henrietta's plan to have him write a regular column in "her father's paper," which might then be picked up by Sunday supplements across the United States.

David and Ray Garnett held the birthday gathering in the tall-windowed, double-height studio that Duncan Grant shared with Vanessa Bell. (Decades earlier, the American James McNeill Whistler had painted there.) They bought wine, rented glasses, and set out bowls of olives. Henrietta mounted the studio's iron staircase carrying an enormous homemade southern-style 1-2-3-4 layer cake with caramel icing—she had packed cookbooks in her steamer trunks. An artistic cake it was, too, decorated with a vixen in a little coat worrying two ducks, an image from one of Ray's woodcuts for *Lady into Fox*. Not satisfied with wine, Henrietta brought spirits and a case of mixers and worked the bar, offering flavorful concoctions that Prohibition's bootleg liquor and bathtub gin had made so necessary in America.

Henrietta slipped into her Roaring Twenties element, but the scene provoked Mina's just-beneath-the-surface anxieties. This was David's world, and among the guests were writers and artists whom she longed to know. Virginia Woolf, "whose recently published *Jacob's Room* [she] hadn't really understood very well," might come and there was John

Maynard Keynes, whose companion starred in Diaghilev's world-famous ballet troupe. Duncan Grant was wonderfully friendly, but the light fare and the heavy alcoholic offerings made for a boisterous blend that was not exactly Mina's style. Henrietta, in contrast, glowed like the sun. It wasn't fair, the way people gravitated toward Henrietta seemingly without any effort on her part. When the phonograph ran down that night in Grant's studio, Henrietta picked up a mandolin. The guests formed a circle as she began to sing.

One of the songs was "Water Boy." Paul Robeson and Odetta later made recordings of this song that were full of yearning and protest, but in 1923 Henrietta, young and white, was singing a chain-gang tune, taking the perspective of a laboring convict. Her performance that night, in all its rich contradictions, was perfect, as Henrietta wore her difference as an American and a southerner channeling rebellion and blackness, sorrow and sex, pursuing and being pursued.

> Water boy
> Where are you hiding?
> If you don't come right here,
> Gonna tell your pa on you.

In the eyes of many Bloomsbury figures, Americans' "New World vitality" was "generally amusing, enthusiastic and tireless" and "sometimes also exhausting and tactless." According to Lytton Strachey's biographer, "a little" of their presence "went a long way." Henrietta never won Lytton over, but many others in his circle could not get enough of her. "Irresistible" was the common refrain. This despite the fact that she was neither bookish nor highly educated, and merely by saying, "Hello, my name is Henrietta," broadcast her roots in a region benighted by slavery, the outrages of lynch law, and an ascendant Ku Klux Klan. Indeed, Confederate talismans were then arriving in Berkeley Street by post. Henrietta received a cross and anchor inlaid with shells from her ailing North Carolina grandfather, symbols of her southern legacy carved while he was a prisoner in the Civil War.

With Bloomsbury as her audience, Henrietta flipped a negative

Henrietta Bingham by Bertram Park, 1923

cultural association on its head. She won cachet by presenting the anomaly of a certified Southern "belle" singing and playing "negro" songs in "negro" style. In the months and years to come, Britons embraced an "imagined south" through music and theater that were bathed in creamy moonlight and populated with carefree "black folks"—but Henrietta's suggestiveness conveyed something more complex, for her unlikely identification with black prisoners reverberated with her barely fettered desires. Dora Carrington described the scene to the writer Gerald Brenan. This letter, from a married woman to her male lover about her lesbian crush—leaving aside Carrington's decades-long attachment to the famously homosexual Lytton Strachey—indicates what scandalous company Henrietta and Mina had stepped into.

> I only know her name is Henrietta. She has the face of a Giotto Madonna. She sang exquisite songs with a mandoline [sic], Southern State revivalist nigger songs. She made such wonderful cocktails that I became completely drunk and almost made love to her in public. To my great joy Garnett told me the other day she continually asks after me and wants me to go and see her.

Carrington had impressed Henrietta, while David—whom everyone thought was sleeping with both Americans—took puckish delight in acting as a go-between. This was emphatically not what Mina had in mind for her "charge."

Lady Ottoline Morrell, who entertained Bloomsberries before the war at her country manor, called Dora Carrington "a wild moorland pony," intense and uncertain, humorous, spontaneous, devoted, despairing, energetic, and frequently unreliable in the interpersonal realm. While studying art in 1911 Carrington lopped off her bushy blond hair to ear length, setting a fashion followed first by art school friends and eventually by the ballroom dancer Irene Castle, silent movie stars, and millions of Jazz Age women. Carrington was twenty-two when she and Lytton Strachey met over a weekend at Virginia and Leonard Woolf's Sussex cottage. During an afternoon ramble, the long-limbed, long-bearded, bespectacled Strachey, attracted perhaps by Carrington's boyish figure and cropped hair, tried to kiss her. She pushed him away in disgust. Confused when someone informed her that Strachey was a homosexual and suspecting she had been toyed with, Carrington swore vengeance. Early the next morning she entered Strachey's bedroom armed with scissors to excise his signature facial hair. As she prepared to snip, he opened his eyes and froze her with his gaze. From that moment onward, so the story goes, she adored him.

David Garnett prized Carrington's "forget-me-not blue eyes" and untutored curiosity. Years later he edited her letters and diaries for

Dora Carrington and Lytton Strachey,
Ham Spray House

publication, revealing her captivating style—and a swarm of inner demons. Virginia Woolf, who had been momentarily engaged to Strachey and remained a close and admiring friend, took a long time to warm up to Carrington, but concluded, "one can't help liking her." Within a year of their first failed embrace, Carrington and Strachey made plans to move to the country together, a thoroughly unheard-of cohabitation that would never escape scrutiny outside the highly liberated Bloomsbury set.

Lytton's career had been slow to start, but at Tidmarsh Mill Carrington created a setting conducive to the writing that soon brought him popular success. She painted, kept a garden, and arranged for friends to visit on weekends. He gave her lessons in French, and read aloud from Gibbon's *The Decline and Fall of the Roman Empire*. Their blink-of-an-eye physical relationship gave way to a committed domesticity. She constantly worried that Lytton would find someone else to share his life with, however, and wished she could satisfy him sexually. "How I hate being a girl," she cried in one letter, "with female encumbrances & hanging flesh." A long, agonized relationship with a fellow Slade School artist, Mark Gertler, foundered under his pressure for physical intimacy. Intercourse, even the idea of it, left her feeling besmirched, and Carrington may in fact have suffered from what is known today as gender dysphoria.

In 1921, Tidmarsh Mill had added some more conventional ballast in the form of Ralph Partridge. The very tall and muscular ex–army officer, an Oxford friend of Carrington's brother, fell in love with her. Increasingly attached to Ralph's companionship, Lytton found him a job at Virginia and Leonard Woolf's Hogarth Press. Ralph doggedly pursued Carrington. Though she had no desire to marry, she acceded, as Virginia Woolf drily remarked, to "a legitimate union" to maintain their "Triangular Trinity of Happiness." Carrington continued using her name, refused to bear children, and made sure her husband accepted Lytton's primacy in her life.

Carrington said that "the discovery of a person, of an affection," was, next to her work, "the greatest thing I care about," and she sought these people beyond her marriage, which sagged beneath Ralph's demands and her resistance. Gerald Brenan, an aspiring writer and a wartime friend of Ralph's, provided an outlet, and it was to him that Carrington wrote, teasingly, of the smashing girl from Kentucky: "Ralph cut my hair too short last week. When it has grown longer and my beauty [has been] restored, I shall visit the lovely Henrietta and revive our drunken passion."

6

O LET'S GET MARRIED

*D*ora Carrington was not the only one with eyes for Henrietta at David's birthday party. Garnett used the occasion to introduce his friends to another protégé, a precocious young artist with a literary bent named Stephen Tomlin. As the years went on, Henrietta kept Tomlin's love letters and discarded Carrington's, presumably because one was a man and the other a woman.

Tomlin was Henrietta's age and the youngest son of an ambitious barrister who later joined the Privy Council. "Tommy," as he was called, attended Harrow School, where he won literary prizes and befriended Sylvia Townsend Warner, the daughter of one of his teachers. Ten years older than Tommy, she became this "successful, popular, and unhappy" boy's confidante. Two miserable terms at New College, Oxford, ended in Tomlin's expulsion, and in 1920 he announced he would study in London under the modernist sculptor Frank Dobson, a darling of the Bloomsbury critics Roger Fry and Clive Bell. In 1921, his college friend Michael Llewelyn-Davies (J. M. Barrie's ward) and a Harrow schoolmate drowned together under suspicious circumstances (they may have been romantically linked), and Tommy suffered a nervous collapse.

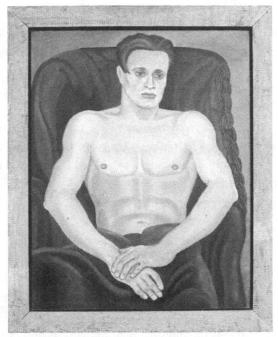

Portrait of Stephen Tomlin by John Banting, 1925

One afternoon in 1922 Tommy and his mother stepped into Birrell and Garnett's shop. Mrs. Tomlin was soon dispatched to a tea party and Tomlin and Garnett passed the next couple of hours looking at art books and debating everything from "Brancusi to Blake." Tommy so charmed David that he lost sight of selling anything. They closed the shop and parted, reluctantly. Eager for sitters, Tomlin soon induced Garnett to pose for him.

Stephen Tomlin stood about five feet six and had a fine torso, which he liked to show off. His classical nose gave him a strong profile, and his sandy hair, brushed away from his face, accentuated his high forehead. It was a face that drew one in, and his charisma was legendary. Tommy loved conversation, and Garnett claimed his laughter conveyed a greater range of expression than any he'd ever heard, from the deepest bitterness to the most mirthful delight. Tomlin's "ambidexterity" in sexual matters was much commented on among the Bloomsbury crowd, and Lytton Strachey found him "exciting—there is strength there—and a mind—a remarkable character." Sylvia Townsend Warner called him "a brilliant creature" who could "argue a hind leg off a donkey," perhaps "the only trait . . . he derived from his father." Besides artistic pursuits, Tommy read widely, composed poetry, and brought the writers Theodore Powys and Warner into Garnett's orbit.

Tommy's appearance in their lives pleased Mina, who, along with Dr. Jones, was pressing Henrietta to try men. But Tomlin came with complications—disapproving parents, limited means, and a terror of loneliness that fueled his promiscuity. Once, while waiting for Tommy in his studio, Garnett imagined him deep in an embrace and wrote on a large wall the names of those who might be detaining him. In characteristic humor, Tomlin painted a fig leaf over the names.

Promiscuity and wit were not enough to protect Tomlin's heart from Henrietta. He later wished that they had run off together and married the day after David's birthday celebration—he was sure they would never have "regretted it." The bachelor sculptor was nimbler than Carrington with her country house and multiple men to manage, and he began seeing Henrietta almost immediately after they met. Mina could be intimidating, and, whatever she said about moving forward from the relationship with Henrietta, her ongoing emotional entanglement often led her to judge Puppin's lovers severely. Tommy's first romantic outing with Henrietta was a double date of sorts, with Mina and David joining the pair. But Tommy, who was "falling badly in love," pined to see Henrietta alone. She sometimes responded warmly but other times with hesitation or made herself unavailable. The early weeks of their acquaintance established Tommy as an insecure lover, alternately thrilling to and resenting Henrietta's power over him. (The dynamic mimicked the role she was playing out with her father.) Tomlin said she had "robbed" him of the "healthy contempt . . . that becomes the amorous male."

Tommy eventually succeeded in getting Henrietta alone in his studio. They discussed psychoanalysis for hours, picking apart each other's dreams, comparing oedipal tensions and the fluidity of desire. It was a heady way of getting at the basic question of whether she found him attractive.

Henrietta was in the early throes of analysis. She was studying her family romance. Jones later argued that this intimacy led Henrietta to favor women as a means of avoiding conflicts with her fantasy lover, the Judge, and her psychotherapist pushed her to explore her attractions to other men. She was a willing, if inconsistent, participant in this heterosexual experiment, and Tommy and Henrietta's mutual enthusiasm for Freud's theories gave the pair a language for discussing who they were and what they wanted. Tommy explained his family conflicts, how his father hated his bohemian lifestyle and accused him of laziness. Henrietta's attitude toward Dr. Jones was so positive that she tried to get Tommy to try psychoanalysis himself, but he couldn't begin to afford the treatment and recoiled when she offered to pay for his sessions.

From October 1922, when Robert vanished in Louisville, through David's birthday party in March 1923, Henrietta's stay in London had been perpetually in question. The Judge told her it was "too self-centered, actually selfish," to remain and the time had come for her to experiment with living untethered from Dr. Jones. On one hand, her father urged her home; on the other a new father figure pressed her to stay and prescribed heterosexual romance. Each way Henrietta turned she felt the demands of others. She threw herself into the affair with Tommy, only to pull away, racked by ambivalence and indecision. Tomlin grew "harried and unhappy." He wanted her time, more of her time; if she came "to live with me now and we both lived to be 80," he told her, "I should still not have had sufficient time really to explore you." He pleaded with her not to leave England: "I love you. You are the best companion I have ever had and the most desirable lover. I have never known anyone with beauty like yours—that drives me nearly mad and yet fills me with deep content . . . I want you so."

Tommy's complaints came in spite of the fact that he and Henrietta saw a good deal of each other. They drove off together, and posted the always-interested David a cheesy souvenir card featuring a couple cozying together on a bench before a mountain with the caption HAVING THE TIME OF MY LIFE IN WALES. When the Sunbeam broke down on a drive into the country, they found an Automobile Association phone box to call for help and remained in the booth, flooding the cramped

space with desire. They took trips to the coast, to Brighton and Rom-
ney Marsh, walking for hours, and scrambled over the spreading green
Malvern Hills dotted with sweet-smelling yellow gorse. Tommy adored
dancing and Henrietta gave him Charleston lessons at nightclubs like
the Ham Bone and the Blue Lantern. In London, they took her *Courier-
Journal* press pass and saw opening night performances for free. He treasured these interludes. As long as they were alone together, conversation
never flagged, but he observed the way she glowed from the attention of
others. Tommy would fall silent, despairing of ever holding her interest.

Tomlin's bronze head of Henrietta—the artistic result of her
sittings—cocks leftward, listening sympathetically, which she so strikingly did to the people she loved. The sculpture captures the hint of a
smile, and a slight double chin. (It also conveyed Tomlin's "refusal to

Bust of Henrietta Bingham by Stephen Tomlin, 1923

flatter his sitters, however close they might be.") He caressed her full cheeks in clay, giving them a smoother surface than he used when rendering David, Duncan, Lytton, or Virginia Woolf. Tommy kept a plaster casting, and Henrietta bought one in bronze for her father, perhaps in a swipe at his possessiveness—for he must think of his daughter's suitor whenever he looked at it.

Jones would have welcomed Tommy to his practice. Indeed, he had acquired yet another patient connected to Henrietta, Mina's former student the poet Eleanor Chilton. The same week Henrietta sang "Water Boy" at David's birthday, Jones wrote to Freud of having now "three cases of female homosexuality," women whose lives were "intertwined with one another," a veritable lesbian laboratory. He told Freud he was finding that the women's identification with their mothers varied surprisingly—with some taking on a masculine and some a feminine position. One of them had described a "typical" mother-daughter beating fantasy. Mina's involvement with both young southerners became a point of discussion; Henrietta and Eleanor represented different aspects of Mina's fantasy self, Jones thought, with Eleanor as the "ironical blond girl" and Henrietta the "blue-eyed ego-ideal." They were tempting but immature outlets for her libido, he said; rather than yield to a man, Mina continued to derive satisfaction from her power over younger, female love objects.

Henrietta was preoccupied by her relationships with the Judge, Mina, Tommy, and David and her commitment to psychoanalysis, but if there was anything that she was truly in love with, it was black music. Listening and dancing to it, she touched pain and exhilaration, and accessed a different world where liberation trumped respectability. It was incredibly sexy. Her extensive knowledge of jazz surpassed that of anyone else in her circle of acquaintance, and this expertise coincided with a dawning realization in the wider transatlantic world that jazz and blues were not mere entertainment but bona fide art. The controversy over these new forms, and the admittance of African Americans into the white provinces of music, dance, theater, highbrow literature—and ultimately, by logical implication, society—made Henrietta, a pioneering connoisseur, all the more exotic and exciting to the people who knew her in London.

The "Negro vogue" known as the Harlem Renaissance was in its early days. Henrietta gathered news wherever possible, including from her father, who told her about an all-black show he took Barry to see in New York. *The Plantation Review* was among the first Broadway productions to play before a racially mixed audience and featured a vaudeville mélange of skits, solos, and song and dance numbers. Florence Mills, then building a following with her birdlike voice and sinuous dancing, and the pathbreaking Louisville-born jazz and blues singer Edith Wilson, had starring roles. An English theater promoter scouting talent in 1922 was so impressed that he signed a deal for the whole troupe to perform in London, backed by Will Vodery's jazz orchestra. Two and a half years before Josephine Baker made her sensational debut in Paris, they would fill out the second half of a variety show incongruously titled *From Dover Street to Dixie*.

Already playing in London in 1923 at a small theater was *Plantation Days*. James P. Johnson, "Father of Stride Piano" and Fats Waller's teacher, led a thirty-two-piece orchestra. Racist hecklers sometimes brought the show to a halt. One night, ignoring the actual rotten tomatoes and probably flashing her press pass, Henrietta beelined backstage to meet the performers. They informed her of the production about to open at the much grander Pavilion Theatre.

Opening night for *From Dover Street to Dixie* brought out the usual black tie and bejeweled audience. The all-white Dover Street section told a Rip Van Winkle tale set in modern-day London. Then came the "Dixie" act that Henrietta wanted to see. A massive sternwheeler paddleboat, the *Robert E. Lee*, dominated the set and one number featured chain-gang escapees in a wildly inspirational dance. *The New Statesman* suggested that Florence Mills's "charm is that she is neither boy nor girl but adolescent." A handful of theatergoers threw boots at the performers, but the general impression was that something new and brilliant had arrived. The celebrated ballroom dancer and film actress Irene Castle wept at the opening. One respected critic deemed Florence Mills, who was sadly never recorded, "by far the most artistic person

Florence Mills, center, in *From Dover Street to Dixie*, 1923

London has had the good fortune to see." Two months in, the show was earning $5,000 a week and playing to full houses—the Prince of Wales attended more than twenty performances.

Londoners embraced this and similar shows that traded on senti- mental and often racist stereotypes about black people in particular and the South in general. At some level Henrietta probably responded to the nostalgia as well, and to the popular interest in primitivism, which was shaped by broader trends in criticism and psychology. The Blooms- bury painter Roger Fry wrote admiringly of African art, and Tomlin, with his mentor Frank Dobson, had recently made a Parisian pilgrimage to see the Musée du Trocadéro's collection of tribal artifacts. Lytton Stra- chey's brother James and his wife, Alix—psychoanalysts then translating Freud's writings for Ernest Jones and the Hogarth Press—collected African artwork, seeing in it "a more direct expression of the Freudian unconscious."

But what Henrietta cared most about was the music and the re- markable talent of the people who played, sang, and danced to it. She knew quality and the most public way she could express her respect for the artists was to throw a party in their honor. In May 1923 Henrietta and Mina had exchanged the respectable but dreary apartment near the Ritz for a "pretty Regency villa" a few blocks from Tommy's Chelsea studio. David, always itching to bring people together, pointed out the advantages of the setting, and promised a hearty Bloomsbury turnout. Here, on a balmy evening at summer's dawn, members of *From Dover Street to Dixie*'s cast stepped into Henrietta's social circle. Such a violation of racial boundaries would have been impossible in Louisville and eyebrow-raising even in New York. In London, including "the colored element" was no less outrageous.

Judge Bingham was in London the night of the party. Stephen Tomlin had no idea how to manage Henrietta's father and David Garnett came to the rescue, chatting him up about politics and the idea of a literary dispatch from London to *The Courier-Journal*. Then Henrietta brought forward the singer Edith Wilson. In segregated Louisville, Wilson's mother had long worked as a cook and laundress for people likely to have been in the Judge's social circle. Edith's light complexion implied a mixed racial heritage, and in fact Confederate blood flowed in her veins as well as Henrietta's. Her great-grandfather was the slaveholding John C. Breckinridge, vice president of the United States under James Buchanan, and later commander of Kentucky's legendary Orphan Brigade—so called because its members felt abandoned by

Edith Wilson

their state's Union government and took up arms against it. At the party, Wilson, Garnett, and Robert Worth Bingham remained in conversation "for some time." Perhaps Wilson told David Garnett of her own claim to literary fame: that her grandmother was the template Harriet Beecher Stowe used for Eliza in *Uncle Tom's Cabin*. "It was an education for me to listen," wrote Garnett, who could not possibly have realized the awkwardness that underlay the "slow ease, the perfect courtesy" Wilson and Bingham maintained from their positions across the gulf of Jim Crow.

Henrietta led her father places he would not tread alone. Breaking down social barriers between the races was a radical idea he had no interest in. Bingham celebrated his own father's night-riding vigilantism with the fledgling Ku Klux Klan in Reconstruction North Carolina, and when an Englishwoman pressed him about the "hideous, horrible lynching of negroes," he retorted, "we would probably stop it when negroes stopped raping white women and girls." Yet Henrietta's influence can perhaps be seen in his financial support for the African American lyric tenor Roland Hayes, the nephew of a waiter at his men's club, who later that year debuted at Boston's Symphony Hall, and in Bingham's calls for moderation when KKK vigilantism surged again in the 1920s Midwest.

The summer heat encouraged informality—some of the men came wearing tennis clothes. The French windows were thrown open and the revelers moved lamps to illuminate the garden. A Romanian-born would-be writer named Jacques Haussmann arrived with Tomlin's old girlfriend Bea Howe. He remembered the American hostesses being "reputedly very rich," and that everybody seemed to have fallen "madly in love with them." Mina took pity on the uncertain young man, and they discussed favorite authors, while Carrington, "shattered by cocktails, late hours," appreciated the "American beauties'" great success. Everyone knew by then that Henrietta and Tommy were lovers, and Carrington assured a friend that her "heart remained intact." In the wee hours, long after Judge Bingham returned to his hotel, Mina's younger brothers, Lincoln and George, visiting from Boston, were rustled from their beds and dressed in "the girls'" pajamas. Lydia Lopokova of the Ballets

Russes led the Kirstein boys in "an impromptu pas de trois" amid the perennials. (It proved a formative night: ten years after this, Lincoln teamed with George Balanchine to found the New York City Ballet.) Lytton Strachey—who accepted American hospitality if not American tenants—served the Kirstein boys drinks and happily fielded Lincoln's queries about his beard. Even later, Henrietta, clad in purple, climbed up on the piano and played her sax.

There is such a thing as social magic, and Henrietta—the sort of person who, as Tomlin wrote, "made the party"—knew how to conjure it, mixing music, food and drink, conversation, seduction, and elements of surprise. The guests—popular Bloomsbury veterans like Duncan, intellectuals like Strachey, famous artists like Florence Mills, or shy newcomers like Haussmann—felt it. David told his mother it had been "the most delightful party I have ever known." Writing to Miss Kirstein, who was sitting for sketches, Duncan Grant called the gathering "absolutely perfect . . . beautiful to look at and delicious to taste." Would she pass on his especial thanks to "Henrietta, as I have always heard her called?" No "Miss Bingham," she.

Henrietta's other success was to further extend her time in London. Her father fussed about his health—doctors were giving him conflicting diagnoses, though his symptoms remain obscure—but he allowed her to stay through the summer. He had been following her "judgment and advice" with respect to the *Courier*'s editorial staff. He fired the managing editor and outlined plans for expanded distribution (midnight trains would run east and west from Louisville), but he would wait until she got home to go over the situation in detail. He also considered a run for governor, ultimately deciding against it. Better to put up a candidate who could "shove Kentucky ahead a generation." His maneuvers fell short, "really a tragedy," he mused to Henrietta. "Perhaps I should have taken it myself." He sought her counsel regarding Robert, and Barry, too. Should he keep Barry home for his senior year? "Darling, my faith, my hopes, [and] my chief hold on life are all in you and for you."

He and Barry would join Henrietta for a few weeks later that summer and then they would *all* sail home. He instructed her to reserve them a table for August 25, 1923, in the *Berengaria*'s upper-level dining saloon.

Tomlin's parents were content to see the American girl move on. Though his mother wrote thanking Henrietta for giving Tommy "his first orders," she coolly noted that she could not judge the likeness her son had sculpted, never having seen Henrietta without a hat. Rather than bring her to his home, Tommy took Henrietta to Chaldon Herring, where he had wintered in a cottage after his time at Oxford. The downs rolled into the sea and barrows sculpted the land. The hermit-like novelist Theodore Powys welcomed "Mad Tom" and his girl, and the whole village turned out to see them.

Her departure set, Henrietta still had six weeks of an English summer before her. She milked it for everything she could. Her $866 in monthly allowance would equal roughly $10,000 in 2015, and Mina's father was similarly generous. Failing to obtain Tidmarsh Mill from Lytton Strachey and Carrington, Mina and Henrietta rented a picturesque abbey in Hurstpierpoint, West Sussex. The country house was justified in part because Mina had the care of Lincoln and George, who studied at the abbey with Alec Penrose, a Cambridge scholar and friend of Tommy's. In London, Maynard Keynes took the boys to galleries and Tommy had them to his studio with its famous fig leaf. The countryside, especially when experienced on horseback, was a tonic to Henrietta's fraying spirits, for the nearer August 25 came, the more anxious she became. Mina sent President Neilson of Smith such a "seductive picture" of the setting that he worried she might never return to Northampton. Tomlin and Garnett were frequent guests, and David began a novel after a morning spent scything the abbey lawn and sipping cold beer from the bottles Henrietta passed around. His subject: the difficulty of fitting "the secret and private nature of physical passion into the social structure."

By midsummer, family obligations broke up Mina and Henrietta's routine, separating them, disrupting various liaisons, and unsettling emotions. Mina's mother, Rose, led her children on a proper tourist trip through England, with stops at St. Ives, Devon, and Bath. Psychoanalysis with Ernest Jones had not resolved her conflicts with her mother, and Mina grew increasingly irritable and insecure. (Dora Carrington could have spoken for either Henrietta or Mina when she noted, "However satisfactory it may be to discover the Freudian motives behind parents [*sic*] madness, I know it is not much consolation when one has to live with the scenes!") Missing David, Mina scolded him for not writing her enough, for standing up Eleanor Chilton, and for not progressing further on his novel. Even if her mother was more exhausting than all his projects and responsibilities put together, David could not help checking Mina sharply: there was "one thing about you that annoys me, which is the American Woman's demand for continual attention and meticulous politeness . . . combined with a total lack of imagination about [a man's] life." She said she wanted honesty about where she stood in his heart, and he obliged, telling her that she was less important to him than Duncan Grant or his wife, Ray. He nevertheless held out hopes of getting Mina into bed. Couldn't she get away for a day or two? "I do want you so much."

The Bingham clan kept chiefly to London except for weekends, when the Judge moved the group to an eighteenth-century castle called Formosa Place across the Thames from the Astors' Cliveden. On Barry's first night in London, Henrietta took him to see *From Dover Street to Dixie*, and brought him along to the Savoy. It impressed him to no end, mingling with Tallulah Bankhead, Adele Astaire, and a sultry silent film actress named Nita Naldi. Barry craved affection and it was easy for Henrietta to please him. Another day they strolled along the Chelsea Embankment, popped into Tommy's studio, and lunched with David at a hideaway called the Dugout. Barry picked her up after her appointments with Dr. Jones on Harley Street, and peering up to the window saw the analyst gazing at him as Henrietta made her way down. It was as close as he ever got to this mysterious personage.

Henrietta's far needier father inserted himself in her social life and commissioned Tomlin to create an eagle-topped gateway for the entry drive at Melcombe Bingham. One evening the Judge burst into David's room so suddenly that he had to cover his papers for fear the publisher would spy the passionate lines he was writing to Mina. Bingham ordered

a chauffeured motorcar to take the family, along with Tommy and David, for a walking trip in the country. David described the unnerving
journey to Mina: "Poor Tommy made occasional efforts . . . such as, 'Do
counties in America vary much in size?' Yet conversation flagged. The
Judge hummed. Barry sat in front. Henrietta looked particularly
murderous." The tension and absurd demands on his time exhausted
Garnett, who vowed to accept no more family invitations from the
Binghams. But David never blamed "dearest Honey, sweetest Puppin,"
whose misery was obvious.

Then it was over. Tommy said his good-byes as she boarded her ship.
"O darling, it was horrible," he wrote later that day. "I thought that the
way I loved you was so quiet and profound that I shouldn't really be upset
by your going away." Henrietta dropped a folded note over the railing,
a gesture that preserved his "wits."

Mina and Henrietta's English friends tried to view their departure
as an interregnum. David, who had been "just crazy to have a car," was
tasked with selling Henrietta's Sunbeam, but in the meantime he ferried
Vanessa Bell and her children to the seaside and sped out to see Tommy
(reduced to a miserable state) in Chaldon Herring. He said Henrietta's
going away was like having his teeth fall out. "The whole of London"
missed them, David told Mina. For her part, Mina was thinking of
taking a publishing job in London to be nearer him, but at other times
she considered cutting off the relationship altogether. Henrietta assured
him this would never happen.

Sailing first-class aboard the *Berengaria*, Robert Worth Bingham was
in a celebratory mood. Henrietta was not. Was she sick or just sulking,
he wondered. He organized a tennis tournament on deck. A member
of the Slazenger family of sports equipment fame umpired. Henrietta,
though an avid player, declined to take part. Neither did she help her
father with an after-dinner benefit he chaired one night during the
crossing. In Louisville she ignored the Judge's suggestion that she write
the history of the cooperative movement in agriculture. (At a tobacco
growers' picnic that summer in Cynthiana, Kentucky, there was a pageant that enacted the "Great Judge" rescuing "Princess Tobago" from

drowning in "mortgages, low prices, and uncertainty.") To join his enterprises in high-minded journalism or cooperative agriculture were objectively honorable tasks, and the fact that a southern patriarch solicited advice from a daughter and extended such an offer remains astonishing. In reality, this feminist scenario stemmed as much from unhealthy family dynamics as progressive ideals, and Henrietta would not commit, especially to her father. Rather than refuse outright and alienate the man who paid her bills, she delayed and deferred.

In September in Asheville, Henrietta steadied the knife as the old Colonel Bingham cut his eighty-fifth-birthday cake. Back at Melcombe, she helped host the former British prime minister David Lloyd George, his wife, and their youngest daughter, who was her age. There was luncheon at Melcombe, a round of golf, and an excursion to Abraham Lincoln's homestead. Germany was the topic of the day. Unable to make payments on its war debt, and beset by terrific inflation, the nation seemed ready to crumble.

But America was booming. The Judge had acquired a fireproof storage business for Robert, and Barry was coming into his own, his exhilarating personality compensating for his shortcomings in the manly arts of sport and hunting. That fall of 1923, Henrietta helped rescue him from the hated Middlesex School, persuading the Judge to hire a tutor who could prepare him for entry to Harvard. In Louisville, he trailed behind Henrietta and her diverting and myopic friend Edie Callahan, a lesbian who guzzled champagne and whose father was a leading Louisville prohibitionist. Edie trained in classical piano in New York before reporting on the Versailles Treaty negotiations for the *Catholic Record*, and in 1923 the Judge installed her as the *Courier-Journal* book editor. Many in Louisville believed she and Henrietta were lovers.

They weren't. Henrietta "declared herself very unsettled and dissatisfied" at home. She was a controversial figure, who lacked all interest in the Junior League activities that occupied her peers. One contemporary who spurned her company said simply that "Henrietta was not congenial. She was real crazy about girls, you see, and I was crazy about boys."

Both to distract from this kind of society and excuse herself from her father's projects, Henrietta needed an occupation, something not too dull or confining, and she proposed opening (with Edie and Barry as assistants) a bookstore near the *Courier-Journal* building in downtown Louisville. (Barry, who wanted to write novels, loved the idea.) In early 1924, "Papa" advanced the money for the Wilderness Road Book Shop, named after the trail that guided pioneers westward from Virginia through Kentucky. David Garnett sent crates of books from London to stock the shelves—surely Wilderness Road was the only outlet in Kentucky to offer Theodore Powys's new novel, featuring an amorous female member of the Salvation Army. (Tomlin asked Henrietta to "boost" Powys "in your papers.") The shop got free advertising in the *Courier-Journal* book section, to which Garnett contributed literary newsletters from London. The competition claimed to be the "Largest Book and Stationery Store South of the Ohio River" whereas the Wilderness Road eschewed all nonliterary novelties.

The shop remained a fixture in Louisville for several decades but only briefly held Henrietta's attention. Through the fall of 1923 and the early months of 1924 she was preoccupied with escape. Stephen Tomlin ached to know when she could return and confided to David, "For me there are two states of being, when I am with her & when I am not." Within hours of her ship leaving port, his letters began streaming across the ocean and overland to Louisville. The arrival of a long letter from Kentucky served to "let loose the dogs of longing at my vitals again." But her letters were too few. If only he could ignore her, "But it's no good trying to reverse our tactical positions. You got me to my knees at the start and I suppose that is where I shall remain."

Trapped in what felt like a desert of news, Tommy pumped information out of David Garnett, who had a more regular correspondence with Mina. After a long walk through the London Zoo, taking measure of eagles for the Bingham gateposts, he and David went to dinner and talked for hours of Henrietta and Mina, making a "decoction of our tears and our Burgundy." David was teasing, but as the weeks went on with no sign that Henrietta would be back in London in January as she had hoped, Tommy pleaded only half-jokingly for Henrietta to at least get some lackey to forward him her schedule. Where did she take her meals? What hours did she keep at the Wilderness Road? What books did she read? How did she entertain the bishops, ambassadors, and financiers passing through her doors? What about her drives with youthful millionaires? Surely he might hear something of her glittering evenings spent "surrounded by adorers of every sex." He had no doubt she was "the triumphant success you always are everywhere," and he did not mind. He only wanted some way to picture her.

Tommy pledged never to smother Henrietta with social expectations and restrictions. His sexuality, hers, and their freedom in love were sacred—even if they provided grist for Bloomsbury's gossip mill. Some considered Tomlin "a prestige bugger"; most acknowledged his bisexuality. Tommy was not terribly stable or mature himself. He wanted "to be anchored to the one strong thing I have come across" in the world.

> I wish more than I can say, and more strongly everyday, that I was "engaged" to you. (I to you, mark you, not you to me. I don't want that. If you had tied yourself in any way I should be in continual agonies of fear that you were regretting and I should hate it.) I use the word "engaged" . . . I don't mean in the matrimonial sense! I mean bound to you in some way.

This murky declaration failed to clear a path between the two of them. An old woman who lived near his studio asked Tomlin where his lass had gone and when he said America, she could not understand why he didn't go after her. He hadn't any money to follow, but if he had it would have meant confronting the Judge directly as a penniless suitor. Besides, Henrietta was nearly inscrutable. He began to suspect she was done with him and tried to stop thinking of her at all.

At Christmas Tommy found himself at the receiving end of Henrietta's legendary generosity. She adored the holiday and sent silk pajamas in which he slept "in exquisite solitude" as well as a shipment from her father's hunting plantation in Georgia. As Tommy and David cracked the "pekon nuts" and sipped the bourbon, David posed a question Henrietta had asked him to present to Tommy: Would he marry her?

My Beloved,

Bunny [David] has told me of the questions in your letter to him. My darling, I haven't written lately because (as I heard nothing from you) I thought my letters had probably become a mere irritation to you. No one knows better than I do how infuriating an unwanted affectionate letter can be. I vowed I would not write again till I heard from you not in the least as a retaliation on you, but simply as a restraint on myself lest I should weary you. My dear I have longed to write. I have thought of you continually and striven ineffectually to comfort myself by writing sonnets about you (as I could not write letters to you). If you want proof you shall have them some day—that is if you can support bad poetry.

I have wanted to hear from you more than I can say. It has been rather intolerable simply hearing of you from other people . . .

I have a curious and constantly recurring dream about you. It varies in detail, but is always the same in general development. It begins in an ordinary sexual way. I am always conscious of being in a strange place, America perhaps, or some house you have taken me to. You at first are always loveable and nude. Later I dress you, usually in some rather surprising and beautiful dress (once it was a very elaborate and be-flounced riding habit). Then you begin to reproach me about some trivial neglect or other, not angrily but persistently . . . and I am conscious of contentment that your rebukes cannot disturb my happiness, when I have you before me to delight in and admire. I dream something like this over and over again. I submit it, darling, to your expert scrutiny.

My angel, how serious is your enquiry as to "whether I would consider marrying you"? You know that I love you, that I have never met a woman that I admire as I do you, that I firmly believe I shall never meet such another. I can imagine no happiness like having you continually by me, for me to admire and love; like sharing to some extent your life and beauty. I want above all things to watch you; to be able to see you going upon your magnificent course. If marrying you meant "possession" in that you would lose your own identity and personality— then I should hate marriage and probably you. But I love you because I believe that impossible . . .

Come back, darling, in January as you said you would. And then, if you really think you know all about me and have no illusions, O let's get married. But I only want to see you again—that's the great thing, to see you and kiss you . . . I enclose a photo stolen from an old album at home of me in a more innocent state. You, darling, will be able to appreciate my development!

It was not exactly a ringing proposal. Henrietta kept the letter and the picture of Tomlin as a boy—in the nude. But January 1924 found Henrietta not in London but in Louisville, evidence of who wielded the power in her life. Marriage was an obvious way out, and the more desperate she felt, the more appealing it must have seemed. Tommy, Mina, her father, Dr. Jones—their expectations and desires, conflicting and unspoken, swirled and eddied around her own. Sometimes they were so tangled that she couldn't think.

Ernest Jones had by no means rid Henrietta and Mina of the complicated feelings they had for each other. People at Smith knew of their year abroad. Suspicion followed Mina back to Northampton, and the burden of secrecy settled over them again in America. David Garnett predicted that Mina would miss him less than he missed her. He felt certain that above all others "the person you'll miss will be Henrietta, and you'll very soon learn our relative importance in your life." Despite all the noise Mina made about moving on from their affair, he was right. That January before Smith's students returned from Christmas holidays, Henrietta visited Mina. After Mina drove her to the station, she took out an old diary and found a few blank pages at the back.

Henrietta said this afternoon that all one can expect in life is a certain inward continuity and she is right. Personal relationships may enrich the consistency of the flux of life, they may even change it but one can never depend on them or expect anything permanent from them. Henrietta I love as I never have and never shall love any one again. A half an hour ago she was here. Now she is gone. To attempt to reason out the significance of these separations is futile. All my life I have been separated from the people I loved though I have had more of her than of Ben or David. Under my care she has changed from a frightened, rebellious child to an independent, reliable girl. Her judgment is unsurpassed. The keenness and directness of her mind carve out infallible opinions. By her alone, could any of my decisions be influenced.

Mina made no further entries in that journal. Perhaps, when she gave it to Smith with her boxes of papers, she did not notice these outlying pages. Or maybe she intended to leave behind this solitary affirmation of her feelings for Henrietta Worth Bingham.

That winter Mina introduced Henrietta to Franklin P. Adams, member of the Algonquin Round Table and an influential columnist at the *New York World*. He dined with the "fair and witty girl from Kentucky," an "old newspaperwoman," Adams called her. Mina journeyed to Louisville, as well, and the women plotted a summer reunion in England. David and Ray Garnett were in Spain and thought of settling there more permanently, renting Carrington's friend Gerald Brenan's Andalusian retreat. David envisioned driving south to Granada with Tommy and Mina—Henrietta at the wheel, of course. "I can't imagine," David said, "a more exciting or amusing trip." (Ray and their children went unmentioned.) David proposed Mina start a magazine that would supply her with a "métier" in England. He was at work on a short story about a scientist seeking to isolate human emotions; he concluded that love could never be disentangled from "jealousy, fear, cruelty, and lust," and was nothing more than "a mixture of other passions." Love was messy and unreliable. But nothing was more important. Writing to Henrietta on the subject of her future, David hoped she had "no doubts what you are going to do" about Tommy. "You shouldn't have."

7

EFFECTS OF HENRIETTA

In January 1924, in Northampton, Henrietta had impressed Mina with her transformation from "a frightened, rebellious child to an independent, reliable girl." The twenty-three-year-old was seriously considering (if not planning) a union with Stephen Tomlin, a momentous step that would shape the rest of her life. But Henrietta failed to return to London in January as she'd hoped, and by late spring a crisis gripped Melcombe. We know very little about what happened, though Henrietta's friends were terribly concerned. What seems clear is that Henrietta's fraught relationship with her father reached a nadir and (the two events are almost certainly connected) Robert Worth Bingham severed all ties with Professor Kirstein.

Given her passionate investment in Henrietta's well-being, Mina may have been destined to come to loggerheads with the other chief force in her friend's life. The rift apparently developed during Smith's spring recess, when Mina made a trip to Louisville. Babes Bingham had died eleven springs ago; her survivors still seemed traumatized, emotionally at sea after their shipwreck. Henrietta had made it clear that she wanted to go back to London while her father adamantly wanted her home with him. It was to some degree a war of wills and the Judge never did "take kindly to defeat." Feelings may have been raw when Mina arrived.

Several accounts of the conflict between these two figures have survived—two only in the oral record. In one Mina the bisexual blue-stocking, in love with Henrietta, seduced the Judge and angled to marry him to get her hands on his wealth and be with his daughter. Bob Bingham had expressed respect for and gratitude to Mina, but there is no evidence that Mina, already well-off, aspired to become part of the Bingham family. Most likely, this story served to besmirch Mina's character in the wake of the discord. In another version of the event, referenced by Frida Laski, Judge Bingham made advances, was rebuffed, and, in his humiliation, banished Mina for good. The final surviving account builds on Henrietta's longtime terror of being "found out" by her father. She told a friend that her window-peeping brother reported to their outraged father an act of lesbian "perversion" (past or present) between Mina and his sister. Robert, especially, had reason to resent Henrietta, the apple of their father's eye.

Of the three accounts, the tattletale brother is the most convincing. It fits the dynamics at work and supplies ample reason for Bingham, disgusted and embarrassed, to blame Mina for everything that upset him about Henrietta's life. Perhaps he did try to woo Miss Kirstein. If so, this could have prompted Robert to "tell" on the professor and Henrietta. Judge Bingham might threaten to report Mina, and her horror of what would happen to her life if word spread that she was a lesbian could spur her to retaliate. Mina had a weapon, too. The Judge's treatment of Henrietta appalled her; she thought he was in love with his daughter. How could Bingham defend himself if Mina whispered to the right people (and she knew a number of those people in the worlds of politics and journalism) about an inappropriate, incestuous relationship with his alluring but neurotic daughter?

Where the truth lies is unknowable, but the rift was permanent, and Mina was "banned from the family circle." Ill-equipped to handle any of the possibilities, Henrietta spun in a maelstrom.

Inklings of trouble in Louisville seeped into the letters Henrietta and Mina sent David Garnett. David pointedly asked for news of "Puppin and how she is handling the judge." Garnett was not one to fret or overdramatize, yet later that spring he told Mina, "Henrietta's letter disturbs me very much." He was "sure that there is only one thing to be done: that it will have to be done in the end and that it would be better to get it over—and that is a complete rupture. Money is of no importance." These were strong words. What could be going on that necessitated such a dramatic break between a parent and child? David promised to "find out exactly how all that business stands" when the "poor badgered" girl got to England in the summer.

In June, Henrietta, her father, and the president of the Burley Tobacco Growers Co-operative Association docked in England at the head of a European tour to broker purchasing contracts. Everyone was abuzz with the latest news of the cold-blooded kidnapping and murder of a fourteen-year-old boy in Chicago by a pair of college students named Nathan Leopold and Richard Loeb. Mina's father, recently elected as chair of Boston's Chamber of Commerce and exquisitely sensitive to negative portrayals of Jews, wrote to his wife of the "perfectly terrible" situation. He made special reference to an unprintable but widely understood aspect of the case, that Leopold and Loeb were "undeniably great perverts," for which "their parents are severely criticized." Linking antisocial criminality and sexual irregularity was commonplace.

While Judge Bingham met with dignitaries and tobacco manufacturers, David and Tommy celebrated the return of their rattled friend. "Henrietta is heavenly," Garnett told his wife, "and was so pleased to be back it was almost painful." The first night they sat outside in the warm air of Brunswick Square, sipping brandy and popping whole cherries into their mouths. But Henrietta's reunion with her lover, the man she had all but asked to marry her, got off awkwardly; neither of them knew how to proceed, and Garnett wrote that they found "it impossible to communicate except by telephone through me. I arrange their meetings, etc." The tobacco mission ended in failure; Bingham's campaign was now in crisis. Grandiose oratory had drawn growers in and the new warehouses made it possible to delay sales, but tobacco prices failed to stabilize.

Detractors pointed to Aaron Sapiro's $48,000 salary and the way Bingham became distracted from Kentucky as he stumped for farming cooperatives from Maine to Georgia. Then came news that he needed to return immediately to the United States: a letter from Garnett to his wife reported that the Democratic Party might nominate Bingham for president. At this remarkable moment in Bob Bingham's life his daughter withdrew from him. She lobbied to stay in London until his return to shoot grouse in Scotland that August. He sailed home without her.

Henrietta had six weeks. It was as if she had burst out of prison, and, rather than carefully consider her options, Henrietta became swept up in a frenetic social life that sparked new sexual encounters. Tommy took her for an impromptu visit to Tidmarsh Mill—Lytton had developed an interest in the well-muscled sculptor. Henrietta brought a basket of cocktail supplies and told David they had enjoyed "much drinking & poker-playing and general friendliness on all sides." Carrington's friend the artist Barbara Bagenal came up in the conversation. "Charming girl," Henrietta pronounced boldly, "have you ever made love to her, Carrington?" That weekend, the seed of Carrington's attraction, sowed at David's birthday party a year before, suddenly germinated.

With her father upset, the question of marrying Tommy lying open and unresolved, and Mina about to arrive for the summer, Henrietta launched an affair with a painter who had a husband, a lover, and the companionship of a gay man who made a display of disliking "that bulky American." Lytton's feelings were not widely shared: his sister-in-law, Alix, was smitten, and after watching Henrietta over the course of an evening, Lytton's lover Philip Ritchie called her "an oasis." At Tidmarsh, Ralph Partridge surmised that the "only safe place for Henrietta was in Lytton's bed, if she wanted a quiet night."

The idea of driving to Spain for the summer never came off. However, after four years of exile in a remote village outside Granada, Gerald Brenan returned to London shortly before Henrietta arrived in 1924. He wanted to complete his biography of Spain's patron saint Teresa—and be near Carrington, whom he had loved from afar since 1920. Henrietta's liaison with Carrington was, consequently, detailed in the snowstorm of correspondence Carrington and Brenan exchanged that summer.

During the same six weeks, Carrington's husband, Ralph (who habitually steamed open and read her mail), took up with David Garnett's sister-in-law, Frances Marshall. In letters to his new girlfriend, Ralph made frequent mention of Henrietta and Carrington's feelings for her. Carrington kept a diary about Henrietta, and shared it with her paramour Gerald, who was initially untroubled by his lover's fascination with the Kentuckian. Regarding their questionable ménage, Lytton had once quipped, "everything at sixes and sevens—ladies in love with buggers, and buggers in love with womanisers, and the price of coal going up, too!"

Henrietta, Mina, and the Kirstein boys had planned to share a house again that summer, but the break with the Judge ruined that idea. Henrietta rented a flat for herself on Cheyne Walk by the Chelsea Embankment. For the Kirsteins, she located a diminutive row house on a quiet Knightsbridge corner. On the only day between her father's departure and Mina's landing, Henrietta and Carrington passed a long afternoon at the empty Knightsbridge house, which, Carrington wrote, "no one knew of but us." Maybe it was then that Henrietta posed in the nude for the painter. She stood confidently, her head tilting as if assessing Carrington, her right hand beckoning, her muscular legs ending in pumps that made them even longer and more erotic. The transactions of that day culminated in something Dora Carrington had never before experienced: "ecstasy . . . and no feelings of shame afterwards."

A thrilling chapter in Carrington's life opened. There had been flirtations with women before, but the overarching theme for as long as she could recall was revulsion toward her body and resistance to physical desires—her lovers' and her own. To awaken such pleasures was a triumph Henrietta surely delighted in. Neither woman made any pronouncements about it but they continued to see each other, with more tentativeness than regularity. In contrast to the urgency and volatility Carrington associated with heterosexual relations, a pregnant hush subsisted between them. "We are the most silent of friends," Carrington remarked. "But I feel sure she is very like her early Italian exterior," with "a goodness that is unusual." Enraptured yet wary, Carrington mused, "Perhaps it's all a delusion, she may of course be quite uninteresting inside."

Henrietta, just twenty-three, was drawn in, as she had been by Mina;

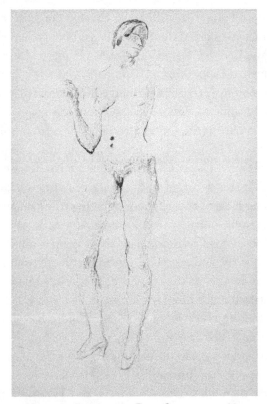

Henrietta Bingham by Dora Carrington, 1924

Carrington was a talented, sensitive, bold yet insecure older woman connected to a sophisticated world. She inspired the painter, thirty, to take driving lessons—of course it wasn't too late! Carrington felt frumpy, but she struck others as perpetually youthful, emanating what one memoirist called a "remarkable impression of sunlight." Within their social circles, both Carrington and Henrietta possessed less intellectual polish than their cohort. Over the years, Carrington worked to bridge the gap through tutorials with Strachey and an eclectic, enthusiastic approach to reading. Henrietta was appealing in part because she seemed not to mind that gap, and had other tools for conveying her intelligence and making herself irresistible.

This passionate connection came about at a time of transition for the occupants of Tidmarsh Mill. Long cohabitation, jealousy, and dis-appointment had weakened their three-legged stool of a household and a fresh start was in order. Ralph's affair with Frances Marshall, a bright Oxford graduate then working at Birrell and Garnett's shop, came as a relief to Carrington. A consensus emerged that extending their cohab-itation required someplace more spacious and less plagued by the cold and the damp. Carrington found a roomy Wiltshire farmhouse some thirty miles from Tidmarsh, which Lytton bought with earnings from his latest biography, *Queen Victoria*. The large windows opened onto a broad, bright green swath of turf. The garden vista was dramatic and romantic—a ha-ha kept the neighbor's grazing cows in lower meadows that stretched to the partially wooded downland hills. With eight bed-rooms, the house could accommodate all its regular inhabitants plus a large weekend party, and everyone agreed that more would be merrier.

Ham Spray House, as they called it, first needed new heating and electrical systems, which hired workers installed. But Carrington man-aged the repainting every room required. Tomlin brought "La Bing-ham," as Lytton called her, from London along with two of Lytton's boyfriends, to add muscle to the communal effort Carrington mustered over several weeks that summer of 1924. Her taste in decoration was less exuberant than what Duncan Grant and Vanessa Bell famously created at Charleston; she took her palette (pink, yellow, white, blue) from Fra Angelico and Giotto. Brushes were distributed and, accord-ing to Strachey, Henrietta "whitewashed unceasingly and never said a word." "Never a drop spilt on the floor," Carrington marveled, "and so economical that one pot of paint lasts her a whole day." Hour upon hour, Henrietta and Carrington worked side by side, sexual tension rising. After breaking for tea, the group set out for a walk. As the others moved off, Carrington drew Henrietta to a side path. Writing to Brenan the following day, she told of their striding

> far across the ploughed fields, through little conifer plantations until
> we came onto "Sheepless Down," and saw faraway in the distance the
> downs of Tidworth and Salisbury. She won me by being completely
> captivated by my downs. I long for you to know her . . . She dresses

badly, talks American, and has a hundred faults but somehow they don't matter, she is so beautiful, and so charmingly sensitive.

Their conversation took Carrington deep into formative sexual memories—bedwetting, a spanking, a peeping Tom—which Henrietta may have asked her lover to consider in relation to her overwhelming physical shame. Meanwhile, among the others, Stephen Tomlin's flirtations matched Henrietta's. An affair with Duncan Grant the previous year and a budding flirtation with Lytton Strachey gave the couple a promising parity. Two hours flashed by, and it was nearly nine when the women returned to Ham Spray all warmth and smiles. Ralph had been waiting impatiently while "the buggers" speculated about what might be taking place and he loudly berated his wife for making them late for an evening party in London.

Soon thereafter, Tommy accepted a potential patron's invitation to spend several weeks on the coast of Italy. The wealthy novelist Leo Myers asked Tomlin and the sculptor Frank Dobson to a sixteenth-century castle overlooking Portofino. Tommy urged Henrietta to join in, and when she wouldn't go he sent letters about the "ravishing little American blond" he met on the train—Henrietta would have found her "distinctly 'bedworthy.'" For Tommy's part, "one or two god-like fisher-boys who spread their nets where we bathe" did "pluck the heart strings a little." But his ruminations came back to Henrietta. He wanted her. "Darling, do try to have some free time when I get back," he pleaded, "so that I can see something of you before your father comes." Henrietta responded positively. Whatever (clearly tolerated) adventures she shared with Carrington, Henrietta's serious relationship with Tomlin was taken for granted and she probably saw more of him, until he left England, than any other lover. Their being together, however, meant that he did not write often, and there is no way to tell what she was thinking about their future. In late July, however, she agreed that they would meet in Paris.

Gerald Brenan claimed he never saw the woman his lover found so delectable, and at first showed no jealousy of her, but in retrospect he realized he "lost half" of Carrington to Henrietta. Carrington had always had enough time to spare, but Ham Spray's renovation, Lytton, Ralph, her own work, houseguests, and this new affair absorbed her every moment. Brenan had a room in town where he worked on his biography of Saint Teresa and augmented his small income by giving Spanish lessons. He yearned to experience in the flesh an affair that had simmered for years at long distance but Carrington kept him at bay. His relationship with Ralph Partridge grew so tense that Ham Spray was off-limits. More than once, Gerald rescheduled his and Carrington's carefully planned dates so that Carrington could instead meet her "charming and intimate friend." After Mina and her brothers arrived and occupied the Knightsbridge house, Gerald offered the women his rooms and his discretion. Even in these circumstances, he did what he could for Carrington.

Believing that honesty enhanced their love, Carrington shared her feelings about Henrietta with Brenan. "I think it's no good being anything but what you are," Carrington told a friend, "and the great thing is never to do anything one doesn't feel genuinely inside oneself." Bloomsbury's informal principle of seizing happiness where one could theoretically made jealousy verboten; nonetheless, Brenan felt wounded and destabilized. Carrington apologized for being "carried away by Kentucky princesses."

Mina Kirstein had her own pain to manage. She was "furious with Carrington" and refused to "come near her." Hurt and angry to see Henrietta involving herself with another woman, Mina did not stifle her disapproval. When Henrietta suggested that a day of manual labor at Ham Spray would do the teenage Kirsteins good, Mina drove out separately and, rather than join the work crew, lay alone on the lawn, reading. Carrington handed pots of paint to the "large American boys," then went off with Henrietta to stroke the hallway's walls pale yellow. Henrietta's aura coated Carrington like the paint on the brushes—"At once I become happy when she is there with me."

Adding to Mina's disappointment, David Garnett and his expanding family had forsaken London for a jewel-like seventeenth-century manor near Cambridge. It, too, required extensive renovations. Thus "engrossed in his domains," keeping bees and writing steadily, David proved an unreliable support to Mina during her summer visit. David and Mina may never have had a physical relationship—a letter he wrote her in the 1970s suggests that they never managed to sleep together. There was her "Puritan" restraint, and one amorous opportunity fizzled when the bed fell apart. Years later, as he considered his and Mina's long friendship, Garnett concluded that the real "obstacle to our becoming lovers was Henrietta"—they were both besotted and couldn't admit it. Mina ultimately found out that David and Henrietta had betrayed her together. Garnett seems not to have had any regrets and later told his daughter that "when he took [Henrietta] to bed, she blushed all over her body."

Sidelined and hurt, Mina felt destined always to be "runner-up" in other people's affections. Her old beau, Ben Huebsch, commented that Mina's going to England looked to him like "annual self-torture." Tommy and Mina grew closer, commiserating about their treatment at Henrietta's hands; he even brought Mina a Manx cat to keep her company. In her memoirs, Mina unkindly labeled Carrington a "permanently adolescent, gamine-type of dabbler in the arts," while Tomlin was a "delightful, talented sculptor."

Mina Kirstein never moped for long. She met with Ernest Jones, sat for a portrait by Duncan Grant, and took tea with David's father, Edward, with whom she discussed the shortcomings of David's female characters in *The Man in the Zoo*. (The novel was dedicated to her and Henrietta.) Grant, then thirty-nine and a veteran of countless affairs and personal dramas, thoroughly enjoyed Mina's visits, from which he learned Henrietta Bingham's whole "hairraising" [*sic*] "history"—the wreck on the train tracks, the sudden Flagler wealth followed by accusations of murder, her father's demands, cloaked in devotion.

In a bold move to distract herself from Henrietta, Mina invited the forty-four-year-old art critic Clive Bell, a Bloomsbury insider (his wife, the painter Vanessa Bell, had a long-term attachment to Duncan Grant), to dinner at her house and also to a party Henrietta threw. Mina loosened up so much that she wrote to him the next day to check her "hazy memory" of what had been said and done. Everyone assumed they'd slept together, and Bell confirmed the suspicion a few weeks

Mina Kirstein by Duncan Grant, 1923

later when he informed Lytton that "Minna's [*sic*] underclothes are the best in America." Clive was taken with Mina and he met her "in a state of pleasing agitation and a dinner jacket" at Kettner's, a venerable locale in the theater district where the king used to dine with his mistresses. Clive had a weakness for intellectual women, and his conversation met Mina's standards, though he was terribly full of himself. Mina went over it all with Ernest Jones. Awed by Bloomsbury figures but disapproving of the group's homosexual irregularities, Jones quipped, "one must expect a man who achieves the rare combination of a Bloomsbury address with [heterosexual] potency to suffer from swelled head in consequence."

Gerald Brenan, poster child for obsessive love, drew a chart on the inner cover of his diary, the X axis representing time and the Y axis measuring the quality of his relations with Carrington. His frustration in 1924 found expression in a downward-trending line noting various temporary separations. He marked the most dramatic descents "effects of H[enrietta]." Carrington admitted, in imperfect French, that the twenty-four-year-old "killed my desires for *les jeunes garçons* pretty completely." "I am impossible." At the same time, she worried whether Henrietta could return her feelings, and compared her posture with Henrietta to Gerald's dissatisfaction with her. "Henrietta repays my affections almost as negatively as you find I do yours." Henrietta didn't respond to letters for days at a time and Ralph pitied Carrington—"nobody loves her and she loves everybody, especially, 'darling Henrietta.'" Being unavailable to those who adored and needed her empowered Henrietta when she was otherwise feeling confused or guilty. Before leaving for Paris and Tommy, this "most Exquisite and charming character" shared a blissful night with Carrington in her freshly painted bedroom at Ham Spray.

Carrington's special diary on Henrietta did not survive, but many of her letters have, and through them one can make out Henrietta's very physical effect on her lovers. Discretion has meant that such effects generally escape historical analysis and description, but that doesn't take away their force. Carrington put into words the feelings and "physical gestures" the Kentuckian aroused in her. Henrietta drove her to constantly think "of certain sensations & wish to God [she] was here so I could repeat them." But Henrietta wasn't there—not enough of the time, anyway, for Carrington or any of the men and women who loved her. The painter concluded to stop "pressing that excelerator [*sic*]," and be satisfied at having known "her as I knew her," but then the longings surged again. "I fear I love her."

The rumors, flirtations, and experimentations of six intense weeks in the summer of 1924 did not alter the perception of Henrietta and Tommy as a couple. A photographer captured them, Henrietta astride Carrington's bob-tailed white mare, Belle, Tomlin riding shotgun behind her, his hands resting easily on her hips as the horse shifted under them. Another snapshot shows them standing before Ham Spray's door—Henrietta in tall gleaming boots and boutonniered jacket, gloves in one hand and long crop in the other—squinting into the sun. She stood above Tommy, gripping his arm. Tomlin grinned, pipe in mouth, hands clasped together like a bride.

In early August the free weeks of summer ended for Mina and Henrietta. Rose Kirstein arrived and set off with her children on a tour of Normandy, Brittany, and Germany. The family shared a sobering experience in Bayreuth—Wagner's controversial Ring Cycle was being performed for the first time since the war. The clerk at the hotel where

Henrietta and Tommy, Ham Spray, circa 1924

they had reserved rooms told them they would be "happier" boarding at the home of "Frau Steinkraus, a co-religionist."

The arrival of Henrietta's "dreadful father and brothers," as Carrington called the Bingham men, bore negative implications. David's advice about making a complete "break" went unheeded. In early August, on the day before the Binghams set off for Scotland, Carrington bid Henrietta a rushed and miserable farewell with Mina and Tommy looking on, equally miserable.

However she steeled herself for the pilgrimage to the Argyll hunting grounds, nothing prepared Henrietta for her father's revelation delivered between grouse shoots on the moors. The family party would return to London sooner than expected because there, on August 20, 1924, Robert Worth Bingham would marry for the third time.

8

AN' I WISH I WAS HAPPY AGAIN

*H*enrietta vomited for five straight hours at the news from her father. "General frightful crises with Binghamesque scenes," Dr. Jones reported to his wife. Mary Lily had been dead seven years, and a fifty-three-year-old man seeking comfort, affection, and support from a respectable Louisville widow made all the sense in the world. Given the pressure Henrietta felt from her father, one might expect her to welcome him finding love—or even just companionship that might ease her burden. Henrietta was thinking of marrying Stephen Tomlin, after all.

But reason had no place in the relationship between Robert Worth Bingham and his daughter. Henrietta's response to Mary Lily had been to pitch a tantrum; this time, the overwhelming emotions left her physically ill.

She was certain the marriage was punishment for frustrating him, for dodging greater intimacy and collaboration in his life and work, and perhaps most of all for loving someone else. Because of the role she had taken on as a child, Henrietta felt guilty if she put anyone ahead of the Judge. In loving a woman, she also violated social propriety, and there was enormous shame in that. If her father suffocated her, suffocation was preferable to alienation, for, notwithstanding Ernest Jones's efforts, Henrietta's childhood wounds from sudden and total loss had yet to heal. Her compensations for that loss made her feel responsible for the Judge, but also for her brothers and the family as a whole. If a stepmother capsized the Binghams' lifeboat, it would be Henrietta's fault for letting her on in the first place.

In June 1924, Bingham had returned to Kentucky without her from the tobacco mission to England. The faltering cooperative endeavor coincided with more thwarted ambitions. Despite his best efforts, his vision of leading American agriculture into a golden age ran aground against resistance, largely from growers themselves, and his attempts at cleaning up state government were backfiring. Kentucky's sitting governor called "Bobbie" a "carpetbagger from North Carolina" who had tricked "a rich old widow" into leaving him a fortune. Back in the United States, the rumors about his possible nomination to the Democratic presidential ticket withered. On one hand, such a possibility would never have arisen without the power Mary Lily's legacy brought him; on the other hand the scandal over her demise might disqualify Bingham from any such high office. He needed Henrietta now. He must have felt dreadfully alone, and he was quick to lay blame: Mina had corrupted her—Mina and the blasted Freudians.

The Leopold and Loeb murder case, called the "trial of the century," was under way that summer in Chicago. Failing to lure Sigmund Freud himself, the defense attorney Clarence Darrow had engaged Freudian-influenced psychiatrists in America to assess the defendants' mental state. In late July, as Henrietta painted at Ham Spray and Judge Bingham, Robert, and Barry crossed the Atlantic for the grouse-shooting vacation, the psychological reports were leaked to the press. Loeb was presented as the mastermind, and the abnormality of the killers was said to be rooted in their upbringing. Sketchy details emerged of the king-and-slave fantasy that threaded their friendship; its specifically homo-erotic aspects were left out of the papers, but rumors circulated widely.

The implication from the psychiatrists was that due to childhood trau-
mas, Leopold and Loeb were not fully responsible for the murder of an
innocent boy—and ought to be spared the death penalty. Judge Bingham was never friendly toward Henrietta's "course"; Freud's shocking
and repulsive theories now splashed before him morning and evening,
seemingly excusing the grossest sin.

From the isolated moors near West Loch Tarbert, with the wedding
nearing, Henrietta wrote wretchedly to Tommy. He ribbed her a little:
"Does an incessant rain accompany your tears?" Perhaps the chill
northern winds had cooled the blood of her "tempestuous family"?
Most of what he wanted to say could not be put in a letter, but she must
know "how I admired you through all that family racket, and how
much I hated seeing you unhappy and ill." He reserved space to complain that the amount of time he spent thinking of her, wanting
her, vastly exceeded "the few minutes I have now and then in your company." Even Tommy's expressions of sympathy echoed the theme she
heard from her father and from Carrington—that she hurt them, denied them.

Henrietta, Robert, and Barry were sure the Judge felt no real love
for his fiancée, Aleen Muldoon Hilliard. Henrietta was convinced that
none of it would be happening if she had gone back to Kentucky with
him in the early summer. The engagement had mushroomed completely without warning, and spun her back to the sadness surrounding
Babes's death and her displacement during her father's marriage to
Mary Lily. In Bloomsbury circles, it was said that her father remarried
"to spite Henrietta because of her coldness to him." David Garnett's
wedding gift to the Judge was a knife.

The announcement took Louisville society by surprise, as well. Six
years Bingham's junior, Aleen Muldoon had known him since he came
to town in 1893. Her Irish immigrant father founded the South's premier gravestone and monument company and a white marble goddess
by Antonio Canova, perhaps a copy of the Hebe that he sold to the
city's library in 1871, decorated their lawn. Spirited and enthusiastic,

Aleen adored parties, and pasted newspaper clippings about them into her scrapbook, where she also maintained a long list of names—her own social register. She enjoyed interior decorating, prized etiquette, and had little use for books or politics. Dark-haired Aleen concluded her "belleship" by marrying the "society man" and stockbroker Byron Hilliard. Her elder sister wed the city's richest bachelor, heir to a banking fortune, and Aleen's two children grew up visiting their aunt and her family at an imposing mansion called "Norton Hall." Still, Aleen's life had its hardships: a hunting accident damaged Byron's eyesight and left him partially paralyzed, unable to work for years, and tuberculosis attacked her teenage daughter. When Aleen's husband died just shy of his fiftieth birthday in 1922, Bob Bingham was among the pallbearers. Aleen's hair was by then prematurely white.

At London's Hyde Park Hotel in August 1924, Henrietta's father drafted, and he and Aleen signed, a prenuptial agreement promising that in the event of his death his wife would receive $1 million and the Melcombe Bingham property. A sizable amount, this was still far less than the half of his estate she would otherwise receive by law. He arranged for their exchange of vows to be held at the sixteenth-century St. Margaret's Church, whose canon (under special license from the archbishop of Canterbury) performed the ceremony alongside the bishop of Kentucky. The Bingham children witnessed the wedding this time, along with Aleen's son, Byron Jr., her Norton sister and brother-in-law, and Babes's sister, Katherine. According to Bloomsbury reports, "They all got drunk." The group was small, but the surroundings dwarfed the Judge's previous nuptials in Kentucky and New York. Westminster Abbey's spires and the Houses of Parliament greeted the group as they came out the church doors. No image accompanied the brief notice that ran on *The Courier-Journal*'s August 21 front page, which also contained an article dismissing Leopold and Loeb's "youthful fantasies as a mitigation in the murder of Bobby Franks." Oddly, no wedding photo has been found among the Bingham papers.

Henrietta's friends worried. Tommy was leaving London to stay with David Garnett but changed plans when Henrietta wired that she needed him in London. Tommy responded that he was "anxious to hear . . . about the wedding and Hymen's attendant Furies." Dr. Jones hoped to have Henrietta in for regular sessions during this period, but she dropped from sight and he sighed to Mina that she "must be leading a pretty complicated life, these days." For nearly two years, he had observed her suffering from a "dread" of "rebuff and desertion" by the father upon whom she remained fixated. A now-familiar form of relief was sex. The satisfaction she gave or got from one person often wounded someone else, however.

Carrington wrote despairingly just after the Judge's wedding that Henrietta had disappeared to Paris with a mysterious "American . . . a girl with lovely red hair." She was roundly hissed in the Bloomsbury set for abandoning Tommy—"Down with the Americans! Abasso gli Americani!" wrote Ralph. Carrington was in fits, and sent alternating "furious and pleading letters." She could only hope that this new passion would fade quickly, as Henrietta admitted her passions often did, telling Carrington, "You must wait, if you can."

Henrietta flaunted her seductive power to keep her own heart intact. Loving many at once and never being totally committed defended her from ever being hurt as she had been hurt at the loss of her mother. She grew up learning to arouse and duck and feint. This rare American on the fringe of Bloomsbury had experiences in love that few her age could match. Henrietta could beguile brilliant and creative people. But she was full of contradictions. Her affairs began passionately but rarely held her attention. They posed too many dangers to her self: they might rival the intimacy with her father; they were often "inappropriate" same-sex loves; and, of course, they might generate feelings intense enough to make her lose control. Granted, Jazz Age sensibilities and the liberated Bloomsberries might have encouraged Henrietta's experimentations; at a deeper level her behavior provided a way to enact rejection, which she did when the desire she provoked became overwhelming. With one lover after another Henrietta acted skittish and immature, ambivalent and distant. She would stop communications altogether and risk driving them away, as she could not with her father. Her intense sweetness combined with powerful defenses, and Dr. Jones found it unusually difficult to "make a deep impression" on her "complicated personality." He apparently did not perceive the connection between the "colossal weight of guilt" Henrietta carried with what one Bloomsbury figure called her acts of "semi-deliberate cruelty." She couldn't help taking responsibility for painful events far beyond her doing (such as her mother's death and her father's marriages), and that guilt made her want to flee, physically, emotionally, or both.

By summer's end, Carrington was indeed hopelessly in love. Her husband, Ralph Partridge, snorted that she looked foolish and "undignified." Lesbian activity was regarded much less sympathetically than male homosexuality by the Bloomsbury circle, and Lydia Lopokova nastily denounced this latest "moral degradation" to John Maynard Keynes, who had been involved with both Grant and Strachey but who married the dancer the following year. Poor Carrington, she wrote, "always wanted to be a man." Carrington wouldn't have cared so much, except that this enticing young person ran through her fingers like water. She seethed, unable to control her "curiosity, and desires to know this creature better." When she and Henrietta spoke by phone in September "her voice of course melted me." Henrietta promised to see Carrington off at Paddington Station one day, and the painter raced along the platform searching for her in vain, finally boarding the train crowded with "beastly little schoolgirls."

> I felt it was some terrible dream and that I would go mad. Suddenly in the distance I saw H walking down the platform very slowly with that enigmatic smile on her face. I pushed the school girls from the carriage door brushed through the parents and dashed towards her. The smoothness of her cheeks again returned and I remember nothing but that she is more lovely to me than any other woman. We talked for one minute. I leap [sic] into the train. She kissed me fondly, and the train moved away. She cannot come this weekend. But seeing her again just for that moment removed all my feelings against her.

Carrington's response to Henrietta had provided a key to a realm of herself she had never known. She wrote remorsefully to Alix Strachey,

"I feel now regrets at being such a blasted fool in the past, to stifle so many lusts I had in my youth, for various females."

Tommy also experienced occasional flights of joy in Henrietta's company only to sink again into depression. Henrietta's adorableness disarmed him; he told Carrington that at their last meeting she was "incredibly beautiful and comforting." For himself, he predicted "an Autumn of despairs," as Henrietta seemed now "completely given over to the ladies." Thoughts of her were "like a mob of starlings always at my head," he wrote, "their cries in my ears, their feathers choking me." He refused to answer when friends banged on his studio door, and he sent his cast of Henrietta's head to Carrington at Ham Spray—he couldn't look at it anymore.

When her father and stepmother arrived in London in late September after a European honeymoon, Judge Bingham called another meeting with Ernest Jones. Unless Henrietta approved it, such a summit today would constitute a breach in privacy, but Henrietta depended on the money her father gave her, and purse strings command attention. The doctor accepted the request.

Earlier that month, Judge John R. Caverly, chief justice of the Cook County Circuit Court, handed down his sentence in the murder-kidnapping trial of Leopold and Loeb. Rather than hanging for their confessed crimes, they were to spend life in prison. Although Caverly cited their age as the deciding factor in his clemency, many blamed Darrow's diminished-capacity argument for what they considered an outrageous outcome, an argument that rested in large part on psychological theories about their upbringing. Bingham was no friend to psychoanalysis. A year and a half had passed since his first encounter with Jones, and at that time the doctor had led him to believe that a month or two more of treatment would put his daughter right. The Judge's concerns were reasonable—of course he would want to know how and when the process would be complete and Henrietta could move on with life. Jones's professional reputation was in question; at the same time, Henrietta's extreme response to her father's marriage seemed to prove that her neurosis remained deeply lodged.

Jones mentioned the encounter several weeks later in a letter to Mina in Northampton. "I really can't write out an account of my interview with the Judge," he told her, "it would be more than an essay, but it was very dramatic! The outcome also was good, and father and daughter parted on the best terms—equally relieved thereby." Certainly, Jones liked to think he contributed to the family peace. Mina was relieved to learn that Henrietta was staying on in England. So, presumably, was Aleen, who set to work in Louisville making "a home for Bob" and had no reason to want her stepdaughter nearby. Jones thought it auspicious that Henrietta dreamed her psychoanalyst was a horse she wanted to take back to Kentucky with her.

Mina returned "lacerated and sore" to the United States that fall of 1924. But just when her romantic life seemed hopeless, Mina encountered someone new. The same fall she first taught Henrietta, Mina had glimpsed a man in a local market on the night of the Harvard-Yale football game. Magnificent-looking in a bowler hat and raccoon coat, he had driven off in "high spirits" in a yellow Stutz Bearcat. Now, in the fall of 1924, they were formally introduced at a Northampton party. Henry Tomlinson Curtiss lived on a nearby farm set on a curve of unspoiled road leading into the picturesque Berkshires town of Ashfield. The barn sheltered horses and a cow. Doves chortled in a restored dovecote and cool woodland cut through by a creek spread out to the house's sides and rear. It was the closest thing to the English countryside Mina had seen in America.

Known to all as "Harry," Curtiss was eight years Mina's senior, Yale class of 1910. His father had partnered with the Boston Red Stockings pitcher A. G. Spalding to create the first large-scale American sporting goods manufacturing company, and Harry worked in the golfing division. He spent winters promoting their equipment in the South and summers working sales in England and Canada. Curtiss claimed in a letter to college friends that he took neither "myself or my golf balls very seriously (though I desire that others shall)," aware that "after my death someone will perfect an even greater golf ball." Mina appreciated his air of an "English club-man," and responded to his Protestant privilege much as she did to Henrietta's. In fact, he reminded her of the

Kentuckian so much that Mina described Harry to Dr. Jones as "a very male Henrietta." She was falling in love.

For two months, Mina kept Harry secret. When she told Jones about him at the end of 1924, he exclaimed, "for a man-hater you are really very flattering to my poor sex!" But Mina worried that the information could derail Henrietta's psychoanalysis—adding fuel to Jones's suspicion that Mina's emotional investment in Henrietta remained too intense. Another hesitation concerned Harry's health; he had spent two years in an Adirondack sanatorium for tubercular patients. Eleanor Chilton, Mina's former student who was at this time in New York, passed on to Jones the news that Mina had fallen for a "beautiful consumptive." Jones told Mina that in making such a selection, she revealed her unconscious ambivalence about men in general. She insisted Harry was strong and well—the far greater obstacle was that he had a wife.

The Curtiss house and land at Ashfield (he called it Chapelbrook and it was used forty years later by Elizabeth Taylor during the filming of *Who's Afraid of Virginia Woolf?*) had been a joint project for Harry and his wife, Esther. She applied her skills to interior decoration and he had gutted and rebuilt the house and tended the land and animals, taking in the clean mountain air his doctors prescribed. Unable to conceive a child and their marriage faltering, the couple spent much of 1923 and 1924 apart. Harry wanted a divorce, but Esther wasn't cooperating. Mina, already under scrutiny for her intimacy with Smith undergraduates, could easily be seen as a home wrecker—behavior that put her teaching position at risk. The local sheriff took the trouble to warn Harry of Massachusetts statutes against "lewd and lascivious cohabitation." It certainly added drama to their affair, but Harry was not a dramatic character. He exuded steadiness and was refreshingly direct. He also took a genuine interest in what motivated people and their relationships. Mina told Jones they had decided not to sleep together until things settled. What a "balm it has been to me," Mina wrote, "to be treated with every kind of consideration, emotional and intellectual and physical."

Harry's existence was unknown to Clive Bell, who had a penchant for bluestockings and with whom Mina had shared a sizzling summer fling. He had not forgotten his "belle et brilliante Mademoiselle," however, and wrote to Mina chattily that winter, adding that her "friend with the Giottesque profile is deep in Sapphistical complications."

In the latter months of 1924, Henrietta retreated from Bloomsbury. She may have been responding to paternal disapproval, or fleeing from the misery and desperation at Ham Spray House and Tommy's studio—or both. Her lovers believed Henrietta was leading their rivals down a familiar path to heartbreak. Carrington sputtered about "American female bitches" and Tomlin envisioned them "sitting round and adoring you with their mouths open." He wrote only half in jest when he observed to Henrietta, "If they only knew what risks they are running—falling in love with you—they would hang themselves before dinner and die happy. I sometimes wish I had done so."

Among the "bitches" was Jeannette Young, Smith class of 1921, who had lived with Henrietta in Northampton at Miss Malby's white frame boardinghouse. She came from railroad money, and possessed slender good looks and a wicked wit. Their friendship endured into Henrietta's later years, steaming up intermittently—or at least arousing the envy of Henrietta's other admirers. Also with Henrietta in late 1924 was the daffy Louisville native Sophie Preston Hill. Once an object of Henrietta's brother Robert's attention, Sophie had lost her fiancé to the war and spent the early twenties in New York selling women's clothes. Sophie lived on nothing, partied all night, and joined the Binghams for dinners and the theater whenever they came to the city. Soon after the Judge married Aleen, Sophie moved to London and got a clerk's job at Guaranty Trust, where the Binghams did their local banking. Sophie accepted Henrietta's lesbian behavior to a point. But a letter Henrietta received from a female lover (likely Carrington), thanking her "for a present that she never hoped to receive," went too far, Sophie told her. Sophie thought such things oughtn't be written down and bluntly called it "unseemly" as well as dangerous.

Mina badly wanted to believe that Harry was dissolving her homosexual interests, specifically her feelings for Henrietta, and for this she credited her psychoanalysis. She wrote flatteringly to Ernest Jones, calling him "my father, my father confessor, my guardian angel and my lover"—leaving us to wonder how literally to take the lover part. Mina wanted to know all of the news Jones had about Henrietta, whose "perfunctory letters" with their "corseted little lines" disappointed and wounded her friend. (At this time and to the end of her life, Henrietta's handwriting *was* remarkably small, neat, and pretty but extremely controlled, as if she were working very hard at it, whereas in her teenage years the letters came off her pen more freely.) Mina simply couldn't help meddling from afar—for instance, she sent Henrietta in London a letter Tommy had written to Mina in Northampton in which he compared his and Mina's situations. It was true that he saw more of Henrietta; but at least Mina knew the one she loved was out of reach and could therefore be "untroubled by hope," while he never knew where he stood from one day to the next. He had seen Henrietta quite a lot in December 1924, but "that is her method, to reinforce the shackles before putting a strain on them."

Dr. Jones did not like what he was hearing in Mina's communications. "So you are appallingly jealous. But of whom?" he wondered. Of Jeannette for her physical closeness with Henrietta or of Jones for being privy to Henrietta's inner life, or of Henrietta for her intimacy with Jones? "I suppose all," he concluded, "but mostly the first," and took Mina severely to task for depending on others to prop up her self-esteem. He also discussed her case with A. A. Brill, the American analyst whom Mina had met on her way to England in 1922. Brill judged Mina to be a "pure homosexual and very narcissistic." She had succeeded in absorbing a few men (Jones was happy to be one) into her ego, but he worried that she identified *with* them, boosting her "homosexuality and masculinity," rather than properly seeing them as objects of her love. Jones was adamant that Mina had more work to do.

Meantime, he fed Mina plenty of intelligence on her friends. He had recently delivered a lecture at Oxford, where Stephen Tomlin appeared and sat with him at the dinner. "I adore Oxford, but heavens what a h-l [homosexual] crowd inhabit it." His mind filling with homophobic Darwinism, he wondered, "What is going to become of life if both sexes bolt from each other like this?" As for Henrietta, he wrote to Mina, it was "difficult to say" very much. "She varies so. But she is doing some real analysis now and then, so we shall see. She is not at all unhappy." All her dreams revolved around Mina versus the Judge.

In December 1924, the Judge and Barry, "backed by every cousin and aunt," were pressuring Henrietta to spend the Christmas holidays in Kentucky. At some point, probably while confronting their father's marriage to Aleen that summer, Henrietta had confided her secret to Barry—that her work with Dr. Jones involved some intervention in her sexuality. She bargained on her brother's sympathy; after all, Barry displayed a measure of gender-atypical behavior. Her liaisons with Carrington, Jeannette, and possibly others that summer and fall notwithstanding, Henrietta led Barry to believe that she had committed to ridding herself of her unruly attractions to women. If she refused to go home, Jones explained to Mina, Barry would "suspect that she is still h-l [homosexual]."

In truth, Henrietta must have felt terribly divided about her life. Psychoanalysis helped her avoid her father and Kentucky, pleased her lover and mentor, Mina, and, ideally would help resolve her anger and shame. At the time, anything so outré as psychoanalysis would have been challenging to discuss, and the world was packed with people who recoiled at her "kind." It is not surprising that she used oblique references to a "course" in psychology or promised Barry she was nearly done with her difficulties. Yet the tension between the mountain of money and time she devoted to a doctor determined to place her on a firmly heterosexual footing and her actions, which tell a story of pleasures given and taken, same-sex encounters she could not or would not control, must have been very great, and could easily have led to feelings of failure, despair, even self-loathing. Ralph Partridge called Henrietta a "brute"—and her bouts of unfeeling behavior may have stemmed from such negative feelings. They could also account for the way Henrietta stopped responding to Mina's pleas for updates.

"Henrietta can at least answer cables if not letters," Jones wrote irritably to Northampton, "and as I hadn't seen her for five hours I couldn't give you the latest of her oscillating decisions. But I say she won't go

[home], so that's what I cabled." In her life as in her analysis, Henrietta struggled to move beyond seduction, to concentrate and commit, to focus on long-term goals and repress impulsive urges. She stayed in England for Christmas, though, and left Barry to suppose the worst.

The week before the yuletide holiday, Carrington invited Henrietta and Tommy to Ham Spray for a night of cross-dressing theater followed by dancing to the gramophone and a midnight supper. Henrietta said she would come but failed to appear, never calling and leaving Carrington and Tommy furious and miserable. David Garnett sent tempting letters offering "an old fashioned Christmas" at his home, Hilton Hall, "in the heart of the shires." A "barrel of ale and a cellar of wine will make you [and Tommy] reel through this day and dance into the night. Mistletoe will hang over your bed and nowhere else." But she turned him down, too. Columbia Records released the Louisville blues singer Edith Wilson's "How Come You Do Me Like You Do?" that year—half of Bloomsbury could have asked her friend Henrietta Bingham the same question.

Rather than go to Ham Spray, Hilton Hall, or home, Henrietta played out a lesbian fantasy in a foreign land with her American set. A few days before Christmas, she drove with Sophie through France to the Riviera. Jeannette Young joined them at Nice's Grand Hotel O'Connor for their own dress-up game. Years later, Sophie's husband, Jacques, recalled a photo from the holiday: Henrietta in full drag—man's trousers, walking stick, and fedora—flanked by her girls. Very Marlene Dietrich, Jacques pointed out. Dietrich was unknown at the time; however, Henrietta's costume was de rigueur in Weimar Berlin's exuberant lesbian and transvestite club scene where the future star was coming of age.

A slender letter from London awaited Henrietta at her hotel after New Year's. "My darling," it began. "For Heaven's sake come back soon." Tommy had come up with an epigram for their relationship: "They that desire and act not, breed Pestilence." He did not begrudge her "breaking hearts in France," but he had already paid dearly for hesitating to press his suit with absolute clarity. He expected she would "pay for it too." If his entreaties burdened her, it was simply her cross to bear as "the loveliest thing in the world."

Will you please marry me when you get back? I am perfectly serious. Please do. I see no objections. It's only this damned hanging about that makes it look difficult. We could have done it March 10, '23 [the day after they met] and never regretted it. There is no project that does not appear especially difficult if one shivers on the brink long enough. Please marry me.

Stephen Tomlin was lovesick and depressed. He was sometimes manic. But he was no masochist. He wanted Henrietta as she was and believed he had a chance of winning her and carving out with her a fair share of happiness. Marriage, in the form Tommy offered it, would shield her from other obligations and supply an irrefutable reason to build a future apart from the man who gave her life and seemed to want to keep her for himself. It could also choke off the flow of money from Kentucky, and although she was not a spendthrift, Henrietta lived well and shared generously with friends. Nothing suggests that a frugal, bohemian lifestyle attracted her. There was also Tommy's instability, and her own. She now had the proposal she had asked for the previous winter, but it was the last letter from Stephen Tomlin that Henrietta kept.

When she next saw Ernest Jones in his office, he announced that Mina was engaged to Harry Curtiss. Mina didn't want to tell Henrietta herself, so Jones drew back the curtain so Henrietta could contemplate the increasingly deserted spot she occupied, bargaining that the emotional strain the news generated would penetrate her defenses. The doctor afterward wrote that Henrietta absorbed "the bigness of it," and appeared not to blame Mina. "No one could feel more responsible for me than Mina," Henrietta told him, "but she would be a fool to let anything interfere with this." The analyst took Henrietta to mean that she fathomed "how true heterosexual love loomed above—overshadowed all other things." It might as easily have referred to a relationship that made Mina happy and concluded her quest for a loving tie with a man. The crossing lines of interest multiply with Jones's own belief that Mina's nuptials pointed to therapeutic "success" that would aid his efforts with Henrietta. Henrietta's worry that Mina "would now despise her" did not disturb him. Mina's news did stir Henrietta's fears of abandonment and prompted "dreams of her mother throwing her into her father's arms." "No harm was done," he concluded breezily. Jones felt Mina's tying the knot would "complete the impression of her father's marriage, and show her how insecure are incest and homosexuality to build on."

"Incest" is a big word. There are two ways to look at that comment from Dr. Jones. From a psychoanalytical point of view, all children harbor incestuous fantasies toward their parents. An analyst would never take Henrietta's dream of her mother throwing her into her father's arms literally. Neurotic female patients repeatedly came to Freud with memories and dreams of "premature sexual experiences" involving fathers and sometimes mothers and other adults. Ultimately he viewed these as fantasies, extensions of the Oedipus complex, and Ernest Jones would have done the same. Freud posited that children first desired their mother and suffered frustration at not having her to themselves. Girls then fixated on the father as a way to indirectly have the mother. Later (in an especially obscure process) the daughter transferred her identification from father to mother—as a way to vicariously possess the father. If Henrietta had yet to complete this "stage" and achieve its heterosexual resolution, this would explain her neurotic, sometimes hysterical symptoms. Henrietta's analyst would likely see her seductiveness and ambivalence about the Judge and other romantic figures in her life as an expression of internal psychic disorganization and immaturity. Her homosexual behavior and panic attacks would resolve when she released her father fixation. Now that these primary erotic objects (her father and Mina) had abandoned her, Jones supposed the chances of a breakthrough were greatly improved.

There is another possibility, however. Could Jones also have been referring to the common meaning of incest—sexual involvement with a family member? What if Henrietta reported memories, accurate or not, about sexual contact with Robert Worth Bingham?

When I began this project, I had no sense that I would ask myself, even briefly, whether my great-grandfather may have committed incest, and while many aspects of Henrietta's story are unsettled, this one is unsettling. Henrietta's father was perhaps unusual for his day in that he wanted to be close to his children. We know he was prone to grandiosity and self-pity and required, especially when lonely and stressed, unquestioning female support. We also know that from an early age Henrietta was alluring and uninhibited. As their intimacy crystallized in the bereavement that followed Babes's death, Henrietta's needs for love and emotional security never commanded the same weight the Judge's did. Henrietta was a child, and in relying on her as a surrogate, her father compounded the damage to her psyche. But I don't think it went further than that. Judge Bingham was a compelling man, an idealist, a passionate advocate for his state and country, a harsh critic of corruption. He was narcissistic and highly emotional, but he leaves an impression of strict physical self-control and moral rectitude.

Still, some psychologists note instances where nonphysical, covert, or emotional incest harms and distorts children and whole families, and the picture drawn aligns closely enough with Henrietta's to deserve consideration. In such cases, daughters enjoy "special status" with fathers who idolize and are in turn idolized by them. They are flirtatious and unusually charming and attractive as children. They have absent or colluding mothers. They are terrified of abandonment, struggle to make healthy romantic attachments, and often fail to establish lives separate from their fathers. Siblings are jealous at the preferential treatment and may feel guilty for escaping this hurt done in love's name. Did Henrietta and her father engage in an unequal but mutual obsession and dependency? I think so. But the shame that comes with breaching the taboo against parents and children having sexual contact, and the lies and secrecy that breach interjects into a family, would be missing.

In the spring of 1925, Jones exuded confidence. If there was still an impediment to Henrietta's progress, it lay with Mina herself. Since he had last written to Northampton, Henrietta had

> made more fundamental progress than in any previous six months. People often do move rapidly in spurts after a long jog-trot. It was

Left to right: Harry Curtiss, Lincoln Kirstein, George Kirstein, Mina, Henrietta

partly induced by an asinine letter from her father telling her to come home and assuring her that ps-a [psychoanalysis] arose from the same evil spirit that led to the rape of Belgium [alleged war crimes at the outset of World War I], and partly to some illuminating experiences here coming at a critical juncture in the analysis. I think she will have done with homosexuality and be ready to move on to the next stage.

How absurd of you to talk about her ceasing to care for you! . . . She not only loves you, and always will, but has a remarkable objective interest in your welfare quite different from the personal value you may be to her. She is freer from the subjective dependence on you, in fact, I am inclined to think more so than you are from her.

Which brings me to the main theme of my letter. She and I both think that you need to clear up still further your relation to her. Your letters give many indications, which I can't detail here, of there being too great an element of dependence on her. Please don't dispute this, but look into it, for there is certainly some truth in what I say. Instead of her being a loved and desirable friend, you <u>need</u> her in too agitated a way, and the feeling is too much mixed with your feeling for Harry for me to be entirely at peace about you. Good thing for you that he isn't an analyst! . . .

The upshot is, don't worry so much about Henrietta. She can look after herself and your job is with Harry—first, foremost and all the time. Whatever you do, leave her out of that. A *ménage a trois* is too ghastly. Don't even want her to "like" him. It's got nothing to do with you what man she likes. She isn't you. She's a friend.

You see, you are such splendid girls that I'm aiming high. I want you both to be healthy, happy, capable and good friends. And at this moment I'm very hopeful all round.

It was strong advice, and in many ways very sensible. Mina was already planning a summer visit to England with Harry after their wedding, and Jones cautioned, "I'm sure it would be better <u>not</u> to stay with her." Besides, who knew where Henrietta would be, as "one can never tell what her erratic papa may do, directly or indirectly."

When the British Psycho-Analytical Society gathered in May 1925 for their regular meeting, Jones, the society's president, raised the subject of female homosexuality. Lytton Strachey's brother, James, was in attendance and quickly recognized that Jones was speaking of Carrington's lesbian lover. He wrote afterward to his wife, ridiculing Jones's claim "that the real reason why she threw over Carrington was because she (Carrington) wasn't a virgin." Jones ignored Strachey's suggestion that a "complete Oedipus complex," by which a child identifies with both parents and develops bisexually, deserved consideration.

Instead, two years into analysis, Ernest Jones believed his patient was moving past her father-driven neurosis. If she was to truly have "done with homosexuality," Mina must cooperate. "You needn't tell me how sweet and lovable she can be," he told Mina. "Of course, H has an enormously strong and deep femininity—that's the trouble. It doesn't show very easily but some day when I've finished some lucky man will get the benefit of it."

In the spring of 1925, Henrietta readied for a return to the United States. Sophie had departed in February, arriving in Manhattan to the first issue of *The New Yorker*. Duncan Grant was drawing Henrietta in preparation for an oil painting—and Tommy said the sketches were

Dora Carrington and Alix Strachey, mid-1920s

"ravishing." (Sadly, they have been lost.) Lytton took her to lunch, pleading mercy for Carrington, who sent one of her glass paintings as a farewell gift. "I dream of her six times a week," Carrington told her friend Alix Strachey, "dreams that even my intelligence is appalled by, and I write letters, and tear them up continually." The diary she kept about Henrietta and planned to use for a "*temps perdu*" of her life since the "American invasion" was cast aside or burned, and she occupied an entire spring afternoon at Ham Spray House constructing an elaborate cardboard coffin for a cocktail shaker Henrietta had left behind. Snow-drops surrounded the cold reflective corpse; the coffin's lid bore an inky cross and "RIP DC." Gerald Brenan tossed in his sleep; in one dream, an especially horrible incubus-like Carrington hung from a tree, disem-boweled, the victim of the South's gruesome and peculiar form of ret-ribution. He did not need psychoanalysis to divine its meaning.

Henrietta also sat for Vanessa Bell, and upon seeing an unfinished canvas, Gerald Brenan asked, "Oh, and what do you think of her? Is she very fascinating? Or have they invented that?"

V[anessa]. Well she is very beautiful to paint. I really did not see anything else that was remarkable. What do you say?

AN' I WISH I WAS HAPPY AGAIN

I. I don't know her. I have only seen her. I thought she moved beautifully.

V. Does she? It is a good thing she is going to America almost at once. I think she has done enough damage. No doubt she will come back just in time to undo everything—I hope Carrington is not very shattered.

I. Carrington? I shouldn't have thought so. She never sees her, I believe.

V. She saw her very recently.

I. Oh! but I suppose it is Tommy who is upset.

V. Probably. But hardly more upset than he has been in the last six months. I have really fancied sometimes he might be going off his head . . . He thinks she might marry him. He goes on asking her. She never refuses definitely. But of course she never would.

More than two years had passed since David Garnett's thirtieth-birthday party with the ingenious caramel cake and the song about the sweat that "run like mine boy." Vanessa Bell and Gerald Brenan agreed it would be "worse" if Henrietta did marry Tommy. With Henrietta gone, Carrington rededicated herself to Lytton and Ham Spray, breaking off her relationship with Brenan. She doubted her ability to share "'intimate' relations with anyone." For Tommy's part, he wailed, "An' I wish I was happy again," quoting (or imitating) the blues Henrietta loved so much.

9

JUG BAND ORDERED

*I*n 1925 Henrietta negotiated a deal that preserved her autonomy and left neither the Judge nor her psychoanalyst pleased. "She must come back in September, that's all there is to it," Jones told Mina. Sanguine as he had been, her work was not complete. "So I am sending her home," he concluded, imperiously, but he imagined it would be for only a short time. In June, there was a family wedding in Asheville, and in July, the Judge had an emergency appendectomy. The house she and her father had furnished and draped together seven years earlier was undergoing a total redecoration under Aleen's direction. When Barry returned to Cambridge in September for his sophomore year, Henrietta had no intention of staying in Kentucky; if she was going to make it in America it would have to be someplace else, and Manhattan was the obvious choice. Like Henrietta, the city was mad for jazz and blues; fretful, joyful notes exploded from theaters and nightclubs and dives. Her father acceded; at least she was away from Jones. By fall, she had an apartment and a job.

John Mason Brown, who held her hand at the movies during their middle school romance, still carried a torch for Henrietta and was eager to help. Brown came to New York in 1923 with a Harvard degree and an undimmed love of the theater, and eventually *Theatre Arts Monthly* hired him as a critic. This highly regarded magazine had broad tastes, embracing young Martha Graham's modern dance, community productions in small cities, Charlie Chaplin, and puppetry. *Theatre Arts* published Edmund Wilson, Thornton Wilder, and Pablo Picasso along-side pieces such as the Howard University philosopher Alain Locke's manifesto for a "Negro drama." Edith Isaacs, its venerable editor, shared Henrietta's interests in African American performers. Isaacs had moved the journal from quarterly to monthly publication in 1924, and hired Henrietta—whom she met through John Mason Brown—to build the subscriber base and sell advertisements. The struggling magazine be-came Henrietta's "little child," a labor of love. The number of advertisers (chiefly theaters and allied businesses) increased; she also persuaded her father to purchase $1,000 worth of shares, which kept the magazine afloat during a particularly lean period. "Dear Judge Bingham," began her tongue-in-cheek note formally thanking him for the assistance. She signed herself "Cordially Yours, Henrietta Bingham." But the job also meant suspending her analysis, and Jones admitted to Mina that he was "gradually coming round to your view of ~~your~~ her father."

Henrietta's elegant, brand-new apartment at 25 Fifth Avenue, just north of Washington Square Park, sat practically on top of Mabel Dodge Luhan's former Greenwich Village salon. Speakeasies, book-stores, clubs (many catering to homosexuals), and theaters—the Prov-incetown Playhouse was then reviving O'Neill's *The Emperor Jones*—were only a short walk away. *The Great Gatsby* was out but selling slowly and, as one of Henrietta's friends wrote, Manhattan was full of the "smell of easy money in the air." At dinner parties, people talked of "oil and mo-tors, of the stock-market and the Florida land boom. Everywhere peo-ple spent money conspicuously and entertaining was extravagant and alcoholic." The following year, in *Vanity Fair*, Carl Van Vechten pro-filed Bessie Smith and other blues queens, performers Henrietta regu-larly saw at night, in the flesh. Young Duke Ellington and Jelly Roll Morton spun at seventy-eight revolutions per minute on her gramo-phone, the music echoing her demons, her terrible fear of being alone, and her need to escape. Langston Hughes, who had only recently won a publishing contract, wrote in his poem "The Weary Blues,"

> "Ain't got nobody in all this world,
> Ain't got nobody but ma self.
> I's gwine to quit ma frownin'
> And put ma troubles on the shelf."

Acceptance of trouble, openness about sex, humor—these were sometimes enough to get her through dark spells. On a slip of pale blue 25 Fifth Avenue stationery, she penciled a fragment of a song by her favorite jug band as the rhythm played in her head.

> Take your time and strut your stuff,
> He's good looking that's true enough.
> Your man is from the East
> So save your grease
> And Mammy don't you give all your lard away.

A man from the East soon presented himself. Jacques Haussmann, one year Henrietta's junior, arrived from England that fall with a job in commodities, a love of the theater, and a novel that Virginia and Leonard Woolf's Hogarth Press had offered to publish. His creative interests combined curiously with his post as a broker for the Continental Grain Corporation. In pictures, the high-browed blond sometimes looks puzzled, even stricken. Half Jewish and self-conscious about it, Jacques subsequently became Jack (or John) and changed Haussmann to Houseman. As John Houseman, he achieved renown. In the 1930s he collaborated with Orson Welles on productions for the Federal Theatre Project, the Mercury Theatre, and *Citizen Kane*. During his long career in entertainment, Houseman produced and directed Broadway plays and Hollywood films and founded the Juilliard School's Drama Division, and at age seventy-one was awarded an Oscar for his portrayal of the biting Harvard Law School professor Charles W. Kingfield, Jr., in *The Paper Chase*.

John Houseman at Chapelbrook, circa 1926

Houseman had first laid eyes on Henrietta in London. A friend of Stephen Tomlin's named Bea Howe brought him to one of the parties where Henrietta entertained the Bloomsberries. Now, after his first few weeks in New York, his spirits were sagging. The bombast that had carried him to America had deserted him, and Bea urged him to break through his gloom by looking up the dazzling hostess from Kentucky. One afternoon after work in October 1925 he stood apprehensively at Henrietta's threshold. Bea had minced no words about her reputation among the Bloomsbury crowd; Henrietta was capable, she warned, of "pure callousness."

"Twelve and a half hours later, a little before dawn," Houseman remembered being driven home to his apartment tower "in the grey open Chrysler in which she boasted she could cover thirteen blocks between traffic lights." Dinner at a stylish café down the street from her place had been followed by cocktails with Florence Mills and Edith Wilson in the break between performances of *Dixie to Broadway*, the latest iteration of the all-black revue. Joined by others in her circle, Henrietta then took him farther north to 135th Street and the crammed dance floor at Small's Paradise in Harlem. The night ended at a "boogie," or "rent party," in which Harlemites, squeezed by exorbitant rents, opened their apartments to paying guests. Houseman described a "dim-lit 'hotbed' railroad flat" on Lenox Avenue, smelling of chitlins and greens. The "latest on wax" or live musicians provided music for dancing. An edgier crowd sought out "buffet flats" that offered sexual encounters of all kinds, cafeteria style.

That night in the fall of 1925, with Henrietta guiding him, Houseman tasted, heard, and saw the Harlem Renaissance. It was a stunning entrée. But over time what impressed him even more was Henrietta's "pure affection," which left him "terribly moved and humble and infinitely grateful." She aroused him as no one had, seeming at times "excessively feminine" and at others like a "delicate, smooth-muscled boy," and he liked to call her by her masculine middle name, Worth. Late in life, Houseman judged that this was "probably the only time and certainly the first I was ever really in love."

A posse of fellow southerners, exiles of sorts, kept Henrietta company and made her apartment their social headquarters: John Mason Brown; an Asheville cousin named Martha Mckee; Sophie Preston Hill; Edie Callahan, the pianist and Henrietta's former partner at the Wilderness Road Book Shop; and Billy Weaver, who worked by day at a bank and at night dressed in tight suits and "danced like an angel." Her Smith College friend and sidekick in Nice over New Year's, Jeannette Young, was also single and in New York, working sales at the Brick Row Bookshop. Mina's former student Eleanor Chilton—a "Southern Poetess" whose cheeks were "perpetually damp with tears," as John Houseman wrote—made frequent appearances. Two or three times a week Henrietta's admirers gathered at 25 Fifth Avenue for cocktails, and eventually made their way uptown to the Plantation Room or any number of "speakeasies and the sultry flats of Harlem tenements," though Houseman felt sex "played only a small part in this [interracial] familiarity." He described a remarkable "laughing night-time intimacy" that flowed between these black and white southerners, a "warm, in-

stinctive communication." The "atmosphere of glamour and gaiety was
no less magical," Houseman wrote, "for being achieved almost entirely
with Bourbon and mirrors."

An only child, Jacques spent his first years moving from one European
capital to the next as his father gambled on commodities futures.
"Lacking security," he recalled, "we lived in a whirling state of conspic-
uous extravagance," in which bespoke cars and half-decorated houses
sometimes vanished without warning to meet margin calls. Sent to
England for school at age seven, he absorbed the "elaborate chameleon
maneuvers" that enabled him to pass with ease through wealthy Gen-
tile circles in spite of his Jewish name. His father's untimely death left
the small family financially exposed. At this point, the blue-eyed teen-
ager was inducted into the Church of England. Although Houseman
completed his secondary education in Britain and even won a coveted
scholarship to read modern languages at Trinity College, Cambridge,
he decided in favor of a career that would enable him to better support
his mother. At seventeen, through the sponsorship of one of his father's
fellow financiers, he went to live on an Argentine estancia to learn the
grain trade from the bottom up. Houseman imagined rescuing his
mother from insecurity and proving himself as a "merchant prince." He
would meet and surpass his father's legendary reputation.

Having worked the wheat harvest and taken it to market, Houseman
toiled at a low level in the international arbitrage department of a Buenos
Aires bank until his mentor procured him an apprenticeship at London's
leading grain brokerage. At night, he worked on a novel, "The Plains,"
which Hogarth Press agreed to publish if the author footed two-thirds
of the cost. Witnessing his disappointment, Virginia Woolf offered to
pass the manuscript to Desmond MacCarthy, an editor at Heinemann.
While he waited for a firm answer from MacCarthy, who also edited the
prestigious *New Statesman*, Houseman reviewed books for the magazine.
Seeing his name in print was thrilling, but Jack remained uncertain
about a literary career. His foreign birth precluded his membership
in London's Baltic Exchange (the freight shipping market with a trad-
ing floor for brokers) but another Jewish friend of his parents' offered

a job at a New York brokerage office. Bidding farewell to MacCarthy, Houseman learned that the editor had lost the manuscript—could he send another copy? Houseman could have, but didn't; the American opportunity seized him in a way he could not fully explain.

Houseman competed for Henrietta's attention alongside Jeannette, Eleanor, and the "lunatic Louisville troop," which Barry sometimes joined from Cambridge on weekends. Henrietta had at least two other men pursuing her: the hometown contender, John Mason Brown; and someone named Alan, who claimed to love her "from the very depths." Alan complained jealously of "M. Boulevard," a play on the name Jack shared with the city planner who laid out modern Paris. Alan was the Kirsteins' Rochester cousin—Mina told Jones she was doing everything in her power to "dilute her h-l [homosexual] whirlpool" with appropriate males.

For their third date, Henrietta and Houseman drove up the West Side to the Claremont Inn, a landmark restaurant modeled on an English Palladian manor. They lunched in a terrace room overlooking the Hudson, Henrietta's suede gloves resting on the white tablecloth. The cool nights had begun and she talked of her horses and foxhunting. They chatted about Bloomsbury friends and figures. "There were people in her apartment when we got back," Houseman remembered, and "we could hear voices and laughter through the door and a piano playing. With her key in her hand, before she opened the door, she asked me to kiss her."

Other Harlem nights differed only in minor details from their first marathon. Some evenings ended in a shoe-box "Village haunt" where Edie Callahan took over when the piano player went home. For three days running, they attended the six-day bicycle race in Madison Square Garden. That fall, with Henrietta, Houseman got his first real taste of American theater; together they saw the Provincetown Players' production of August Strindberg's *The Dream Play*, the New York premier of *The Green Hat*, starring Katharine Cornell (Henrietta befriended her) as the scandalous Iris Storm (a role Tallulah Bankhead acted in London), and the comic Beatrice Lillie (also later a friend of Henrietta's) singing about a "nigger gal in Tennessee" in *Charlot's Re-*

view. Henrietta and Jack had their favorite speakeasy, Giovanni's, on Park Avenue, and some nights they gussied up for fancy meals at Delmonico's or Voisin's. While Henrietta saw much in him to like, Houseman remembered being preoccupied with his inexperience on these dates—he was a virgin.

With Christmas approaching, Henrietta left for home. The air was sucked out of Houseman's life. Then came a telegram: JUG BAND ORDERED HURRY LOVE H. A second cable conveyed Judge Robert Bingham's invitation to spend the holiday with his family.

Henrietta had singled Houseman out. Jack described an "enchanted" Christmas with the Binghams, misty as a fairy tale. Louisville in no way resembled the sunny southland of popular song—"far away from snow and ice, / It's a perfect paradise." Snow in fact had fallen on Melcombe. The severe brick house came into full view as Henrietta drove him past formal gardens and around a final dramatic bend. The "pillared mansion" stirred childhood memories of luxurious Houseman family vacations. He called the "real" black servants "delicious chocolate-coloured, inarticulate gibbering niggers [who] wander about the house doing things," and upon whom Henrietta showered "rich presents of 'flannin' pijamas [*sic*] and gorgeous blouses for Christmas."

The back-hall cheeriness contrasted with the family dinner on Houseman's first evening. Henrietta sat at one end of the gleaming dining table set with sterling and crystal and her father sat at the other. Aleen, sturdy and unremarkable, was placed beside the Judge. The mood tightened as Robert came to the meal already in his cups. The enormous table, a lake of veneer into which evenings sometimes tipped and drowned, was traded in the mornings for breakfast with Henrietta in her sun-filled corner bedroom, cousins and brothers crowding in as servants bore trays of food. Henrietta presided from her satin-quilted bed

against a backdrop of family portraits and dozens of bright-colored horse-show prize ribbons on the walls. Afterwards, in pale tan jodhpurs, she led me up through frozen, powdered snow along trails in the hills from which we could look down on the shining curves of the

Ohio River, stopping off at the stables and at neighbors' houses for juleps on the way back. The rest of the day was filled with parties, from which we came home only to change our clothes and start out again.

The festivities of Christmas night concluded in Henrietta's room in the wee hours, John in his evening clothes, she dressed in black, the coal fire making their faces glow. She took his head in her hands and ran her fingers through his hair and pulled him to her mouth.

He asked for no more. But his presence in Louisville suggested serious intentions. He was the "young man she had brought home from her travels," an English-accented, smooth-mannered small-time financier of indeterminate birth and nationality and yet her chosen suitor.

Dizzy from lack of sleep, constantly and agreeably hung-over, I was living a dream in which Henrietta and the New World were deliciously confused—a dream of riches, glamour, and unlimited opportunity. Watching her in the full radiance of her position as the King's Daughter, heiress-apparent to so much splendor (including ownership of one of the most influential papers in the country) I began to indulge the rosy fantasy of one day entering this world at her side, of sharing in all this luxury and authority without effort or struggle—as her consort.

But self-doubt nipped at Houseman's heels. The Harvard-educated husband of one of Henrietta's friends "was now about to become the youngest partner ever to be received into the House of Morgan" while he had a "humiliating position as a junior apprentice with an alien firm of Jewish grain-merchants." Houseman gripped his highball and bore up under the questions of curious locals. Being with Henrietta made him "completely happy," yet swells of insecurity pulled him this way and that. He felt sure that a person of Henrietta's concentrated glamour, "strength," and "depth and generosity of character" would quickly tire "of my incompleteness, my inherent bourgeoisie and vulgarity."

In Kentucky with Henrietta, Houseman got to hear more of the music she was so mad for. On his last night in Louisville she took him

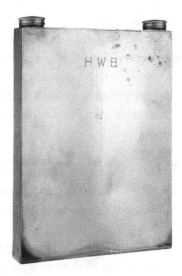

to a dance at a nearby country club. An enormous silver-plated flask—nothing like the dainty containers that flappers tucked into their garters—rode along with them in the car, making their night glow. Rather than return home, they sped past Melcombe and continued through the black night for what seemed like hours,

> past deserted houseboats frozen in the ice, then inland between farm-houses and silos till we came to a shack that stood alone in a field of corn stubble. Under a kerosene lamp, seated on apple-boxes, with two jugs of corn-liquor between them, were four men in ragged overcoats, their black faces barely distinguishable under their hats. This was the Jug-Band that Henrietta had promised me. They started playing as we came in, their instruments an empty gallon jug, a wash-board, a loose-strung bass and a guitar which was played at the same time as the nose-whistle . . . They played for us to dance at first; then, later, when the second gallon of corn was almost gone, they started to sing lewd, low-down blues, heavy with hate.

The two of them sat in that lean-to and drank it in. Boxing Day was dawning when the wheels of Henrietta's car crunched over the frozen field and back onto the ribbon of macadam. Houseman was stunned, shivering with "voluptuous excitement." In the months and years that followed, the mere recollection of Henrietta at the wheel with the long silver flask on the seat between them, glancing at him with her violet-blue eyes as they drove through the snow on a black night in Kentucky turned Houseman's "bowels to water" and provoked "orgasms of uncontrollable, delicious weeping."

Houseman's visit marked the beginning of his years as Henrietta's "young man," her intended in the eyes of family and friends. His letters and memoirs brim with Henrietta—irresistible, generous, warm, laughing, and "terribly troubled, always"—and with his own insecurities. He shared Mina's view of Henrietta as a "fantastically gifted writer" beset by "deep and violent conflicts," and beneath "the energy and the charm," Houseman recalled, "ran a stream of despair in which she would suddenly sink and drown before your eyes." In he went after her, but unlike Stephen Tomlin, Jack Houseman could possibly amass the kind of money that would ease a break with her father.

Money, at least in Jack's view, was central. Henrietta's father "spent money as I have rarely seen it spent, massively and deliberately." The complicated relationship between Robert Worth Bingham and his daughter came to a head with John Houseman's visit to Melcombe. Three years earlier, when she had gone to London with Mina, he declared that no one in Europe was good enough for her. In early 1925, the prospect of losing Henrietta to an upstart grain trader (or to anyone) was unbearable. As Henrietta readied to go back to New York, the Judge brought her before him for a private talk.

His blunt proposal set her wheels spinning for the next several months—and underscored how highly he prized her and how critical she was to him even after his remarriage. "If she agreed to return and live at home he would make her his associate and, later, his legal successor as publisher of *The Courier-Journal*." Her twenty-fifth birthday was approaching. He believed in her talent. In his view, what more important duty could she have, could there be? He wanted an answer in March, when they were to meet in Florida.

Trunks were packed, farewells bidden. Jack's train to New York pulled out of the station at Louisville. They would not be separated long. Henrietta was to follow, stopping first in Chicago to see her Callahan cousins and aunt. Jack had just settled into his compartment on the Pennsylvania Railroad car, when,

> at the last moment, after a series of mysterious feints and substitutions in which a number of black maids played an agitated and conspiratorial part, [Henrietta] emerged smiling and alone, just as my train was pulling out, from the drawing-room of the car next to mine.
>
> Here we spent the night together. While we were in the diningcar the porter had made up our berths. We lay back, after we had passed Pittsburgh, sprawled side by side in the dark, with the sweetish odor of bourbon around us and the mass of the upper berth hanging low and heavy over our heads, secure in the closeness and warmth of each other's bodies. We talked through the night, over the pounding of wheels, changing positions when we grew numb or felt the desire to kiss, getting up now and then to refill our glasses and, when the train stopped, crawling over to the window to peer out from under the drawn shade at the grey, deserted platforms or the snow-covered fields beyond the misted panes.
>
> It was past midnight and we were well into our second bottle when Henrietta began to talk about her childhood.

She unburdened herself about the collision with the train in Pee Wee Valley and the way she found herself "occupying the dead woman's place at her father's side" until he decided to marry again. Henrietta told Houseman about Mary Lily's death and the aftermath, during which she buried her resentment and returned to the center of her ambitious father's brittle but gilded life. She told of trying to break loose at college and afterward. But the sense of entrapment and desperation remained. Houseman had teased her about the "hideous gloom" that sometimes hovered over her spirits in New York, and Henrietta herself had written to Bea (who passed the letter to Tommy, who then told Carrington) of her plan to return to England, where people could understand her, where "she could save her soul."

Henrietta had confessed her troubles to Jack—or rather some of them. The implication was that he might help her escape from what he called "the emotional maze her father had built around her." Houseman was poorly prepared for the hero's part, but he was in love and the possibilities were tantalizing. It was the middle of the night in the Pullman sleeper car. Snowflakes brushed against the window. Tucked together into the lower berth, they finally quieted and drifted off. Houseman remembered, as if "in a dream, Henrietta opening her dress for me to put my hand on her breast" and "waking to find her crying in her sleep and the tears sliding, warm and slightly salt, across her cheek into my mouth."

10

A RED DAMASK SUITE

*I*t was no dream, and Henrietta's confidences and physical overtures on the Pennsylvania Railroad sealed something in her relationship with Jack—a "secret treaty." Almost as soon as they arrived in New York, she presented him to Mina, whose involvement in her life had now extended over five years. The year 1926 began with both women headed for marriage, and the couples celebrated New Year's Eve on the town in New York. Bea Lillie, whom Noël Coward called "the funniest woman in the world," headlined in a musical review with the explosively popular Paul Whiteman Orchestra. Houseman passed first muster and Mina and Harry invited him and Henrietta for a country weekend at Chapelbrook.

When Mina's Saturday classes ended, the foursome made the drive from Northampton in deep and falling snow, using farmhouses, stone walls, and trees to guess at the vanished roadway. As the house came into sight, the car slumped into a ditch. They made the final leg on foot, wading through waist-high drifts, carrying groceries and liquor bottles. Mina erased almost every trace of Henrietta from her archives, but she turns up in a Chapelbrook scrapbook, standing in the snow in puff-legged riding breeches, smiling through her squint as she holds a horse by a rope, her other hand beckoning a shepherd dog.

Mina professed to like Houseman, and, keeping in mind Jones's warning about caring too much what her friend thought or did, she turned over to Harry the role of advisor to the younger couple. Harry imparted lighthearted wisdom: Henrietta must keep constantly before her "the holy trinity" of Father (Jones), Son (Jack), and the Holy Isaacs (her editor at *Theatre Arts Monthly*). But Houseman was "the greatest of these."

In early 1926, Houseman began traveling extensively for his firm. Separation burnished his romantic visions. He began at the Chicago Board of Trade's commodity pit, and from there he visited every major North American port for wheat exports—Montreal in the east, New Orleans and Galveston to the south, and on the Pacific coast, Seattle, Portland, and Vancouver. Jack improved his margins by following the grain to the source, to prairie elevators and regional hubs like Kansas City, where he spent weeks putting deals together. One winter night he and Henrietta spoke by telephone—he was in a Vancouver hotel room, she in her Fifth Avenue flat and about to go up to Harlem. Henrietta had loved the telephone since the seventh grade when she dated John Mason Brown. It afforded intimacy across space without words on a page. But Jack hated it. He said her deep voice sounded "indifferent," and hung up feeling frantic about her. Unable to distract himself, Houseman composed a long letter promising to be less "repressed and a rather less dangerous person for you to marry."

Jack worked with renewed purpose. Besides proving himself worthy of his father's reputation for trade, he needed to demonstrate that he was not the "international fortune-hunter" Henrietta's relatives feared. Her father's "perfect courtesy" in Louisville "stretched tight over an abyss of jealousy and suspicion," and Houseman wanted to meet the elder man on his own terms. Jack described a twenty-eight-year-old Chicago trader who had cleared $300,000 in ten days, and declared, "I am a very dynamo." His orders, sent to the New York office, made the transcontinental telegraph wires crackle with "vitality," and he predicted that "we will be successful, grossly and flamboyantly so."

Not that life would be a shallow, philistine affair. Houseman was turning out short stories that Henrietta read and critiqued. He asked her to submit one called "Titanic Blues"—also a blues song recorded in 1925 by Virginia Liston—to Alfred A. Knopf at *The American Mercury*. Henrietta was enthusiastic, but it never appeared in the magazine. He directed her to pass his manuscript for "The Plains," to whomever she thought best. On solitary nights in the hinterlands, he worked on a new novel, and she read his chapters as he sent them. *The New Statesman* published a story that also appeared in a volume of the year's best short fiction. Jack would have preferred to earn his living by writing books, but didn't think his writing was "of that kind." He said Henrietta must prepare "to marry a Mammon. Do you mind?"

Isolated and starved for companionship, Houseman reveled in grandiose dreams. While he might one day write something truly good, he expected to "leave the culture in our ménage in your hands." He talked of spending a few more years in the grain trade, long enough to get truly rich and retire at thirty-two. They would travel to China, Siam, and Spain. Then she could be a "lady-farmer" on an estate with a barnful of horses while publishing "all the best books"—or a newspaper if she liked—somewhere far from Kentucky. The power and distinction offered by her father (and which part of her seemed truly to want) could be hers with Jack instead. Houseman assured her she deserved nothing less.

Just how Henrietta responded to this portrait of their future is lost with her correspondence, which Houseman apparently destroyed. But his letters point toward persistent concerns Henrietta had, not about money or occupation, but about sex. Their kisses, embraces, caresses—she seems to have initiated them all, and by his own account, Jack often became "sullen and repressed" in her company. When she sought advice, Harry lent his authority to what Mina and Ernest Jones had preached for years: "If you are to find happiness it is in this way," he said, urging her commitment to a man. "Conquests, Henrietta, are not new to you but I'm quite certain that the quality . . . inherent in this one is. It is tender and intense and wholly lovely—and it's young and fresh too." "Go slow," Harry counseled, and "keep the physical in check yet awhile, or it will blow you both up."

Henrietta absorbed Jack's discomfort, as anyone who kisses someone can. He admitted to inhibitions, to being ashamed of his virginity and terrified that impotence or clumsiness would drive her away. Her friends told Henrietta to try "sounding him out . . . to ascertain whether or not his fear is based on any actual experience with a woman." Harry felt certain that with her "sure hand," Jack could be brought into line, indeed to "completely capitulate—and with such a flood as to probably carry him over and through his fear." He would learn gradually about her sexual needs and how to meet them. Houseman required guidance, reassurance, letters, and time together—familiar obligations that drove her away from her father and other lovers—and without these Jack felt punished and enervated. He tried to feel confident in their treaty, and kept telling himself that as their mutual need advanced it would resolve in marriage. Once wed, his "shyness in the flesh" and her "idleness in ink" would no longer pertain.

At the end of February 1926, Henrietta left New York to meet Judge Bingham in Florida. (Aleen remained behind.) Father and daughter approached the Izaak Walton Club on Useppa Island, where millionaires angled for marlin and tarpon, from opposite political poles. The Judge was celebrating a reduction in income and inheritance taxes recently signed into law by President Coolidge, while Henrietta brought eyewitness reports from the work stoppage in the textile mills of Passaic, New Jersey, a few miles from New York City. Henrietta became swept up in the crisis, joining the organized relief effort that sustained more than 15,000 strikers and their families during a months-long protest pocked with police brutality and martial law.

"Amuse yourself in Florida, darling," Jack wrote resentfully from damp, chilly Vancouver. His letters had been coming steadily, sometimes twice a day, but Henrietta kept none from her tropical sojourn, where she may have told her father that Houseman had asked her to marry him. This was sure to produce the greatest reaction. She had made no final commitment to her beau, nor could she tell her father no about the newspapers—it would be foolish to cut off that possibility. Before she decided what to do, Henrietta wanted to complete her psychoanalysis. The Judge's response is not known, but Henrietta's friends, who witnessed the father and daughter together during this time, intimated that he cast a shadow over her life. Jack wondered "what arrangement she had made with her father or what price he had exacted for letting her live away from him in London" for the rest of the year.

Whatever she did, it worked. Mina would be pleased. Her father got a part of what he wanted—she wouldn't marry yet, at least. Jack was pushed aside; unless he abandoned his job and joined her in England, they would be separated. Houseman alternated between imagining "storms of fury" raging in "the paternal breast" and bitterly picturing his beloved dancing "your damned Charleston in the garconnieres and garrets of Bloomsbury with all your new steps." However she finagled it—the public word was that she was going over to foxhunt—Jack felt "terribly afraid of the future" and begged her to be faithful to him. Her relatives continued to regard him as her intended, and when he came to Chicago from Vancouver, Henrietta told him to visit Aunt Katie, who was still sighing about "poor John Mason Brown." Henrietta's cousin Laurence unnerved Houseman over drinks after squash at the Saddle and Cycle Club when he asked "with a leer, after 'that Jewish bitch Mina Kirstein.'" The family had lined up against Mina, and Houseman, half-Jewish and passing among Gentiles, shivered.

Henrietta called Jack to Louisville in advance of her departure. Talk had begun about Derby hopefuls and fairylike dogwood blossoms and purple buds dotted the bare Cercis branches in the woods. Edie Callahan invited them over for a respite from the Bingham hothouse. Stephen Tomlin's heavy iron gates had at last gone up at the foot of the driveway, their severe stone eagles guarding each coming and going. Having rushed Jack through them on the way up the hill, Henrietta talked of completing her psychoanalysis before they married. She seemed so certain, so reasonable, yet Houseman could not help worrying when, the night before he left, Henrietta began to cry as they kissed. "I think I shall never forget the feel of your tears," he wrote next day. Why did she cry? She must help him understand. He was in love, and the further they went physically, the emptier he felt when they were apart. He knew her skin, and, "instinctively," her "core," yet there was a "whole Henrietta" that eluded him. These elusions were to some extent mutual. Henrietta claimed that he "sucked up [her] personality" while keeping his own shut away. They were not in the best of shape to bear a transatlantic separation.

The 1926 General Strike in Britain delayed Henrietta's crossing, and Houseman pressed her to wait out the event with him in Chicago, where he was stuck. All she had to do was run down from her apartment, get lunch "at the bootlegger's," and hop the Twentieth Century Limited to the windy city. Come, Jack pleaded, "for the sake of the Lord Jesus Christ." What could stop her—not "propriety," as Henrietta had passed through "grave dangers" in that realm and remained, he believed, "pure." Instead she went up to visit Barry at Harvard and asked Jack to meet her at Chapelbrook, where she wanted to see Mina and Harry before she sailed. Harry's divorce would be finalized in the spring and a June wedding was planned. Louis Kirstein said he would not attend—Harry was not Jewish and his divorce damaged his standing. If Jack resented Henrietta for not giving him time alone with her, he appreciated Mina's part in their relationship. "God bless her," he wrote, "I think she loves us loving each other."

Jack implored Henrietta not to let him be shy in Northampton. He later mourned their history of long absences and "horrible half-meetings, those snatched furtive caresses" that left neither of them satisfied or reassured about how they would fit together. He blamed his self-consciousness "for the many things I never said to you, the kisses I never gave you." Whatever "spiritual and physical intimacy there is now between us, was your doing, was brought about because you were the one who had the courage to break down the hideous barriers that might have separated us beyond all hope."

Then she was gone. He was in Chicago's Drake Hotel, reading Carl Sandburg and escaping to symphony concerts and plays. A movie studio convention had taken over the hotel's third floor, and the flamboyant Hollywood wardrobes and heavy security amused the regular clientele. The future producer and director experienced a moment of prescience, writing, "I have often told you the movies was about the right level for me." Years later, Houseman's filmic eye framed his recollection of their latest separation:

> Those who accompany departing travelers through the humiliating efficiencies of our new giant airports can have no idea of the emotional part New York ship-sailings, with their accompanying alcoholic rites, played in our lives in the twenties and thirties. Henrietta's farewell party on the Aquitania, celebrated in her deluxe, flower-scented cabin with floods of champagne, bourbon and bootleg gin, was a classic of its kind. Around midnight, after the champagne had run out and the second call of "All ashore that's going ashore!" had been ignored, Mina and Harry appeared, took a quick, distasteful look around at the delirious retinue, kissed Henrietta goodbye and left. I started away with them but half-way down the gangplank I turned and went back, fighting my way through the din of gongs, against the stream of departing guests, to Henrietta's cabin. She sat dazed and smiling on the bed and as I kissed her . . . through the taste of Bourbon, I felt the warm, quick, eager motion of her tongue deep inside my mouth.

Jack sweated out the summer in New Orleans and Galveston, buying and shipping wheat while consuming great gobs of literature—in New York Henrietta had been his books—and composing letters to her every few days. Her inadequate responses drove him mad. He might hear of trips to the theater, of encounters with famous writers (H. G. Wells), and that she was unhappy—but not why! Did her sadness have one whit to do with their separation? At one level, he wanted her to suffer as much as he did. He also wanted her to get to her work with Ernest Jones. Knuckling down to difficult tasks was not Henrietta's forte, and it tormented Houseman to hear she was spiriting the newlyweds Harry and Mina around the countryside. They visited their favorite innkeeper at the Spread Eagle and marveled at David Garnett's house, garden, and boys. They laughed and drank. Henrietta left behind a 78 rpm record. On one side "Zeb Tourney's Girl" recounted a violent hillbilly feud, and a rendition of the standard "A Letter Edged in Black" completed the other. This tune contained lines that rang familiarly to Henrietta over the years: "Come home, my boy, your dear old father wants you / Come home, my boy, your dear old mother's dead." David played the songs on his gramophone for weeks.

Harry managed the troika tenderly. He never tried to make Mina give Henrietta up. His awareness of his mortality and his unhappy first marriage motivated him to love without fear. Ernest Jones—who saw both Mina and Henrietta on track for well-adjusted lives—gave Harry his blessing. (The doctor was less hopeful about Mina's other student, Eleanor Chilton, who was seeing a married Princeton professor with two children.) In Paris, the trio united with Mr. and Mrs. Kirstein, who had boycotted Mina and Harry's wedding. Harry took his bride into a Parisian lingerie shop to order a trousseau of handkerchief linen underclothes. Rose Kirstein considered this effeminate and said so. A perfectly preserved pair of fine cotton ladies' drawers and a delicate wool mesh undershirt, each bearing Harry's monogram, were among the clothes Henrietta kept for years afterward, turning up in the trunk she left behind in Melcombe's attic. Whether worn by husband or wife, Henrietta either filched a set or Mina shared them with the girl she loved.

The Judge, Robert, Barry, Aleen, her children, Byron and Alice, and her niece made their way to Europe that summer, joining Henrietta in Paris and crossing paths with the Kirsteins. (Mina's brother Lincoln was at Harvard with Barry and jealously dismissed him as the unattainable golden boy, rich, bright, popular. Lincoln wrote in his diary that he once overheard Barry say that a "psychological play" another undergraduate had written to share with a group of "homosexual friends" was "awfully merry.") From Paris, the Binghams departed for the Alps. In August, Bob and Aleen Bingham marked their anniversary with a return to Guthrie Castle's haunted walls and damp, bracing moors.

With so much travel, Henrietta saw little of Ernest Jones, but the summer of her separation from Jack yielded a remarkable piece of theater, a "psychological play," in fact, that dramatized insights she had gained since coming to Europe with Mina. On a Swiss hotel's blue writing paper, Henrietta and twenty-year-old Barry sketched the first scenes of a four-act play in which the fates of an elder sister and a younger brother hang in the balance. Barry kept the rough sheets (some in Henrietta's hand, some in his) to the end of his life, tucked away in a closet, the closely written, penciled pages browning and crumbling at the edges.

"Shadows" presented a family in the process of entombing itself. A widowed and well-off southern patriarch, Philip Castleman, cruelly (though perhaps unwittingly) stifles his offspring in the service of his narcissism. An alcoholic eldest child, Philip Jr., never finished college and has fallen prey to a fortune hunter named Maud. The next child is Gordon, the only girl but in fact an honorary boy with a masculine name to herald her exceptionalism. The younger son, Maurice, has college before him and shows promise as a composer. A "confirmed old maid of twenty-five" named Rita is Gordon's lesbian friend and knows the Castlemans well enough to speak her mind. She and Gordon hope to see Maurice study music in Paris.

The brothers despise each other. Philip Jr. cannot win his father's approval and subverts the wunderkind, Maurice. How nice, Philip says sarcastically, to be "born with an artistic temperament," since it appeared to be "the safe way to get about everything you want in the world." Maud pretends to be merely a friend and not in pursuit of the eldest Castleman son; she objects that music training abroad would squander money that Philip Jr. should by rights inherit. Maurice would pick up the mannerisms of "cheap artists," she predicted. Free-floating homophobia packs Philip and Maud's dialogue. "There must be something wrong," Maud observes, "with a boy that can't get along at school." This conventionality repulses Maurice more than it hurts him, for he penetrates Maud's craven motives and laments his brother's feeble character.

The father, oblivious to the tension swirling between his children, sees only what he wants: "Thank God I have you children to care for, now that I'm only an old worn-out man that has nearly lost the enchantment of life," he tells his offspring. At another point he reminds them, "How empty my life would have been without you three children, since your mother died." But it is Mr. Castleman who demands care and attention, and his hypocrisy with respect to Gordon focuses the drama.

At twenty-four, Gordon is a remarkably independent woman of business. She has held a management position at a mill owned by another family and drawn accolades from her employer—an unlikely scenario for 1926, but no more than a female newspaper publisher. She loves her work. Furthermore, she needs it, and recognizes that something turns "sour and ugly when I have to be dependent on other people, and I hate it."

> **Rita:** But some day you'll fall in love, dear, and it will all be different.
> **Gordon:** Oh, no it won't be different. The man I love will love me because I am a wild, ambitious, unbridled creature. Whatever happens, I'll never lose my ambition.

Gordon is given a professional opportunity farther from the Castleman seat in Virginia, but her idle elder brother insists that her duty lies at home with their father. In fact, Mr. Castleman nurtured his daughter's modern temperament. Sounding unnervingly like the young Bob Bingham during his courtship of Babes Miller, he calls Gordon his "experiment"; Mr. Castleman envisioned raising "a woman so independent mentally that she could do whatever she chose with her life." Females of his own generation "had their schemes and plans," but he never met one who applied herself beyond the confines of marriage and social relationships, a woman "who had what could truly be called ambition."

As Maurice says, his sister absorbed "most of the ambition for all three of us." But her presence was too "soothing" and "adorable" for Mr. Castleman to tolerate losing. While he admitted that it would "be unreasonable of me to object" to the new job, he also realized that "the loneliness" of the idea "almost overwhelms me. You see, I had hoped to have you at home after you got through college." Only one thing looms more terrifyingly within the father's breast. If Gordon took a husband it "would mean that she and I could never be as close together, again," a "final . . . breaking of old ties."

And then he betrays her. Having noted early in the play that his daughter's "very strong personality . . . is anything but disturbing to me," Mr. Castleman seizes upon Gordon's alarm about Maud's ill intentions after she broaches the subject of Philip Jr.'s infidelity to his fiancée, a dear family friend. Her father tells Gordon she is being "merely feminine," catty, and irrational. In the name of protecting her, he pinions her wings. "I have never seen you so hysterical," Mr. Castleman pronounces, and "I can't think of letting you go away in autumn if you're not going to be your old calm reasonable self."

In the final act, Philip elopes with Maud while Maurice returns to college, and Gordon remains behind at home to prop up their father. Gordon, formerly striving professionally, is domesticated, managing the household for a man. Mr. Castleman welcomes the prodigals back to the big house, where Maud makes Philip Jr. her puppet. In a matter of months Gordon's "former youth and warmth" drain away. Cloistered and benumbed, she toasts her father's bread just so, hoping to be "as efficient a piece of machinery as possible," a Cinderella in reverse, for in conceding to her father she hopes to preserve Maurice's freedom to pursue *his* dream. But Maurice experiences a mental break, passing five days shut up in his dormitory room composing a full symphony in a fog of inspiration. He emerges just in time to take—and fail—his examinations. In despair and shame, Maurice sets fire to the sheet music and leaves school, resigned to a job back home at the Castleman firm.

Father "tries to fill his life up with all our lives," Gordon observes; "it frightens me in a way." And it's never enough; he is "lonely all the time." Barry and Henrietta's modern gothic tale asked how they could hold on to themselves when tasked with shielding their father from grief, isolation, and scandal. How could they save themselves from becoming mere shadows of their dreams—or his?

Henrietta posed a similar question to John Houseman from the "spinach-green" mountains of Switzerland. Having toured England and France with Mina and Harry, then the Alps with her family, Henrietta proceeded to spend several weeks in Scotland with the swarm of her father's guests. Taking the fifty-five-room Guthrie Castle as his base, the Judge went on daily grouse shoots and entertained with help from nine servants superintended by Henrietta and, to a lesser degree, Aleen. Her father's vacation life in the 1920s consisted of shooting excursions complete with his own hunting dogs shipped from America, guests coming and going, packed lunches and formal dinners, cocktails and reels, and visits to neighboring villages and towns where Bingham curried favor with local lairds and made himself available to newspaper reporters. And he urged Henrietta to give up her own plans to be a part of it. She derived some satisfaction from this life of privilege with its distractions and amusements—as well as the sense of responsibility her father conferred on her. But it left her dizzy, unfocused. She was not seeing Ernest Jones, which Houseman had understood to be the purpose of her presence in Europe. Jack expected her back in November, and they had talked of her spending the winter with him in Vancouver. However, by the time the Binghams cleared out of the castle, Henrietta foresaw staying in England through the winter of 1926–1927 (and foxhunting season). She would really buckle down with Jones. She knew her father would detest this plan and she asked Houseman what she ought to do.

Jack was in New York negotiating with his superiors at Continental Grain—he wanted a raise in light of his success and the personal hardship that came with chasing wheat across North America. Over eggs and toast with Mina, he told her about Henrietta's indecision and the lengthy and furious "No!" he had composed but not yet posted. Mina said he must come see her and Harry at Chapelbrook. They could talk it all over.

Between horseback rides through meadows and cooling dips in the amber waters of the swimming hole, Mina told Jack things he'd never known about the creature who had taken over his life. "One of your most nefarious traits," Houseman wrote to Guthrie Castle, is "that you spoil the world for anyone who has been intimate with you. You are far too exciting." Mina excelled at tête-à-têtes, and one evening in the churchlike great room where Duncan Grant's portrait of her hung over the fireplace, Houseman sat on a stool at her feet. She was a "teacher and counselor giving advice" but also a "former lover passing on rele-

vant emotional data" to him as Henrietta's "suitor." In the hazy August
Berkshire foothills, Mina spelled out Henrietta's undependability,
her lesbian behavior and her panics, which she believed grew from her
maltreatment by a neurotic and selfish father, and how vital it was for
her to sort these things through before she married Jack. According to
Mina, seducing women allowed Henrietta to identify with her father
(acting a man's part, sexually) without threatening their fundamentally
incestuous bond. Mina

> delivered her relentless diagnosis in more realistic and clinical terms
> than I had ever allowed myself to use . . . She reminded me that being
> in love with Henrietta meant loving two quite different and unrelated
> persons: the one, warm, strong, gay and tender, constantly surpris-
> ing you with her intelligence and generosity; the other idle, violent
> and fitful, capable of almost any treachery and cruelty in her flight
> from terror and her compulsive appetite for personal power. She was
> telling me nothing I did not already know and had not sensed about
> Henrietta from the beginning. And once the first shock was past I
> found myself listening to her with mixed feelings of gratitude and re-
> sentment—of despair over my imminent loss [of a reunion] mingled
> with a sense of relief that the decision had been made with no act of
> volition on my part.

Jack was too dazed, too desperately in love to find fault with these in-
trusions in his and Henrietta's affairs, to suspect Mina of sabotage, or
to question the alignment of Henrietta's thinking with Mina's. Later
that year, Jack noted Mina's penchant for "promiscuous dramatization,"
but he told Henrietta that Mina's confidences made him "love you
more passionately, I think, than before."

But Houseman was shaken. Could they be happy? Could he satisfy
her? Soon after the weekend in the mountains, he spent an entire day
in a Chicago bookstore surreptitiously reading the sexologist Havelock
Ellis's advice book to couples, *Little Letters on Love and Virtue* (1922).
Ellis emphasized the erotic needs of women. And, like Stephen Tomlin,
Houseman teased her with reports from his travels. In New Orleans he

found his way to the "Rue Royale," where "the local Bloomsbury" types gathered. An effeminate young man with a pale forehead and a "soft voice . . . wants me ever so badly," he reported; the fellow handed him a sheaf of his poems, but Jack cut off the encounter.

Jack assured Henrietta that he did not think it was "essential" to "lose your oddities." Mina knew her so much better, though, and she said she must. Where Henrietta herself stood on the question remains impossibly buried, but Houseman was clear in condemning her entanglement with the Judge. Jack refused to advise her "in the matter of your father." He found their "constant muffled conflicts" maddening. Now he must wait six more months before he saw her. He tried to have faith. "You believe, don't you, that I have a greatness in me?" he wrote Henrietta anxiously. "You do love me, deeply, don't you?"

The extended stay in England threatened to place Henrietta among the scandalous and unproductive expatriates depicted in Hemingway's *The Sun Also Rises.* Her expensive Fifth Avenue apartment stood empty, though Jeannette Young, Sophie Preston Hill, and Billy Weaver still gathered there, and Houseman described a drunken Billy one night petting with a man who might have been Carl Van Vechten. Jeannette finally located a rich Denver couple to take over the lease. Family members referred euphemistically to Henrietta's "lessons" in London, but her Chicago cousin told Houseman that the Judge had come to his wits' end and was cutting her off. Henrietta would be forced to come home.

With Thanksgiving 1926 approaching, Henrietta cabled her father that she would stay on in London. Bingham was furious and desperate and summoned Houseman for a conference. Jack predicted another round of "family turmoil and bitterness" and winced to think of Henrietta "devoured by grotesque panics." She was being portrayed "as the colonel's granddaughter indulging a caprice, or as a rather sinister neurotic," yet she was "neither and both," and he loved her. The Judge was furious, but so was Jack.

> Until you and I have been together again I do not want to see him.
> It infuriates me, beyond words, that you should be having these con-

flicts with him just now—of all times. I would do anything in the world to stop them; I have thought of writing to him—did I not realize how useless it would be; how utterly alien I am—how completely incapable I am of understanding these Bingham conflicts, these intricate patterns of intrigue that you find it necessary to weave around each other.

The separation was almost unbearable. Although Houseman tried to encourage her ("There is nothing you cannot achieve if you want"), the idea that Henrietta might now quit her analysis exasperated him. "You have been doing it for three years," he reminded her, "in fragments, never finishing it." To give up would be "another defeat, another weakness."

The possibility had hung over her for years, but in late 1926, Robert Worth Bingham cut off Henrietta's funds, which came both from his pocket and from the trust her mother had left. Houseman learned about it from Bea Howe and immediately offered to set up an account for her and advance whatever she required. His business was speeding along and it was "ridiculous that you should be in want," he wrote. Henrietta refused. She was seeing Jones three times a week, calling it "painful as hell." By the new year her father relented, and her allowance flowed once more, but Jack was making ground, clearing $8,000 in Vancouver over nine days—about as much as her father earned from his newspapers in a week. In a few more months Jack and Henrietta would break bread together, maybe even bread made from grain he had shipped around the globe. They could be in a position to break from Robert Worth Bingham, too.

For her birthday in January, Jack told Henrietta to pick out "a dog to live with" as his gift. It might calm her. She selected a border terrier named Caesar (the breed was used to flush foxes from their dens) and brought him to her snug, respectable two-story house in Kensington. But Henrietta was not leading a quiet life. Besides the daredevil English foxhunting that obsessed her—clearing huge walls and yawning ditches at breakneck speed—she cast her spell on Carrington's friend Alix Strachey. In late 1926 Carrington complained to Lytton that his sister-in-law "disgraced herself with Kentucky." Alix, a trained psycho-analyst and translator of Freud's works, was reportedly Henrietta's "dog, her slave, etc." David Garnett saw little of "Puppin" as he stayed mostly in the country, but he informed Mina that Henrietta treated the older Alix unkindly. In their autobiographical play "Shadows," Gordon remarked to her brother Maurice, "It isn't good to care too much for people; it may make everyone unhappy."

American music rang in Londoners' ears. Florence Mills and Edith Wilson and the Plantation Orchestra were back as "The Blackbirds of 1926" and the performers, especially Mills, took the city by storm. The platform gave her a chance to speak more directly than most black entertainers then dared, telling readers of *The Sketch* that "Down South it's still terrible. There isn't slavery any more—not real slavery—but there's something very like it." Mills "shut her eyes quickly. A line of black lashes over a delicate coffee skin." "But it's all going to be better." Mills's poignant anthem "I'm a Little Blackbird Looking for a Blue-bird" collapsed the ravages of racial prejudice with the sorrows of any-one who ever felt outcast. Henrietta understood at both levels, and applauded progress toward racial justice. While her 1923 party had been one of the first to showcase the performers, in 1926 the band-wagon was crowded with admirers—any number of occasions might have been the one where David Garnett saw the Kentuckian, at what he called a "Blackbird party."

Nonetheless, at bottom, Henrietta felt alone in London. "I used to nearly perish with loneliness," she later remembered, "on long evenings in the spring when the twilight seemed to last for hours." Stopping in Kensington Gardens, she watched men sailing their yachts in the Round Pond and strolled "around the more fashionable squares," peer-ing into the "windows at the servants relaxing over their supper." Her privilege left her longing for the pleasure of leisure well earned.

In April 1927, Jack pried from his employers a month's leave of absence. The couple would spend two unchaperoned weeks in England and sail back to America together. Henrietta took the terrier Caesar to meet his ship, and they drove from Southampton through the warm drizzle to

London in her long-hooded Bentley coupe. She was thinner and glowing, her eyes dancing between him and the road, her gloved hands cool on the wheel. Knowing how nervous Jack would be after close to a year apart, Henrietta consulted with Dr. Jones. Houseman accompanied her to his office and waited for his turn with the psychoanalyst. "It was sort of an indoctrination," Jack explained, complete with explicit sexual advice on how he ought to proceed. The doctor wanted to fortify him, but for an anxious lover the setting was nearly terrifying. Before they parted, Jones pronounced Henrietta's beau "psychologically smart and penetrating," and "off we went to Brighton and lost our virginity."

At the grand redbrick Hotel Metropole, they booked into an overdecorated "red damask" suite with a crystal chandelier and a view of the English Channel. They took dinner in their room and chased it with brandy. The time had come for the great event—almost a medical prescription in the context of Jones's treatment. Jack had to stare down his terror of fumbling in his efforts to give her pleasure. Henrietta was no rookie in the bedroom, but the buildup to this particular encounter was unlike any other in her admittedly broad experience. Henrietta's humor carried them through; they survived the night and Houseman remembered it all with a sort of miserable delight.

Next morning they walked along the pier. At the arcade, wooden skee balls clunked into their catchments. Back in London, crab apples were in flower. They met Bea Howe, who had introduced them, for champagne at the Café Royale. David Garnett groused that Henrietta did not return his calls. He did not meet Houseman, and knew only "his sex—which is something." She immersed herself in Jack, the two of them lingering over breakfast together at the house on Aubrey Walk, playing tennis and drinking lemon squash in the afternoons, walking Caesar through Kensington Gardens. They made a driving tour of the Cotswolds, stopping for a tramp through fields around Long Compton. When they wanted to lie down and kiss, they leashed Caesar to a tree.

Word spread among the Bloomsberries that Henrietta was marrying and leaving England for good. Since the summer of 1922, she had spent three-quarters of her time as an expatriate; England was more "home" than Kentucky and New York combined. The next step was to confront Louisville with her fiancé. She wanted him to escort her to the Kentucky Derby. Jack worried that he couldn't get away from work, and in the midst of their reunion he fell to brooding about her slipping into another round of excitement that didn't include him. Mina saw everything resolving happily, but David Garnett demurred. "And so he's an American and she is going home for good," he wrote Mina in May. "I don't believe in such finalities, and I daresay we three shall [be] drinking MORE cocktails together in the 1950s. At all events your ghosts will often be with me then, as they continually are now. For strangely enough you and she are milestones in my life; and I am very very fond of you."

The composer Richard Rodgers and the lyricist Lorenz Hart shared Henrietta and Jack's steamer back to the United States. Their hit that year, "My Heart Stood Still," encapsulated love's vaunted powers: "A house in Iceland was my heart's domain / I saw your eyes, now castles rise in Spain." But Henrietta and Jack were quarrelling. One night in the smoking room, he burst out angrily, insulting her in public. Shocked by his own behavior, he blamed himself for shutting off "the first rate emotions." His fear and guilt may have sabotaged their relationship; Jack confessed to being a "rotten lover," self-pitying and no fun.

On May 14, 1927, they attended the fifty-third Derby, which went off under gathering clouds and a crowd of seventy-five thousand. When Henrietta's grandfather died the following day in Asheville, it was the end of an era for the Bingham family. The Judge had been bankrolling the military school for years and soon it would be shuttered. After the funeral, Henrietta and her father took the train to New York, meeting Barry. They put themselves up at the Waldorf Astoria, though they also had the run of a plush new yacht named *Eala* (Gaelic for "swan") for late-night parties. Henrietta was given a "luscious great silver fox fur." Jack felt threatened and they fought again. Henrietta became distraught.

Jack's gloom, his swings between adoration, verbal abuse, and self-flagellating apologies gave Henrietta pause. "What rot!" she liked to say. When she wanted clarity about the future, marriage appeared riskier than ever. Her hesitation wounded him anew, and his overwrought responses spooked her. They escaped the city to Chapelbrook, looking for relief. On June 8, 1927, after two short days together and while the nation anticipated Charles Lindbergh's return to America after his record-breaking flight, Houseman departed for Kansas City—his summer posting for the Continental Grain Corporation. "My darling," he began,

for (these two months) I have been too preoccupied with my own complainings, too solicitous of my own tender pride, to consider objectively just what you and I, my darling, have been doing to each other all these weeks. Now that I am suddenly shaken out of my complacency (for there can be no worse complacency than a querulous one) I am disgusted at the mistakes which I, on my part, have committed from the very first days when I did the lazy thing and came and surrendered to you, shamelessly jangling my chains of accumulated loneliness and aching virginity—and the innumerable times when with a little more courage and a little effort, I might as well have made you come to me and reassured you and led you—and I remained, instead, impotent and querulous and sullen and watched you go away from me . . .

I know our possibilities of misery too well ever to want to hold you, even for an instant against your inclination. And I shall keep the promise I made to you in Hanover Square, that I would walk out of your life gracefully the instant I saw no hope in our relationship. I love you Henrietta . . . with all my body and all my soul . . . I loathe myself for breaking down in New York when I should have helped you. But I know how very much, in intimacy, I can give you, when your dying terrors do not throw their last desolate, impassable chasms between us, and that my love could give you something deeper than passing compliments.

But Houseman's faith waned in the Plains. He enumerated his demons: "infantilism"; "the grotesque wheat-devil" (the manic pursuit of riches); "the ragged Kerstein [sic] complex" (Jewish self-loathing); "lingering shadows of impotence neurosis"; and various "envies and sundry anxieties." All "embittered my desires."

The end came like the cloudburst of a long-building thunderstorm.

In late June 1927, he returned to Louisville. Incapable of responding to Henrietta's caresses, Jack jabbered about ambition—his, hers.

> There you are, with everything, all the potentialities in the world. If your life should be a failure it would be a terrible tragedy—a most pitiful waste. And except that we love each other I have so . . . criminally little to offer you. It's not simply a question of money . . . in every respect I am a doubtful quantity. In marrying me you are taking a risk, so big, so wild (I mean that quite seriously) . . . and you want success terribly.

Henrietta felt sick with other people's expectations. She might never meet them. The sun had set hours before. "You don't know what you're missing," Henrietta told Jack. He never forgot her words. Henrietta and John Houseman cared deeply for each other, but the drama and insecurity and recrimination were too much and perhaps too familiar for her to consecrate with matrimony.

Part Three

You are aware of what other historians so easily overlook—
that it is impossible to understand the past with certainty, because we cannot divine men's motives and the essence of their
minds and so cannot interpret their actions. Our psychological analysis does not suffice even with those who are near us in
space and time, unless we can make them the object of years
of the closest investigation, and even then it breaks down before the incompleteness of our knowledge and the clumsiness
of our synthesis.

—SIGMUND FREUD TO LYTTON STRACHEY,
DECEMBER 25, 1928

11

HUNTING

*E*rnest Jones lamented that the long affair with Houseman failed to end in marriage. Mina and Harry decided, however, that Henrietta and Jack "could have made each other as miserable as any two people" they knew, owing chiefly to Houseman's "neuroses." He had been "hard where he ought to be soft," Mina wrote, "and soft where he ought to be hard." No such critiques saddled Henrietta; the breakup was proof of her "maturity and reliability." She certainly exuded these qualities during visits to Chapelbrook in the summer of 1927—Mina called her a "beautiful, calm, composed and wise young woman." Mina felt vindicated, but each time a visit from the unequalled Henrietta ended, sorrow washed over her. Harry and Ernest Jones were pressuring Mina to have a child, but Henrietta had long since occupied that role; she was "miracle" enough. Mina had her students, even exceptional ones like the poet Anne Morrow, who later married Charles Lindbergh. And she had Harry. But her longing for Henrietta spilled into her letters to Ernest Jones. He told her Henrietta must "try the cold world alone now for a time. I have brought her from women to men, but she finds the latter a strange animal that takes a little getting used to."

Believing Henrietta should marry "as soon as possible," Mina set about plotting a match. This person should be Henrietta's equal in charm, intelligence, and wealth. He should be heterosexual, for Mina dreamed of a marriage like hers, not the "lavender" type sometimes entered into for social cover by "sapphists" and "buggers." And the couple should settle far from Kentucky, perhaps in England, which Henrietta loved and her Anglophile father could not oppose. Harry cautioned that Henrietta could never be "a free person" until she confronted "the financial issue." Either the Judge must cut her off or make clear exactly what he was willing to give her. In Mina's opinion, three years of marriage to Aleen—a potentially stabilizing force—had not altered his obsession with Henrietta or his toxic effect on her spirit, and she predicted that

> no matter what Judge Bingham promises to do he will break his promise as soon as he is outside of Henrietta's influence. The man is obviously unbalanced and becoming more so all the time and to test one's strength of character by one's ability to cope with complete unreliability would seem to me about as sensible as judging one's architectural capacities by building a house on the sands by the sea.

Mina was convinced that Henrietta required a man to stand between her and her father; it was the sole way to break his hold.

The two women went on a hunt for candidates. Mina regarded Henrietta's ability to contemplate other partners as evidence that she had gained wisdom through therapy, though it also fit her old pattern of changing lovers, or taking multiple paramours at once. She and Mina contemplated Ivor Churchill, the second son of the Duke of Marlborough and Winston Churchill's cousin. His mother was the American beauty Consuelo Vanderbilt and he took an interest in modern art. Henrietta genuinely enjoyed him, but would he marry her? With women, Henrietta had no difficulty playing the seductress, acting upon her desire; with men, she wanted to be "sought after." Mina told her reprovingly what she had endured "to achieve Harry."

Mina wanted to set her up with a "clever and original" aspiring architect, a "virile young man" whom Lincoln Kirstein had met at Harvard. The Curtisses invited Philip Johnson to Chapelbrook that fall with the idea of introducing them. But Johnson and Henrietta were not to meet, at least not in 1927, as Henrietta was in England during his visit—and Henrietta was hardly Johnson's type. ("Boys don't fall in love with boys," his father insisted, even though a Boston neurologist told Philip to accept his homosexuality.) While Mina barked up this unlikely tree, Henrietta was getting "perpetual letters" from a "Miss Lehmann," to whom she had entrusted her Bentley in London, arousing Mina's "petty jealousy." She admitted as much to Jones, but reflected that "Henrietta has always had men and women in love with her, and derived an abnormal satisfaction from it. Now I suppose she will derive a comparatively normal one."

Henrietta's willingness to express desire was part of her appeal. She was freer, by dint of her money and her courage, than most in 1927, by which time the liberated flapper figure had moved closer to the cultural center. More and more young women played sports, smoked cigarettes, drove automobiles, wore revealing dresses, and danced, danced, danced— things Henrietta had been doing for years. More of them were having sex before marriage, too, and more wives braved divorce when matrimony failed them.

For all Ernest Jones's efforts, Henrietta's actions suggest she could not or would not make her prodigious desires conform to the dominant code. She had intimately witnessed the arrangements at Tidmarsh Mill and Ham Spray House, had risked her own and her family's reputation by loving women as well as men, and had even found male lovers who tolerated her female ones. She needed to be desired to feel alive, but her long-term relationships made her feel trapped. Henrietta's lesbian affairs, even after years of therapy, frustrated Jones and Mina, and possibly Henrietta herself. If she *could* love men, as Jones felt certain she could, why on earth didn't she stick to them? Attracting male admirers may have been a survival skill for Henrietta; but unless Mina, Jones, Tomlin, and Houseman were badly mistaken she wasn't faking her heterosexual involvements.

There was an urgency to this matter. She was twenty-six and her peers were all married or about to be. Her brother Robert had fallen for a Scottish girl on board a ship the previous year, and the wedding was planned for August in Edinburgh. Meantime, Barry, who had finished his third year at Harvard, sometimes gave off contradictory signals about his own sexual preferences, but a Radcliffe girl he was dating had the potential to become serious. Henrietta's willful singlehood invited questions and speculation, even if Robert's union was scarcely a cause for celebration. The wedding dinner the Binghams hosted at the Caledonian Hotel featured six courses and four wines, but "a more depressing event I've never encountered," Barry wrote to his sweetheart. The bride was no catch, and the Scottish and American parties "stared at each other in mutual mistrust." In the midst of this summer of nuptials, Henrietta tested what her father would put up with to have her near him. She asked "Miss Lehmann"—the twenty-four-year-old English actress who had the use of her Bentley and had sent so many letters to her while she was in America—to join the family party as it moved from Edinburgh to grouse shooting near Guthrie Castle. They were more than just friends. A framed photograph of Beatrix stood on Henrietta's dresser to the end of her life.

Auburn-haired Beatrix Lehmann was almost universally known by her own request as "Peggy," in memory of a treasured pony. Her genius for "comic devilry" ensured she got a measure of attention, though her sisters were thought to be prettier. A brother, John, was Barry's age and went on to a distinguished career as a man of letters. During World War I, Peggy disguised herself as a boy so she could attend Scout activities. Their father served as a Liberal member of Parliament from 1906 to 1910, but his sense of humor—he parodied Sherlock Holmes for *Punch* as "Picklock Holes"—made him more engaging than Judge Bingham. However, while Bob Bingham brought down hundreds of grouse on the moors of Scotland, Parkinson's disease crippled Rudolph Chambers Lehmann.

Peggy attended the Royal Academy of Dramatic Arts and first appeared on the London stage at twenty-one. She was likely introduced to Henrietta through Tallulah Bankhead, whom she understudied in three different productions. There were all-night escapades with Bankhead, who would suffer pre-opening-night "nerve storms" and insist "that she couldn't be left." Peggy, living on a meager allowance, meanwhile had "stockings to mend, bills to pay (impossible) and understudy (70 pages) to learn." According to contemporaries—and by the standards of the era—Lehmann was remarkably open about her lesbian leanings. "Tallulah must have been in love with her," recalled Bankhead's co-star Glenn Anders. "We were together all the time."

In September 1927 while Peggy was in Scotland with the Binghams, her sister Rosamond promoted her novel in the United States. *Dusty Answer*, set largely at a university dormitory for girls, featured a protagonist swerving between same-sex attractions and heterosexual courtship. American sales were strong, and Henrietta insisted the author meet Mina and Harry. They welcomed Rosamond warmly at Chapelbrook, but Mina was not pleased to learn of the growing intimacy between Henrietta and Rosamond's sister. John Houseman, who heard that Henrietta was "very much in love" with the actress, was especially hurt.

The *Glasgow Bulletin* covered the vacationing American press baron and his party, and ran a photo of "Miss H. Bingham" and "Miss P. Lehman [*sic*]." Striding together in their tartans, walking sticks in hand, they flank a shotgun-toting "Mr. Phillips (who evidently objects to the 'snapshotter')." The image captures Henrietta's crosshatched social world. Wogan Phillips, heir to a shipping fortune, had a fling at Oxford with Lytton Strachey's lover Roger Senhouse. Henrietta's father was pictured alone, aiming his double-barreled Purdy from a high stone butt. His solitary masculine stance over the Earl of Airlie's estate is the reverse of Henrietta's no less masterly sociability.

That same day, Henrietta sat shoulder to shoulder with Peggy, on the moor alongside a chauffeured automobile, their legs tucked sideways under them. The photographer caught them in conversation, cigarettes in hand and nipping dark liquid from small glasses. Aleen's adult children and nieces perch on the running board—they frequently enjoyed the Judge's hospitality, although one niece observed that he was "rather a formal person." Bingham gave his sporting stepson, Byron, a job in the printing business Robert had abandoned, and permitted him to take long hunting vacations. When Aleen's daughter, Alice, wrote

Grouse shoot, 1927

home to Kentucky she did not mention Miss Lehmann, but said, "Ma was thrilled" to be invited to lunch at nearby Airlie Castle. (Aleen matched Henrietta's father's delight in the British peerage.)

Henrietta stayed on in Britain after the shooting party, foxhunting and spending time with Peggy, and realizing that Ivor Churchill was a "no go." November brought a season of mourning when the thirty-one-year-old sensation Florence Mills succumbed to tuberculosis. Her fellow "Blackbird" Edith Wilson followed her casket at the largest funeral Harlem had ever seen. The darkness intensified in January 1928 when Harry Curtiss contracted pneumonia. He and Mina were on their usual New Year's visit to New York, and his tuberculosis-scarred lungs could not combat the infection. He died ten days later in an oxygen tent, aged thirty-nine. It was a vast loss. Peggy's sister, Rosamond, called Mina's "just what marriage should be, how I wanted mine to be. You had gone through so much to achieve such peace——oh Mina!" Rosamond wrote that Henrietta was "broken," but Mina destroyed all her sympathy letters. Henrietta briefly touched down in the United States during the summer of 1928, and went to see Mina, still numb, at Chapelbrook. "All I wanted was to be Harry's wife," Mina wrote, "and anything else I may be seems unimportant and futile."

In 1928, Rosamond Lehmann and her lover, Wogan Phillips, second Baron Milford, rented what Dora Carrington described as an "absurd little cottage with roses and arbours" in the village of Quainton, Buckinghamshire. Amusingly, the unmarried couple shared the place with Peggy and Henrietta (who wanted a base in hunt country) in order to keep up appearances. The foxhunts were held several mornings a week. Locals watched the dogs and riders set off after gathering at a manor house. The bugle cry, steaming horses, tumbling hooves, five-foot-plus fences, mawlike ditches, and inevitable crashes had Henrietta hooked. Riding to hounds, as only the English did, was an almost sexual act, full of grace, passion, and conquest. And she did it well. She arrived home exhausted and exhilarated, often after dark. Her Smith friend Eleanor Chilton had moved to England, and snapped Henrietta's picture in Quainton, smiling and robust in her tailored breeches and hunting coat. Eleanor also photographed her with Peggy outside the house on a sunny winter's day. The pair had emerged into the

Eleanor Chilton's photo of Henrietta and Peggy, Quainton, February 1929

brightness from beneath a thatch roof so low they would have had to duck. Henrietta grasped Peggy's arm assertively with one hand and readied a cigarette with the other. Two men stared at them from the village road.

Like Henrietta, Peggy was an entertaining companion, adding spark and cleverness to a group. She could turn her mordant humor against herself, loathed sentimentality, and insisted on her independence. According to Rosamond's biographer, Peggy suffered "almost invariably unhappy love-affairs," limited by self-described "'cynicism and bullet biting.'" But the relationship that began while Henrietta was at least informally engaged to John Houseman persisted through the decade. The women treated the bond provisionally. A character in Rosamond's 1930 novel *A Note in Music* talked of caution with respect to intimate ties: "one sees to it that no relationship shall sweep one beyond the balancing point where possession of oneself ceases and suffering begins."

London roared with manic revelry. The novelist Anthony Powell remembered late 1920s parties surpassing those of any other era. Henrietta and Peggy moved through "lower" Bloomsbury gatherings peopled with the younger set that admired Woolf, Strachey, the Bells, and so on, and parties thrown by hosts

> of far less distinction, probably fairly rich in contrast to the guests, though not in any high range of richness and . . . often unknown to many of the invitees. Fancy dress was the rule rather than the expectation . . . Hostesses were for some reason often well-to-do lesbians; less frequently male homosexuals

who were somehow connected to the arts. The preferred nightspots were the Cavendish Hotel's Lobby Bar, where the American pianist sang "Ol' Man River," and a basement club called the Blue Lantern with an "intellectual tinge" favored by Tallulah Bankhead and a bi- and homosexual crowd.

During her time with Peggy Lehmann, Henrietta wrote a clutch of newspaper articles, light profiles of interesting personages in her English social orbit. They were exclusives, for *The Courier-Journal* and the North American Newspaper Alliance, a press agency that offered syndicated material to some fifty U.S. papers. (Robert Worth Bingham sat on the board.) Henrietta's upper-class subjects exhibited energy and self-reliance, traits calculated to appeal to American readers. In late 1928, she called on Virginia-born Nancy Astor, who sat in the House of Commons—"a splendid example of what a woman can do in the political world." A committed advocate of women's suffrage, Astor lamented, "'Do you realize . . . that the French women do not even want the vote?'" Two weeks later, Henrietta's profile of Lord Burgh ran in *The Courier-Journal*. This officer of the Scottish Black Watch regiment had opened a millinery shop off Brompton Road in Kensington. American readers might have appreciated that in spite of his distinguished family (an ancestor was the first husband of one of Henry VIII's wives) he needed "to make a living" to keep his castle.

In 1929, Henrietta sought an interview with the media-shy Countess of Oxford, Prime Minister Herbert Asquith's widow. Due to her diminished income, the countess, already a prolific author, announced that she would advise clients "Upon Matters of Taste in Furniture, Colour and Decoration." (Henrietta would also have known her as a passionate rider—a foxhunting accident had disfigured her nose and upper lip when she was younger.)

[A]part from their incredulity that Lady Oxford should increase her heavy duties and obligations, her friends and the general public were interested that a woman of her social and political importance would enter business.

I determined to go to Lady Oxford's house on her first morning "at home," though I was warned by friends that "Margot" didn't care for newspapers and their representatives.

The door was opened by a dignified butler, obviously an old family servant. He preceded me up the staircase, and left me in a large room on the second floor.

I had barely had time to notice the parchment colored walls and Adam ceiling when Lady Oxford entered, smartly dressed in a black skirt, black and white woolen jumper and small black felt hat.

She asked me in her rather deep, musical voice why I had come and when I answered that I wanted to interview her she said abruptly, "Well you must leave at once . . . I have never been interviewed and I am much too busy to start now, even if I wanted. Goodby."

Henrietta knew how to project a charming American naivete. "I suppose my face betrayed my disappointment," she wrote, "because Lady Oxford looked at me intently for a moment and then said in the kindest voice imaginable, 'Perhaps I can help you. Tell me exactly what you want and I will do what I can. You are young, and young people shouldn't be unhappy.'" The countess proceeded to hold forth on mixing Chinese antiques with Chippendale pieces. Moments later Margot Asquith ushered Henrietta into a bedroom of mirrored walls that concealed closets along two sides. Against one wall stood her bed, and near it John Singer Sargent's drawings of her daughter Elizabeth and son Anthony, a filmmaker Henrietta knew. Lady Oxford "had to hasten off to luncheon with Queen Mary," but turned back to share her "secret" with the reporter. "My tea is brought to me at 6 each morning."

Henrietta's ingenuous writing betrays her as a novice; she appeared to be merely dabbling. But the profiles kept alive the possibility of playing a role in her father's growing empire and kept her allowance flowing. (In 1928–1929 she received the enormous sum of $24,000 from her father, although her brother Robert took in nearly three times that amount during the same period.) Henrietta then turned her hand to a more serious writing project for the North American Newspaper Alliance, "How Europe Handles Crime and Criminals." She praised institutions where prisoners received training in useful trades that could ease their return to society, and pointed out the benefits of separating youthful offenders from adults. The articles posted statistics on death, recidivism, living conditions, and work. From Paris, Henrietta drubbed the French for breaking prisoners' spirits with meaningless labor in

penal colonies. Psychoanalysis may have lain behind Henrietta's interest in this subject. Psychiatric medicine was adopting Freudian ideas,
and in the United States psychiatrists in some prisons sought to "cure"
convicts. She told a friend of helping a shell-shocked mental patient
with agoraphobia and claustrophobia, and, as the 1920s drew to a close,
Henrietta toyed with the idea of being "a prison commissioner." Nothing her father did could entice her to move home.

On Thanksgiving Day, 1928, Henrietta addressed a letter to "Dear
Ernest." She wanted to "celebrate . . . in a more substantial way than
my usual daily realization of all that you have done for me." She had
not forgotten that she still owed him money; if he kindly sent the balance due she hoped to pay in full that winter. Then she invited the
doctor and his wife to spend a Sunday at the cottage in Quainton.

Jones may not have always collected from his American patients—
Eleanor Chilton continued seeing him in the late 1920s and owed money
ten years afterward—but he benefited from his sessions with them in
other ways. In late 1927, the *International Journal of Psycho-Analysis* published his article "The Early Development of Female Sexuality," based on
"five cases of manifest homosexuality in women." Jones deemed three
of the analyses complete and said two had been "carried to a far stage."
He was at pains to point out that only two of the subjects were openly
hostile toward men, but he failed to mention that at least three of the
women—Henrietta, Mina, and Eleanor—were Americans connected
with Smith College and personally involved with one another.

"I have very little talent for originality," Jones told Freud in 1910; his
"ambition" was "rather to be 'behind the scenes' and 'in the know.'"
However, by the late 1920s, Jones had aligned himself with Karen
Horney and Melanie Klein, who were questioning certain aspects of
Freud's theory. A schism was brewing, and his 1927 essay echoed their
challenges to the oedipal sequence and the importance of penis envy.
Psychoanalysis was breaking into the educated mainstream, although
the scientific community questioned the movement's methodology, including Freud's use of single cases to make broad assertions. Jones's *five*
cases gave him a more substantial basis for his propositions.

A thicket of theory and assertion mars the essay—Ernest Jones could not match Freud's literary flair. He posed the question: "What differentiates the development of homosexual from that of heterosexual women?" In the "normal" process the girl renounced her erotic attachment to her father and transferred it to "more accessible objects" that would complete an "adult plan" of coitus, pregnancy, and motherhood. Instead, Jones found that his homosexual female patients alternated between same-sex "potency" and paralyzing fear of *aphanisis*—the loss of all sexual pleasure. "*Faced with aphanisis . . . they must renounce either their [born] sex or their incest.*" According to Jones, girls who guarded the erotic tie to the father and identified with him were renouncing their sex and therefore developed "neurotic" lesbian tendencies. Jones further divided the homosexual women he treated into two groups: those who envied and sought the status and power of men—he was thinking disapprovingly of feminists—and those who pursued relationships with women as a means of enjoying "gratification . . . at the hand of an unseen man (the father incorporated into themselves)." Given that at least three of his patients were daughters of wealthy men without whom education, travel, and other freedoms would have been difficult, his observations about their dread of paternal "disapproval" and "desertion" seem more obvious than insightful.

It is impossible to imagine Judge Bingham absorbing such material. One family member said he was too squeamish about sex and bodily functions even to discuss where the cream in his coffee came from. Did Henrietta wade through it and agree with Jones, as Mina seemed to, or think it "revolutionary," as Eleanor Chilton said she did? Whether or not Henrietta recognized herself in his lesbian taxonomy, her "gratitude and devotion" toward Jones was real and she credited her doctor with her sense of well-being, such as it was. His claim to have "brought her from women to men" strained credibility, however, and the essay did not touch on his effort to reorient patients' sexual behavior.

Ignoring such a scholarly précis was not difficult, but Robert Worth Bingham surely took in the facts surrounding the breakthrough lesbian novel that was published in 1928. At the outset of Radclyffe Hall's *The Well of Loneliness*, Sir Philip, an English country gentleman, dotes on his unusual daughter, whom he named Stephen, taught to ride, and whose "inversion" he compassionately observes over the years. The child's mother blames Sir Philip for the young woman's aberrancy—her masculine physique, her abhorrence of women's clothes, and her rejection of an eligible suitor. When her father dies, Stephen discovers the German psychiatrist Richard von Krafft-Ebing's *Psychopathia Sexualis* and other treatises on "abnormal" sexuality, interlined with Sir Philip's handwritten notes. Her father had understood her. But not her mother, who banishes Stephen upon discovering her affair with a married American woman. After this, Stephen, wearing clothing fashioned by a men's tailor, seizes love and an expatriate domestic life in Paris with a member of a female ambulance unit. As Hall conceived of it, her protagonist bore a tragic burden. The aim of the book was to stir sympathy and call for justice for those "afflicted" with an inborn homosexual identity.

The Well of Loneliness disturbed and fascinated contemporary readers, though Henrietta may have found Virginia Woolf's *Orlando*, published the same year, more enjoyable. The title character of that novella changes from male to female over historical eras and is the more popular book today. But *The Well of Loneliness*, with its direct plea for tolerance, spoke to the personal and social plight of sexual nonconformists. Hall based her argument on the theory that inversion was congenital, a position Freud dismissed. But if such a condition could not be blamed on the individual, or even their upbringing, if it were simply a naturally occurring variation that society had rendered a curse, then condemnation, legal suppression, imprisonment, and "punishing treatments" were acts of cruelty.

An international legal battle over obscenity and artistic freedom surrounded *The Well of Loneliness*. Hall had won the James Tait Black Memorial Prize for a previous novel, and within months of release, *The Well* had been widely reviewed, censured by moralists, defended by leading British writers, dropped by its British publisher, printed in Paris, subjected to seizure at the port of Dover, and raided in bookstores. Courts ruled that it was "disgusting" and "prejudicial to the morals of the community" and banned it in Britain. The American press followed the scandal and its cross-Atlantic iteration. Although slated for release by A. A. Knopf, adverse publicity led that house to conclude that "no American publisher could now handle it except as pornography."

Covici-Friede, an upstart U.S. firm, published *The Well of Loneliness* in late 1928, anticipating a challenge from the infamous New York Society for the Suppression of Vice. This "serious novel on a forbidden theme" (*Book Review Digest*) about a "congenital invert" (*New York Herald Tribune*) generated a great deal of attention. By the time the publishers came before the court, the book had sold more than twenty thousand copies. Prominent American writers, including Upton Sinclair and F. Scott Fitzgerald, wrote in support of its publication. In a surprising ruling in April 1929, about the time Lady Oxford and Henrietta discussed interior decoration, a New York court ruled in the publisher's favor. Nine days later, Henrietta's ship docked in New York. The next day a full-page ad ran in *The New York Times* celebrating "The Most Controversial Book of the Century—Suppressed in England and Vindicated by an American Court."

The photo of Hall that was published in countless papers reinforced an image of lesbians as "man-like" in clothing, appearance, erotic desire, and ambition. In fact, Hall's story depicted femme types, as well, but alleged they were often "normal" or at least bisexual, besides which they could "pass" in the wider society without drawing attention. Henrietta certainly played with gender stereotypes. Feather boas and the mules she wore for Carrington's sketches pointed in one direction; cummerbunds and the man's suit, hat, and cane she donned on the Promenade des Anglais in Nice pointed in another. She usually styled her hair long enough to tuck a few pieces behind the ear, but in the late 1920s she cut it very close to the head like a "marquee vamp."

That was a look Henrietta's father despised, and late in the decade he made his expectations clear. After the breakup with John Houseman and Peggy Lehmann's repeated stays at Guthrie Castle, Robert Worth Bingham could not pretend away his daughter's interest in women or blame it on Mina Kirstein Curtiss. Freud's focus on the psychic ramifications of early relationships between parents and children upset Edwardians like Bingham, but if he had studied the works of Krafft-Ebing and Havelock Ellis, he might have felt relieved of responsibility for her condition.

In any case, he surely recognized at some level that Henrietta's lesbian relationships made it less likely that she would marry and leave his orbit. The Judge relaxed considerably during this period and gave his implicit blessing to her "close friendship" with Miss Lehmann. But even if he and other people knew or thought they knew about his daughter's sexual predilections, Bingham demanded that her clothing and public demeanor not prove it. Plausible deniability was essential. Henrietta must never outwardly affiliate with a group Radclyffe Hall's protagonist called "maimed and ugly" perversities of God's creation. "It nearly broke her heart when [her father] jumped on her" about her attire, her friend Sophie remembered. "She got so that she dressed" in "a skirt, always a skirt," except of course when she was riding to hounds, which meant jodhpurs and spit-shined black boots.

12

SPEED SIX

The contentious father-daughter dance that had dominated the 1920s settled into a calmer routine toward the decade's end. Both parties saved face; Henrietta was given personal latitude and her father received regular visits that restored his sense of intimacy. They would spend about six weeks each year together, usually during the late spring. She would arrive with fanfare in time for the Derby, and during the annual shooting parties in Scotland each August or September, she was also an integral part of the planning for his large groups of houseguests. Miss Overman, her father's secretary, noted how well the publisher seemed upon his return from Guthrie Castle in 1929. His health was not consistently strong during these years, and seeing Henrietta always did him "a lot of good."

Black Friday in October 1929 and the ensuing free fall in the stock market had little immediate impact on the Binghams. The Judge's portfolio shrank dramatically, but he could afford the losses. The greater adjustment for the family that year was that Barry was in Louisville writing news headlines at the radio station his father had established in 1922. The novel Barry produced in Switzerland and Asheville in the eighteen months after his 1928 graduation from Harvard went into a drawer. He couldn't bring himself to alter the ending, as a potential publisher requested. His father had given him a grace period, but when literary success was not forthcoming, Barry kept his promise to try his hand at journalism. The demands on him at work were not heavy, and when Henrietta's ship docked in New York, he went to meet her. They lingered in the city, seeing her friends and visiting favorite speakeasies. In Louisville, Barry remarked to his girlfriend that "Father has gotten so pleased with having Henrietta at home, that" even though he seldom drank "he opens up some marvelous Rhine wine" each night at dinner. The wine didn't alter the fact that Aleen rivaled "the chloroform sponge to produce complete unconsciousness."

There may have been fewer dinners together than the Judge would have liked. Rather than staying with him and Aleen, Henrietta was Barry's guest at a Tuscan-style cottage next door, which Bingham had recently purchased. It was the ideal *garçonnière* and Henrietta assumed responsibility for all domestic and social arrangements. It was heaven for Barry. When possible, they ate at "Fincastle," as the house was called, and joked about "sever[ing] all ties with the family." Over Derby, they hosted their "blotto cousin" Laurence from Chicago with "a swell married lady." The couple drank "a quart of whiskey" and they "discussed sex in all its manifestations, and stayed up til four o'clock in the morning." Henrietta's luggage included gifts—for Barry a kinky, limited-edition illustrated volume titled *De Sade: being a series of wounds inflicted with brush and pen, upon Sadistic Wolves garbed in Masochists' Wool.* Barry amused her with the sheet music for "Baby Eyes" and "Midnight Melody," maudlin songs he wrote in collaboration with WHAS Radio's hillbilly host, "Happy" Jack Turner. All this fun contrasted thuddingly with the volume Mina sent Henrietta that spring. *Olive, Cypress, and Palm: An Anthology of Love and Death* contained poems Mina selected over her two years of mourning Harry. The compendium is so weighted with grief it almost hurts to lift it.

To people at home, Henrietta's English life seemed willfully odd and unanchored. Her unease mounted in spite of Barry's and Edie Callahan's efforts, and she was drinking heavily to get through the weeks.

One evening in the powder room at the Louisville Country Club, Henrietta made a reckless and unwelcome pass at a fetching debutante. The girl tore out of the bathroom and leaned over the grand staircase and shouted, "Henrietta Bingham just kissed me on the lips!"

Such an exclamation was not forgotten easily, and such behavior (which would not cause a stir at a "lower Bloomsbury" party) could not be overlooked in Louisville. Henrietta announced an earlier-than-scheduled return to England. She talked of taking Peggy Lehmann to see Berlin's cabarets and soak up the midnight sun in Sweden. Barry and Edie, caught up in her plans, arranged to join the pair. With sadness, the Judge wrote to his sister in Asheville, without mentioning the illicit country club kiss, of course. He had counted on making the Atlantic crossing with Henrietta and having her at his side for several months in a row, "but she has made up her mind and I can't do anything about it."

On July 13, 1930, Henrietta walked into Bentley Motors' London showroom and drove off in a six-and-a-half-liter Speed Six Mulliner drophead coupe, winner of the previous year's twenty-four-hour Le Mans road race. It was a wildly powerful machine; perhaps it distracted from her dependence on the man whose money had paid for it. In short order the boot was packed with suitcases and supplies, and Henrietta and Peggy were off to Stockholm, attracted by a grand exhibition of modern design. Following that, they installed themselves at a Baltic resort. Sweden was "the greatest fun," Peggy told her sister Rosamond; the country was full of perfect blondes, replete with good food, and amazingly free in its social mores. Peggy's brother, John Lehmann, then working for Leonard and Virginia Woolf at the Hogarth Press, forwarded their mail from London as they made their way south, via Berlin, with its open transvestite balls and lesbian bars that went well beyond Bloomsbury's experiments. (Two years later, Peggy would return to Berlin seeking German film roles.) In Munich she and Henrietta attended a vast avant-garde production called *Totenmal*, or *Call of the Dead*, mounted by the lesbian dancer Mary Wigman with over-the-top lights, dances, unaccompanied choirs, and masked men reading the letters of soldiers lost in the Great War. It was a staggering work of "peace propaganda" even as the Nazi party closed in on political control. The couple was deliriously happy in Munich. "Henrietta," Peggy wrote to Rosamond, "has been adorable and the best of travel companions (and often unspeakably funny!)."

The party doubled when Edie Callahan and twenty-four-year-old Barry joined them. The Speed Six easily mounted the Alps. But Peggy grumbled that Americans, grouped together, resembled "a lot of screaming peacocks." She knew she sounded like a snob, yet it came as a relief when "time and money" cut short their journey before they reached Vienna and Budapest. They would spend a few days in Paris and then cross the Channel. The Binghams were on their way to Scotland; Henrietta and Barry could not slip that noose, but Peggy agreed to join them and urged Rosamond and Wogan to come along. The shooting was good, and she added to Rosamond, "You'd love the Judge."

Peggy's show of enthusiasm for Judge Bingham, whom she had first met at Guthrie three years earlier, marked a departure from the antagonistic stance of Henrietta's other friends and lovers toward a man who seemed at best overbearing and narcissistic and at worst Mephistophelean. In bringing Miss Lehmann once more into the house party, Henrietta asserted a relationship that was both unmistakable and unmentionable. On this point, she and Robert Worth Bingham had come to terms.

One person who did not appreciate Barry and Henrietta's gay travels through Europe and the British Isles in 1931 was Mary Clifford Caperton. The blonde Virginia-born classics scholar had won a prestigious postgraduate fellowship to the American School in Athens after graduating from Radcliffe in 1928, and after that worked as an editorial assistant at Houghton-Mifflin in Boston. Mary had been Barry's sweetheart through most of their time in Cambridge and yet no proposal had resulted. She worried he was slipping away.

Mary understood that to have Barry she must show him a life that was better, somehow, than the one his sister offered. Henrietta was Barry's boon companion, his supporter and protector in a world he often felt didn't understand him. Mary could not compete directly with Henrietta's "curious glamour." Ultimately, Henrietta became the antihero in their epic romance—at least in Mary's telling. This proceeded gradually (but not coincidentally) as Judge Bingham shifted his vision of the family's future toward a scenario that privileged not his daughter but his younger son.

The first thing Mary Caperton knew about Henrietta was how intimate (one of her favorite words) brother and sister were. For a long time in Cambridge she hadn't the "vaguest idea" of Barry's "situation or home life." But he drove a Stutz and spent holidays abroad, while she, hailing from a proud and penurious Richmond clan, washed her own sweaters and attended college on scholarship. She claimed ignorance of the Bingham newspapers in Kentucky and the scandal over Barry's stepmother's death. He did tell her about his persecutions at Middlesex and the lark he had with Henrietta and Edie Callahan, running the Wilderness Road Book Shop in Louisville. Barry loved theater and books; he also concocted gin in his Harvard bathtub. Weekends meant finding a good place to drink and good people to drink with, and he liked driving a carload from Harvard twenty miles outside of Boston to the parties thrown by an older friend of Henrietta's. The scene was a bit wild for Mary—the married hostess overserved them and "made up to some of the girls." Mary coped with the heavy drinking by periodically retiring to the powder room to vomit. The hostess left her alone, she said, seeing she was "obviously not available" for that kind of experiment.

Mary's first encounter with Henrietta came at a humiliating moment, which may have contributed to the anxiety she felt about this sophisticated older person. In the spring of 1928, Judge Bingham loaned his yacht to his children with the understanding that Barry would escort Aleen's niece to the Harvard-Yale Regatta. Feeling left out, Mary allowed a Boston eye doctor she dated to escort her to New London, but at their hotel his importunate demands led her to pack her bag and seek refuge with the Binghams. Henrietta was unofficial captain of the ninety-three-foot craft, and Mary threw herself on the mercy of this "mysterious, fascinating creature" who ran with such a daring European crowd.

A few months later, after graduation, Barry sailed to Europe with Henrietta, Edie, and his Harvard classmate Francis Parks. Mary was traveling that summer, too, seeing Europe for the first time before reporting to Athens for her fellowship. Barry, Edie, and Francis took Mary along with them to Paris, where they danced and drank at Ada "Bricktop" Smith's gay-friendly nightclub in Pigalle. The redheaded, freckled American singer and dancer had performed with Florence Mills and Edith Wilson, and given the Prince of Wales lessons on how to dance the Black Bottom. She was Josephine Baker's Parisian mentor and sometime lover, and knew Henrietta well. Bricktop called Barry "my honey boy."

Over the next months, Barry drifted from Mary, as he wrote his novel and then repaired to Kentucky to start work at the radio station. He took the job lightly at first, referring to his colleagues as "nice tacky people in spectacles who are embarrassingly obliging to me," and chuckled "over the mannerisms of the 'artists' who come in to broadcast." In the fall of 1930, he started as a cub police reporter at the newspaper and found, to his surprise, that he enjoyed it. He began showing an interest in management, and he appealed to Henrietta for support when their father hatched a plan to purchase the *Courier*'s chief competitor, the *Louisville Herald-Post*, and operate it as a Republican organ. Henrietta had backed Barry up—they both thought it would end in embarrassment.

Not long after, personal loss jerked Barry into a new sense of reality. An automobile crash killed Francis Parks; the aspiring writer had a letter from Barry in his pocket when he died. After the funeral, Barry wrote to Mary that Parks "never had to grow out of . . . the college phase." Had Barry? He seemed to want to, and in early 1931, he took Mary to a Manhattan speakeasy and proposed. They spent the night at the apartment of Jeannette Young, Henrietta's friend from Smith.

Robert Worth Bingham spared no expense for the wedding, held in Richmond in June 1931. Aleen assumed responsibility for the out-of-town guest list and china patterns. The Depression had thrown 20 percent of the country's population out of work, but the previous decade had rewarded Robert Worth Bingham handsomely. *The Courier-Journal* and *Louisville Times*'s combined daily circulation had doubled to more than 200,000, while the Sunday edition had almost tripled to 160,000. When the Bank of Kentucky and Louisville Trust Company failed in

December 1930, thousands of citizens lost their "Christmas savings" accounts, and the Judge offered to refund each depositor half his or her account. He gave out more than $200,000.

As Barry's nuptial day approached, Henrietta scrambled to sort out her feelings. Though her bond with Barry was potent, family weddings conjured loss, pain, and distrust. She wanted Barry to be happy, yet the idea of "stomp[ing] up the aisle" of the church as Mary's old-maid bridesmaid was unbearable. She cabled her regrets to the Capertons without giving a definite reason for her absence. Mary was relieved. She imagined Henrietta detained by some new "Hunting Field romance." She was so "decided," Mary told Barry, that they ought not "urge her and worry her again." Barry would not hear of anything so "unsatisfactory." He cabled Henrietta that she absolutely must be there with him. She did appear, and hosted a party for the bride and her attendants.

After the wedding, the Judge took Henrietta to New York and escorted her aboard the *Aquitania*. Posing on deck, Henrietta looked proper in a dark suit and white gloves and white corsage, with her wrist linked through her father's arm. Consulting Dr. Jones and seeing Barry's union may have prompted a renewed foray into traditional matchmaking, for when Judge Bingham and Aleen arrived in England later that summer, she introduced them to a British army officer named John Starling. His father was a respected physiologist, but Jones, writing to Mina, judged the man "very far from . . . another Harry."

Mary and Barry spent the summer of 1931 honeymooning through Europe, and after a Scandinavian cruise, they made their way to the French Riviera. To Mary's dismay, Barry summoned his sister. Starling came with her. It's possible they were engaged—from the Côte d'Azur, Starling wrote to Judge Bingham, thanking him for his "complete understanding" and "tremendous encouragement." "I have great hopes for the future," he wrote. He complimented Bingham's prizewinning hunting dogs (they had been shipped to England for grouse season) and looked forward to shooting partridge together in September.

In Venice, the foursome made their base at Harry's Bar, a gem with a few tables and natural light during the day. Venice was "crawling with homosexuals," Mary recalled, and at Harry's one night, Starling was

Henrietta with Barry and Mary Bingham, Italy, 1931

propositioned. The captain's violent response, shouting threats to "flatten the bugger," left them all upset. The next day, seemingly to make up for the disturbance, Starling presented Henrietta with a jeweled bracelet—which Barry discovered he had charged to the Bingham hotel bill. Henrietta dropped him and the party broke up.

Barry had no thought of Henrietta leaving, though, and the new Mrs. Bingham couldn't help resenting it. Somewhere in Italy the three of them posed before a rustic fountain. Barry, tanned and smiling, sat between the women, at precisely the same distance from each and touching neither. Henrietta wore clothes she couldn't be seen in at home, white wide-legged trousers and men's-style espadrilles, a pale shirt, a shining white silk men's tie, and a black skullcap, and leaned coolly against the rim of the fountain while Mary and Barry perched on its edge, like teenagers. Mary's bare legs are clenched together against the camera's gaze, her pocketbook set carefully at her feet.

Henrietta possessed an alchemical ability to conjure adventures and intimate companionship, but her talents were gaining no purchase outside lovemaking and riding to hounds. She had produced no books, no

plays besides the incomplete and unproduced "Shadows," no new the-
atrical or cultural journal, and of course no husband or children. Meanwhile, children were something that Mary eagerly offered to Barry.
The newlyweds settled in Louisville across the lawn from Melcombe.
Mary's bounden duty and delight was to make her husband feel adored
and at the center of something noble and satisfying. (It was a skill she
hammered into her daughters a generation later.) Barry was assuming
responsibilities his sister, endowed with equal intelligence, had run
from. Within six months of his marriage, he was writing occasional
editorials. Robert was "a miserable disappointment" and by this time of
little consequence in the family, but Henrietta maintained a strong
presence. The Judge "really thought Henrietta could be prepared to run
the newspapers," Mary recalled, shaking her head, but she "never could
have set herself to that kind of work."

Henrietta's younger brother had married a brilliant and unusually
strong-minded woman who would go to battle for him—mostly in ways
he liked (for he hated conflict) and sometimes in ways he didn't. Mary
was astute enough to perceive that if Barry proved himself, he could
have almost everything his father had amassed since his days as a
teacher at the Bingham School. She didn't win over Aleen—who lost
her own daughter to tuberculosis in 1931 and considered Mary's giving
birth within a year of the wedding unseemly. But Barry's new wife
delighted the Judge. He applauded her "absolutely normal" pregnancy.
"I admire and respect her as much as I love her," he told Henrietta.
The new bond between father and son never bridged their differences
in personality or the abandonment Barry experienced as a child, but the
Judge found it more gratifying than he ever imagined to watch Barry
"take hold," get married, and have "nice children." One month before
Mary gave birth, the publisher took out a large life insurance policy on
Barry, and when Mary went into labor in May 1932 as her husband lay
ill with scarlet fever, Judge Bingham drove her to the hospital. They
named the baby Robert Worth Bingham III. "My father had the high-
est expectations of Henrietta. He thought she was brilliant," Barry
later observed. But he and Mary were relieving her from the succes-
sion. Perhaps there was freedom in that.

13

MISS AMERICA

*H*enrietta meanwhile endured a series of blows that included the increasingly dire economic crisis and the unwinding of her relationship with Peggy. She had spent Christmas 1931 with the Lehmanns, where the family theatricals involved John comically cross-dressing as their American-born mother. For Henrietta, the cheer came aided by quantities of alcohol. Peggy noted her sweetness and the "largesse and generosity" she brought to the holiday, but none of the Lehmanns could miss the way she applied "herself with religious and fanatical fervor to all bottles."

The New Year brought bleak news. In early 1932, Lytton Strachey died following months of unexplained suffering from what doctors later identified as stomach cancer. He was fifty-one. The loss sank Carrington like a stone. Facing life without Lytton was unbearable. Six weeks afterward, despite the vigilance of Ralph Partridge, Stephen Tomlin, David Garnett, and other friends, Carrington put on Lytton's violet dressing gown and shot herself in her Ham Spray House bedroom. It was a terrible end to a rich and troubled life.

Henrietta felt increasingly unmoored—she had seen how love was easily torn away, even from Mina and Carrington, who had painstakingly crafted homes and cultivated partnerships. Foxhunting offered Henrietta a distraction and a separate community of sportsmen and -women, but she suffered a serious concussion when her horse took the bit and bolted, unseating her on a paved road. Peggy's appraisal of her life could easily have expressed Henrietta's own: "getting uglier and more lonesome every moment. Always falling in love with the wrong people. It is small consolation that they return the compliment." Peggy at least had her acting (although roles were few) and she had managed to write a subtle and affecting novel, *But Wisdom Lingers*, which Methuen published in 1932. Secretly in mourning over her female lover's early death, the protagonist flees to an isolated Cornish village, pursued by a mystified male admirer. Few copies sold. Even fragile Eleanor Chilton had published fiction, poetry, and critical essays. Henrietta determined to do something, and aimed for a spot in the clerical pool at the British Foreign Office (higher positions were closed to women). She enrolled in a training program to learn speed typing and shorthand.

Personal disappointments aside, the Great Depression gripped the transatlantic world. The stock market crash of late 1929 initiated a long, steep slide that only reached bottom in mid-1932. Citing losses and suspended dividends from the securities he had acquired from Mary Lily's estate, Henrietta's father cut her allowance from $950 to $500 per month. He put his yacht up for sale, and reduced his servants' wages by 20 percent. *Courier-Journal* employees saw pay cuts of 10 percent. John Houseman—who had ridden the crest of the commodities market, breaking ranks with Continental Grain to form his own firm, Oceanic Grain Corporation—was bankrupt by 1930 and was counted among the millions of unemployed. His marriage to a glamorous stage actress named Zita Johann was spiraling downward. Shantytowns sprang up, including one in Central Park.

New York's popular governor Franklin Roosevelt took an activist approach to the emergency. Robert Worth Bingham knew him from the Democratic convention of 1928, at which Roosevelt nominated Al Smith. Three years into Herbert Hoover's presidency, the publisher wrote to Roosevelt, calling him "the best hope, not merely" for Democrats, "but for our country." After three Republican administrations, economically strapped American voters were expected to embrace a strong candidate from the opposing party, and Bingham pledged to FDR "all of my energy and every resource I have." Voters in Kentucky and the rest of the South needed reassurance that the Harvard-educated northerner, called "pink" by some for supporting organized labor, wasn't a demagogue, and Bingham worked the back rooms to line up Kentucky's Democratic delegation in advance of the 1932 Chicago convention. This time, Henrietta was enthusiastic about joining his efforts and helped to rally a group of FDR-friendly publishers. The FDR drumbeat coincided with what Peggy Lehmann called "a complete change" for Henrietta. While in the United States that summer, she suspended her aspirations to a Foreign Office position and remained stateside through the election, working for the campaign, partnering with her father's project and hoping for a political solution to the national crisis.

A different sort of hope was also at work in Henrietta's reversal. In 1931, the actress Hope Williams had signed an eight-by-ten publicity shot "For Henrietta" that showed a gamine blonde with an Eton crop, looking as if she had jumped off the set of *Peter Pan*. The playwright Philip Barry (whose 1939 play *The Philadelphia Story* starred Katharine Hepburn in her landmark role) first spotted Williams as a New York City society wife in an amateur performance and gave her a lead part in *Holiday* (1928), which he wrote especially for her. That year Williams separated from her husband, a well-off physician, for reasons of "incompatibility." Her Broadway appearances for Barry led to other roles, including one opposite the comedian Jimmy Durante in Cole Porter's 1930 revue, *The New Yorkers*. Hepburn, a frequent understudy, lifted from the older actress her trademark swagger and "bantering nonchalance." The younger actress admitted to stealing "a great deal from Hope. She was the first fascinating personality from that period, 1929 to 1932, which wasn't really ready for her," adding, in a code that probably referred to her sexuality, "she was a woman who blossomed with a little more than she was supposed to." Hope's rise brought her to the attention of Tallulah Bankhead, as well. A longtime friend of Tallulah's recalled that in 1931, "all the top-drawer lesbians—social ones— were making a play for Hope . . . and that led to quite a long affair."

Hope Williams, 1931

Peggy Lehmann minced no words at the news of Henrietta's attachment to the star. She told her sister that her ex was "living in Homo-sin with Tallulah's best girl." Amid the election-year campaigning, Hope and Henrietta devised a western vacation adapted to the lyrics of Cole Porter's "Let's Fly Away," which Hope had performed onstage and could no doubt sing in her sleep. In the Absaroka Range, near the showman Buffalo Bill Cody's settlement and the Yellowstone preserve, Hope hosted Henrietta and Edie Callahan on a backcountry horse-packing trip. They camped in meadows, hiked peaks, and angled for trout in mountain streams. The small party had its own wrangler and cook, and menus featured fresh-caught fish and champagne.

Henrietta brought home a heavy silver cowgirl belt, and her snapshots show Hope duded up in rolled jeans, a beaded leather jacket, and a man's cowboy hat. In England, Peggy Lehmann admitted to "ride-'em-cowboy" fantasies. "I should think," she wrote to Henrietta, "it was the ideal country for bringing out most any girl's subconscious wish for spectacular masculinity."

Many of Henrietta's friends and lovers—Peggy Lehmann, Tallulah Bankhead, Hope Williams, Bea Lillie, and Katharine "Kit" Cornell—belonged to a transatlantic lesbian and bisexual theater set whose roots reached back to Isadora Duncan and Eva Le Gallienne. During the twenties, when a "riotously promiscuous 'lesbian chic'" flourished in select crowds, the theater- and later film-going public could be teased with the possibility of same-sex female relationships as long as no one named it outright. Greta Garbo and Marlene Dietrich took the game to new heights with audiences in the 1930s, but hard times brought a resurgence of traditional social mores, and the relative freedom of these actresses with regard to sexual identification dramatically diminished. Silence reigned and the performers took immense care to cover their tracks. Hope Williams was always intensely private, but (under an open sky) in the summer of 1932 Henrietta had reason to feel happy. Hope had money and success, and promising roles ahead. As the election neared, Williams rehearsed for a play set in Paris and written to capitalize on the expatriate craze. The script was by the *New Yorker* humorist S. J. Perelman—his recent credits included the screenplay for the Marx Brothers' film *Horse Feathers*—and his wife, Laura, and Williams led the cast as an American fashion writer.

Henrietta bounced between Hope and the Judge, who spent much of his time after Labor Day in New York, coordinating with the campaign from his apartment at the Park Lane Hotel. Eleanor Roosevelt took tea with Bingham and gave assurances of victory over Hoover. The connections he'd made during his cooperative agriculture campaign gave Bingham standing among rural constituencies, which he fully exploited. Many in the Roosevelt camp felt that not only the welfare of Americans but the broader world might depend on the 1932 election. Peggy Lehmann wrote to Henrietta grimly from Dresden, predicting "a sad future for all and sundry. What an age to live in!" Henrietta helped her father to prepare for an Associated Press board meeting on election coverage protocol, as well as the candidate's October visit to Louisville. FDR's train rolled into town carrying both Kentucky senators, the mayor, and the governor—a remarkable show of bipartisan unity, for these dignitaries had often been political rivals and had not always met Bingham's sniff test. *The Courier-Journal* estimated that more than fifty thousand onlookers lined the streets for his motorcade and Henrietta joined five hundred Democrats at a luncheon before his speech.

Talk of a reward for the Louisville publisher began well before the election. After FDR's success at the polls, the Binghams and Roosevelts went south to their respective Georgia retreats—the Kentuckians to the quail-hunting plantation the Judge owned near Albany and the president-elect to Warm Springs. They met at "The Little White House," as it came to be known. Roosevelt cited Bingham for having worked "hard and faithfully," and though Bingham had long insisted that he had no thought of holding public office, he got himself on the list of possible nominees for secretary of state. Some of his advisors felt a cabinet post would compromise his "independence" as a publisher, indeed they worried that any presidential appointment would damage his stature as a newspaper owner, and, in the end, Senator Cordell Hull of Tennessee was chosen for that post. But Barry believed another premier diplomatic spot was the best fit of all. The ambassadorship to the Court of St. James's united his father's ambitions for public honor with his love of the English. And it felt natural after the social and press connections he had developed during his many sojourns to the United Kingdom.

What made the London opportunity even more desirable was its confluence with Henrietta's course. Roosevelt's campaign revived not just a nation mired in hopelessness, but also Bob Bingham's dream of pursuing the public good with his daughter at his side. His son would manage the papers in Louisville (with close guidance from the top executives) and Henrietta would be doing something equally great— with him. Her deep social knowledge would help him. Her presence would comfort him. Urgent queries meanwhile arrived from Peggy

Lehmann. "What do you do with yourself all day—and night?" Was Henrietta "rich, poor, happy, miserable, in-love, out-of-love, analysed, unanalysed?"

The alternating suffocation and fear of abandonment that had dogged Henrietta since her mother's death came to a head once more. She had spent years resisting a life swept up in her father's world. But she also realized that working as a secretary or in a prison system would be odd indeed, given her lavish allowance—and possibly unseemly. Her resistance remained, and as her father was lobbying the president-elect, she seesawed back to John Houseman.

His grain business gone, Jack returned to literature, and playwriting in particular. His income had dropped from tens of thousands to a mere few hundred dollars a year. He sold his Deco furniture and moved to a farmhouse an aunt rented in New City, north of Manhattan. Houseman began to translate and write plays, including one with Lewis Galantière, a banker at the Federal Reserve who later translated Saint-Exupéry. During the very cold and isolated winter of 1932–1933, Jack met Henrietta in the city. He berated himself much as he had five years before—he was "an awful, bloody fool" to have let her go, though now they could experience "the increased fire of rediscovery, the deep delights of recognition." The hour they spent in Pennsylvania Station before she returned to Louisville to manage the "political situation" was for him "sublime, unalloyed ecstasy." "I continue to love your eyes, and to be with you, within reach of your hand, is a joy which leaves me, when it is over, limp and sick." "To believe" in the possibility of a future together was not, he assured her, "to be pinned down!"

But who was pinning down whom? Much later in life, Houseman saw 1933 as Henrietta's turning point. The London post was apparently the Judge's for the taking, but according to Houseman he said, "Daughter, I'm not going to accept the position unless you come with me." In Henrietta's lover's mind, it was psychological blackmail. With her, and only with her, would her father gain an honor that would cap his career.

She hesitated.

Over lunch with Jack marriage came up—again.

"Look, I know it didn't work before but would you marry me?"

According to Houseman, it was Henrietta who asked. Marriage would have kept her in the States, called her father's bluff, and placed her in the midst of the theater world she loved. (Jack's next project was right up her *Theatre Arts* alley, directing an all-black cast for the premiere of *Four Saints in Three Acts*, composed by Virgil Thomson with a libretto by Gertrude Stein.) Houseman later wondered whether she had been suggesting a "lavender marriage" for social and professional protection. He wasn't sure, but in his telling, his response left no room for discussion.

"Absolutely not."

But it was Houseman who wrote of the "deep delights" of recapturing what they had together. Henrietta kept that letter to the end of her life. It is plausible that in the heat of rediscovery, and witnessing her uncertainty and fear about following her father, Houseman was the one who made the proposal. Whichever the case, he remembered her having "a bad time deciding" whether to yield to "the temptation to be the ambassador's wife—he was married but she was the one who was to be the top girl." If Jack had posed the question, Henrietta had a choice, but if Houseman had in fact turned her down, Henrietta's feelings must have been grievously mixed as Roosevelt's inauguration neared.

It may have been during this period of strain that Henrietta risked her reputation—and her father's. At a Louisville Junior League ball she clumsily tried to seduce a younger woman whose prominent family owned the Four Roses bourbon distillery. Miss Jones did not holler to the assembly as the girl at the Louisville Country Club had, but gossip spread. That such behavior could cause Henrietta to be expelled from her father's entourage, or damage his chances at the Court of St. James's, may have been the point.

One week into his term the president announced his diplomatic selections. Henrietta had acceded to her father's entreaties. Another publisher, Josephus Daniels of Raleigh's *News and Observer*, won quick approval from the Senate Foreign Relations Committee to represent the United States in Mexico. When Bingham's file came before the committee, the chair put a hold on the nomination, citing his "anti-American attitude" with respect to British war debts. Bingham had promoted a policy of debt relief, which would assist agricultural interests by increasing exports. But British debt forgiveness had little support in America. Then darker allegations surfaced. Abraham Flexner, a distinguished former Louisvillian who founded the Institute for Advanced Study at Princeton University, contacted the committee, claiming to have evidence of "scandal and disgrace" that made Robert Worth Bingham unfit for the appointment.

Applause and approving shouts punctuated a speech impugning the nominee's character by Representative Albert C. May of Kentucky. May called "Robert Worthless Bingham" a "slacker" who refused to serve in the war (this was unfair) and whose wife's "mysterious" death provided the "filthy lucre" to buy a newspaper that May, a Democrat, accused of playing "political harlot of the Republican party." Henrietta's father maintained what he hoped would appear to be an honorable silence, but the allegations floated for days before the Foreign Relations Committee reconvened.

At the same time, Dr. Ravitch, the dermatologist who had left Louisville in the wake of Mary Lily's death, and whose own career had suffered for it, was sending disquieting letters and demanding money. "I was told several times you had a habit of forgetting friends," he wrote ominously from Los Angeles. "I am really sorry that I ever consented to do for you what I did." Bingham turned to FDR's speechwriter, Raymond Moley, to save his nomination. Moley's counterattack included a statement from Dr. Hugh Young on Johns Hopkins letterhead citing Mary Lily's alcoholism; an offer from one of the pathologists asked to examine her exhumed organs to testify that no poison had been detected; placating committee members with hundreds of endorsements; and placing both Kentucky senators before the committee on Bingham's behalf. In the end, Bingham was approved without fully reviving the details of Mary Lily's death, but no amount of time could erase the old blot—Roosevelt himself gleefully called his ambassador "my favourite murderer," though presumably never to his face.

Growing as anxious and furious as he had been twenty years earlier when his mother-in-law challenged his honor, Bingham collapsed. Even Henrietta could not prevent it. Young had him hospitalized at

Johns Hopkins. After several weeks' recuperation, he boarded the brand-new cabin liner *Washington* bound for England with Henrietta and Aleen. The former New York governor Al Smith presided over a dockside ceremony in which forty-eight young women released homing pigeons, one for each state. Dozens of alternating American and Union Jack flags decorated the pier at Plymouth when they landed. A battery of cameras captured Henrietta shoulder to shoulder with her father, beaming like the sun.

Two days later London's *Daily Sketch* pictured her standing erect alongside a broad walk in Hyde Park as though reviewing a string of blanketed Thoroughbreds being led by their grooms to the auction house, Tattersalls. MISS AMERICA LOOKING OVER LONDON read the headline. In the photo spread, the ambassador's daughter towered above a small image of Bingham and a slightly larger portrait of his cocker spaniel, Dandy, then stuck in quarantine. A few days later, she watched her father's coach enter the gates at St. James's Palace to present his credentials to King George V. Next came her presentation at court, wearing a body-skimming pale pink crinkled crepe gown. A studio portrait for the occasion was widely published. Candid shots showed her hunting in Buckinghamshire and hacking in Hyde Park. The park was just

Ambassador Bingham with Aleen and Henrietta
arriving in England, 1933

across the street from Prince's Gate, J. P. Morgan's former London home, which served as both embassy and ambassadorial residence. The British papers loved that she rode to hounds and cited her familiarity with British and American theater. Hope Williams visited at the embassy, and the whole family went to a play starring Peggy Lehmann as Emily Brontë. Ceremonies piled on one another, and on July 4, 1933, the ambassador's "chic young daughter" greeted 2,500 guests for the traditional Independence Day reception in the embassy garden. She was "just keen about everything," Aleen said, attending receptions at Parliament and serving tea to the ambassador of Argentina.

Or was she? Tracing Henrietta's life through the late 1920s and early 1930s is challenging—almost all her correspondence was destroyed. But a letter Henrietta wrote to Stephen Tomlin coincided with her 1933 reentry to London. Following Henrietta's departure for New York in 1925, Tommy and Carrington (possibly brought together by their heartbreak) had a brief sexual relationship. In 1927 he married Lytton's niece, the model and novelist Julia Strachey, but the union was effectively

"Miss America" in London, 1933

over by the time Henrietta returned to England, done in by infidelity, heavy drinking, and depression. The losses of Lytton and Carrington were open wounds for him, and Henrietta could sympathize. She was warm, a little wobbly herself, but, as ever, immensely good company. Two days before her presentation at court, Tommy was in the country at a friend's family estate and Henrietta wrote to him from his studio—a telling reprieve from Prince's Gate. The letter contained a story heard from a mutual friend who used to get in trouble for "piddling in the old man's" flower beds. When his mother would chase after him with a poker, his refuge was to slip under her skirts. She had other news, but "it would take too long to give details . . . and as the details are all the main points I will let it keep." Would he please come back soon—"when I'm depressed there's no one to talk to and when I'm happy there's no one to be happy with me."

Houseman had predicted Henrietta would be "top girl." Barry's wife, Mary, described Henrietta's importance at 14 Prince's Gate, where she held sway in the kitchen and explained all manner of customs and expectations to Aleen. Henrietta knew "the Prince of Wales and all those people that Aleen had never known," Mary added. "I imagine there was a good deal of tension on that score in the embassy." Ten years earlier she had concocted caramel cake for Bloomsbury; now Henrietta planned menus with the embassy's French chef. At one affair, the heir to the throne, soon to be Edward VII, was served "soufflé Henrietta."

For the first time since college, perhaps, Henrietta had a clear and publicly acknowledged role, and the embassy brought perquisites she appreciated. Her father basked in her companionship, and the two of them spent quiet weekends in the country and slipped out to movies and theater openings. (Aleen stepped back, apparently willingly; there were many other occasions where only the ambassador and his wife were included.) Henrietta directed her own social life from a powerful perch. The Bloomsbury painter Duncan Grant—his bottomless sense of fun intact—skipped back into her life, starting a portrait of her and irritating Vanessa Bell, who seemingly never met an American she liked. David Garnett lunched with the family and had his first meeting

with Mrs. Bingham. He judged her to be a "rather shy lady" who "felt it difficult to live up" to the charismatic Henrietta. While Aleen adored the pomp and whirl of her well-staffed embassy life and sent home an album of large photographs of the interiors at Prince's Gate, Garnett believed that in a crowded room the ambassador's wife "would be overlooked and would rejoice that she was."

One evening soon after settling into London, Henrietta threw a dinner party while her father and Aleen were attending a diplomatic function. The guests included the comedienne Bea Lillie and Noël Coward, the tart-tongued playwright and actor whose productions lit up both the West End and Broadway. The company was "delightful," as David remembered, and they stayed on after the meal only to be startled "near midnight by a tap on the door."

"May we come in?"

It was the Ambassador and Mrs. Bingham. We welcomed them and I think made them feel that their appearance at the end of the evening had added to the enjoyment of the younger people. When the time came for departure I was taking leave of the Ambassadress and that good lady protested feebly, "But you know, I've no right to be here at all."

"Well, now that you've found your way, I do hope we shall often see you here again," said Noël Coward, who was standing next to me.

His wit was rather cruel since its essence was the truth: the lady was a nonentity in her own house, but she looked at him full of humble gratitude.

In 1924, the prospect of the Judge's marriage had induced a five-hour fit of vomiting, dredging up grief about her mother, anger about Mary Lily, and the terror of being left behind, left alone. Almost a decade later, her father made Henrietta's status clear.

Those first months were in fact a "bad time," for the ambassador. He suffered fevers no one could explain and used his frailty—as he often did—to bind Henrietta to him in this moment when he was perceptibly weaker. He was unable to attend the London Economic Conference, which convened to address Europe's war debts and monetary stabilization. He tried to keep a hand in the negotiations from his bed and wound up irritating some of FDR's delegates. Raymond Moley, who participated in the summit, returned to Washington irate, dubbing Bingham "the horizontal ambassador."

Dr. Hugh Young arrived from Baltimore and, with Henrietta, escorted Bingham to a private Welsh clinic. He was given a strict diet and ordered to avoid strenuous activity. Henrietta applauded her father's role in getting Roosevelt elected—banks were stabilized, emergency relief was reaching millions of needy citizens, and farmers were getting federal price guarantees and subsidies—but what if the job he had taken with her support cost him his life? She went off alone during the days to hike in the nearby Clwydian Range. On the back of her map, she wrote out the lyrics to a hit song from the year her mother died, when Henrietta and her father mourned and clung to each other, cementing the bond that she would spend so much of her adult life trying and failing to break.

> The hot winds that come to thee
> The desert sands all go from me,
> I bid them to tell thee that I love thee
> Speaking my soul to thee.
> Hot sands burning fire my veins with passion bold
> Love I'll love thee till desert sands grow cold.

Tenderness mixed with tension. At some point, Bingham or his secretary purged nearly all his correspondence with his children, but a handwritten note from Henrietta on embassy stationery was kept. It accompanied "a small gift to greet you when you awake—with my very best love, H."

By fall, separated from Hope, and with matters with Tommy going nowhere, Henrietta went back to Ernest Jones. Asked by *The Sketch* for a favorite verse, Henrietta quoted Ralph Hodgson's vision of escape: "BABYLON—where I go dreaming / When I weary of to-day, Weary of a world grown grey." Eleanor Chilton and her husband, Herbert Agar (his 1933 study of the American presidency won the Pulitzer Prize), saw a good deal of Henrietta. Eleanor was in contact with Jones as well and visited the analyst and his wife at their country home. Eleanor recognized her old rival's "great competence and poise, and really amazing gifts of insight and understanding," but she also judged Henrietta "a very defenceless [*sic*] person . . . susceptible to influences of

Eleanor Carroll Chilton Agar with Ernest and
Katherine Jones, at the Plaat, Elsted, 1933

all kinds." Henrietta did Eleanor a good turn, however. Her father hired Herbert as a policy advisor, and in 1935 the Agars transferred to Louisville, where Herbert oversaw *The Courier-Journal*'s editorial page.

Roosevelt's administration, focused primarily on domestic issues, allowed trade protections to stand despite protests from economists and advisors like his envoy to Britain. Bingham wasn't always in step with the president. Apparently without authorization, he discussed an American plan to aid currency stabilization. It came to naught and embarrassments like this made him appear ineffectual. *Fortune* ran an article critiquing presidential appointments of wealthy donors to important embassies, labeling Roosevelt's man in London "neurasthenic," "lacking in diplomatic savoir-faire," and in need of "help and advice." (This particular article did not find its way into the ambassador's bulging scrapbook.) Even more troubling, the head of the German delegation to the Economic Conference divulged Hitler's plan to enhance the nation's *Lebensraum* (living space). In October 1933, Germany withdrew from the World Disarmament Conference and the League of Nations, dealing a blow to the postwar hopes for peace.

One perquisite of embassy life was the international clipping service the Judge engaged to document his time in office. In 1933, Henrietta asked to be sent any news of Hope Williams, and accumulated a stack of cuttings. In December, as Prohibition came to an end, Henrietta sailed for New York for the premiere of *All Good Americans*, in which Hope's fashion writer character loses her lover to a "Kentucky heiress" (one of Henrietta's Bloomsbury nicknames); Hope's face appeared across the pages of *The New York Times* and the *Herald-Tribune*, and the syndicated column "New York Day by Day" nominated her for the "most swaggery walk." Readers were reminded that the social register dropped Williams when she hit the boards professionally—acting simply wasn't done in her class and neither was divorce. One critic noted Hope's short, "icy coiffure," and some reviewers complained that her performance lacked emotional range. The play ran forty performances— and when Henrietta returned to London the clippings stopped. The affair ended like a star dying on a cloudy night. It must have been a sad time all around; Williams appeared only once more on Broadway, and her lone Hollywood role was as a mannish pianist in Noël Coward's 1935 film, *The Scoundrel*.

Henrietta returned to the embassy that winter ahead of her father, who remained in the United States to consult with the president as well as doctors (his health remained weak). When the household at Prince's Gate reassembled in March 1934, Anglo-American ties showed signs of strengthening—at a personal level, at least. Through one of his lovers, the Prince of Wales met the divorcée Wallis Warfield Simpson, a distant cousin of Barry's wife, Mary. Generally enamored of Americans, Edward enjoyed sitting with Henrietta at a dinner that spring and asked her for an invitation to the embassy. Henrietta managed the preparations and the prince stayed until after midnight, declaiming upon the dangers of revolution and the threat of "social parity." Before leaving the embassy, the heir to the British throne issued the ambassador a coveted invitation to visit him in Cornwall. Edward and Wallis's Nazi sympathies already troubled some in America (though not most of the leadership at the State Department) and the ambassador included the conversation in his official diary.

Robert Worth Bingham liked to note Henrietta's "extraordinary effect" on others partly because it affirmed and explained the effect she had on him. A diplomatic dinner at the Soviet embassy placed Henrietta with Ambassador Ivan Maisky on one side and on the other a man who spoke neither English nor French. Henrietta began conversing in Russian. (Where she picked this up is unknown, but she was planning and possibly took a trip to the Soviet Union during this period.) After dinner, guests swarmed her and her father. Henrietta's magic worked on diplomats just as it had on Carrington and Stephen Tomlin when she sang "Water Boy" in Duncan Grant's studio.

A full decade had passed since then. At thirty-three, she was hardly the ambassador's "young daughter." Her cheeks had slimmed, but Henrietta's skin remained milky and unlined. She wore her hair longer, waved at ear level, and her sleekly tailored clothes set off her still-boyish physique, a contrast to silver-haired Aleen's ample bosom. A photo from

1934 shows Henrietta on a garden bench, her head tilting at the same angle Stephen Tomlin carved it—vulnerable, sympathetic, knowing. In one hand she holds a cigarette; the other rests protectively on Caesar's successor, a wire-haired terrier named Hope. Barry, wearing tweeds and spectator brogues, sits cross-legged at her feet (he and Mary were then visiting). When they wrote "Shadows," brother and sister had struggled against their wounded and imperious father, but as he weakened, their ambitions appeared neatly joined to his. Henrietta acted as his consort and "wonderful comfort and support" in the world of international diplomacy, where he butted heads with the Department of State. Barry, meanwhile, spent seven months as *The Courier-Journal*'s White House correspondent, soaking up the New Deal Brain Trust atmosphere.

A 1934 profile of the ambassador for Birmingham's *News-Age Herald* only briefly mentioned the "ambassadress" before moving to the "congenial relationship" between Bingham and his daughter. The journalist described Henrietta and the Judge's morning ritual of "cantering along the bridle paths" of Hyde Park, and repeated Bingham's tale of one evening finding himself seated beside a lady whose name he had not made out during the "hubbub of introductions." The lady "'started off by saying nice things about you, Henrietta,'" he said, turning to his daughter, "'and from then on we were fast friends!'"

14

A JOYOUS AND SATISFYING LIFE

*A*mong the multitude of receptions held at 14 Prince's Gate in 1934 was one for the "girls" of the U.S. Wightman Cup tennis team. They were in England for the annual competition, modeled after the Davis Cup, pitting Britain's top players against America's. That particular year, the U.S. women "were expected to lose by a large margin." The warm welcome they received from the Binghams, their "pride in American tennis," and their sincere "interest in our fortune in the matches" surprised the group. The gloom lifted a little. Led by Helen Hull Jacobs, the team went on to upset the Brits.

As a teenage competitor in Louisville, Henrietta had accumulated at least a dozen tennis trophies and knew all about Jacobs—anyone following tennis would. The Associated Press named her 1933 female athlete of the year. Jacobs appeared on court in shorts at Forest Hills (today's U.S. Open), the first woman to do so at a time when players wore stockings and skirts below the knee. Critics saw the move as dangerous to society: one female competitor's father opposed the abbreviated costume because he wanted his "girl to grow up a woman." Helen gained few followers at the outset, but she refused to turn back. It gave

Helen Hull Jacobs by Dorothy Wilding, 1935

a competitive advantage: you could see your own feet and no lunge was too long in shorts. A few weeks before she and Henrietta met, no less a figure than the Prince of Wales judged shorts acceptable for female players, perhaps agreeing with a *Daily Mail* cartoonist that Helen Jacobs at least "looked better in shorts than any man we could think of."

On July 4, 1934, Helen was moving forward in her Wimbledon bracket when she attended the embassy's annual Independence Day garden party. Guests in morning coats and sleekly fitted dresses thronged the lawn behind 14 Prince's Gate. Mary and Barry were on hand from Louisville, and Henrietta arranged for a musical ensemble to play what one newspaper called "plantation airs." Jacobs grew up on her mother's romantic tales of Kentucky and Virginia, where an ancestor served as a delegate to the 1776 Continental Congress, and she always "expected to find the inhabitants of these two states" special, "a race unto themselves." Robert Worth Bingham addressed the crowd in his top hat, and at some point Henrietta turned her electric blue gaze on the player about to face off against Dorothy Round, England's skirted champion.

Helen Jacobs had none of Mina's refined intellectual aspirations, Tomlin's brooding cleverness and conversational gifts, Carrington's rumpled bohemianism, or John Houseman's self-consciousness and way with words. Like Hope Williams, Helen was a star in her own right, but as a tomboy who spent her childhood in Arizona and San Francisco, she was well beyond the purview of the Social Register. Her driven approach to life (she competed fiercely in middle school to surpass the smartest boy) took her to the apex of her sport. She was not inclined to question authority and approached the world with guileless sincerity and a gee-whiz appreciation of her good fortune. That she was sexually interested in women seemed not to disturb her, but the twenty-six-year-old tennis player had never fallen in love like this.

While Henrietta watched the women's final at Wimbledon, she penciled a menu, including baked grapefruit and sole *grillé*, on the back of her ticket book. But more than a fine meal was in store. After Jacobs lost to Round in three hard-fought sets, Jacobs and Henrietta escaped together. A news report noted that the runner-up "rested . . . with Miss Bingham, daughter of Mr. Robert Worth Bingham, the American Ambassador in London, at her [weekend] home at Sunningdale." The "special relationship" developed quickly with other members of the Bingham household. Helen's strict regimen and fierce determination embodied the Joan of Arc–like female warrior type Robert Worth Bingham idealized and for years tried to make his daughter fit. She promised to be a positive influence on Henrietta, who struggled with self-discipline and focus. Whereas Henrietta drank (heavily at times) to ease her anxiety and boredom, Helen sipped sherry—and not even that during training. When she departed for New York and the U.S. Open Tennis Tournament, a mass of cut flowers from the ambassador filled Jacobs's cabin. In thanking him, she pledged to do even better in England next year.

Helen easily took the 1934 singles trophy at Forest Hills in September, but that was because her greatest opponent, Helen Wills Moody, was out of competition. Moody had apple cheeks and a pretty smile (contrasting with Jacobs's square-jawed look) and did not consort with the other women players. She earned the name "Little Miss Poker Face" for her coolness on the court. During the 1933 U.S. finals match against Jacobs, Moody had been trailing badly when she suddenly forfeited, citing pain in her back. Tennis fans were skeptical. "Some ten thousand people had seen her walk off that court," the sportswriter Paul Gallico noted, "apparently without so much as a limp." Jacobs won points for her grit—she had entered the same tournament against her physician's advice after he diagnosed an "acute inflammation of the gall bladder"—but the forfeiture robbed her of a sense of complete victory over her archrival. The press exploited the drama, including the contrast between the happily married Moody and Helen Jacobs: the latter, reported New York's *World Telegraph*, "isn't keen about the boys." And while Jacobs publicly denied a feud, she privately referred to "that foul woman who calls herself a lady."

Henrietta sailed for America after Wimbledon, too, staying with Jeannette on Long Island and seeing Mary, Barry, and her nephews, Worth and Barry Jr., who were vacationing there. She was almost certainly following Helen, whom she called by her family nickname, "Hono." Henrietta's return to London was repeatedly delayed and her tracks vanished altogether for a time, upsetting the ambassador. Finally, she and Helen surfaced in London in November 1934.

Helen planned to spend the off season writing a novel set at a Nevada mining town (her father had been a mining engineer) and a military school for boys. She was also fielding a volley of offers to "go pro." As a radio commentator, she could bring in $1,000 per week during matches, but strict rules prevented amateurs from taking income from sponsorships or tournament play. Sponsors could cover tournament expenses, but devoting oneself to the sport required a steady stream of funds. Helen, having already worked briefly at the *San Francisco Examiner*, and authored a volume, *Modern Tennis*, hoped she could support her career with freelancing and other publishing ventures.

No doubt both women realized that Robert Worth Bingham could be of real assistance to Helen, and on November 8, her father's sixty-third birthday, Henrietta brought her to the embassy for tea. The women were very much together, for the next day Henrietta visited Helen's flat,

Peggy Lehmann in tow. Two days after this, Henrietta read through draft pages from the novel. "Think with her help and discussion I can make a go of it," Helen wrote in her journal. By the next week, she had dined twice at the embassy, with Henrietta's father reading aloud to them from Edgar Wallace's popular tales of colonial Africa over after-dinner coffee. On November 16, Helen wrote, "Stayed with Nat"—a family nickname for Henrietta. London's *Daily Mail* ran a photo of Helen leaving the embassy for tennis practice, noting that she was there as the "guest of Miss Bingham, daughter of the American Ambassador." Henrietta's friends would have read the coded meaning behind the innocuous phrase.

The Judge had demonstrated at Guthrie Castle that he could tolerate a female companion of Henrietta's—or at least that he was capable of looking the other way in the face of a lesbian relationship. Helen's presence, however, excited and soothed both father and daughter, and her infatuation with Henrietta developed alongside her intimacy with the whole household. Jacobs gained not just a lover, but a base, a family, and a male mentor to replace the father from whom she was estranged. Ambassador Bingham "seems really to enjoy me," Helen wrote in her diary. Bingham knew he could better manage Henrietta if he enlisted her lovers as allies; Helen recorded private conversations with the ambassador in which he told her how marvelous his daughter was and how "he feels the need of H's presence and trusts her judgment."

Helen witnessed Henrietta's anxiety spike over her father's health and the stress of his work, and saw Nat bear the brunt of his complaints or frustration in ways that appeared to Helen unjust or out of proportion. Bingham's high-strung and demanding behavior had posed a burden to his family members for decades, but Helen, who admired him greatly, could not make sense of his negativity. "Wish A[mbassador] were never annoyed," she wrote after an evening out with the two of them. "It is not right he should be, and that in turn worries H, whose nerves are in too tense a state at present to endure it."

But Helen did not complain. She soon had her own "little room" at Prince's Gate (which helped immensely with her expenses). More significant, still, she assumed the status of honorary daughter to the man she called "H.E." (for His Excellency) or, prosaically, "Pa." Henrietta had her "best girl" living under her father's roof. Aleen embraced Helen's celebrity aura. One day she got to meet Gary Cooper, with whom Helen had a tennis date. (Hollywood was mad for the sport.) When London's social season opened in June 1935, Aleen presented Jacobs to Queen Mary at St. James's Palace alongside a group of American debutantes. On one occasion, police pulled Helen over for speeding home from practice at Wimbledon and they let her go, assuming that as a member of the ambassador's family she enjoyed immunity. Publicity about this transgression upset Helen but did nothing to threaten her place at the embassy.

A particular alignment of conditions—the ambassador's protection and the dominant culture's absolute insistence that homosexuality never be acknowledged publicly—enabled Henrietta and her lover to make a home together. Still, it was an extremely daring arrangement. The women divided time between London and a complex of timber-and-brick Tudor cottages with undulating thatch roofs and diamond-mullioned windows in the village of Long Crendon, Buckinghamshire. This was renowned Bicester Hunt country and Henrietta could stable her foxhunters on the premises. She already had one terrier named Hope and found a purebred puppy for Hono, officially named "Letitia of Crendon" though they called her "Scrap." Judge Bingham leased the house (known in the area as "Madge's") for a country retreat and footed the cost of additions to the stables and a new lawn tennis court where Helen could train. He spent weekends with them, sometimes without Aleen, and whenever he needed Henrietta, they came back to their quarters at Prince's Gate. Henrietta always felt best when the outdoors, animals, and physical activity were part of her daily life—training horses, long walks with the dogs, and gardening steadied her and kept her demons in check. The intimacy and happy associations ringing around the farm in Long Crendon made for what Helen called in her diary "a joyous and satisfying life."

This cordon of immunity existed in a context of the outer world's denial of their intimacy and the silence of even the nearest members of the household—"His E" and Aleen. Helen mourned the "apparent necessity of keeping secrets" even as they flouted convention. The pretense could be overwhelming, and, as Helen noted telegraphically in her pocket diary, it "destroys so many illusions."

Nonetheless, Henrietta swept her off her feet. They had their portraits taken by the society photographer Dorothy Wilding. They went walking in the Cotswolds, lodging at Lambs Inn, a romantic complex composed of fifteenth-century weavers' cottages. They toured Westminster where they witnessed the opening of Parliament from the royal box. At the British Museum they researched a section of Helen's novel set in Jamaica and consulted Ernest Jones with respect to a character's

Henrietta Bingham by Dorothy Wilding, circa 1935

medical condition. Helen played tennis several times a week, often with the famed "Big Bill" Tilden, but also with Henrietta. Nat was "a natural," Helen wrote.

Horses became a point of shared delight. Helen's equestrian inexperience showed the first day when the family horse, Melcombe, which Henrietta described as quiet as a lamb, took off on a fifteen-minute tear through Richmond Park. "You didn't fall off," Henrietta remarked with a wink when it was over. In late 1934 and early 1935, the ambassador and Aleen spent several months in the United States. For Christmas, Henrietta and Helen drove the Bentley to Cornwall, rented horses, and galloped along the dunes. On Christmas Eve they trailed behind a foxhunt. Helen's legs were adapting to the saddle and she dreamed of riding to hounds with Henrietta. They passed days-long stretches in Long Crendon, where Helen completed her manuscript and they rode for hours, Henrietta pointing out the covert where the most spine-tingling chase of her life had begun. Tennis season approached too fast for Helen to risk her first foxhunt—perhaps next winter, Henrietta told her. But Helen had "seen enough to realize that however thrilling tennis competition might be, it couldn't hold a candle to the excitement of a long run [on horseback] and the thrill of personal risk in taking a post and rail which you knew was probably too big for you; the satisfaction of clearing a brook and hacking home after a good hunt."

Exhilaration on the downs, dunes, and bridle paths was matched in bed. One evening, after they attended separate dinner engagements, Nat appeared at Helen's door and the women fell into each other's arms. "A pretty nice surprise," Helen wrote. "I, as usual, couldn't speak." Helen's frank temperament distinguished her from Henrietta's earlier loves, but the spell she fell under was the same. Helen wondered what she "would do" without "my only love." "After marvelous night stayed in bed till 11:30"; Henrietta had gone and Helen was "lonely now." Nat was so lovely to look at, "an aristocrat from head to toe." Her kindness exceeded anyone's. She was entranced by her tones as David Garnett and Jack Houseman had been. At some point, modesty drove Helen to make excisions to her pocket diaries, yet through vigorous ballpoint scratches, some words ("Nat is the best [illegible] have ever known") are nevertheless discernible. In her mid-thirties, with the Jazz Age years behind her, Henrietta retained her seductive power. "Wonderful scenes tonight," Helen wrote on another occasion before closing her eyes.

Henrietta mixed her glamorous brew for a dinner at Prince's Gate, given during her father and Aleen's absence. Champagne, dancing, late-night poker, and a guest list that included Edward, Prince of Wales—to which Douglas Fairbanks, Jr., asked to be added—made for a "glorious success." Edith Wilson, then in London touring the newest "Blackbirds" revue, was a likely guest and attraction for the prince, who escorted Helen into the dining room. That night the athlete broke with her usual abstemiousness and put away three glasses of champagne. The couple spent the next evening (Henrietta's thirty-fourth birthday) reviewing the party, doubtless discussing the American divorcée who had stolen the prince's heart. (Whether Wallis Simpson attended, as well, is not known.) A few days later, Henrietta joined Edward's party at Fort Belvedere, where hot dogs were on the menu. These combined risibly with his tartan kilt and atrocious bagpipe playing. Helen stayed behind—there were places they could not appear together in public—and envied Henrietta's time seeing royalty up close and her ability to report back information that might be useful to the United States. Later that year, Robert Worth Bingham criticized Edward to FDR as a "German protagonist."

Henrietta kept score, point by agonizing point, at the 1935 French Championship at Roland Garros Stadium in June. (Mussolini was massing for an attack on Ethiopia, forcing Henrietta's father to miss the tournament.) Helen failed in a grueling semifinal battle with the German Hilde Krahwinkel Sperling. After more than a year *hors de combat*, Helen Wills Moody was about to emerge from her San Francisco "lair" and a Wimbledon rematch was anticipated. "If I had been Jacobs," the sportswriter Paul Gallico imagined, "I should have shaken in my shoes." Helen nonetheless played solidly through the early Wimbledon rounds, hiccupping only when faced with Sperling, fresh from her Paris victory. Helen confided her worries to "H.E." On the night before the semifinal the Binghams distracted her with rubber after rubber of bridge. The following morning, "Pa" pulled her aside and pointed at the newspaper account of her most recent match. It noted how very few errors Helen had made. "There you are," he said. "See that it says that tomorrow." With her second family watching from the grandstand, Helen did just that, winning two sets 6–3, 6–0. Meanwhile, the other Helen dispatched her opponent in the other semifinal. On Center Court, Jacobs would have the chance to prove to all, including her lover and the British royal family, that she could beat Moody at her best.

"In all the history of sport, there has never been such a complete and dramatic vindication in trial by combat," one writer claimed. Henrietta could scarcely breathe; she gripped the pencil and scorecard and marked the progress of battle. It seemed impossible, but in the third set, with Helen Jacobs up 5–2, it was match point. Moody slung a lob off a

Helen on Henrietta's hunter Stinger, with Aleen and "Pa" at Long Crendon, 1935

difficult shot and Jacobs came up for the kill. Helen Moody saw her chances fade to a vanishing point. The ball nicked the tape at the top of the net and dropped—on Jacobs's side. The match turned from there. Henrietta fought back tears as Helen gave up five games, the set, and the championship. Moody had won, fair and square. "Finals," Helen wrote in her diary that day. "Could have beaten the bitch."

The family retreated to Long Crendon to work off the disappointment. The press captured the ambassador and Aleen posing with their guest astride Henrietta's horse, but Henrietta herself stayed out of the pictures. She led daylong rides over the countryside and pulled Helen into bed—and into the garden where the fruit of their joint labors, a profusion of lupine and sweet peas, bloomed. In August, Henrietta, Helen, and the ambassador left for America, while Aleen stayed in London to undergo surgery. The nature of the "operation" is not clear, but it was typical of the marriage that her husband moved ahead with his affairs.

On the crossing, Henrietta's father enthralled Helen with stories he'd told a hundred times. There was the tale of his great-grandfather William Bingham arriving almost penniless from Scotland at the wrong port and having to walk from Wilmington, Delaware, to Wilmington, North Carolina. A gold ring found on a forest path enabled him to buy a horse and ride the rest of the way. The Judge described his terror as a child when his father appeared at the door in a hooded Ku Klux Klan costume—but also how the Klansmen, in blackface, supposedly infiltrated a meeting of Republicans and ex-slaves, heroically foiling "plans to burn four houses, all barns" and do violence to Confederate veterans' "wives and daughters." He retailed the time when he was mayor of Louisville and a "drunken, wife-beating street sweeper" walked into his city hall office and drew a pistol. Bingham told of knocking him down and wrenching the weapon away. His assailant scrambled ignominiously out the window.

When the steamship docked in New York, the news photographers were there and the *New York Post* ran a photo montage headlined A LORD [comedienne Beatrice Lillie's son], A (TENNIS) QUEEN AND AN AMBASSADOR ARRIVE. Henrietta was not named, but in the photograph Robert Worth Bingham and Helen flanked the woman they both loved.

They met Barry at the Plaza. It was one of those "glorious nights," when Helen felt fully bonded to Henrietta and the world they made together, and a reprieve before another tournament for Helen and another departure for Henrietta. The good news for Jacobs was that Moody, resting on her laurels, sat out the tournament at Forest Hills, but then Henrietta went to Virginia Beach, where Mary and Barry and the boys were vacationing. This separation pained Helen, who grew miserable and anxious. By the quarterfinals her lover and the ambassador were in place, though her own family remained in California. "Pa here—thank god," Helen wrote in her diary. Two days later Jacobs cruised to victory over Sarah Palfrey, setting a record for consecutive U.S. titles. That night at the Pierre, Helen "got a glow on sherry." The couple then pointed south for a leisurely drive to Louisville.

Henrietta steered along the James River to Richmond and then east through King William County to Williamsburg, where Helen's forebears lived in Revolutionary times. They strolled around the colonial Governor's Palace with its formal gardens and incongruous cupola, appreciating John D. Rockefeller's recent reconstruction. In Staunton, Virginia, they knocked at Stuart Hall's school office, passing the tennis court where Henrietta briefly reigned as champion, and toured the hushed, empty buildings. Nat led Helen to the room she lived in when her father courted and married Mary Lily.

Either Henrietta did not divulge the anger and ambivalence she felt twenty years earlier, or did so with much sympathy for her father, because Helen's adoration of the Judge never waned. Helen's eagerness to please and support Robert Worth Bingham aligned with Henrietta's. For Henrietta, Helen signified a purpose beyond nurturing her father. Helen looked up to Henrietta as a model of good taste and captivating charm, a companion who delivered immense physical pleasure. Nat took charge of the player's financial affairs, read her drafts, and coached her when her regular teachers were not available. Helen was thankful and emotionally direct. The balance seemed near perfect and it was about to get even better.

15

OUR HOUSE WITH OUR HORSES

$\mathcal{H}$elen longed to see Kentucky—and her fame would make her a winning guest. Though Mina had visited Melcombe in 1924, it was the first time Henrietta had brought a current female lover home. It was a courageous move, and how Louisville society would respond remained open to question. Mary and Barry threw them a mint-julep party in the stately limestone Greek theater the Judge had recently commissioned from Carrère and Hastings—notably the same firm that two decades before had designed Whitehall as Mary Lily's Palm Beach wedding present. Herbert Agar was running *The Courier-Journal*'s opinion page, and he and Eleanor hosted a dinner at their home. And, of course, there were tennis games. Helen offered Barry and Mary pointers and Barry boasted that he aced her—once. An exhibition match was arranged at Melcombe's En-Tout-Cas court overlooking a formal garden with flagstone walks, a quiet fountain, and bursting perennial borders. At night, they returned to the empty house—empty except for the somewhat diminished servant staff. Helen found the mansion "impressive and dignified" but lacking charm, adding that it had one thing in particular to boast: "I love its woman."

Henrietta knew her father's time in England was coming to an end. According to standard protocol, serving ambassadors submitted their resignation upon the reelection (or defeat) of the president who had appointed them. FDR was expected to win easily in 1936, and in late 1935, the Judge contemplated a return to Kentucky. Henrietta's post-embassy life and how Helen might fit into it hung in the air. Her father had purchased a large plot of land two miles from Melcombe Bingham, but she didn't like the idea of living there. A house had already been built for Robert, which Aleen's son and his wife currently occupied. Henrietta wanted no part of a family compound. She and Helen had been "happy and proud" in England, more so than any time in Henrietta's life. As summer slipped into fall, Nat and Helen weighed the idea of establishing another home together.

The Iroquois word that "Kentucky" derives from—"Ken-tah-ten"— has been translated as "Land of Tomorrow." Whether tomorrow would mean Kentucky for Henrietta had been in question since she first left Smith College. Barry lobbied hard for Henrietta's landing at home; he wanted her near for his own sake and understood her need for breathing room from their father, Aleen's children, and Louisville society more generally. In the dry autumn air, Henrietta drove Helen into the countryside, in the direction she had taken John Houseman to hear the jug band play that dark and frozen Christmas. Miles from Melcombe, in a place called Goshen, they happened upon a jewel, a fine brick house dating to 1812 built by an early settler who named it "Harmony Landing." Barry described it for the ambassador: the property was set on a "high bluff, at least two hundred feet above the river, with green fields below that run right to the river's edge. From the top you can see for a good twenty miles up and down the river and the whole place is enough to take your breath away." Much of the farm's two hundred acres had been converted to a country club golf course, but the Depression and the club's location sixteen miles from Louisville sank the venture. An octagonal shelter originally built to cover an amusement park merry-go-round had been moved to the club and would make a signature horse barn. Henrietta and Helen imagined breeding Thoroughbreds and pedigreed dogs and riding their hunters across the rolling countryside.

His Excellency complained about the delay in Henrietta's return (she was to have joined him in Scotland for his grouse-killing spree, and Robert and his wife were inadequate substitutes), but Barry told the Judge that his short-term loss would be a long-term boon. "I believe she has had as good a time as she has ever had here," Barry wrote of his sister. "She talks about coming back to make her headquarters here in much more definite terms than she has ever done before." Henrietta "wouldn't consider coming back, of course, until you finish your job in London." The ambassador would not like the distance this rural outpost put between him and his daughter, but Henrietta was prepared to deploy principal from her trust to make up the difference between the price of Harmony Landing and the parcel he had already purchased for her. A bourbon tycoon was interested in purchasing the surplus land nearer Melcombe, though Aleen's son, Byron, enjoyed living next to the unoccupied acreage and was making negotiations difficult. Barry felt the new scheme was worth the trouble. The other property "has the most peaceful and impressive atmosphere of any place I have seen, and H felt at once that she would rather live there than anywhere in the world."

In November 1935, Henrietta stood with her father in London, receiving guests for the annual Thanksgiving Dinner. His speech contrasted Britain and the United States, "the two great Democracies," with Nazi Germany and Fascist Italy. The democracies must exert "their great weight throughout the world on the behalf of peace," he said. The residents at Prince's Gate felt grave concerns about what lay ahead, but Helen and Henrietta were comforted by the vision of another place they might call "our house with our horses."

Helen was hell-bent on riding to hounds during the winter of 1935–1936, and they spent as much time as possible in Long Crendon. Learning the sport from Henrietta was, she said, like learning the chop shot from the tennis great Bill Tilden. The teacher took the risks seriously, though; Helen had much at stake. "Since you are fool enough to hunt," Henrietta said, "you must hunt Stinger." He was steady enough to carry even an inexperienced rider over five-foot-high fences spanning up to eighteen feet of terrain. Under orders from Nat, Helen insured herself heavily against an accident, and, unbeknownst to Helen, Henrietta ordered the groom to gallop Stinger early the morning of that first hunt—this would take the edge off his speed. The red-coated masters snapped their whips and the hounds whimpered with excitement. Helen survived, and over the season the women took part in many hunts. Both had falls, but the most severe injury came one December day when Henrietta was kicked in the stomach at the stable. Terrified, Helen swore, "I could have shot the horse if I'd had a gun."

At Henrietta's insistence, the family celebrated Christmas 1935 in Long Crendon. She put up stockings and decorated the tree. On the political front, there was much to be thankful for. A cascade of progressive policies came out of Washington in 1935: the Works Progress Administration would soon give work to thousands of unemployed, including artists, writers, and actors; American unions could engage in collective bargaining for the first time; Social Security promised dignity to the elderly. Helen was delighted with her gifts from Nat—including perfectly tailored foxhunting clothes. In his diary, the ambassador noted that Henrietta "did everything possible to make us all happy." He repaid her with a beautiful gray horse. A deal would not close on the Goshen farm until the spring of 1936, but Henrietta was studying Thoroughbred bloodlines and plotting a breeding program.

Their blissful-sounding life together—writing and riding, walking the village lanes and country fields with Hope and Scrap, giving brilliant dinners followed by blackjack, and passing quiet evenings with H.E.—had difficult moments, of course. Henrietta drank more than Helen liked, and, after pressure, agreed to stick mostly to beer—which was less alcoholic but also extremely unladylike. Henrietta probably enjoyed that. Helen had a tendency to impose her teetotaling regime on her lover, but Henrietta had not given up nightclubs and music and dancing and the drinking that came with them. "Must stop being trying about trivial things (cocktails)," Helen once lectured herself in her journal. There were jealousies, too, such as a night where, after dinner at the Savoy with Peggy Lehmann and another guest named Percy, they all returned to Madge's. Helen grew so upset at something she witnessed happen that she fled to the darkness of Stinger's stall, where she stroked him until her composure returned. Both Peggy Lehmann and Henrietta experienced heterosexual attractions; Helen possibly did not. Percy may have been a man—or Henrietta and Peggy could have been flirting. On another night, Helen restrained Henrietta after a man shot "lecherous glances" at them. Nat fired off a few choice words, but Helen knew "what a mess" a public fracas could "precipitate."

Henrietta saw little of Mina or John Houseman in the embassy period, but it is safe to say she was a regular topic of discussion between her former lovers. At one point Houseman visited London and pronounced that Henrietta was clearly enjoying "being an English lesbian." Meanwhile, Jack and the widowed Mina initiated a "sporadically intimate" relationship sometime in 1934, and Mina inaugurated one of American theater's great collaborations by introducing him to her Ashfield neighbor Archibald MacLeish. MacLeish needed a director for his play about a suicidal tycoon in the wake of the stock market crash. The fact that it was in verse meant that *Panic* (1935) had little chance of popular success, and it ran only briefly. But Houseman cast twenty-year-old Orson Welles in the lead role, and the two began a partnership that continued with an acclaimed all-black *Macbeth* for the Federal Theatre Project's New York Negro Unit, the Mercury Theatre's blackshirt *Julius Caesar*, and the Mercury Theatre of the Air's legendary *War of the Worlds* broadcast. Houseman and Welles's collaboration (Houseman was by this time the producer) ultimately collapsed in acrimony during the creation of *Citizen Kane*. Mina herself joined the Mercury Theatre of the Air as a researcher. She also weathered a late-term abortion. Attractive as he could be, Jack did not inspire sufficient confidence in Mina for her to bring his child into the world.

Mina returned to England in the spring of 1936 to see David Garnett and pick up the threads of her affair with the Bloomsbury art critic Clive Bell, who sent a bouquet of lilacs to her hotel. She responded with a note counting the "days since an accomplished hand has stroked my lovely spine." Henrietta, by contrast, was more rooted than she had ever been. She wanted Mina to meet Helen and witness the home she had made. Life at Madge's Farm in Buckinghamshire was the closest thing she had to Chapelbrook—and her relationship with Helen the nearest she had come to Mina and Harry's marriage. Nat celebrated Mina's arrival with a thirty-three-year-old bottle of bourbon, older than Helen herself. Phyllis Gomme, who had helped Henrietta decorate Madge's and was planning interiors for the Harmony Landing house, joined them and the low-roofed living room filled with laughter.

Mina then took Henrietta and Helen to meet Charles Lindbergh and his wife, Anne. Anne Morrow had been a star student of Mina's at Smith, graduating in 1928. Hoping to avoid public attention as the man convicted of kidnapping their baby neared execution, the couple rented Long Barn, a secluded spot belonging to the writer Vita Sackville-West and her husband, the diplomat Harold Nicolson. At first the aviator seemed "stiff and disinterested." He was famously introverted and unworldly, and had never heard of Helen Jacobs, but she didn't mind. He "unbent" when Henrietta mentioned the traffic-free route they had taken to Long Barn. A navigator at heart, Nat pulled out her maps and marked the roads. Lindbergh said to Mina, "She seemed like a sensible girl."

Robert Worth Bingham's extravagance with respect to Madge's and the decoration of Harmony Landing provoked Aleen, even though Henrietta frequently turned down offers of more money from her father. To smooth things over, Helen invited Aleen to join her and Henrietta in Budapest for the 1936 Hungarian national tennis championship. Their suite in the Ritz overlooked the Danube and Helen played well, but it shocked the travelers to hear Hitler described by a fellow dinner guest at one event as a "very kind man." In the final match, Helen appeared tired and took a bad beating. The tennis season (next up was the French Open) suddenly looked doubtful. Aleen departed and Henrietta, worried about Hono's health, took her to the Alps. "Nothing but bed. Happy with N," Helen wrote simply one day. Jacobs called the ambassador "an angel" for allowing Henrietta stay with her—but then Italy annexed Ethiopia and he recalled Henrietta "home to London." They went.

As the 1936 Wimbledon tournament neared, it seemed that Moody would not compete, giving Helen Jacobs perhaps her greatest chance at the All England title, although her doctor advised against her playing. Jacobs's response was "Nuts to him." On July 2, Henrietta, her father, and Aleen watched the semifinals from the green-and-silver-cushioned armchairs of the Royal Box. Helen was "perfectly trained and showing impeccable match play temperament," defeating Jadwiga Jedrzejowska in straight sets. Especially after the British women fell out of the bracket, the audience embraced Helen, who had come so close to triumph so many times. One of Queen Victoria's granddaughters leaned over to the ambassador and whispered, "She's got to win."

The final, between Jacobs and the German-born Hilde Krahwinkel Sperling, was held on July Fourth. Political overtones weighed heavily since Hitler viewed competitive sport as a metaphor for national power. (Jacobs's surname sometimes led people to assume she had a Jewish background, and she witnessed Aryanization at work as Jewish players were disqualified from representing Germany and non-Jews were pressed to proselytize for the Nazis.) The day before, the Englishman Fred Perry had defeated a homosexual German player, who was later imprisoned on a morals charge.

A crowd of twenty thousand witnessed the match, with its pounding rallies of up to thirty shots. Helen took the first set 6–2, her shorts fluttering as she bounded across the court. Sperling dominated the second 6–4 and they battled into a third, with Jacobs breaking Sperling's serve but giving up several match points. It was match point again when one of Sperling's slashing backhands tore toward her. It went into the net, giving Helen victory at Wimbledon. At last. *The New York Times* reported that Jacobs "made one exultant leap" as the stadium burst into "probably the most wholehearted ovation Wimbledon will ever know." A female reporter from the Associated Press watched Helen peel the tape from her blistered fingers and toes. Asked how she had achieved her triumph, Jacobs looked up at the stands and replied, "I think the hunting I did the past year was grand training." As she achieved the long-sought title of her career, she publicly credited her lover the best way she could.

British papers ran large photos of the champion in shiny black hunting boots and cravat, seated casually out of doors at Long Crendon with her host, the proud American ambassador. One article did quote Henrietta saying she was "so excited" toward the end of the match "that she doesn't remember a single stroke." Deploying the code surrounding homosexuality, the column mentioned that the "two girls are almost inseparable."

Jacobs was riding high. J. B. Lippincott & Co. rushed her memoir, *Beyond the Game*, to press in time for the U.S. Championships at Forest Hills. (Henrietta received passing mention, and Helen fought to keep a chapter that her editor had advised cutting, which detailed her friendship with Ambassador Bingham.) She landed on the cover of *Time*.

Only separation from Henrietta darkened Helen's world. "Can't bear the idea of not seeing H for weeks," Helen confided to her diary toward the end of the summer of 1936. She toured the West Coast, was given a parade in her hometown, and promoted her book, but she felt "in [a] state of static emotion, uncomfortable, unkind." It was heartbreaking when, instead of joining Helen in San Francisco, Henrietta headed with Barry, Mary, and Edie Callahan to a fishing camp in Quebec's Laurentian hills. Helen wondered if "some attractive creature" was competing for her lover's affection.

Not only did Henrietta's desires range widely, but her history suggests that the more tightly she was held the more restless she became. That summer of 1936, Nat did in fact show interest in someone other than Helen. Jack Houseman's visa had expired, and he repaired to Canada pending a resolution of his legal status. Driving along the Saint Lawrence River, he noticed "a speeding black foreign convertible which seemed curiously familiar," and in Montreal at the Ritz's front desk he found a cable from Leslie Howard (whom he had cast in *Hamlet*) alongside a letter bearing Henrietta's "small crabbed writing." Mina had informed Henrietta that Jack was in the neighborhood, and they spent several days together, breaking off from Mary and Barry to lie in the sun in forest clearings surrounded by tall timber. "Certain things had not changed at all: the color of her eyes and skin, the warmth of her voice, the way she wore a tailored suit and her hands on the wheel of her car." Nevertheless, Jack decided that he "was no longer in love with her." Mary Bingham remembered differently: Houseman seemed miserable and Henrietta ultimately "rebuffed him."

By late fall, Helen was in Louisville. The couple celebrated Roosevelt's 1936 landslide with Mary, Barry, and the *Courier-Journal* staff. The ambassador remained in London, fearing war and urging the "girls" to come back quickly. (Franco had just unleashed his coup in Spain.) The women drove to Goshen after a late autumn snowfall. The fairways spread grandly above the river where Thoroughbred foals might one day gambol. On November 8, 1936, they cabled HAPPY BIRTHDAY to the ambassador, signing themselves HENRIETTA-HELEN. They would be with him soon. This was to be their last English foxhunting season.

Bingham's posting at the Court of St. James was drawing to a close amid flaring tensions. The British monarchy was in a full-blown constitutional crisis over the relationship between the new king, Edward VIII, and the American Wallis Simpson. Bingham and others in the United States were upset by Edward's unscrupulous public behavior and fascist leanings and did not trust Simpson, either. Beyond Britain, the ambassador told the president he saw "grave reason to suspect that Hitler and Mussolini are beginning to work together on the basis of dividing up the world between them." FDR asked him to remain at Prince's Gate for the time being, but he would likely depart by mid-1937. Mary was expecting a third baby and Bingham anticipated spending more time with his grandchildren. He also hoped to mold the political landscape of Kentucky while he had the strength.

Barry unexpectedly objected to these plans. Instilled from his earliest youth was the need to defend his father's integrity, and he argued for departing immediately or remaining in London through the whole of Roosevelt's second term. "Lord Bing" must not give his enemies the opportunity to criticize him for clinging to his office or accuse him of staying just long enough to enjoy the upcoming coronation of Edward's brother following the king's abdication to "marry the woman I love"; he must occupy it forcefully or yield to his successor. It may have been that Barry had gotten his sea legs in Louisville and didn't especially want his father back running things. But he spoke most clearly on behalf of his sister. Henrietta had done her duty and more. Barry was maturing rapidly, learning to manage his father in ways that maximized his freedom at the newspaper and also Henrietta's leeway to thrive outside the paternal shadow. If the Judge decided to stay on, he would have to do without Henrietta's "wonderful support and comfort." She was coming home even if he didn't. Barry's strongly worded brief took the ambassador aback and he ultimately retracted his request to be relieved.

In January 1937, Stephen Tomlin died suddenly of pneumonia, following years of manic periods, suicidal urges, and limited artistic output. That same month, disaster in Louisville also upended the routine in Long Crendon. After an unremitting rainfall, the Ohio River climbed its banks and ran over great swaths of the city. *The Courier-Journal*'s offices were underwater, and management scrambled for alternate printing facilities. The devastation and mounting deaths made international headlines, and Henrietta's father felt it was his duty to be there. At the height of the crisis, Mary's water broke and Barry navigated the car over narrow two-by-fours on a washed-out back road to get her to the hospital. When it was over, he cabled "Katynat" (another of Henrietta's nicknames), ISNT IT GRAND BIGGEST PRETTIEST GIRL EVER SEEN LOVE BARRY.

When flooding at the power station cast Louisville into darkness and cold, Bingham received permission from the secretary of state for emergency leave. Of course he wanted Henrietta with him. Helen's corner of the triangle was never equal to his, and she had to agree that Henrietta's "place is there." Still, Hono was angry; "Papa is so cheerful about going it nearly drives me nuts," she confessed. Her diary entries during those winter weeks teem with dark crosshatches. On his way out of the country, Pa presented Helen with a cream-colored Labrador puppy "to keep me company while they were gone." Nork Chief, or Guil, as Jacobs called him, "became the dog love" of her life.

By the time Henrietta and her father arrived in Louisville, 230,000 evacuees were already returning to their homes. Henrietta stayed only briefly. She and Helen had one month before leaving Madge's for good. Helen departed from her usual telegraphic diary entries.

> Packing, packing, and in every box that goes some of Long Crendon seems to leave. I cannot bear to think that these last few days are the end . . . I shall never think of it as anyone's house but ours. Even the dogs seem to know that something unpleasant is happening. So much is bound up with L.C.—hunting, hacking through the lanes, taking pictures in the fields, coming home from town or America, down the hill by Dodwell's Farm or over Thame bridge . . . shopping on High St. looking perfectly horrible; nat [*sic*] feeling the breasts of chickens in Baileys and I buying film and sweet-pea seeds from Brank and Walker. Having high tea after hunting and drinking chocolate and watch[ing] the late riders coming home. Hearing the horses going by at exercise while we breakfast. Nothing will ever be just like it.

A crowd of Aleen's relatives arrived in London for the coronation of George VI and Elizabeth, which Aleen and the ambassador attended. The others viewed the royal procession from a high window. There was general relief about the new king, but at Prince's Gate hopes for a peaceful resolution to European tensions were fading. Bingham told the American Society's July Fourth banquet about the enemies of concord, "people who regard war as a cult . . . and who only listen to the argument of force." It was a difficult season for Helen, as well. An injured shoulder resulted in her worst competitive performances since 1930. She hated going into games without "my chick," as she did at Roland Garros in Paris that spring, and she lost in the quarterfinals. When Wimbledon started up the next month, the shoulder continued to trouble her and she was defeated in the round of eight.

The ambassador suffered from "bloody dictators" and from the abandonment he always experienced when Henrietta left him. The State Department slapped him with the requirement that his speeches henceforth be preapproved in Washington following some that were deemed excessively anti-German. The day the *Aquitania* bore Helen and Henrietta away from Southampton, he had to turn his eyes from the dock. He was exhausted. For months he had been running a low-grade fever. Doctors could discover nothing wrong, but in July they observed swelling around his liver and spleen. Bingham's condition worsened dramatically in August and he sailed suddenly for America. As press reports appeared suggesting FDR had recalled him, Henrietta and Barry met his boat in Quebec and took him straight to Johns Hopkins for medical consultations.

He must have feared he might not live much longer. From Johns Hopkins, Bingham went to the Greenbrier resort in White Sulphur Springs, West Virginia, where he and Mary Lily had signed their prenuptial agreement in 1916. With lawyers and Barry at his side, he came to a settlement regarding his estate. Reversing his plan of dividing his assets into thirds for his offspring, the Judge executed a complex instrument that made Barry and Mary's children beneficiaries of all voting shares of Bingham company stock. Barry would control the trust up to his father's death. Henrietta would have no share in the business, although the will granted her title to Harmony Landing and his quail plantation. Robert got far less—his standing debts were forgiven. Barry would also oversee for his brother and sister twin trusts that supplied $15,000 income per year from the Courier-Journal and Times Company earnings. Suddenly Barry was the only real heir.

Bingham booked passage back to England, but he was too weak to board and returned to Baltimore. Unable to pretend to serve the office he had once passionately sought, he penned his resignation. The Massachusetts businessman Joseph P. Kennedy, who had waited impatiently for his chance at the post, visited Bingham's bedside, where the Kentuckian told him he still hoped some treatment might "knock out the trouble."

Helen and Henrietta spent Thanksgiving at the hospital. As a last resort, surgeons opened Bingham's abdomen. It was riddled with cancer, later identified as late-stage Hodgkin's lymphoma, explaining his progressive weakness, recurring fevers, and weight loss. He never recovered consciousness. Henrietta, Barry, Bingham's sister Sadie, along with Aleen and her son and Hugh Young, were at his side when he died. When Dr. Young left the room to address reporters, thirty-six-year-old Henrietta clung to her father's old friend for support. The news appeared the next day on page one of *The New York Times*. On a loose sheet of diary entries from December 1937, Helen Jacobs wrote the header, "1937 Year Papa died at Johns Hopkins. I last to talk to him."

16

MY NERVES ARE BAD TONIGHT

*J*n the late 1930s the world turned crueler toward Helen and
Henrietta's kind, and reproducing Madge's Farm in the Kentucky countryside proved more challenging than either woman had
imagined. After a decade of relative visibility, lesbians and gay men
faced a widespread backlash that painted them as suspect and degener-
ate. Family wealth insulated Henrietta and Helen had achieved international stardom, but no less a source than *The New York Times*'s front
page described new methods to correct "overfunctioning" adrenal
glands in lesbian and bisexual women. Female athletes, once seen as
representing joyful heterosexuality, were subjected to increasingly negative innuendo. New York City used its liquor licensing authority to
shut down nightclubs and bars frequented by homosexuals (often abus-
ing and arresting patrons in raids) and put new statutes on the books
against representing "sex perversion" on stage. Hollywood instituted a
production code that banned homosexuality from the screen. One historian has described the "closet" as an invention of the 1930s, '40s, and
'50s state, medical, military, and cultural authorities that forced often
quite visible, non-self-hating sexual nonconformists "into hiding."

Many in the gay world felt compelled to exercise greater caution in their activities and apply rigorous self-editing to their writings in order to eliminate evidence of homosexuality.

There was no question of Helen Jacobs appearing with the family as they left Johns Hopkins to face the press or being seen with them on the funeral train that bore Robert Worth Bingham's body from Baltimore to Louisville. Helen could not hold Henrietta by the hand nor grasp her arm at the funeral, presided over by Bishop Woodcock at Calvary Church on Fourth Street, where four decades earlier Bob and Babes exchanged wedding vows. On the way from the sanctuary to the gravesite, the cars passed houses and shops trimmed with wreaths and Christmas lights. Then half-frozen clods of earth fell on the casket on a soft slope of Cave Hill Cemetery, where his remains were laid next to those of Henrietta's mother. He had ordered Babes's stone to read "Loveliest and most beloved." Nat's calm deserted her and Helen recalled that she was "highly emotional," strong words for Jacobs that suggest more than ordinary grief. In the past, this state of mind had produced tantrums and uncontrollable purging. Henrietta would have no easier time letting go of her tie to her father in death than in life.

"Lovely" was a favorite word of his. He called Henrietta "the loveliest daughter God ever gave a father," and for almost as long as she could remember, she had been the target of adoration and extraordinary need. Having spent so long loving, fighting, avoiding, comforting, serving, and forgiving him, Henrietta felt deracinated, flying like so much turf under a racehorse's hoof. Her friend Ivor Churchill, whom she had once imagined marrying, reached out with prayers and sympathy. Knowing something of how she and the ambassador were knitted together, Churchill consoled, "You have deep currents of fortitude, because you are your Father's daughter." Helen could not "get used to his being gone" either, but it's not clear how much help she could give Henrietta, who resisted depending on others—or others depending on her. When Christmas came it was nothing like England. An expansion project at Little Melcombe had driven Mary, Barry, and the children across the lawn—and Henrietta and Helen were merely Aleen's guests. Nothing felt right.

The day "King of Swing" Benny Goodman broke the race and genre barrier at Carnegie Hall with a jazz orchestra that included black musicians, Nat and Hono visited Pa's frozen gravesite. The sound Henrietta had loved for two decades had achieved the pinnacle of acceptance, but she missed the moment, remaining in Kentucky through the winter to supervise the renovation at Harmony Landing and struggling, as Helen wrote, through periods of "misery when [the] situation seems to have no solution."

The Goshen house, barns, and 450 acres of fields and woods would need to carry Henrietta through her loss. She and Helen surveyed miles of white board fences going up, the newly sown bluegrass, and the home filling with antiques they had selected. The dogs trotted toward the merry-go-round barn with its lattice of rafters. The place could be a refuge, Helen thought. "Nothing but the elements can touch us here," she wrote, "and even they are limited."

In the spring of 1938, movers placed Louis XV fauteuils and a Heppelwhite sideboard in her new home. Henrietta was starting afresh, which may explain why she left the two steamer trunks from London behind at Melcombe. Hats, gloves, and woolen socks, along with tea cozies, driving maps, and silk corsages, bottles of cough medicine, and shoes Nat wouldn't need on the farm, were forgotten in the garret. So were Stephen Tomlin's and John Houseman's ribbon-bound love letters, which she may never have read again—but which could not have entirely escaped her memory.

There was a great deal to do to manage a new household and supervise the farm. A string of English broodmares, some descended from a winner of the British Triple Crown, would soon give birth in Goshen's green fields. There would be colts and fillies to break and train, and stud fees to pay for the next year's breeding rights. She pored over *Blood-Horse* magazine and attended the yearling sales in Lexington, Kentucky, the navel of American turf culture. She needed to build a reputation, and by dint of geography, sex, and sexual preferences Henrietta was a rank outsider. Yet her charm and gut-level understanding of horses as athletes gave her confidence. She would concentrate on breeding mares and selling the yearlings and keep a few horses to race for the

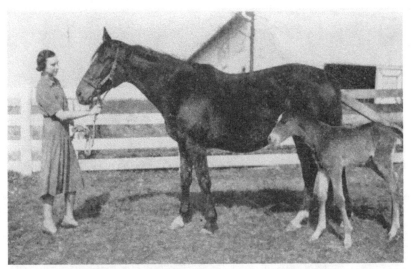

Henrietta with one of her broodmares, circa 1938

joy of it. On the sunny winter day a star-faced filly was born to one of her dams, Henrietta posed with the pair and sent the picture to Mina.

But Thoroughbred racing is called the sport of kings with good reason, and the barriers to success loomed high for a woman in the late 1930s. The $15,000 annual payout stipulated by her father's will was a sum roughly equal to her annual pre-Depression allowance and could not be expected to support her lifestyle and a farm operation. Nat looked to yearling sales, boarding services for other people's broodmares, and staple crops to offset Harmony Landing's costs and her own expenses.

The demands the business would make on her pocket were at the forefront of her mind in early 1938 when Henrietta and Helen journeyed to Georgia to assess the quail-hunting escape she inherited from her father, with its thousands of acres, white plantation house, pecan groves, skeet shooting tower, sawmill, and elaborate bird dog kennels. The pointers barked as the groom saddled horses for a final shoot. Helen begged to adopt a puppy in the Judge's memory even though Henrietta warned her they made poor pets. Maintaining the quail plantation made no sense; in the absence of its master it was put on the market to

Henrietta with her nephew Worth on Jubilee, in a Harmony Landing hay field

help fund Harmony Landing. Nineteen thirty-eight was not a propitious time to list a rich man's folly, however, and it took years to sell.

Henrietta and Barry now had a chance to build a relationship beyond the emotional collusion and madcap escapism that defined much of their youth. Barry's children came to Harmony Landing often—Henrietta arranging egg hunts and pony rides. He lacked her way with animals, but Barry adored the track, had a regular bookmaker, and sometimes attended early morning workouts now that his sister had Thoroughbreds in training and could talk a streak about bloodlines, owners, trainers, and jocks. Once, when Mary took the children to the beach in Florida, he packed a bag and spent the week at Harmony Landing so he could "really stay at the house" and luxuriate in his sister's company. He named her treasurer of the Courier Journal and Louisville Times Corporation. Henrietta, who now wore reading glasses, attended business meetings, and the executive editor, Mark Ethridge, and his wife, and Eleanor and Herbert Agar (then opinion editor), attended informal gatherings at Harmony Landing within view of her big octagonal barn.

Yet life in Kentucky could be stultifying and unnerving. Helen was made to feel "queer" when she shopped for farm groceries and hardware supplies in the small town of LaGrange. Aleen, occupying the big house now, and without the mitigating presence of the Judge, could be difficult to bear, while Mary had a way of making Helen and Henrietta feel uncomfortable. Her braininess alienated Mary from Louisville's clubby female networks, and, dependent on Barry, she resented the attention he gave Henrietta. She also found Henrietta's desire for women embarrassing, and perhaps immoral. Mary's sister (who had married a local stockbroker and aspired to be a decorator) gave them a dinner party, but conversation was stilted even on safe topics. Privately Helen angrily pronounced Nat's taste far superior to their hostess's. Dull evenings and heavy drinking took their toll—Mary's sister, like many in the local society, was often drunk.

In March 1938, *Barry Cort*, the novel Helen had begun when she first moved to London in early 1935, and which she dedicated to "H.W.B.," was published pseudonymously. Its release coincided with a sickening sense of anxiety when a volume of Helen's diary, with its frank passages about her lover, went missing. The social tightrope she and Henrietta walked was not for the fainthearted. But in New York before Helen's departure for the tennis season in Europe, they reveled in a safer, more stimulating circle. Henrietta found a pair of musicians to entertain at a small party that included Hope Williams, Bea Lillie, and Dorothy Parker.

Nat would not be with Helen in England this time. Getting even a modest horse-and-farming operation up and running required close attention. Moreover, traveling together without the protection Pa and his household afforded was guaranteed to attract negative notice. It is possible that Henrietta saw need for the separation. Even if the relationship with Helen were completely satisfying, the tennis player's presence at Harmony Landing generated "tremendous curiosity," Mary recalled. Gossip held that Henrietta had settled in the next county over from Louisville because the city police department threatened to expose her misdoings if she resided in their district. Such rumor and speculation about Henrietta was annoying at best and more often mortifying. Exhaustion and anger about the pretense they were forced into may have led Henrietta to act recklessly. While riding the elevator up to a party at Louisville's Pendennis Club, Helen and Henrietta embraced long enough that the doors parted onto the ballroom to reveal a deep kiss. It was "little short of scandal." For Helen to spend "weeks and months" at Harmony Landing was undeniably detrimental to the Binghams' profile.

In London, Helen swayed queasily without her Bingham anchor. She called at 14 Prince's Gate, where Joseph P. Kennedy and his large family were installed, but the place felt chilly and inhospitable. (Freud and his family, aided by Ernest Jones, took refuge from Nazism in London that summer—Hitler's party denounced psychoanalysis as a "pornographic Jewish specialty.") Helen tried to focus on her task. She trained with her close friend "Big" Bill Tilden, whose prowess on the court no longer protected him from demeaning comments about his "fairy" ways—he was banned from teaching at Hollywood's tennis clubs when he moved there in 1939. When not playing, Helen wrote freelance articles, but she was depressed and empty without her "Kentucky love." "Everything," Helen wrote, "is an effort." She resented the horrible distance and enforced public silence about the person who mattered most to her; when asked about *Barry Cort*, Helen did not deny having authored the book. She and Henrietta were exposed; *The New York Times* pointed out that the dedicatee was "probably" the former American ambassador's daughter, with whom the athlete had been "close friends for a number of years."

When Jacobs reached Wimbledon's final round, a rematch against Helen Wills Moody and their first meeting on the singles court since 1935, Henrietta cabled from Louisville, PLEASE REMEMBER THE TITLE IS MORE YOURS THAN HERS. DEFEND IT DARLING ALL LOVE. The score in the first set was tied 4–4 when a prior strain in Jacobs's Achilles tendon ripped. Though the injury was obvious to the spectators, Wills took no notice. Jacobs stubbornly played through a second set despite pleadings from officials, losing 6–0 but proving she could take her beating outright.

Nat ordered flowers for Helen's stateroom, and made sure their reunion in New York was "heavenly" even if Jacobs had to hobble with a cane. They drove upstate to Lake Minnewaska so that Hono could recuperate before the U.S. Championships. Six weeks later, Jacobs entered the tournament as top seed but fell in the third round, a thudding disappointment as she had dominated Forest Hills throughout the decade. (That she played at all is astounding; recovery from a ruptured Achilles tendon normally requires six to nine months.) Pressure mounted for the thirty-year-old player whom Edie Callahan had nicknamed "Madam Queen" to retire or go professional.

That fall, Helen played a charity match for the Louisville Community Chest, but winter in Goshen was no longer an option. She went back to work on the novel she had begun in 1937 about her Revolutionary-era forebears, and arranged to lodge in Williamsburg, conduct research at the College of William and Mary, and absorb the colonial Tidewater atmosphere. At night, she wrote in a creaky eighteenth-century house at an antique desk Henrietta had given her. She found a new patron in Mrs. Archibald "Mollie" McCrae, who with her husband, a Pittsburgh industrialist, had restored the nearby 1750s mansion Carter's Grove. Mrs. McCrae (noted for her frequent tipsiness) and her daughter, Sally Eddy, were both recently widowed; they were also avid riders and supplied their famous visitor with mounts for the local foxhunt.

Henrietta and Helen spent their fifth Christmas together in 1938. Theirs was by far the most sustained of Henrietta's many liaisons, but it was fraying. Around Valentine's Day, they watched Helen's Labrador compete in the Westminster Kennel Club show at Madison Square Garden. What should have been a thrill—Guil won reserve champion for his division—was overshadowed by the "queer situation" surrounding Henrietta's old friend Jeannette Young. "Not too happy," Helen wrote in dismay. What exactly transpired is unclear, but it seems that Helen was jealous of Jeannette, for immediately after the show, Henrietta departed for Harmony Landing—the pretty Jeannette in tow. Helen

quickly sought other companionship. Upon returning to Williamsburg, Helen joined the household at Carter's Grove much as she had
the embassy five years before. Sally Eddy became "my S."

Sally accompanied Helen to Kentucky in the spring of 1939, ostensibly to help sift through documents held in a local archive. The trip
went better than Helen could have hoped. "Heavenly to see Nat," she
wrote, and their first ride was perfection. Louisville's best department
store dressed a window with Izod tennis clothing designed by Helen
and of course she was still in demand on the court. A young Louisville
attorney made a fourth one day, and joined the group at Harmony Landing for cocktails afterward. It was pitch-dark when he dropped his car
keys in the driveway. A staggering search turned nothing up, and
Henrietta offered him a bed for the night. He watched as Helen
and Henrietta climbed the graceful staircase and closed the door to
Henrietta's room.

This year, 1939, would be Helen's final season of international competitive tennis, and Henrietta was to join her in late June for Wimbledon. But as Helen trained in London, Henrietta's vague and limited
communications left her lover feeling "utterly in the dark as if I were a
stranger." Mina, Stephen Tomlin, Carrington, and John Houseman
would have understood. Nazi Germany absorbed one piece of Europe
after another. Fellow players talked of fleeing the continent, and even
in Long Crendon "alarm" was palpable. Then Nat sent word that she
would not make the journey. Mary had suffered a late-term stillbirth,
and as with the 1937 flood, duty to family trumped all else. "I can't bear
the way we are drifting apart," Helen wrote, "not in mind but—in body."
The tournament ended for Helen in the quarterfinal round. The women
reunited at Forest Hills, where Helen battled through the championship
match, buffeted by almost gale-force winds, until she was narrowly
beaten. At Harmony Landing they absorbed the Nazi-Soviet pact and
the German invasion of Poland. How prescient His Excellency had
been and how he would have raged had he been there. When she left for
Virginia, Helen said it was "like leaving home in which one has always
been contented and happy."

Whatever their earlier hopes, Helen Jacobs and Henrietta Bingham could not replicate the near-constant cohabitation they had enjoyed from late 1934 through the end of 1937. For Henrietta, having multiple guests to stay with her, men as well as women, supplied plausible deniability about her sexuality while addressing her need for companionship—and pleasure. In Williamsburg in late 1939, Helen commented that Sally was the "most beautiful rider I ever saw, except Nat," but she twisted uncomfortably, accusing "bloody" Jeannette, once more in residence at Harmony Landing, of preventing Henrietta from writing to her.

Nat's humor and the women's affection could still overcome these hurts. Years later, Helen culled her papers carefully, destroying all but one of Henrietta's letters and redacting diary passages. Their love for each other and life together permeates her little locked journals. The single letter was simply too funny to throw out, too emblematic of the woman she adored. In it, Henrietta assumed the persona of her black Labrador Melania. Melania and Helen's champion cream Labrador produced one litter together, but like her mistress, Melania had other mates. A neighbor's black dog jumped the fence to consort with her, with predictably mixed results:

> Dear Madam, I have tried to write sooner but somehow or other didn't feel quite up to it.
>
> The fact of the matter is, Madam, that I woke-up one morning and found nine black sausages in my basket. Was I surprised!
>
> You see I didn't really like that black gentleman who used to call on me at the Farm (what a climber he was, though—up and over the fence in a jiffy) and as you know I have always had a soft spot for Guil. But there you are—such is life.
>
> Speaking of Guil, he isn't speaking to me but I've told him the whole thing was just as much his fault as mine. You know Madam how really affectionate I was to him on several occasions.
>
> That black-haired blue-eyed Kentucky bitch upstairs says she is going to drown the sausages. Well, Madam, I implore you to let me keep two or three for a little while—because unlike some people I know my Tits are not exactly Tiny.

Helen spent the Christmas holiday in Williamsburg with Sally. Henrietta came right afterward to hunt on her new horse, Bloomsbury, to celebrate the arrival of 1940, and to toast her thirty-ninth birthday on January 3. Miss Henrietta, as everyone back home called her, brought a carful of wrapped packages, and Robert, adrift after the breakup of his marriage, joined them from New York. Helen led the siblings on long rides over the land she'd come to know almost as well as Buckinghamshire. Several weeks into the visit, however, Robert—or maybe his drinking—became intolerable and Nat drove him back to the city. A few nights later, Helen walked into her house through a broken-in back door and found Henrietta, smashed on booze. "Could beat her for her condition," Helen lamented. "Want that elegance back."

Henrietta's dependence on alcohol must have been escalating dangerously, because Helen took it upon herself to write to Barry about the incident even though she knew Nat would despise being exposed this way.

Helen visited Kentucky in February, where Aleen was organizing a local chapter of the relief organization Bundles for Britain. She was there again in April, and one cold, bright Saturday at the Keeneland racecourse, they cashed winning tickets on Henrietta's filly Crumpet. Another of Nat's Thoroughbreds, named Blue Harmony, seemed equally promising. But a preponderance of fillies at Harmony Landing presented a challenge. "Fillies are all right for racing," she told a reporter, "but they don't bring much at Saratoga when compared to the colts." War talk was getting hotter all the time (Barry funded Herbert Agar's move to New York to help guide the interventionist Century Group) and in the locker room after the Forest Hills final, Alice Marble, who had just beaten Helen, asked her, "What's left for us now, with international tennis on hold?" "I'm going to hang it up for a while," Helen replied. "I'm going to join the service, if they'll have me, and do whatever I can to help."

It was an impulse countless Americans shared in 1940 and 1941. Barry enlisted in the Navy. With Henrietta's family, friends, and the nation distracted by international events, Harmony Landing seemed to stretch farther from the world. Helen worried constantly about Nat.

She had lost weight and was fighting sustained periods of depression. Pineland, the quail plantation in Georgia, fetched a bottom-feeder's price and war would only harm her equine investments. Living openly with Helen (or any female lover) in Goshen was a lost dream. More and more, with a mixture of shame and defiance, Nat sought comfort in the bottle, to the point of blacking out. As F. Scott Fitzgerald explained, "There was a kindliness about intoxication, that indescribable gloss and glamour it gave, like the memories of ephemeral and faded evenings." Helen left Kentucky with an uneasy mind, and afterward wrote affectingly to Nat of her devotion.

> I haven't forgotten your promise to go to the doctor for me, and give me a report. I don't like to be tiresome about it, but I want to put my own mind at rest. Such wonderful days are ahead for all of us, beloved, if you will only feel well again . . . Horses from Harmony Landing would be world famous, flowers and Labradors from chez Hono likewise, and we will grow mellow together. We will throw historic, brilliant parties, and pool our brains to think up all sorts of fun, and I will be your farm manager when you need one, and put you to sleep when you need that, too. We can be happy and proud together, darling.
>
> But even if you don't like this plan, I am beside you, behind you, and on top of you (if you want. Naughty Hono!) You can do and say nothing to stop the constant flow of deep and growing love that goes out to you from my heart every time I look at you.

In this one letter from a female lover that Henrietta kept, Helen conceded that they could not share Harmony Landing or any home, but her pledge transcended whatever impediments or furies plagued them, and Helen underscored her "constant love and adoration," no matter what other people thought.

Henrietta went north in the summer of 1941 to market five yearlings at Saratoga (Louis B. Mayer bought one) and watch Helen play at Forest Hills. Barry, Mary, and the children were about to move to Washington, D.C., for his job in naval public relations, and he asked Henrietta to join them for a week at the beach in Chatham, on Cape

Cod. Helen did not receive an invitation—such offers never came to them as a couple. In Chatham, Henrietta suffered a breakdown. What precipitated the event or even how severe it was is not recorded, and with Helen then keeping her diary only irregularly, shedding light on Henrietta's darkening life becomes more difficult. Whatever happened, it upset Mary terribly, and Barry felt compelled to take his sister to a Massachusetts sanatorium.

The "Chatham" cycle, consisting of drinking, obstreperousness, and miserable remorse, repeated, with variations, throughout the war years. It was a time during which Henrietta grew estranged from a number of the key figures in her life and felt sidelined, rejected, and abandoned, unsure what contribution she had to make to the world. Barry left to study the British civilian defense system and Mary edited *The Courier-Jounal*'s book page and sat in for him on the newspaper's editorial board. Henrietta was patriotically growing "marihuana," as her Department of Agriculture permit called hemp, to help fill the Navy's demand for rope when hostilities interrupted imports. Helen spent 1942's summer months in Kentucky lecturing for the American Women's Voluntary Services, but she took extra measures to distance herself from Henrietta to maintain appearances. She rented a nearby farmhouse and looked for a place of her own to buy. But Nat did not come around very much, and it all seemed "v. strange and lonely" in Kentucky, Helen wrote. Henrietta was "unwell" (likely a euphemism for intoxicated) for Helen's first party, and an out-and-out argument concluded with Helen wringing "a great moral triumph" from her lover. Henrietta may have promised to stop drinking. But the gloom persisted. Jeannette Young arrived for a stay and fabricated a poster with a caricature of Harmony Landing's mistress looking down at the mouth. The heading read, "No Fun on the Farm."

Adding to Helen's miseries in Kentucky, her well water made her seriously ill. She took refuge at Harmony Landing, and Sally Eddy came from Williamsburg to nurse her. Wartime gas rations and other limits on transport made shipping yearlings to Saratoga impossible, but Henrietta got so stir-crazy she left for Lake Tahoe, where her brother Robert was living. Back in Virginia that fall, Helen enrolled at William and Mary to strengthen her application to the Navy's new "Women Accepted for Volunteer Emergency Service" (WAVES). Henrietta registered for a Navy assignment, as well, but Mary was dubious: "I'm afraid the WAVES is much too strenuous for H. even if she is offered a job—and so far nothing has come through for her." Before the fall semester was out, Helen was posted to Navy Public Relations and sent to basic training. Meanwhile, Henrietta grew thinner and Edie Callahan wrote to Barry in London, concerned whether her old friend was able "to live by herself on the farm here."

It was a valid question. In the fall of 1942, Mary was left to manage another alcoholic "eclipse" and hired a professional nurse to ensure that Nat ate. Jeannette stepped forward and took Henrietta to stay with her in Chicago. There she found a physician she trusted who identified a thyroid problem, and warned that alcohol combined with poor nutrition was affecting her liver. She was to follow a strict diet, cut out all hard liquor, and drink no more than one or two bottles of beer each day. This regime the family called (sometimes affectionately, sometimes sardonically) Henrietta's "beer wagon."

Mary doubted such organic explanations for Henrietta's failure of self-control and dismissed her sister-in-law's "vague and emotional shibboleths of psycho-analysis." Possibly Henrietta was in consultation with Jones, though no letters from the war era remain in his papers. Still, Nat stuck to her new regime and Mary said "that odd and sad feeling of banishment from her actual self which has haunted all of us since Chatham" lifted.

Henrietta sent Barry wartime care packages loaded with caviar and fruitcake from Marshall Field's, and Mary and the children cut their Christmas tree at Harmony Landing, the boys going at the trunk with their little hatchets. Nat selected for her nephew Worth an edition of *Huckleberry Finn* with Norman Rockwell illustrations. A handwritten note at the head of one chapter explained, "this is one of my favorite books written pby[*sic*] M.T., and one of the passages I like most is this: Huck Fin[*sic*], a boy of about 12, and a slave named Jim have run away down the river on a raft. Huck, dressed as a girl, has gone asore [*sic*]." Cross-dressing, interracial escapades, and humor—it was a perfect

Henrietta in American Women's Voluntary Services uniform, 1943

concoction to share with her nephew—and her note, composed without the care she applied in her letters to adults, vividly conveys her handicap in written communications.

Barry's gift to her, a Raoul Dufy print she had once admired, moved Henrietta nearly to tears.

Several months later, dressed in a belted American Women's Voluntary Services uniform and hat, her nails neatly manicured, Miss Henrietta Bingham went before a parent-teacher assembly to drum up land and volunteer agricultural labor for the United States Crop Corps, a national program that eventually yielded millions of tons of produce, and used women and teenagers to help farmers harvest and process the 1943 crops. Women were great "assets" in war production, she told her listeners, and in the rural cog of that machine, they could lead the now), her face shining and flushed from the wind and the sun (and from the bourbon in the long silver flask that I remembered from Prohibition days) and the violet-blue eyes the memory of which . . . used to turn my bowels to water and send me into orgasms of uncontrollable, delicious weeping.

We slept together, and made love rather predictably in a motel in western Kansas, where we spent our first night. The second night, somewhere in Oklahoma, after eleven hours of driving, we slept together without making love.

Watching her steer up into the Rockies, "her slender strong hands on the wheel and the way her lips parted in a half-smile when she was going over eighty," he called Henrietta "a ghost," but one who produced "a spasm of longing so sudden and so intense that it left me quite dizzy."

Henrietta plowing by mule, Harmony Landing

charge. "It would be a national disaster to let this potential food supply rot in the fields," she warned. "It is clearly up to you and me."

Henrietta wrote to Barry that it made her "deeply grateful to find myself useful." Some days, riding the plow over Harmony Landing's rolling hills felt exactly right. Other days, she bleakly monitored the price of horsemeat, unsure she should continue to keep her mares. The hemp crop took up fields she needed for corn to feed the hogs—what should she do? Her volunteer work handling "thousands of frantic women who think they are going to starve to death come summer if they don't have a garden" was clearly "unenviable." Barry wrote encouragingly of her staying "on the wagon with such determination . . . this time" and of hearing from third parties about the "civic-minded Henrietta Bingham."

Still, she felt trapped. Ivor Churchill had written in 1937 upon the Judge's death that she had "qualities that are intended for greatness. They will serve you as you pass through this deep valley of the shadow." Now, if she were lucky, she might be sent to observe farming programs around the country—not the role she imagined for herself in the war, or in life. "I may get into politics yet," she told Barry ruefully.

These were long nights alone at the farm. She couldn't help comparing herself with her younger brother, her sister-in-law, and especially her lovers. Mina Curtiss produced a radio program based on soldiers' letters home. Helen spent the summer of 1943 in Navy training at Smith College—a highly stimulating nearly all-female environment replete with purpose and the possibility of romance. She hoped to ship overseas, but first she was asked by her superiors in the Navy to write a novel. They gave her three months.

By Your Leave, Sir, a wartime pulp romance aimed at recruiting women for service and published by Dodd, Mead & Co., went through several printings and drew on the lives of Henrietta, Helen, and Mina. On a hemp farm overlooking the Ohio River, Becky McLeod mourns her fiancé's death in a London air raid. Becky enlists, leaving behind her mother and new suitor. An intimate relationship develops with a roommate during training in Northampton, and Becky is never more joyful than in her company—a theme Helen left undeveloped. An androgynously named local intellectual, Alex Mecklin, writes a syndicated column about the war from her picturesque New England farm and receives Becky in her vaulting, book-lined library, a dead ringer for Mina's barn room at Chapelbrook. The women are at odds; Alex disapproves of females in the armed forces, whereas the chance to "step into the unfamiliar ways of a man's life" thrills the young Kentuckian. Alex experiences a change of heart when she witnesses Eleanor Roosevelt reviewing the graduating trainees, but she reminds Becky that military life, no matter how rewarding, must not get in the way of marriage.

While Lieutenant Jacobs breathlessly composed her story, Henrietta fixed suppers for Edie Callahan, who had lost her cook, and stayed up late reminiscing about Harlem and Greenwich Village. Helen said she missed her: "You can imagine what I would give for a look at the country and a horseback ride and broo in the boo," their term for a roll in the hay. But Helen was preoccupied and Henrietta was stuck. Some weekends Henrietta hosted her nephews, Worth and Barry Jr., who rode horseback, fired her shotgun, and gorged on farm cream and butter. Before bed, she taught them card games and scandalized them by explaining the mighty hard time she had finding workers who wouldn't infect the milk cows with venereal disease. To her brother in London she wrote, "I would give anything to see what it is all like now."

One spring moonlit evening in 1943 Henrietta left her cook by the kitchen radio and strode out to the sheep pens with a pail of warmed milk. The ram had done his duty that winter and she had delivered two score lambs. Some needed bottle feeding. The animals knew her and scarcely rustled in the straw. "An old rooster dozes on a post," she wrote, describing the scene to Barry. "The cats lie curled up in the straw, the mules carry on conversations in odd tones as the lambs play follow the leader on and off the fat backs of the ewes." Then "the most harrowing screams . . . weird, terrifying wails that might have come from the dungeon at Guthrie [Castle]" broke the serenity at Harmony Landing. The barn cat had a challenger. Henrietta sank to the ground as the toms "fought all over," even to the rooftop. It was an apt metaphor for the battles that could erupt in her.

John Houseman reappeared in her life. Although Voice of America recruited him to develop overseas programming, he was ultimately turned down because of his foreign birth. Houseman had deserted Hollywood after his feud with Orson Welles, but he decided to go back, bringing with him his close friend and collaborator, the composer Virgil Thomson. Henrietta invited them to stop and visit on the way out west. She could use the help.

"The haying season was on," Jack wrote. "Virgil and I pitched in the mornings and after lunch I rode around the farm with He while she proudly showed me the colts she had bred. We a bourbon in the evening"—the beer wagon being abandone temporarily. Henrietta was the perfect hostess, exuding and the glamour and the warmth" she always had. She ev an evening of gospel music by the local Apollo Quartet fo Thomson especially liked "John the Revelator." As the depart, Henrietta unexpectedly volunteered to go alo

And here we were, sixteen years later, with the top wind in our faces as we took turns driving thro heat of the endless wheat-fields of western woman in her early forties with a strong, grace

17

THE NOT AT ALL SOLVED
PROBLEMS OF HENRIETTA

*O*n Henrietta's return from this interlude in the summer of 1943, she looked "awfully pretty and well." And yet the 1940s burned almost unbearable memories of Henrietta into those who loved her. Time and again, Henrietta lost her compass, and her irresistibility slid away. Each time she pieced herself together again she experienced humiliating remorse for losing control, and close by was the fear that another eclipse was closing upon her.

Like countless others living in the middle decades of the twentieth century with nonconforming sexualities, Henrietta used alcohol and drugs to numb herself against the judgments and disapproval. Henrietta's sexuality was largely seen as the cause of her addictions—for the more than a dozen breakdowns and at least half a dozen hospitalizations between 1940 and the late 1960s. The prejudices even of well-meaning physicians who cared for Henrietta compounded her difficulties, often insulting and frightening her, and confusing her family, as well.

Nat was far from well after her time with Houseman. He had slept with her, but Jack was not in love. Indeed, perhaps for the first time she could remember, nobody was in love with her. Her father's death had left her bereft of that backstop as well. Within days she had stopped eating and drank herself into another weeklong breakdown. Mary went around the house securing wine closets and the like, only to have her sister-in-law order the locks sawed off. Mary summoned the chair of the University of Louisville department of psychiatry, who ordered intravenous feeding, round-the-clock nurses, and heavy sedation. Dr. Spafford Ackerly also suggested a newly developed therapy using electrical shocks to induce convulsions. Nat adamantly opposed this idea, which struck Mary as pure mulishness.

Henrietta recovered quickly. Her financial worries were mounting, however, and her breakdowns and medical bills only added to them. She hosted Thanksgiving dinner, appeared in style at the fall Breeder's Luncheon at Churchill Downs, and escorted Worth and Barry Jr., aged ten and eleven, to a high school homecoming football game. Her brother had a short leave from the Navy for Christmas of 1943, and though Dr. Ackerly advised against travel, Henrietta was bent on celebrating her birthday and seeing him off in New York. Staying in Louisville would be too lonesome. Barry's last night in the States ended disastrously. It was as if the cats were loose in the barn again, and Mary, furious at having her leave-taking spoiled, had to beg Barry's forgiveness for the "ugly and cruel things I said about Nat." He urged tolerance. He and Mary were so lucky, he reminded her. Nat did not have their good fortune in marriage and their clear purpose in life. "It chills and disturbs me to think that I can't convert even a small part of my happiness into some form of benison for people close to me who need it as badly as poor Nat does." But having witnessed his sister's descent, he promised Mary he would write to her from London with "as strong a plea as I knew how to make for the electric therapy."

Barry still carried the deep memory of running to Henrietta for protection, love, and understanding. They shared family secrets and could finish each other's sentences; Henrietta made him laugh like no one else could and sotto voce "naughtiness" peppered their conversations. Barry's daughter, Sallie, recalled, "Mother couldn't pry them apart."

But in the six years since the Judge died, Barry had "taken hold" and she had not. Leaving aside the tension her lesbian relationships caused, the war exposed a chasm between the siblings with respect to community influence and stability. He fathered four children, deployed the paper's political leverage, sat on boards, led public fund-raising crusades, involved himself in progressive racial reform groups, and won honors such as Kentucky "Man of the Year." Mary took on board work, spoke before the Women's Action Committee, and spent her days at *The Courier-Journal.* In contrast, Henrietta managed an expensive and unwieldy farm, a place that had once felt like a dream but increasingly conjured the terror of abandonment she had carried since childhood. She still needed approval, especially male approval, and in some measure Henrietta transferred this need from her father to Barry. Meanwhile her hedonistic impulses persisted—running out of control especially when that approval was threatened or withdrawn. While Barry was home, he smoothed things over in his special way, but he no longer needed her as he had. But Mary, insecure about Henrietta's bond with her husband, exercised her primacy over "Miss Nat" in a thousand small ways.

That fall, Dr. Ackerly prescribed Henrietta the barbiturate secobarbital (or Seconal) to assist with her withdrawal from alcohol, but probably also to ease her anxiety and depression. These were the "dolls" made famous in the 1966 novel *Valley of the Dolls.* Few in the 1940s grasped their addictive properties or the danger of psychotic behavior when the patient stopped taking them, but it was well known that combined with alcohol they could cause death. Barry's early 1944 letter, conveying his belief that his sister's brain was malfunctioning and urging her to undergo electroshock therapy, was followed by a severe overdose—possibly an attempt on her own life.

When she at last replied to Barry months later, Nat was with Jeannette Young in her parents' Lake Shore Drive apartment, looking down on the city spread below.

> I had given the electric therapy treatment deep consideration even before your letter arrived and I have thought a great deal about it since. It might help and god knows I would do anything to avoid these cycles

of depression and their serious consequences to my personal relationships, aside from the many other angles which I am very conscious of.

However it doesn't seem sensible to take the treatment for a condition at a time when it doesn't exist. Unfortunately it doesn't act as an
insulation against future troubles.

Naturally I can't guarantee that the periods of depression won't
return at intervals, perhaps for some years to come, but I do believe that
with more self control and foresight I can avoid the recourse to alcohol
which I realize, only too well, prolongs the agony.

Please I beg of you dear not to worry and don't imagine that I am
constantly battling temptations which I am not, or that I take the situation too lightly because I don't . . . So much love darling and please
write when you have a minute. Devotedly, Nat

The war dragged on but there were bright spots and tenderness. A fiery
colt from Harmony Landing Farm began winning in Chicago. She collected purse money and made good on some substantial wagers, returning to Louisville in triumph. She also helped care for her beloved elderly
aunt Sadie, who still lived alongside the Bingham School barracks, then
falling to ruin beneath the kudzu vines. Henrietta monitored Sadie's
tippling and lent a hand where she could. One summer, Mary asked
her to take the boys with her to Asheville, but she kept them home
when Jeannette Young joined the party. It was the kind of small blow
Henrietta suffered countless times.

Barry's return from the Pacific in late 1945 ended the wartime
correspondence with Mary and with his sister, and Henrietta's subsequent movements and activities blur and fade in the absence of letters.
No diaries or memoirs of her later lovers have been found, and oral
history, a smattering of photographs and financial reports, along with a
series of agonizing letters Barry exchanged with various physicians, are
all that remains. Lacunae open up, sometimes covering years at a time.
A clutch of farm-related documents, clippings, and track photographs
tell of her breeding a mare to Count Fleet, 1943's Triple Crown champion, and of Snow Boots (a colt she bred) breaking a speed record at the
Seabiscuit Handicap at Santa Anita. Given that she actively operated

Harmony Landing during a highly turbulent decade (economically and personally), Henrietta should have taken pride in some of her accomplishments. But she dipped again and again into her dwindling brokerage account to keep it all going, and life at Harmony Landing—or Louisville—had proven detrimental to her well-being. Henrietta could still make others happy for short periods (Mary marveled at the way she hosted at Harmony Landing, creating an air of welcome and charm as well as extraordinary "well-ordered and excellent" "cordon bleu" dinners), yet she may not have been able to bring herself to fully commit to a life rooted in Kentucky with its conservatism and the constant reminder of the position and influence that might have been hers. Fantasies of a better place, a place where she was appreciated more and could love freely, hummed in her head—irritating, mesmerizing, and inescapable. In 1945, she considered renting out the place.

Henrietta once told Herbert Agar she "meant not to allow the war to interfere with her life in any small particular," but of course it had. Once it ended, everyone seemed to be moving, reconnecting. Herbert, who had served in London in press relations and as the wartime American ambassador's special assistant, deserted Eleanor for the daughter of the English architect Edwin Lutyens. Eleanor never recovered. She died four years later, at fifty-one, her vision cruelly impaired by anorexia nervosa. Eleanor's unpublished poems, photograph albums (with pictures of Henrietta intact), and first editions by the likes of Edna St. Vincent Millay were given to the library at Smith College.

On advice from Edmund Wilson, Mina gave up teaching and began translating the letters of Marcel Proust. In 1946, she wrote to David Garnett for help cutting through the red tape of postwar travel restrictions. She wanted to visit England and then spend a season in France interviewing Proust's surviving correspondents. (During the war, Garnett managed to scandalize the remnants of Bloomsbury by marrying Angelica Bell, the daughter of Vanessa Bell and Duncan Grant. She was more than a quarter century his junior.) Mina hoped David would exert himself on her behalf "when I tell you that your darling Henrietta reappeared in my life after seven years of silence and that I took a great deal of trouble for her." But Mina liked taking trou-

Mina Curtiss, Chapelbrook, 1950s

ble for Henrietta; specifically, she referred her to her former analyst and the president of the American Psychoanalytic Association, Bertram Lewin.

Mina's reappearance among the Bloomsberries naturally brought Henrietta to their minds, and in 1950, Clive Bell asked her how to respond to questions. "When I talk of you to your English friends, they often enquire, at the end of our conversation, after Henrietta. Am I justified in saying that she is a Dipsomaniac?" Mina rose hotly to Henrietta's defense. "I don't think Henrietta should be labeled anything so ugly as the word 'dipsomaniac.' I would say that in the most tragic and painful fashion she, from time to time, drinks herself into a stupor. In between times she is as delightful and charming as ever."

In the midst of consultations with Dr. Lewin, bouts with alcohol, and interludes of sobriety, Henrietta broke down again in 1948, and the University of Louisville's Dr. Ackerly proposed a frontal lobotomy. Henrietta fought him on this and Barry arranged for a member of Harvard University's psychiatry department to examine her in Louisville and give a second opinion. Dr. Harry Solomon noted her periods of despair, her decade of psychotherapy with Ernest Jones, and six months' treatment more recently in New York. Psychotherapy appeared to have had little impact on her depression and addiction. He recommended that before resorting to surgery she attend Alcoholics Anonymous and spend three or four months in a sanatorium. Nothing about this was satisfactory to Henrietta, who went straight to see Solomon in Boston. He then recast his recommendation—she should continue her work with Lewin and avoid alcohol altogether. Barry felt helpless, unable to force Nat into treatment or even to get clear medical advice. His frustration had already made him turn his attention to the broader issue of mental illness. "I can think of no group," he told Mary, "whose unhappiness so deeply stirs me as those who have some form of mental illness, and the slightest contribution toward relieving their spiritual agony seems to me to offer rich rewards."

In 1950, when her last yearlings were born, Henrietta put Harmony Landing on the market and moved her English furniture to a handsome midtown Manhattan building on Fifth Avenue. Robert was in New York, too, and so was Mina and some of her old friends from the theater world. And, as important, she could access her analyst, Dr. Lewin.

Henrietta found a new partner. Coiffed and slender, with widespaced brown eyes and perfect lipstick, Dorothie Bigelow Holland was older, almost sixty. A lifetime New Yorker, she starred in Cole Porter's first Broadway musical and with Mae West in a successful Arthur Hammerstein play with a "lavender tinge." She performed with Humphrey Bogart for Guthrie McClintic and in a musical revue with Bea Lillie. Her final stage success had come twenty years before in the New York premier of Ivor Novello's comedy *The Truth Game*. How her marriage ended is not known. Others described Dorothie as timid, and perhaps some emotional difficulty prompted her retirement from the boards, but she found other ways to support herself. In the 1930s, she copyrighted two plays and patented her own lingerie strap holder; she later offered private piano and voice lessons. Dorothie knew everyone in the gay theater world, a community that made New York feel safer for Henrietta. "It was certainly a lesbian relationship," Mary recalled, grateful her sister-in-law was out of Kentucky and had "somebody that she loved and would more or less take care of her." Mina (never short on judgments) couldn't bear Dorothie. She called her Nat's "gaga companion." During the 1940s, '50s, and '60s, Mina's fiercely protective instincts compelled her to conceal or seek to repair loved ones' homosexuality. She worried about letters referring to Proust's homoerotic interests and refused to acknowledge the same-sex partners of her closest friends or of her flamboyant brother, Lincoln. Mina tried repeatedly to get Lincoln, a central figure of New York City's mid-century gay community of artists and dancers and writers, into psychoanalysis.

DOROTHIE BIGELOW

Henrietta's glass painting of Dorothie Bigelow Holland

In 1949, Phillips Exeter Academy expelled Henrietta's seventeen-year-old nephew, Worth. His new school, Lawrenceville, was near enough to the city that he spent some weekends with Henrietta. Worth's rebellious streak showed up during the war, when he and his brother invited the son of Melcombe's groundskeeper to swim in their Olympic-size pool, a breach of racial etiquette that prompted Mary to drain the pool. Henrietta had always liked Worth and he was "very, very fond" of her. She shared his outrage at racial injustice, and one Sunday after he returned to his dormitory Worth wrote his "wonderful aunt" about a "good, heart-rending short story" he had just read. "The Vigilante" described "the lynching of a negro," Worth explained. "Steinbeck has written another masterpiece of understatement, putting himself wholly in the place of a member of the mob. Tragic! We must add it to our collection."

The South remained home to Helen Jacobs, who continued in the Naval Reserves, posted to the Dahlgren, Virginia, proving ground. She wrote steadily, publishing juvenile novels and pulp fiction largely centered on the tennis world, and sent Henrietta a copy of *Gallery of Champions*, her 1949 compendium of essays on female tennis greats, with a fond inscription. Henrietta had heard her talk about each of these players, but it was painful to think too much about their past, and Madam Queen kept her distance. Helen reached the rank of Navy commander, but left the service in the early 1950s, ostensibly because of financial cutbacks, although she may have been purged along with thousands of suspected homosexual military personnel during the anti-Communist hysteria provoked by Senator Joseph McCarthy.

Peggy Lehmann's acting career was compromised by her leftist politics and her unusually open bisexuality. However, 1960s and '70s British television provided roles that engaged her comic abilities and milked her eccentric profile, and fans of the original *Dr. Who* TV series celebrate her campy (and suggestively lesbian) portrayal of Professor Amelia Rumford.

Barry saw Henrietta whenever he was in New York, and she filled a table at a fund-raising dinner in the city for Adlai Stevenson's 1952 presidential campaign, for which Barry was a key advisor. Henrietta invited the actress Tallulah Bankhead, who was then applying her bitchy wit to radio and television programs. Another guest of Henrietta's recalled that Bankhead took him to be Henrietta's "boyfriend" and, enjoying the chance to make mischief, Tallulah grabbed Nat's pearl necklace. "You promised these to me. When we were in England, you promised these pearls to me." Henrietta laid her violet-blue gaze upon the star she'd known for more than three decades. "I never did anything of the sort," she replied unsmilingly. Stevenson endured politically damaging slurs about his sexuality as well as his liberal politics and Henrietta had to be careful to avoid public insinuations, even when made in fun.

During the time Henrietta was in New York, Mina and the French poet Saint-John Perse enjoyed a long and satisfying affair, and she described him as the third great love of her life—after Henrietta and Harry. For John Houseman, who endured his share of "red trouble" when McCarthyism raced through Hollywood, a passionate liaison with the screen actress Joan Fontaine was followed by marriage to a former model with a French title, who had a job in Philip Johnson's architectural office. She "made me think of Henrietta Bingham," he wrote, "whom she in no way resembled," but they shared a "curiously seductive confusion of laughter and melancholy, inertia and liveliness." Hot war in Korea, Cold War with the Soviets, and "lavender" raids at home led Jack, in a letter to Mina, to decry "this world of fear and horror and violence." In 1953, he came east to stage Shakespeare's tragedy *Coriolanus* and Mina brought Henrietta to the dress rehearsal. It was the last time he saw her, but for both Jack and Mina she was the standard by which all later loves were measured.

The move to Manhattan and the relationship with Dorothie could not fully drive away Henrietta's depression, which, combined with prescription drug abuse and alcohol addiction, at times became perilous. Money problems and interactions with Barry, who seemed to inadvertently activate Henrietta's shame and anger, were triggers. In 1950, the *New York*

Times real estate page had noted that "Miss Henrietta Bingham has sold Hominy Landing Farm," the misspelling catching her low drawl. The buyer later flipped the property (making a mint in the process and exposing her lack of savvy). Plans were announced for a new country club bounded by luxury house lots—it was another embarrassment. Nat grew sleepless and agitated, ran a high fever, and medicated herself into the "acute toxic psychosis" that landed her in the hospital. She escaped to her apartment, but two days later Dorothie had to call the doctor. It took four hours to sedate and strap her into a straitjacket and return Henrietta to the private clinic opposite Gracie Mansion. She fought her doctors at every step. Dr. William Hall Lewis explained to Barry that

> for the first time, the occasion was opportune for the use of measures which she would not have accepted voluntarily. By sedation, intravenous and other measures, and especially electroshock therapy, we were able to get benefits which were most essential and also promised a more balanced temperament for some time in the future. It was a difficult and arduous process because her reactions necessitated continuous sedation with intravenous and [forced] tube feedings until response to the therapy could be obtained.

When Barry arrived, Henrietta threatened to "go out the window" if he didn't get her released. His sister's condition remained so volatile that Barry took steps toward her involuntary commitment in a state institution.

The possibility of a commitment alarmed Dorothie. She contacted the only person she could think of who might rescue Henrietta. Mina, hearing of the electroshock therapy and commitment papers, announced to David Garnett, "I am goddamned if I'm going to let Barry lock her up just so that he isn't financially or morally responsible for her when there is no reason in the world, rich as he is, that she shouldn't at least have what peace of mind she can." Mina never could resist a crisis. However, by the time she reached Henrietta she had somehow gotten home and was under the care of nurses.

In explaining his patient's condition Dr. Lewis cited the traumatic

loss of her mother, "social activities in London" (a euphemism for homosexual relationships), and the fact that she had never married. He did
not mention depression and anxiety, which had gripped her since adoles-
cence but overtook her during the war. Homophobia and its effects
were wholly outside his analysis. Nor was he at all concerned about
the sedatives and amphetamines she took. Lewis suggested that con-
cussions sustained from riding accidents in the 1920s and '30s left
her brain susceptible to psychosis, which a viral or bacterial infection
or alcohol consumption might set off. Encephalographic tests could reveal an organic root for her distress, he said, and Barry clung to the
hope that a partial frontal lobotomy, which *Time* called a "tension-
relieving brain operation," could help his sister. Some forty thousand
of these surgeries were performed in the United States, often on schiz-
ophrenic patients in mental hospitals but also on noninstitutionalized
individuals diagnosed with depression and other vague challenges.
A milder temperament was the aim, but the procedure sometimes left
its subjects severely impaired. Henrietta refused to consider the tests,
fearful of what they might lead to and angry, perhaps, that the com-
plexities of her life were being reduced to long-ago bumps on the head.
She harbored a "haunting fear," Lewis noted, "of temporary and permanent confinement."

Being single marked Henrietta as outside social norms, and marriage
was a remedy she had long contemplated yet never tried. Her attraction to
women clearly would not desert her, but men were appealing, too, and
a wedding ring offered protection to generations of gay men, lesbians,
and bisexuals, especially in the 1950s as Communist subversion and
sexual "perversion" twined together in the public mind. Dr. Lewis had
just made his observations about Henrietta's single state when she traveled to Asheville to visit the ancient Aunt Sadie. While there, Henrietta,
fifty-three, met and became engaged to a dark-haired man with a
genial face named Benjamin Franklin McKenzie.

Henrietta had long been a pincushion for her nephews' unthinking
barbs about old maids. In the late 1930s and early 1940s they liked to
sing a folk song called "Henrietta's Wedding."

You've been invited to Henrietta's wedding
No one knows who her husband can be—who can it be?
They say she's started to buy all the bedding
But the husband's a deep mystery.

McKenzie was, and is, a mystery. Mary Bingham called him a "barkeep."
Mina referred to him as a "head-waiter" at a nightclub. Henrietta's
niece talked of "whatever his name was," and one nephew believed the
man had worked as a fishmonger on Fulton Street. More than ten years
her junior, McKenzie had two marriages behind him and children to
support. Barry flew to Asheville to deliver the kind of private talk
wealthy families give potential in-laws about their black sheep: Henrietta's finances were not at all as they might appear, he warned; moreover
she had been very ill. Mina was equally appalled by the engagement, and
in a boiling letter to David Garnett, lamented that Puppin was "gushing
like a school girl"; the man, Mina said, was an absolute dolt. They wed
in June 1954 at a New York courthouse just weeks after first meeting.

Newlyweds Benjamin Franklin McKenzie and Henrietta, with Barry,
Dorothie, and an unidentified guest, 1954

Mina arrived home in a state of despair from the reception that
Katharine Cornell and Guthrie McClintic hosted for the couple. She
dialed Jack Houseman in Malibu, longing to speak to someone who
could understand. He was out, but she left word. Jack didn't call back
and afterward wrote to apologize.

> Dearest Minnie, It was very ugly of me not to call you that week-end.
> But, believe me, I had not the slightest desire to hear of Henrietta's
> nuptials and I seriously doubt it would have done you any good to
> repeat their horror to me over the long-distance telephone . . . She
> belongs, for us both, to the "*temps perdu*," where she plays a warm and
> moving and very special part: we share a little guilt about her—in
> that we allowed her to bewitch us with her deepest weakness no less
> than with her very real and positive charm. We share, too, the sick-
> ening regret (directly related to the fascination in which she held us)
> that she should have fallen from the exaggerated [*sic*] hopes we held for
> her to her present level of banal and pitiful imbecility.
>
> And that's that . . . and there is nothing we can do to repair or
> atone for that particular piece of our experience.

The announcement in *The Courier-Journal* gave no details—the
couple might as well have eloped. McKenzie's name appeared without
family, job, or connection. Nor were they Mr. and Mrs. McKenzie; it
was daring indeed for Henrietta to keep her name. At a Louisville
party where the newlyweds were spotted, another guest surmised that
the Bingham black sheep had "married a gay guy." By Labor Day it was
over. McKenzie departed for Florida (she said he took one of her cars)
and Henrietta was left holding an expensive white clapboard house she'd
purchased in Fairfield, Connecticut, and a harborside restaurant Frank
was planning to operate. The divorce, on grounds of desertion, went
through four years later.

In August 1955, Henrietta landed in England for the first time since
she and Helen left in 1937 aboard the *Aquitania*. When David Garnett
heard that voice on his telephone, "unchanged, with warmth and affec-

tion," he felt as if he had opened "a door onto a scene in 1923." David's literary career had continued to flourish, and America and its people still fascinated him. He was at work on his second volume of recollections, which opened after World War I, and seeing Henrietta was, in a sense, research. David hoped she would come to Hilton Hall and meet his wife and daughters, including the striking, dark-haired ten-year-old named Henrietta. But Mina, in a letter, insisted that any visit must be brief. Puppin wouldn't eat at regular hours and demanded iced beer to drink. She sometimes became "painful beyond belief," a "crashing boor." David could not imagine it. Mina had always been jealous of his friendship with Henrietta and was taking David to Venice with her that summer. It would be just like him to invite Henrietta to join them, but he mustn't. Mina said their old friend and lover would bring "back a thousand things I don't want to think about."

Henrietta waited for Garnett in her suite at the Hyde Park Hotel, where her father had always stayed. His blond hair was silvered now and she kissed him once, then took him in fully with her eyes and kissed him again. David found her still "handsome," though the beauty was gone. At lunch they talked of her marriage and she brought the same "humor and intelligence" she had always had to any conversation, but it puzzled him when she said she hoped to marry again. "This was not entirely a joke," he confessed to Mina, "though I took it as such." After lunch, they went by cab to the Royal Automobile Club to get her a driving license. Passing by Piccadilly Circus, she turned to him and confessed, "I haven't the slightest idea where we are." Surely she hadn't forgotten Piccadilly Circus and Green Park! Then Garnett absorbed "a deeper vagueness behind her words. She had forgotten why we had come out and where we were going."

Such "vagueness" may have come from drinking. A "goblet" of sherry preceded lunch, and what else she consumed is not clear, but with a damaged liver even small quantities of alcohol may cause dramatic effects. "Everything you have said is all too true," he lamented to Mina. "There is a sort of glaze over her that makes her like royalty," David observed, "I don't mean our present ones but George III, Victoria, Edward VII."

Henrietta recovered herself, though, and made her way to Sussex, where seventy-six-year-old Ernest Jones and his wife hosted her for a week. She still adored Jones. The second volume of his *Life and Work of Sigmund Freud* came out that year; the first had kissed the bestseller list simultaneously with Alfred Kinsey's *Sexual Behavior in the Human Female*. What advice could he have for the patient who had captivated him so many years ago? Did she tell him about her despair, her dependency on pills, her "nihilistic" behavior that led to a straitjacket and worse, her anger and pain over Barry? Did he reflect on his approach to her case? Henrietta's dramas had always fascinated Jones; his accessibility had made her feel safe. Whatever its limitations, psychoanalysis had given her an approach to her interior life and she stood by it. Barry, on the other hand, felt Jones took his sister "apart and never quite put the pieces together again."

Henrietta visited Thame, where in 1923 she and Mina had spent country weekends. She stood before the Spread Eagle and snapped her Kodak. Carrington had been completing the tavern's sign the day she and Mina first came to Tidmarsh Mill as prospective tenants. The inn-

Henrietta's Kodachrome of the Spread Eagle Inn,
Thame, 1957

keeper at the Spread Eagle had written a memoir featuring Henrietta and Mina, whose "beautiful faces and clothes, and air of love and baths and comfort" made them "the first decent people to grace" the hostel, which became a Bloomsbury favorite.

In Dorset, she saw Stephen Tomlin's friend Sylvia Townsend Warner. Her short stories appeared regularly in *The New Yorker*, and the women exchanged disingenuous assurances that they hadn't altered "in the slightest." It was true that Henrietta's eyes were still a startling blue, "her voice the same rich low bellow." And her seductiveness had not gone—Warner watched Henrietta seize flirtatiously upon her partner, the poet and antique dealer Valentine Ackland, "con amore."

This may be the last time Henrietta's name appeared in the diary or letters of a writer or artist. Through the 1950s and '60s she was less remembered, less recorded, certainly no longer on the cultural cusp. How long Henrietta saw the psychoanalyst Bertram Lewin is not certain, but her visits to doctors filled more and more of her time. She kept up with Jeannette Young and corresponded occasionally with Helen Jacobs. Summers she spent on the Connecticut coast, where the Westport Country Playhouse mounted shows starring Lillian Gish, Claudette Colbert, and her old friend Bea Lillie. Mina met her for lunch or dinner when she was in the city for appointments or on her way to or from France on her research trips. The Civil Rights movement was heating up in the news; there were movies and plays to see, and visits from Barry and occasionally Worth or Barry Jr., both of whom attended Harvard in the 1950s. Embarrassing stories accumulated and she became a dreaded guest at family weddings; you never knew what she would say or do.

Henrietta spent Christmas 1955 in Louisville, and soon after celebrated her fifty-fifth birthday at Melcombe. In Montgomery, Alabama, thousands of black residents were boycotting the segregated bus system, which gave rise to conversations between Henrietta and her brother and nephews. Then Barry took her aside for a serious discussion. In the wake of the marriage to Benjamin McKenzie, her finances were in disarray. Following his attempt at firmness, Nat drank beer after beer, seeking insulation from the cracking shame that alienated her from the most important man remaining in her life. Before bed she swallowed a fistful of capsules. Perhaps she had come to that pitch-black point Fitzgerald described in his essay about breaking down: the feeling of "being the unwilling witness of an execution, the disintegration of one's own personality." Late the next morning, no one had seen Henrietta and a servant was sent in to rouse her. She didn't move. An ambulance bore her comatose form to the hospital as her nephews and nieces watched, aghast. Mary went into the guest room and emptied Henrietta's wicker pill carrier, revealing "a veritable pharmaceutical establishment" procured from half a dozen physicians and pharmacies. She found stimulants such as Dexedrine and Dexamyl, which Henrietta took to face life each morning and to control her appetite, along with sedatives—Seconal, Dormitol, and Dormison—which she needed to close the world down again. Pharmaceuticals have their own cold poetry.

Henrietta's overdoses and loss of bodily dignity had a chilling effect on those closest to her. Barry woke in cold sweats from nightmares in which she took her life or simply passed out, setting fire to her bed and burning down her apartment building. Certainly, he experienced the despair that comes when we cannot save the people we love.

Dorothie was a loyal presence in the 1950s and '60s and for much of the time lived in an apartment connecting to Henrietta's, but ultimately she could not manage her care without help. Beginning in the summer of 1967, Barry paid a younger woman to sleep at Henrietta's apartment, oversee her medication, take her to the park, movies, and museums, and sometimes accompany her to inexpensive seaside hotels. In December 1967 the caregiver wrote to Barry that Henrietta was "at her very best . . . she talks about Proust, James Joyce, Dylan Thomas, and it is a pleasure to see her so completely changed." Henrietta trusted this person enough to reflect aloud on her long-standing internal difficulties. This educated Frenchwoman felt she had gotten a "glimpse into the not at all solved problems of Henrietta." However, any "hopes of a lasting betterment have shrunken to a minimum" and she thought it "a pity that Doctor Jones' Analysis was not completed."

In June 1968, Henrietta rose from bed one night and fell to the floor. Next morning, Dorothie helped the maid gather her up and looked into

milk   Sugar
Barley

Note paper
cigauttes
gin
hair pins
oil
med. dropper
aspirin
Phenodorm
Soneryl
amytal

Henrietta's shopping list, 1960s

the frozen eyes that had captivated so many. An autopsy showed a massive internal hemorrhage, caused by an acute gastric ulcer. No church service was held. At the small graveside ceremony, Henrietta was interred beside her father, a man she loved and fought and never escaped. Whether Dorothie made the trip to see her burial no one could tell me, and Henrietta Bingham's other known lovers—Mina, Tommy, Carrington, Jack, Hope, Peggy, Helen—were dead or scattered far from Kentucky. But each January 3, until Dorothie herself died in 1986, she had bright carnations laid on Henrietta's grave.

Those who loved or knew Henrietta well confronted the question of how to manage the presence of this alluring but troubling figure in their pasts. Mina soldiered onward as a *femme des lettres* (after Proust she wrote biographies of the French composer Georges Bizet and the Russian empress Anna Ivanovna). In 1978, she published a well-received volume of memoirs that mentions Henrietta not once. She appears a single time in Mina's unpublished recollections despite being, by Mina's own account, the first great love of her life. A friend watched as Mina fed the fire with old letters in the mid-1960s, a "selfish" act, he thought, especially for a person who had become a biographer. Although views about homosexuality were shifting, Mina continued to protect Henrietta—or was she protecting her own reputation from the erotic response Henrietta had long ago aroused in her?

In 1962, Helen Jacobs was inducted into the tennis hall of fame. She, too, pursued her writing to retirement, living outside New York and working for Grolier Encyclopedia's sports department, and later in the decade, the Sports Writers Guild honored her alongside the lesbian tennis champion Billie Jean King. Unlike Mina, Helen let her (albeit redacted) account of their affair remain in the diaries and photograph albums her surviving partner turned over to the International Tennis Hall of Fame. John Houseman cut long passages about Henrietta from his 1972 autobiography, *Run-Through*, yet she survived into print, meriting a place in the index, a vivid character who exerted immense sexual and emotional pull on him as a young man.

In 1968, seventy-six-year-old David Garnett began collecting Dora

Carrington's letters and diaries, and in them he reencountered Puppin. Even though the journals the artist kept during her affair with "Kentucky" were gone, the letters indicated that Henrietta had affected her as no one else had. Garnett, always tolerant, was quite happy to include Carrington's lesbian relationships, and the new wave of feminism made Carrington's independence and sexual frankness marketable. When *Carrington: Selected Letters and Extracts from Her Diaries* was published in 1970, the Upper Grosvenor Galleries mounted the first retrospective of her paintings. By the time Michael Holroyd's biography of Lytton Strachey and the film it inspired—*Carrington*, starring Emma Thompson—came out in the 1990s, Carrington's artwork, like Bloomsbury art generally, was experiencing a boom. Paintings she had practically given away commanded hefty prices. But Henrietta never made an appearance on the silver screen. Christopher Hampton's screenplay originally included her, though he ultimately found the "polymorphous" aspect of Carrington's life too unwieldy and Henrietta was cut before production began.

"Miss Nat's" marginalization and diminished status as a member of the Bingham family helped make possible the idealized narrative Barry polished for the benefit of his own children. He wanted to inspire them to continue his commitment to using their media businesses (television was added in 1950) to improve the lives of Kentuckians. Notably, Barry never spoke fondly of the Judge. His father's passion for Henrietta had always made him uneasy—and sometimes angry, other times jealous. Yet he and Mary resolutely championed Robert Worth Bingham as a public-minded publisher and promoter of American internationalism, an ambassador whose clear-eyed view of the Nazi threat deserved greater credit than he got while he was alive. That his father had wanted Henrietta to follow in his footsteps as a leader of one of the most powerful newspapers in the South was forgotten, or characterized as an inexplicable lapse in judgment. Barry had assumed this formulated version of his legacy, and he and Mary expected their sons to do likewise. Henrietta (not to mention Mary Lily) could not be reconciled with Barry's heroic version of his father's biography. She was, with Robert, who had succumbed to emphysema in 1965, virtually expunged from the Robert Worth Bingham archive Barry donated to the Library of Congress in the 1970s.

Yet tucked in a box deep in a cupboard in Louisville rested the decomposing manuscript of the play Barry and Henrietta wrote, in which the patriarch martyrs his children to his narcissistic fantasy of intimacy. This stifling dynamic had forever subverted Henrietta, and Barry was too sensitive not to feel a little guilty that he had been able to pass through that fire where she had not.

The Judge's naked ambition and the manner in which he got his fortune begat strains and questions that did not, of course, die with him. The rancorous family feud that broke up the Bingham media properties in 1986 prompted new probes into the past, including Robert Worth Bingham's 1916 marriage to Mary Lily. Barry spent a small fortune and his last years compiling elaborate documentation aimed at stopping publication of one book and refuting the claims of others. Given the nature of Henrietta's sense of duty to the father who needed her too much, she might have done the same.

POSTSCRIPT: EXTANT

In the 1950s, the CBS Radio program *This I Believe* asked citizens to read brief essays on "the rules they live by." The broadcaster Edward R. Murrow invited Barry Bingham to contribute his voice to the chorus. Barry had recently returned from a stint in Paris as chief of mission to the Marshall Plan and might have been expected to comment on his devotion to postwar American internationalism.

In spite of its name, *This I Believe* strove for a secular tone and discouraged statements of religious faith, but if Henrietta tuned in for her brother's broadcast she heard a man renouncing the folly of his youth and rededicating himself to the service of God. Here was "Baby Eyes" Barry, not known for his piety, expounding on the Parable of the Talents and the duties incumbent on the privileged. The Gospel story he told turns on the fate of three servants given differing amounts of currency ("talents") during their master's absence from home. The servants who added value to the money they were entrusted with were rewarded, whereas the servant who buried his talents for safekeeping was "cast . . . into outer darkness." In Barry's reading, the master is God on Judgment Day. Those who started with more should have more to show for themselves than those who began with less. He linked this to the childishness that marked American society as a whole but particularly infected the "generation of Americans who grew up after World War I." The jazz babies embraced a "feverish" and "fruitless" pursuit of happiness. Barry concluded that the only answer lay "in God, whose service is perfect freedom." Henrietta could be forgiven for feeling that the dichotomy her once-adoring brother drew between responsibility and immaturity left her on the wrong side of heaven.

Henrietta was "something else," audacious enough to press her lips to those of an unsuspecting Louisville debutante and capable of delivering matchless "ecstasy" to Dora Carrington. Her gifts—as a person of enormous charisma, who commanded love and attention—were roundly acknowledged in her first four decades. In late middle age, however, Henrietta was reframed as the outcast servant who had wasted her potential.

Henrietta rightly turned down the chance to join Robert Worth Bingham's tobacco crusade or succeed him as the publisher of *The Courier-Journal*. But in her way, she did become the "ambitious, unbridled creature" he wanted his daughter to be. She compensated for her early losses (and perhaps for her dyslexia) with a magnetism that might have fitted her for leadership, but such roles would have meant an even nearer identification with her complicated father. Not that she wasn't powerful. "Henrietta used power much more the way men do," her niece Sallie recalled, "to try to get what she wanted." Even in her declining years, Henrietta remained impressive. "When she was in a room," her friend Sophie's husband, Jacques, said, trying to explain Henrietta's appeal, "you knew it."

Henrietta's "oddities," as John Houseman called them, were slow to enter my consciousness. (Vladimir Nabokov used the same word in describing the homosexual elder brother he nearly expunged from his memoir.) At some gut level I always knew Henrietta was "different," as people say with a downsliding inflection to their voices. Whenever I asked about her, I was told she was a great horsewoman whose beautiful farm was now a country club we didn't belong to and which I never visited. I was in my late twenties and conducting an oral history interview with my grandmother, Mary, when she volunteered that Henrietta "was, you know, an invert." It was just a phrase about a minor character in her life story. But it was an ugly label: although I had never heard it, I understood at once what she was alluding to.

Around the same time, *The Courier-Journal* ran a review of *The Art of Dora Carrington*, one of many books published in the 1990s as scholarly and popular attention focused on sexual identity in general and the Bloomsbury Group in particular. The reviewer quoted the author's description of "two frankly erotic, sensual" nudes Carrington made of Henrietta "in a most revealing and unselfconscious stance." I bought the volume and took in the provocative high heels and strong legs, never dreaming that another of my great-aunt's lovers, the tennis star Helen Hull Jacobs, was still alive in East Hampton, Long Island.

Helen Jacobs once exclaimed in her diary, "Wish I could figure my Nat out." There is no single explanation for what made Henrietta the charming, tantalizing, maddening, and self-destructive force she was. Her mother's death before her eyes left an open wound—and an opening for an unusually close partnership with her father that both empowered her and made her weak. The Judge loved her unsparingly and offered her one platform after another, all of them at his side. He may not have been able to tolerate a husband for Henrietta, but he did tacitly legitimize her love for Helen Hull Jacobs. There was no preparation, however, for a world without her father's protection and gravitational pull. She remained a remarkable figure, but homophobia and her struggles with commitment compounded the obstacles she faced in building a happy life without him. Psychoanalysis could give Henrietta a safe place to explore these conundrums and a framework for understanding her drives and conflicts, but it did not banish the anxiety and depression that stalked her. Alcohol abuse and the drugs prescribed by quacks, as well as by doctors sincerely trying to help her, made things much, much worse.

We have flickering images of Henrietta, mostly through longing gazes. "Prudence dictated that [homosexuals] remain unobtrusive and leave behind as little incriminating evidence as possible," the historian John D'Emilio has written of the challenges of piecing together lives like hers. The letters found in Henrietta's trunk proved her allure. Being from men, they were safe to keep. But these men did not adorn her Upper East Side bedroom in 1967. Portraits of Hope Williams, Katharine Cornell, Beatrix "Peggy" Lehmann, and Dorothie Bigelow Holland were there, suggesting much, proving nothing. The heartbreak, frustration, and even cruelty some lovers suffered at her hands may have prompted them to destroy the evidence. Carrington probably burned her diary of "the American invasion" or ritually buried it alongside Henrietta's cocktail shaker. The archives of Mina Kirstein Curtiss and John Houseman contain not one letter from Henrietta. This was partly discretion and partly because Henrietta's later breakdowns alienated anyone who had experienced her glamour, her warmth, and her diaphaneity.

The "whole Henrietta" remains out of reach. She would not want to be delivered or pinned down, anyway. The former is insulting and the latter always scared her. Yet she is now without question extant. The trunk is open.

This volume is, in a sense, another lover—pursuing her and being pushed away. Henrietta leaves us with a series of sounds: unceasing calls to "come home"; ice clinking in emptying highball glasses; a saxophone note trailing away as the party ends; a tennis racket smashing a ball; a powerful car engine sighing as it's shut off; pills rattling in a bottle. She took freedom as far as she could. She gave pleasure. By not living the brilliant life expected of her, she disappointed her father, her brother, her lovers. Henrietta's charm and best efforts could not dissolve the pain she spent years trying to escape, but in her return to us again she may, even briefly, find acceptance.

NOTES

ABBREVIATIONS USED IN THE NOTES

Names

DC	Dora Carrington
DG	David Garnett
EMB	Eleanor Bingham Miller
EJ	Ernest Jones
FM	Frances Marshall (later Partridge)
GB	Gerald Brenan
HLM	Henrietta Long Miller
HWB	Henrietta Worth Bingham
JH	John Houseman (previously Jacques Haussmann)
JMB	John Mason Brown
LS	Lytton Strachey
MCB	Mary Caperton Bingham
MKC	Mina Kirstein Curtiss
RP	Ralph Partridge
RWB	Robert Worth Bingham
Tomlin	Stephen Tomlin
WMB	William Marshall Bullitt
WRK	William Rand Kenan

Books

AFT	Campbell, Walter E. *Across Fortune's Tracks: A Biography of William Rand Kenan Jr.* Chapel Hill: University of North Carolina Press, 1996.
BB	Bingham, Barry. *Barry Bingham: A Man of His Word.* Samuel W. Thomas, ed. Lexington, Ky. University of Kentucky Press, 1993.
BTG	Jacobs, Helen Hull. *Beyond the Game: An Autobiography.* Philadelphia: J. B. Lippincott, 1936.
CC	*The Complete Correspondence of Sigmund Freud and Ernest Jones, 1908–1939.* R. Andrew Paskauskas, ed. Cambridge, Mass.: Belknap Press of Harvard University Press, 1993.
FF	Garnett, David. *The Familiar Faces.* London: Chatto and Windus, 1962.
OPL	Curtiss, Mina. *Other People's Letters: A Memoir.* Boston: Houghton Mifflin, 1978.
Patriarch	Tifft, Susan E., and Alex S. Jones. *The Patriarch: The Rise and Fall of the Bingham Dynasty.* New York: Summit Books, 1991.
RT	Houseman, John. *Run-Through: A Memoir.* New York: Simon and Schuster, 1972.
RWB	Ellis, William E. *Robert Worth Bingham and the Southern Mystique: From the Old South to the New South and Beyond.* Kent, Ohio: Kent State University Press, 1997.

Newspapers

CJ	*The Courier-Journal*, Louisville, Kentucky
NYT	*The New York Times*

Unpublished Material

Albert interview	Sophie and Jacques Albert, interview, February 27, 1987, courtesy Susan E. Tifft and Alex P. Jones
HHJ diary	Diary of Helen Hull Jacobs, Helen Hull Jacobs Papers, International Tennis Hall of Fame and Museum, Newport, Rhode Island
JH interview	John Houseman interview, February 4, 1987, courtesy Susan E. Tifft and Alex P. Jones
MCB oral history	Mary Caperton Bingham, oral history with author, 1993–1994, AP
MEM	Memorandum on "The Binghams of Louisville" by David Leon Chandler to the Macmillan Publishing Co. from George Barry Bingham, Sr., April 27, 1987, FHS

"Run-Through," Box 51, folder 6, John Houseman Papers, Department of
JHP-UCLA Special Collections, Charles E. Young Research Library,
University of California, Los Angeles
TOR Transcript of Record, Court of Appeals of Kentucky,
containing Transcript of County Court Record, Jefferson
Co., Ky., August 28, 1917

Manuscript Collections and Repositories

AP Author's possession
Berg-NYPL Henry W. and Albert A. Berg Collection of English and
American Literature, New York Public Library
BFP-FHS Bullitt Family Papers, Oxmoor Collection, Filson Histori-
cal Society
BHP-LOC B. W. Huebsch Papers, 1893–1964, Manuscript Division,
Library of Congress
Charleston-KCAC The Charleston Papers, King's College Archive Centre, Cam-
bridge University
FMP-HAJTC Florence Mills Papers, Helen Armstead-Johnson Theatre
Collection, Manuscripts, Archives and Rare Books Divi-
sion, Schomburg Center for Research in Black Culture,
New York Public Library
FP-KCAC Papers of Frances Catherine Partridge, King's College Ar-
chive Centre, Cambridge University
GBB-FHS George Barry Bingham, Sr., Papers, 1861–1989, Filson His-
torical Society
GBP-HRC Gerald Brenan Collection, Harry Ransom Center, Univer-
sity of Texas at Austin
GFC-HRC Garnett Family Collection, Harry Ransom Center, University
of Texas at Austin
GFP-NWUL Garnett Family Papers, Charles Deering McCormick Li-
brary of Special Collections, Northwestern University
HHJ-ITHFM Helen Hull Jacobs Papers, International Tennis Hall of
Fame and Museum, Newport, Rhode Island
EJP-BPAS Ernest Jones Papers (P04), Archives of the British Psycho-
analytical Society
EJP-LOC Ernest Jones Papers, Manuscript Division, Library of Con-
gress
JHP-UCLA John Houseman Papers, Department of Special Collections,
Charles E. Young Research Library, University of Califor-
nia, Los Angeles
LEK-HBS Louis E. Kirstein Collection, Business Manuscripts Collec-
tion, Baker Library, Harvard University

LKP-NYPL	Lincoln Kirstein Papers, Jerome Robbins Dance Division, New York Public Library
MCB-FHS	Mary Caperton Bingham Papers, 1850–1995, Filson Historical Society
MKC-SCA	Mina Kirstein Curtiss File, College Archives, Smith College, Five College Archives & Manuscript Collections
MKC-SSC	Mina Kirstein Curtiss Papers, 1913–2005, Sophia Smith Collection, Smith College
MKC-Yale	Mina Kirstein Curtiss Papers, 1896–1985, Beinecke Rare Book & Manuscript Library, Yale University
RNL-KCAC	Papers of Rosamond Nina Lehmann, King's College Archive Centre, Cambridge University
RWB-FHS	Robert Worth Bingham Papers, Filson Historical Society
RWB-ADD-FHS	Robert Worth Bingham Added Papers, 1894–1944, Filson Historical Society
RWB-ADD-FHS2	Robert Worth Bingham, Additional Papers, 1790–1936, Filson Historical Society
RWB-LOC	Robert Worth Bingham Papers, 1856–1939, Manuscript Division, Library of Congress
SBP-Duke	Sallie Bingham Papers, David M. Rubenstein Rare Book & Manuscript Library, Duke University
SCA	Smith College Archives
STP-ULASC	Samuel W. Thomas Research Collection and Archive, University of Louisville Archives and Special Collections

PROLOGUE: HEREIN LIETH HID A CREATURE

3 *"eyes like Henrietta's"*: Royden Peabody interview, November 30, 2005, AP.

3 *"purple eyes with tangled lashes"*: MCB to GBB, quoted in Sallie Bingham, *The Blue Box: Three Lives in Letters* (Louisville: Sarabande Books, 2014), 213.

4 *"violet-blue"*: JH, *Front and Center* (New York: Simon and Schuster, 1979), 109.

4 *"Brilliantly blue"*: FF, 9.

4 *"She looks the memory . . . little girl"*: Eleanor Chilton, untitled poem, Class of 1922 Collection, and untitled poem (January 1922), Eleanor Chilton Papers-SCA.

4 *"should preach, her voice is so divine"*: HHJ diary, February 6, 1936.

4 *"Giotto Madonna"*: DC to GB, May 31, 1923, GBP-HRC.

4 *"faintly husky"*: FF, 12.

4 *"Kentucky princess"*: GB to DC, June 23, 1924, GBP-HRC.

5 *"a three-dollar bill"*: Barry Bingham, Jr., in Marie Brenner, *House of Dreams: The Bingham Family of Louisville* (New York: Random House, 1988), 215.

5 *"never be married . . . be a lesbian"*: Eleanor Bingham Miller interview, September 21, 2008.

5 *"close friends for a number of years"*: "Helen Jacobs Discloses Her Authorship of Novel," *NYT*, April 8, 1938.

8 *"catching a glimpse . . . overtake you"*: Tomlin to HWB, September 1923, AP.
8 *"not fundamentally a very serious person"*: MCB oral history.

1. COQUETTING

11 *"fool"*: W. W. Davies to RWB, January 10, 1901, RWB-FHS.
11 *population*: U.S. Census Bureau, 1880.
12 *For five summers in the 1880s . . . parkways*: George H. Yater, *Two Hundred Years at the Falls of the Ohio: A History of Louisville and Jefferson County* (Louisville: 1979), 118–23.
12 *An Irish immigrant great-grandfather . . . Democrat*: "Dennis Long: Pioneer Manufacturer and Railroad Promoter, Built Louisville and Jeffersonville Bridge," undated newspaper clipping, Long Family Material, GBB-FHS; "Samuel Miller Meets Death," *CJ*, February 3, 1895; Dan Walsh, Jr., "Noted Characters Memorable to Louisville," *CJ*, August 13, 1916, typescript GBB-FHS.
12 *"an exclamation in the language of High Victorian Gothic"*: GBB, "Memories of a Louisville Childhood," in *Remembering Barry Bingham* (Louisville: privately printed, 1990), 12.
13 *For the better part of a decade . . . Asheville for a change of air*: "Another Appalling Accident Added to Already Long List of Horrors," *CJ*, December 16, 1893; "Samuel Miller Meets Death," *CJ*, February 3, 1895; Walsh, "Noted Characters," *CJ*, August 13, 1915, "Big Four Bridge," *Encyclopedia of Louisville*, John Kleber, ed. (Lexington: University Press of Kentucky), 89.
14 *"acute melancholia . . . passing over his body"*: "Samuel Miller Meets Death," *CJ*, February 3, 1895.
14 *"My whole heart throbs for you"*: RWB to EMB, February 3, 1895, RWB-ADD-FHS.
14–15 *Bob Bingham's childhood . . . his second wife*: RWB to Margaret Mitchell, February 16, 1937, RWB-LOC, and Ellen Louise Axson to Woodrow Wilson, *Papers of Woodrow Wilson*, vol. 3, 280; *RWB*, 12–13. Elvira "Vy" Woodward Bingham separated from her husband in 1921 and died in 1932 in South Carolina.
15 *All the Bingham men . . . left by his mother*: For Worth money and RWB's educational finances, Supreme Court of North Carolina, August Term 1901, In re Will of J. M. Worth, in MEM, Part II, Vol. A, exhibits 5G and 6D, AP, FHS. Jonathan Worth, John Milton's elder brother and North Carolina governor 1865–68, helped found the Cedar Falls Manufacturing Co. before the Civil War. The mill supplied clothing to Confederate forces. Jonathan died in 1869 and Bob's grandfather assumed control of Worth Manufacturing.
15 *large loans . . . years to pay off, if it ever did*: Affidavit in Transcript of Record for the Worth Inheritance Litigation, MEM, exhibit G; *Patriarch*, 31–32. The move west also came in the midst of a bitter dispute about ownership of the academy name, see Robert Mason, "The Fall of the House of Bingham," *Virginia Quarterly Review* (Winter 1989), 165–75.

15 *"a sour, dyspeptic small-town pedant"*: Wolfe, quoted in David Herbert Donald, *Look Homeward: A Life of Thomas Wolfe* (New York: Little, Brown, 1987), 63.

15 *Bob was perfectly willing . . . tragedy*: *Patriarch*, 31–32.

15 *"had bred a considerable measure of contempt"*: RWB to EMB, March 1, 1895, RWB-ADD-FHS. On the youthful Bingham's effect on women, Hugh Young, *Hugh Young: A Surgeon's Autobiography* (New York: Harcourt, Brace and Co., 1940), 504.

16 *"distrustful and suspicious . . . defeat very kindly"*: RWB to EMB, August 1, 1895, RWB-ADD-FHS.

16 *"my present position . . . business standpoint"*: RWB to EMB, October 10, 1895, RWB-ADD-FHS.

16 *"as I have remarked . . . continued disapproval"*: RWB to EMB, August 23, 1895, RWB-ADD-FHS.

16 *subscription to* The Courier-Journal: RWB to EMB, December 10, 1895, RWB-ADD-FHS.

16 *"perhaps the richest man"*: *CJ*, May 17, 1896.

16 *Babes's mother was said . . . warning against indebtedness*: loan and advice, J. M. Worth to RWB, March 10, 1896, Affidavit in Transcript of Record for the Worth Inheritance Litigation, Memorandum exhibit 5G; mourning attire and Worth will, *Patriarch*, 37.

16 *"Dame nature holds . . . by gum"*: W. W. Davies to C. B. Robinson, January 11, 1907, quoted in *RWB*, 24.

17 *"a great deal of money"*: RWB to EMB, May 23, 1900, RWB-ADD-FHS.

17 *Instead of inheriting . . . grandfather's wealth*: Will and codicils of J. M. Worth, Randolph County (NC) Wills, 1775–1902, State Archives of North Carolina.

17 *"Bob seems to care . . . Grandady [sic] himself"*: Berta Boyd to RWB, April 26, 1900, quoted in *Patriarch*, 40.

17 *"the most contemptible thing in the world"*: RWB to R. T. Grinnan, April 9, 1900, RWB-FHS.

17 *On January 3, 1901 . . . legacy he sought*: MEM, 67–70; Superior Court of Randolph Co., NC, July Term, 1902, In the Matter of the Last Will and Testament of John M. Worth, deceased and Consent Order, R. W. Bingham etc. vs. Hal M. Worth etc.; Circuit Court of the United States for the Seventh District of North Carolina at Greensboro, re RWB etc. vs. Worth Manufacturing etc.

17–18 *Babes admired her husband's . . . prominent ancestral origins*: *RWB*, 20–21, n. 23 and 24, 207; RWB scrapbook, unnumbered, c. 1899–1900, AP; *Patriarch*, 39–40; EMB engagement book 1912–1913, AP; photo album presented to RWB by People of St. Columb Minor, August 2, 1922, AP; Henrietta Long Miller to RWB, und. [c. 1905], RWB-ADD-FHS; RWB to R. Diamond, September 4, 1905, RWB-FHS.

18 *habit of practicing public speaking . . . train his tongue*: Royden Peabody interview, November 30, 2005, AP.

18 *"badtempered [sic] fool . . . meanness of temper and disposition"*: RWB to EMB, March 19, 1899, RWB-ADD-FHS.

18 *"You are so perfect . . . want you with me"*: EMB to RWB, July 5, 1906, RWB-ADD-FHS.

18 *In 1905 . . . documented in Kentucky*: Tracy Campbell, *Deliver the Vote: A History of Election Fraud, an American Political Tradition, 1742–2004* (New York: Carroll and Graf, 2005), 113–36 and *RWB*, 32–34.

19 *"invest Babes [sic] money . . . without her help"*: HLM to RWB, und. [1905], RWB-ADD-FHS.

19 *Henrietta associated the birth . . . almost never cried*: *BB*, 202 n. 8; trust agreement, October 18, 1906, folder 527, BFP-FHS; inheritance, *CJ* clip [1922] in Long Family papers, courtesy Royden Peabody; codicil 6 to will of July 22, 1913, HLM file, BFP-FHS; withdrew, EMB to [Colonel] Robert Bingham, April 3, 1910, RWB-ADD-FHS and RWB to Katie Callahan, May 11, 1906, RWB-FHS.

20 *They had just moved . . . popular man's untimely death*: Campbell, *Deliver the Vote*, 130; *RWB*, 36–46; Yater, *Two Hundred Years at the Falls of the Ohio*, 42; *Encyclopedia of Louisville*, 70.

20–21 *"coqueting" . . . No one was to speak of it*: EBM to RWB, und. [c. 1907], RWB-ADD-FHS.

21 *Beargrass Creek*: GBB, "Memories of a Louisville Childhood," 15; *BB*, 25.

22–23 *An extended family party . . . it was no use*: *CJ*, April 28, 1913; *Louisville Post*, April 29, 1913; Brenner, *House of Dreams*, 100.

23 *In going through her possessions . . . remember*: lace, with attached note, AP.

23 *slip away . . . waltzing, twirling*: Patriarch, 49.

24 *Shock rendered Barry . . . scarcely walk*: *BB*, 30, 36; Brenner, *House of Dreams*, 99–100; *Patriarch*, 52.

24 *high school career with a bender*: Albert interview.

2. PRETTY BOXES

25 *"I am just hungry . . . my lovely darling"*: RWB to HWB, August 15, 1914, AP.

26 *"Honey"*: HWB to RWB, July 1, 1915, RWB-ADD-FHS.

26 *"yiked my yooks . . . by the time he was 16"*: HWB to RWB, und., RWB-ADD-FHS.

26–27 *His father . . . respected local family*: George Stevens, *Speak for Yourself, John: The Life of John Mason Brown* (New York: Viking, 1974), 12, 13–14, 20, and Herbert Warren Wind, "Circuit Rider," *The New Yorker*, October 18, 1952, 44–81.

27 *Over their eighth-grade winter . . . tasted better*: JMB diary, January 14, 17, and 25, February 21 and 25, and March 4 and 5, 1915, FHS; Melville Otter Briney diary, June 20, 1914, Melville Otter Briney Papers, FHS.

27 *Henrietta dropped . . . remained in pursuit*: JMB diary, September 21, 1915, FHS and JH interview.

27 *Hiawatha*: JMB diary, FHS; *Caron's Louisville City Directory*, 1915.

28 *"lovely mother's horrible mother"*: Albert, interview, and A. F. Callahan to RWB, August 30, 1904, and April 30, 1908, *RWB*, 24.

28 *"I'm getting . . . securities back"*: HLM to [?], December 1915, HLM file, BFP-FHS.

28 *His response, that . . . trusteeship of Babes's estate*: RWB statement, unsigned, regarding "Securities Belonging to Mrs. Bingham in the Possession of Fidelity Trust Co.," AP and HLM Codicil No. 4, will dated July 12, 1912, HLM file, BFP-FHS.

28 *"short or anything of that kind"*: WMB to Helm Bruce, October 31, 1914, HLM file, BFP-FHS.

28 *Bob's mother-in-law . . . moved Babes's remains*: Helm Bruce to HLM, June 23, 1914, HLM file, BFP-FHS; Cave Hill Cemetery ledger, October 21, 1913.

28 *In a final offer . . . could not work*: John Barr to WMB, July 3, 1915, HLM file, BFP-FHS; WMB to W. W. Davies, July 19, 1915, HLM file, BFP-FHS.

28–29 *"frantic joy" . . . "Good Lord no!"*: W. W. Davies to HLM, July 22, 1915, HLM file, BFP-FHS. Davies noted that when Bob advised his wife to place her assets in a trust, he released his spousal share—one third the value of her real estate and one half the value of her personal property.

29 *"the wealthiest woman in the United States"*: Patriarch, 56.

30 *"not heavily endowed with brains"*: Clarissa Anderson Gibbs, in Campbell, *AFT*, 161; voice, *Wilmington Star*, in Campbell, *AFT*, 44.

30 *Other friends swept her . . . as much as $100 million*: Sidney Walter Martin, *Henry Flagler: Visionary of the Gilded Age* (Lake Buena Vista, FL: Tailored Tours Publications, 1998), 135–50, 178, and Campbell, *AFT*, 112.

30 *"so small of stature"*: *Palm Beach Life*, February 15, 1916, quoted in Campbell, *AFT*, 174.

30 *"$100 million"*: *Louisville Evening Post*, September 24, 1917.

30 *"a quiet steed . . . riding is my only amusement"*: HWB to RWB, July 1, 1915, RWB-ADD-FHS.

30 *Robert escorted . . . Kenan professorships*: Patriarch, 61, Campbell, *AFT*, 171–73, and Col. Robert Bingham to Chancellor E. K. Graham, October 6, 1915, and und. [1917], Chancellor's Records, Wilson Library, University of North Carolina at Chapel Hill.

31 *"fortune hunting"*: Col. Robert Bingham to UNC Chancellor E. K. Graham, und. [1917].

31 *"P. S. Have you . . . Mary Lily yet?"*: HWB to RWB, September 8, 1915, RWB-ADD-FHS.

31 *That fall of 1915 . . . spelling contest*: *Caron's Louisville Directory*, 1916; HLM to [?], December 1915, and HLM to Fidelity Trust, [April] 1916, HLM file, BFP-FHS; tennis *CJ*, September 27, 1917, and trophies, AP; algebra, HWB to RWB, September 8, 1915, RWB-ADD-FHS; 1915 Collegiate School *Transcript*, Vol. 1, no. 1, and Vol. 2, no. 2.

31 *"Of course you have brains . . . development"*: RWB to HWB, January 16, 1920, AP.

32 *"a real Virginia playboy"*: GBB, in *Patriarch*, 52; tennis, University of Virginia yearbook, 1916.

32 *As she settled . . . Sadie, from Asheville*: Travis J. Tylsinger (Stuart Hall) to Susan Tifft, February 6, 1987; Campbell, *AFT*, 176; *RWB*, 57; November 1916 clips, RWB-FHS.

32–33 *The Judge told reporters . . . erased Bingham's debt*: *CJ*, November 16, 1916; interview with William Rand Kenan, 1917 Notebook, folder 1928, BFP-FHS; RWB to Keith Bullitt, December 18, 1916, HLM file, FHS.

33 *Henrietta first confronted her new . . . sputter apologies*: *CJ*, December 3, 1916; Campbell, *AFT*, note 86, p. 363; Brenner, *House of Dreams*, 109.

33 *"They don't want . . . to come home"*: Albert interview and *Patriarch*, 64.

33 *Invitations had gone out . . . became unforgivable*: Ellen Barret Wood, quoted in Brenner, *House of Dreams*, 109; *CJ*, January 2, 1917; TOR, 80; Campbell, *AFT*, 181; Mrs. Dr. [Rev. Peyton] Hoge, WMB pocket diary, folder 1928, BFP-FHS.

33–34 *Barry remained . . . for the winter season*: Albert interview; Brenner, *House of Dreams*, 124; Young E. Allison to RWB, January 27, 1917, RWB-FHS; interview with Mrs. George Davis, MLKFB Case, BFP-FHS; *Palm Beach Daily News*, February 14, March 2 and 15, 1917; Martin, *Henry Flagler*, 153–56.

34 *"Don't forget I am thinking . . . time here"*: RWB to HWB, March 15, 1917, AP.

34 *The Palm Beach paper . . . luxury shops*: *Palm Beach Daily News*, February 14 and March 21, 1917; William Rand Kenan in WMB pocket diary, folder 1928, BFP-FHS; "Bing," *Inlook: Stuart Hall Catalogue*, Campbell, *AFT*, 182.

34 *"found Whitehall . . . shallow and ostentatious"*: GBB memorandum to family, August 30, 1985, box 65, STP-ULASC.

35 *"payroll"*: WRK, WMB pocket diary, folder 1928, BFP-FHS.

35 *Louisville house . . . stepchildren*: Winfrey P. Blackburn, Jr., and R. Scott Gill, *The Country Houses of Louisville, 1899–1939* (Louisville: Butler Books, 2011), 247; Laura Moore Gavin to Mrs. Robert Love Kenan, September 21, 1941, Kenan-Love Papers, Southern Historical Collection.

35 *age limit*: Reserve Corps recruiting station to RWB, April 26, 1917, GBB-FHS.

36 *Perhaps Hoover*: RWB to Herbert Hoover, May 28, 1917, RWB-FHS.

36 *Returning to Louisville . . . paid for a new car*: WRK and Mrs. George Davis, WMB pocket diary, folder 1928, BFP-FHS; Campbell, *AFT*, 183; *Patriarch*, 65–66; Albert interview; Jennie C. Benedict, *The Road to Dream Acre* (Louisville: Standard Printing Co., 1928), 67–69.

36–37 *It probably did not please . . . $5 million*: TOR, 76, 85; WRK to Sarah Kenan, July 20, 1917, BFP-FHS; Campbell, *AFT*, 185, 187; GBB and HWB to RWB, July 2 and 4, 1917, RWB-ADD-FHS; Cave Hill Cemetery records, July 5 and 12, 1917, and W. W. Locke to RWB, July 5, 1917, RWB-FHS; *CJ*, July 27 and 28, 1917; *Louisville Post*, July 27, 1917; RWB to Haywood Parker, October 27, 1917 (copy), AP.

37 *"everybody knew right away"*: Carrie Cox, quoted by Mrs. James B. Skinner to Sam Thomas, March 18, 1982, box 63, STP-ULASC.

37 *"great trouble"*: Hugh Young, draft section on RWB from his memoir, with Aleen Bingham to Hugh Young, February 6, 1940, GBB-FHS.

37 *"her habit was to lie . . . to be discussed"*: GBB memorandum to family, August 30, 1985, STP-ULASC.

37 *enter a sanatorium*: Hugh Young, draft section in RWB from his memoir, with Aleen Bingham to Hugh Young, February 6, 1940, GBB-FHS.

37 *"I know what you are going thru"*: George M. Ward to RWB, July 19, 1917, RWB-LC, in *RWB*, 60.

37 *"Have kept my promise"*: MLKFB note, AP.

38 *"My dear Mr. Kenan . . . Ravitch"*: M. L. Ravitch to WRK, July 4, 1917, MLKFB File, BFP-FHS.

38 *Mary Lily could have engaged . . . two-hour intervals*: Bingham wrote that his wife "flatly refused to have anybody" but Ravitch in charge of her care, and to call in new physicians "would have disturbed and distressed her," RWB to Judge George Rountree, June 11, 1918 (copy), AP.

38 *Her nurse . . . "before I began to wait on her"*: Eva Mueller statement, MLKFB Case, BFP-FHS.

38 *"While the injections . . . get alarmed"*: M. L. Ravitch to WRK, July 10, 1917, MLKFB File, BFP-FHS.

38–39 *After Mary Lily . . . "doing nicely now"*: RWB to WRK (telegrams), July 13 and 16, 1917; RWB to Sarah Kenan and Graham Kenan, July 16, 1917; WRK to Sarah Kenan, July 20, 1917; Ravitch to WRK, July 20, 1917, all from MLKFB File, BFP-FHS.

39 BINGHAM WILL CONTEST THREATENED: *Louisville Evening Post*, August 27, 1917.

39 *"Mr. Davies . . . could not come into her house?"*: TOR, 73–85.

39 *"from beginning to end . . . hounded to sign"*: "Unseen Witness" to Helm Bruce, September 6, 1917, MLKFB Case, BFP-FHS.

40 BODY SECRETLY EXHUMED: *CJ*, September 22, 1917.

40 *"badly scared Negroes"*: Hugh Young, Notes made on the case of Mrs. Mary Lilly [*sic*] Bingham, March 13, 1933, Alan Mason Chesney Medical Archives, Johns Hopkins University Medical Institutions, MEM, in *Patriarch*, 73.

40 MRS. BINGHAM WAS DRUGGED!: *New York American*, in Brenner, *House of Dreams*, 121. The *New York Herald*'s headline,"Impression Grows Mrs. Bingham Killed by Poison," is mentioned in RWB to Bessy [Mrs. Hugh] Young, October 22, 1917, AP.

40 *"I almost fainted"*: Albert interview.

40 *"Dearest Dad . . . live on that"*: HWB to RWB, und. [1917], RWB-ADD-FHS.

41 *"Please honey . . . about your trip"*: HWB to RWB, November 19, 1917, RWB-ADD-FHS.

41 *"criminal slanders . . . the country"*: RWB to Judge George Rountree, October 24, 1917, AP.

41 *"showing the effects of strain"*: RWB to Bessy [Mrs. Hugh Young], October 22, 1917 (copy), AP.

41 *"steadfast and manly conduct"*: George Gordon Battle to RWB, September 26, 1918, AP.

41 *"terrible episode," "never recovered"*: GBB memorandum to family, August 30, 1985, box 65, STP-ULASC.

41 *"monstrous," "villainous"*: George Gordon Battle to Judge Alexander Humphrey, July 15, 1918 (copy), AP. Some Kenan family members wanted to pursue Bingham. William Rand Kenan lived through the gossip columns' innuendo with respect to his sister's virtue in the years before Flagler married her, and

knowing that anything related to Standard Oil was subject to public odium, he had no interest in a fight. His biographer suggests that Will Kenan and his brother and cousin did not see eye to eye about the case (Campbell, *AFT*, 188–90).

41–42 *"bursting," "I am afraid . . . if I stay much longer"*: HWB to Sadie Bingham Grinnan, und. [December 1917], RWB-ADD-FHS.

42 *"crushed"*: MKC to EJ, September 23, 1922, EJP-BPAS.

42 *center on their basketball team*: Louisville Collegiate School *Transcript*, 1918.

42 *"loads and loads . . . now and then"*: GBB diary, February 20, 1919, AP.

42 *five-man band . . . Swiss dirndl*: GBB diary, February 8, 1919, AP.

43 *"instruments for public . . . fair-dealing everywhere"*: RWB, *CJ*, August 7, 1918; Haldemans, *Patriarch*, 78–79.

43 *"I am not myself a trained newspaper man"*: RWB to Marshall Humphrey, October 18, 1921, Marshall Humphrey Papers, FHS.

44 *"Lord Bing"*: Ray Reibel to GBB, September 15, 1977 (copy), box 63, STP-ULASC.

44 *Henrietta competed . . . dominating city tournaments*: trophies and Second Kentucky Army Horse Show program, June 24, 1920, AP.

44 *"as a gentleman . . . as a student"*: University of Virginia dean to RWB, March 4, 1918 (copy), box 63, STP-ULASC.

44 *"redeeming myself in your opinions"*: Robert to RWB, November 6, 1917, RWB-ADD-FHS.

44 *enrolled in flight . . . never graduated*: RWB, 68.

44 *"strange, fantastic existence"*: JH to HWB, August 12, 1926, AP.

44 *Parties . . . only horse manure*: Albert interview; Brenner, *House of Dreams*, 43; *The Jug Bands of Louisville*, compiled by Laurie Wright from material supplied by Fred Cox, John Randolph, and John Harris (Essex, England: Storyville Publications, 1993), 19.

45 *Before her 1920 high school . . . she could remember*: Krausgill Piano Company, March 1, 1920, Receipted Bills G-P, RWB-ADD-FHS; Peggy Gilbert (1905–1997), saxophonist, *NYT*, February 25, 2007; Louisville Collegiate School *Transcript*, 1921; Joan Marie Johnson, *Southern Women at the Seven Sister Colleges: Feminist Values and Social Activism, 1875–1915* (Athens: University of Georgia Press, 2008).

3. DETRIMENT TO COMMUNITY

46 *Henrietta and more than five hundred freshmen*: Smith College annual report 1920–21.

46–47 *Henrietta lodged . . . part in special outings*: Helen Lefkowitz Horowitz, *Alma Mater: Design and Experience in the Women's Colleges from Their Nineteenth-Century Beginnings to the 1930s* (New York: A. A. Knopf, 1991), 162; Catalogue of Smith College, 1920–21, SCA; "Regulations of the Department of Hygiene and Physical Education," 1918, SCA.

47 *"moral degenerates," "not legitimate"*: "Your Daughter: What Are Her Friend-ships?" by a College Graduate, *Harper's Bazaar* (October 1913), 16, 78, in Horo-witz, *Alma Mater*, 283.

48 *On the first day . . . late summer heat*: oral history with MKC, 1971, 5–6, SCA.

48 *"homesick, frightened, and miserable"*: MKC to EJ, September 23, 1922, EJP-BPAS.

48–49 *"Go on home, you dirty" . . . "czarist"*: MKC, "Chosen?" *Massachusetts Review* (Summer 1983), 426, and "The Past and I," 50, 51, 66, MKC-SSC.

49 *tantrums, the threat of which*: Martin Duberman, *The Worlds of Lincoln Kirstein* (New York: A. A. Knopf, 2007), 4, 9.

49 *"as beautiful . . . her own vanity"*: MKC, June 1918, diary 1918–1919, MKC-SSC.

50 *"domestic science and manual training"*: Rose Stein Kirstein to Louis E. Kirstein, July 26, 1914, LEK-HBS.

50 *"How interesting . . . peddlers"*: MKC, "Chosen?" 428.

50 *required Christian vespers*: MKC, "Winter Letters," MKC-SSC.

50 *convinced a dozen students . . . "consider taboo"*: MKC, "The Past and I," MKC-SSC, 121–23; MKC, "One of the Little Foxes," *The Seven Arts Chronicle*, 2 (September 1917), 667–69; MKC, English 25 paper (1916), MKC-SSC.

50 *"combined a strong . . . humor"*: MKC, "The Past and I," 124, MKC-SSC.

50 *"that salvation . . . were synonymous"*: MKC, "The Past and I," MKC-SSC.

50 *Mina's unfeminine radical . . . "can't take long"*: "The Follies of 1918 or How Doth the Busy Bolshevik (An Agitation in 2 Spasms)," by Nell Battle Lewis, MKC-SSC. The author became a crusading journalist in her native North Carolina, pressing for women's and labor rights, and against the death penalty. She proved far more radical in many respects than the butt of her satire.

51 *"bloated capitalist"*: Frida Laski to MKC, September 4, 1921, MKC-SSC.

51 *"Jewish end," "go on being a Christian"*: Frances Hackett to B. W. Huebsch, April 15, 1921, Huebsch Papers, LOC.

51 *"sought education; he did not sell it"*: Henry B. Adams, quoted in MKC, "Henry Adams and Failure," M.A. thesis, Columbia University, 1920, MKC-SSC.

51–52 *In the fall of 1920 . . . "take me"*: MKC to Louis E. Kirstein, September 21, 1920, MKC-SSC; MKC, February 24, 1919, diary 1918–1919, MKC-SSC; Patri-cia Fowler Scriggins to MKC, May 2, 1977, MKC-SSC.

52 *"a young woman . . . as an instructor"*: Rose Stein Kirstein to MKC, January 13, 1923, MKC-SSC.

52 *"only natural . . . great deal to me"*: MKC to EJ, September 23, 1923, EJP-BPAS.

52 *"a friendly warning"*: Dean of College—Administrative Board Minutes, Novem-ber 19, 1920, SCA.

52 *nearly one in five first year students*: Smith College President's Reports (1920–1921 and 1923–1924), SCA.

52 *"in such . . . and I with her"*: MKC to EJ, September 23, 1923, EJP-BPAS.

53 *"ecstatic," "was persuaded"*: GBB diary, summary of 1921, AP.

53 *While wading . . . from Kentucky and from Henrietta*: GBB diary, summary of 1921, AP; MKC to William Allan Neilson, June 13, 1922, MKC-SSC; *BB*, 37–39.

54 *Louisville car dealership*: Caron's Louisville City Directory, 1921.
54 *Tobacco prices* . . . *own career*: "Warn Tobacco Raisers Against Lawlessness," *NYT,* January 6, 1921; Aaron Sapiro to RWB, June 4, 1921, RWB-ADD-FHS2; *RWB*, 76–77.
54 *"Between the claret* . . . *of this day"*: HWB, GBB diary, 1921, AP.
54 *"effeminate"*: Ray Alkison Spencer to RWB, Middlesex Records, in *Patriarch*, 85; GBB diary, 1921, AP.
54–55 *In London* . . . *young Virginia Woolf*: GBB diary 1919, notes on 1921; MKC to LEK, July 5, 1921, MKC-SSC; LEK to MKC, July 26, 1921, LEK-HBS; Harold Laski to Oliver Wendell Holmes, June 26 and July 7, 1921, *Holmes-Laski Letters* (Cambridge: Harvard University Press, 1953), 342–50.
55 *"with repressions* . . . *wisdom teeth"*: Frida Laski to MKC, September 4, 1921, MKC-SSC.
55 *Mina didn't have a man* . . . *unbearable*: Frida Laski to MKC, March 16, 1922, MKC-SSC; http://law2.umkc.edu/faculty/projects/ftrials/shipp/lynchingyear .html, accessed July 22, 2014.
55 *dressed head-to-toe in violet*: Memories of Sally Mason Clark and Clarice Young '22, 1952 Reunion Book, SCA.
55 *"I have kissed* . . . *like you"*: Chilton, "To Mina" (1921) and "Sonnet," volume labeled "Mina S. Kirstein, June 1922," MKC-SSC.
55 *"silence bared its teeth, and bade," "tension at my heel"*: Chilton, "Sonnet," October 30, 1920, in "Mina S. Kirstein, June 1922," MKC-SSC.
55 *"years to understand"*: Chilton, "Sonnet," London, July 14, 1921, "Mina S. Kirstein, June 1922," MKC-SSC.
56 *"But now* . . . *hence their worth"*: Chilton, "To H.W.B. In Reply," Eleanor Carroll Chilton Papers, SCA.
56 *"reconciled"* . . . *much more engaged*: RWB to HWB, October 5, 1921; HLM to HWB, December 16, 1921; HLM to HWB, January 30, 1922, AP.
56 *couples retiring to automobiles* . . . *during dances"*: "Both Jazz Music and Jazz Dancing Barred from All Louisville Episcopal Churches," *CJ*, September 19, 1921; Marshall Winslow Stearns and Jean Stearns, *Jazz Dance: The Story of American Vernacular Dance* (New York: Da Capo, 1994), 109–10, and Court Carney, *Cuttin' Up: How Early Jazz Got America's Ear* (University Press of Kansas, 2009).
57 *"unsupervisable automobile,"*: Horowitz, *Alma Mater*, 316, 308.
57 *scored a small victory*: Smith College Annual Report 1921–1922.
57 *"an invalid," "You must* . . . *well and strong"*: HLM to HWB, December 16, 1921, AP.
57 *Her $450,000 estate* . . . *loved as a child*: "Miller Estate Worth $450,000" [1922] clipping from Long family scrapbook, AP.
57 *"get the poor* . . . *their salvation"*: RWB to HWB, October 5, 1921, AP.
57–58 *To advise him* . . . *farmers in Maine*: *RWB*, 85.
58 *"Look at her eyes* . . . *you are really like"*: Chilton, untitled poem, January 1922, Eleanor Carroll Chilton Papers-SCA.

58   *Dr. Marion Leeper, a local practitioner*: MKC to Miss Clark, June 28, 1922, SCA.

58   *if the authorities . . . for all involved*: e-mail with Nanci Young, Smith College Archivist, November 26, 2013.

59   *"Detriment to Community"*: Dean's Administrative Board Minutes, June 23, 1922, SCA. Violations are described in the college's *Customs and Regulations, 1921–1922*, 6–7.

59   *"cut quite a figure"*: My grandmother Elizabeth Brent Simms Stenhouse (1902–1966), Smith '24, overlapped with Henrietta and described her this way (conversation with Edith S. Bingham).

59   *"I tried to teach . . . lie with me"*: DG to MKC, August 18, 1924, Berg-NYPL.

4. AN AMERICAN GIRL OF TWENTY-ONE

63   *"period of instability"*: Smith College Annual Report, 1921–1922, 25.

63   *"For Henrietta . . . happy year"*: copy of George W. Cable, *The Amateur Garden* (New York: Charles Scribner's Sons, 1914), AP.

63–64   *Mina arranged . . . offer with Mina*: Huebsch to MKC, June 28, 1922, BHP-LOC; MKC to William Allan Neilson, June 13, 1922, SCA; LK diary, July 7, 1922, box 1, folder 6, LKP-NYPL.

64   *Upon renewing her teaching contract . . . years' service*: MKC to Neilson, February 25, 1922, Neilson Folder, SCA; Neilson to MKC, March 3, 1922, MKC-SSC.

65   *"like a streak . . . crush on Henrietta"*: HWB and GBB diary, 1922, AP.

65   *inside jokes*: Sallie Bingham interview, December 13, 2005, and MCB oral history.

65   *"perfectly . . . from end to end"*: HWB and GBB diary, 1922, AP.

65   *"gray as a badger"*: Ibid.

65   *"a triumph . . . and good spirits," "dreaming spires"*: Ibid.

66   *"found out," "could hardly . . . touch her"*: MKC to EJ, September 23, 1922, JP-BPAS.

66   *stepped off the train . . . "more to complain about"*: MKC to Louis and Rose Kirstein, September 10, 1922, MKC-SSC.

66   *"Petroushka"*: MKC inscription, May 4, 1923, in *Love Poems of John Donne* (London: Nonesuch Press, 1923), AP.

66   *"always . . . 'two ladies alone'"*: H.D., *Tribute to Freud* (New York: Pantheon, 1956), 74.

68   *Before and during World War I . . . could go astray*: Ann Douglas, *Terrible Honesty: Mongrel Manhattan in the 1920s* (New York: Farrar, Straus and Giroux, 1996), 122–29, and Christine Stansell, *American Moderns: Bohemian New York and the Creation of a New Century* (New York: Henry Holt, 2000), 302.

68   *Bookstores routinely . . . "Hysterical Women"*: Brenda Maddox, *Freud's Wizard: Ernest Jones and the Transformation of Psychoanalysis* (New York: Da Capo Press, 2006), 168.

69   *"contrary sexuals or inverts"*: Brill, "Conception of Homosexuality," 335.

69 *no one could . . . impetuous, and unreliable*: Jennifer Terry, *An American Obsession: Science, Medicine, and Homosexuality in Modern Society* (Chicago: University of Chicago Press, 1999), 292–96; Kenneth Lewes, *The Psychoanalytical Theory of Male Homosexuality* (New York: Simon & Schuster, 1988).

69 *"an active homosexual . . . manifested itself"*: MKC to EJ, September 23, 1922, EJP-BPAS.

70 *"became very intimate . . . physical one"*: Ibid.

70 *A "beautiful and clever" . . . to male clients*: Sigmund Freud, "The Psychogenesis of a Case of Homosexuality in a Woman," *The Standard Edition of the Complete Psychological Works of Sigmund Freud*, vol. 18, trans. and ed. James Strachey et al. (London: Hogarth Press, 1955), 147, 161.

70–71 *Mina explained . . . "in itself unhealthy"*: MKC to EJ, September 23, 1922, EJP-BPAS.

71 *live contentedly with her "perversion"*: Ines Rieder and Diana Voigt, *Die Geschichte der Sidonie C.* (Vienna: Zaglossus Verlag, 2012).

71 *Freud surmised . . . "problem of homosexuality"*: Freud, "Psychogenesis," 150, 151; Terry, *An American Obsession*; Chandak Sengoopta, "Tales from the Vienna Labs: The Eugen Steinach-Harry Benjamin Correspondence," *Favourite Edition* (published by the New York Academy of Medicine) 2 (Spring 2000), http://www.academia.edu/192188/_Tales_from_the_Vienna_Labs_The_Eugen _Steinach-Harry_Benjamin_Correspondence_, accessed July 22, 2014.

72 *"disgusted"*: A. A. Brill, "The Conception of Homosexuality," *Journal of the American Medical Association* 61 (1913), 335.

72 *"in general amenable . . . uncontrollable impulse"*: EJ, "Some Practical Aspects of the Psycho-Analytical Treatment" (1914), in EJ, *Papers on Psychoanalysis*, 2000 ed. (New York: William Wood, 1923), 318.

72 *Besides . . . money was on his mind*: Brome, *Ernest Jones: Freud's Alter Ego* (New York: Norton, 1983), 137, 142.

72 *"because I love" . . . "home of my own"*: MKC to EJ, September 23, 1922, EJP-BPAS.

72 *"something that we . . . something we are"*: Ann D'Ercole, "Postmodern Ideas about Gender and Sexuality: The Lesbian Woman Redundancy," in *Sexualities Lost and Found: Lesbians, Psychoanalysis, and Culture*, ed. Edith Gould and Sandra Kiersky (Madison, CT: International Universities Press, 2001), 192.

72 *"pale and ravishing"*: JH, "Run-Through," JHP-UCLA.

73 *a bisexual culture . . . often overlapped*: Lillian Faderman, *Odd Girls and Twilight Lovers: A History of Lesbian Life in Twentieth-Century America* (New York: Columbia University Press, 1991), 66, 69–77, 91; Stephen Tomlin to HWB, July 11, 1924, AP; Kate Summerscale, *The Queen of Whale Cay: The Life of a Great American Eccentric* (New York: Penguin, 1998), 56–59; Hazel V. Carby, "'It Jus Be's Dat Way Sometime': The Sexual Politics of Women's Blues," in *Unequal Sisters: A Multicultural Reader in United States Women's History*, eds. Vicki L. Ruiz and Ellen Carroll Dubois, 2000 ed. (New York: Routledge, 1994), 330–41.

73 *"both for her inversion . . . symptoms"*: EJ to Freud, February 15, 1923, *CC*, 510.

73 *"greatest piece of public . . . ever done"*: *CJ* employees to RWB, October 10, 1922; Emma Charlotte Backus, "The Princess of the [Tobacco] Pool: A Pageant of the Magic Leaf (Lexington, Ky.: The Burley Tobacco Growers Co-operative Association), RWB scrapbook 1922–30, AP; and *The Producer's Program: Fifty Golden Years and More* (Lexington, Ky.: The Burley Tobacco Growers Co-operative Association, 1991), 27–35.

73–74 *"Well on his way to Hell,"* *"haggard old man"*: RWB to HWB, September 17, 1922, AP.

74 *Robert vanished . . . into the state*: RWB to HWB, October 25, 1922, AP.

74 *He cabled Henrietta . . . "collapsed completely"*: Ibid.

74 *"child stabbed me . . . climax of the fight"*: RWB to HWB, November 12, 1922, AP.

74 *"course . . . in psychology"*: RWB to HWB, October 30, 1922, AP.

74 *"until early in December . . . every angle"*: RWB to HWB, October 25, 1922, AP.

74–75 *"I have made up . . . from the wreck"*: RWB to HWB, October 30, 1922, AP.

75 *"Thank God . . . to save me"*: RWB to HWB, November 12, 1922, AP.

75–76 *"terrifying accident"* . . . *"without even a scar"*: RWB to HWB, November 12, 1922, AP.

76 *"the loveliest daughter . . . a father"*: RWB to HWB, November 12, 1922, AP.

76 *"there never was such material to build on"*: EJ, in RWB to HWB, January 15, 1923, AP.

5. FREE ASSOCIATIONS

77 *"actively homosexual . . . specially interesting" work*: EJ to Freud, February 15, 1923, *CC*, 510; EJ, "Psychoanalysis in Psychotherapy," *Papers on Psychoanalysis*, 301; Maddox, *Freud's Wizard*, 170–71.

77 *"Irresistible"*: Maddox, *Freud's Wizard*, 164.

77 *"on their own ground"*: Ibid.

78 *"murky reputation"*: Ibid., 107. Jones's character and early career: Maddox, *Freud's Wizard*, 75, 80; Brome, *Freud's Alter Ego*, 67, 70, 102, 135, 179–80; EJ to Freud, October 17, 1909, 30.

78 *"will-power and self-mastery"*: EJ, *Free Associations*, 96–97; 113–14.

78 *Winnicott tried to lay out . . . to the unconscious*: Winnicott, in Janet Malcolm, *Psychoanalysis: The Impossible Profession* (New York: A. A. Knopf, 1981), 142–44.

79 *"lively, directive . . . lives and families"*: *Analyzing Freud: Letters of H.D., Bryher, and Their Circle*, ed. Susan Stanford Friedman (New York: New Directions, 2002), xxiv–v.

79 *Dreams were key . . . analytical insight*: Ken Robinson, Archivist Emeritus, British Psychoanalytical Society, interview, May 3, 2010; Brome, *Freud's Alter Ego*, 135, 179–80.

79 *"world of phantasy . . . pleasurable this may be"*: EJ, *Papers on Psycho-Analysis*, 317.

79 *"widowers . . . in the love of the wife"*: J. C. Flugel, *The Psycho-Analytic Study of the Family* (London: International Psycho-Analytical Press, 1921), 158, 226.

80 *"consider apt subjects . . for them"*: RWB to HWB, und. [c. February 1923], AP.

80 *"valuable to us newspaper owners"*: RWB to HWB, March 9, 1923, AP.

80 *"true romance"*: RWB to HWB, January 16, 1923, AP.

80 *"any man . . . result for humanity"*: RWB to HWB, November 12, 1922, AP.

80 *"preserve enough . . . anything worthwhile"*: RWB to HWB, June 14, 1923, AP.

81 *"cut him off entirely"*: RWB to HWB, February 24, 1923, AP.

81 *"disturbing the peace" . . . treating a woman honorably*: RWB to HWB, March 9, 1923, AP.

81 *"the best American . . enough for you"*: RWB to HWB, March 14, 1923, AP.

81 *"tall dark American girl,"* "reductio . . . *fidelity in love"*: FF, 9–10.

82 *"inexhaustible charm,"* *"jingle"*: F. Scott Fitzgerald, *The Great Gatsby* (New York: Charles Scribner, 1925), 121.

82 *"pudding"*: Jane Garnett to author, September 2008.

82 *"oval face" . . . "strength of personality"*: FF, 9–10.

82 *"Henrietta . . . or yours for her"*: DG to MKC, und. [1923], Berg-NYPL.

83 *"a stray kitten . . . to be adopted"*: DG, *Golden Echo*, 252.

83 *"wrong or maladjusted with either"*: FF, 13.

83 *"Did I tell you . . . week ago?"*: DG to MKC, January 17, 1923, Berg-NYPL.

83–84 *"Our relationship . . . sanctity of marriage"*: MKC, *OPL*, 14–15.

84 *"I will not have . . . help it"*: DG to Ray Garnett, und. [1923], box 32, folder 22, GFP-NWUL.

84 *"pouncer"*: Frances Partridge in Gretchen Holbrook Gerzina, *Carrington: A Life* (New York: W. W. Norton, 1989), 96.

85 *"exquisite American girls"*: DC to GB, March 1, 1923, GBP-HRC.

85 *"appallingly stupid and vulgar,"* *"Americans must . . . detestable people"*: DC to GB, February 6, 1923, GHP-HRC.

85 *Touring the two women . . . living in his home*: DC to GB, March 1, 1923, GBP-HRC.

85 *spoke a foreign language*: MKC, "Slices of Life," 9–10, courtesy Lynne Robbins Knox.

86 *"lavish hospitality"*: FF, 10.

86 *"her father's paper"*: DG to Ray Garnett, und. [1923], box 32, folder 22, GFP-NWUL.

86 *David and Ray Garnett held . . . necessary in America*: FF, 10–12.

86 *"whose recently published* Jacob's Room . . . *very well"*: MKC, "Slices of Life," 9–10, courtesy Lynne Robbins Knox.

87 *"Water Boy"*: DG to MKC, March 9, 1962, Berg-NYPL.

87 *"New World vitality . . . a long way"*: Michael Holroyd to author, June 11, 2008.

87 *"Irresistible"*: Ralph Partridge to Frances Marshall, August 7 [1923], FP-KCAC.

87 *Confederate talismans . . . prisoner in the Civil War*: Robert Bingham to HWB, March 14, 1923, Southern Historical Collection, University of North Carolina, Chapel Hill.

88 *Britons embraced . . . "black folks"*: Brian Ward, "Music, Musical Theater, and the Imagined South in Interwar Britain," *Journal of Southern History* 80 (February 2014), 45.

89 *"I only know . . . to go and see her"*: DC to GB, May 31, 1923, GBP-HRC.
89 *"wild moorland pony"*: Morrell in Gerzina, *Carrington*, xvi.
89 *Carrington was twenty-two . . . adored him*: Ibid., 69–70.
89 *"forget-me-not"*: DG, *The Flowers of the Forest* (London: Chatto and Windus, 1955), 10.
90 *"one can't help liking her"*: Gerzina, *Carrington*, 126.
91 *"How I hate . . . hanging flesh"*: DC, in Gerzina, *Carrington*, 93.
91 *"legitimate union"*: Woolf, in Gerzina, *Carrington*, 275.
91 *"Triangular Trinity of Happiness"*: DC to Strachey, in Jane Hill, *The Art of Dora Carrington* (London: Thames and Hudson, 1994), 82.
91 *"the discovery of a person . . . I care about"*: DC to GB, in Ibid., 82.
91 *"Ralph cut my hair . . . drunken passion"*: DC to GB, May 31, 1923, GBP-HRC.

6. O LET'S GET MARRIED

92 *"successful, popular, and unhappy"*: Sylvia Townsend Warner, *Garland of Straw* (New York: Viking Press, 1943), 138.
93 *One afternoon in 1922 . . . pose for him*: FF, 1–9.
93 *Garnett claimed his laughter . . . mirthful delight*: FF, 1–9.
93 *"ambidexterity"*: Ralph Partridge to Frances Marshall, September 4, 1924, FP-KCAC.
94 *"exciting . . . a remarkable character"*: Strachey in Holroyd, *Lytton Strachey: A New Biography* (New York: Farrar, Straus and Giroux, 1994), 586.
94 *"argue the hind leg . . . from his father"*: Warner, *Garland of Straw*, 138.
94 *Tomlin came with complications . . . over the names*: FF, 1–2, 12–13.
94 *"regretted it"*: Tomlin to HWB, January 2, 1925, AP.
94 *"falling badly in love"*: Tomlin to HWB, March 26, 1923, AP.
94 *"healthy contempt . . . amorous male"*: Tomlin to HWB, May 9, 1923, AP.
95 *"too self-centered, actually selfish"*: RWB to HWB, February 24, 1923, AP.
95 *"harried and unhappy . . . to explore you"*: Tomlin to HWB, April 13, 1923, AP.
95 *"I love you . . . I want you so"*: Tomlin to HWB, August 27, 1923, AP.
95 *"HAVING THE TIME OF MY LIFE IN WALES"*: Tomlin to DG, June 26, 1923, GFP-NWUL.
95–96 *When the Sunbeam broke down . . . holding her interest*: Tomlin to HWB January 1, 1924, AP; Tomlin to HWB December 15, 1923, AP; Tomlin to HWB, September 2, 1923, AP; Warner, *Garland of Straw*, 139; Neville Jason, *The Sculpture of Frank Dobson* (London: Henry Moore Foundation, 1994); "Cocktails with Elvira: Elvira Barney and Her Circle," http://elvirabarney.wordpress.com/tag/hambone-club/, accessed July 22, 2014.
96–97 *"refusal to flatter . . . might be"*: Oliver Garnett, "The Sculpture of Stephen Tomlin," B.A. thesis, Cambridge University, 1979.
97 *"three cases" . . . "typical" mother-daughter beating fantasy*: EJ to Freud, March 8, 1923, CC, 513.

97 *"blue-eyed ego-ideal"*: EJ to MKC, October 21, 1924, EJP-LC.

97–98 *Her extensive knowledge . . . knew her in London*: JH interview.

98 *"Negro vogue"*: Langston Hughes, Allen Woll, *Black Musical Theater: From Coontown to Dreamgirls* (1989; New York: Da Capo Press, 1991), 60.

98 *all-black show he took Barry to see*: RWB to HWB, November 12, 1922, AP.

98 The Plantation Review . . . From Dover Street to Dixie: Woll, *Black Musical Theater*, 96–98; Steve Tracy, "Stafford and Wilson: Trailblazers in a Brave New World," liner notes for *"Ain't Gonna Settle Down": The Pioneering Blues of Mary Stafford and Edith Wilson* (Archeophone, 2008). Wilson signed to Columbia Records as their first female blues singer and proved an early mistress of double-entendres. Her style was less earthy than Bessie Smith's, which might have alienated the *Plantation Review*'s white market.

98 *A massive sternwheeler . . . inspirational dance*: Brian Ward, "Music, Musical Theater, and the Imagined South," 55; "Eccentric Steps" footage from *Dover Street to Dixie*, http://www.britishpathe.com/video/eccentric-steps, accessed July 22, 2014.

98 *"charm is that . . . adolescent"*: No author, *The New Statesman*, November 8 [1923], clipping, folder 9, FMP-HAJTC.

98 *Irene Castle wept*: Irene Castle to Florence Mills, June 1 [1923], folder 4, FMC-HAJTC.

98–99 *"by far the most artistic . . . to see"*: St. John Irvine, in Bill Egan, *Florence Mills: Harlem Jazz Queen* (Lanham, Md.: Scarecrow Press, 2004), 92.

99 *Roger Fry . . . collection of tribal artifacts*: Roger Fry, "The Art of the Bushmen" (1910) and "Negro Sculpture" (1920). For more, see Gretchen Gerzina, "Bushmen and Blackface: Bloomsbury and 'Race,'" *South Carolina Review* 38 (Spring 2006), 46–64, 279; Garnett, "The Sculpture of Stephen Tomlin."

99 *"more direct . . . Freudian unconscious"*: Perry Meisel and Walter Kendrick, eds., *Bloomsbury/Freud: The Letters of James and Alix Strachey, 1924–1925* (New York: Basic Books, 1985), "Introduction," 47.

99 *"pretty Regency villa"*: LK, *Mosaic: Memoirs* (New York: Farrar, Straus and Giroux, 1994), 59.

100 *"colored element"*: D. J. Taylor, *Bright Young People: The Lost Generation of London's Jazz Age* (New York: Farrar, Straus and Giroux, 2007), 6.

100 *Confederate blood . . . John C. Breckinridge*: Tracy, "Stafford and Wilson."

101 *"It was an education . . . perfect courtesy"*: FF, 14–15.

101 *"hideous, horrible . . . women and girls"*: RWB diary, October 30, 1934, in Ellis, *RWB*, 197.

101 *Henrietta's influence . . . Symphony Hall*: Roland Hayes to RWB, December 28, 1923, RWB-LOC.

101 *windows were thrown open*: FF, 14.

101 *"reputedly very rich . . . love with them"*: JH interview.

101 *Mina took pity . . . "heart remained intact"*: RT, 46; and DC to GB, July 1, 1923, GBP-HRC; DG, *Carrington: Extracts from Her Letters and Diaries* (New York: Ballantine Books, 1970), 257.

102 *"an impromptu pas de trois"*: LK, *Thirty Years: The New York City Ballet* (New York: A. A. Knopf, 1978), 6–7.

102 *clad in purple . . . played her sax*: *RT*, 46.

102 *"made the party"*: Tomlin to HWB, May 9, 1923, AP.

102 *"the most delightful . . . ever known"*: DG to Constance Garnett, July 1, 1923, GFC-HRC.

102 *"absolutely perfect . . . heard her called?"*: Duncan Grant to MKC, August 12, 1923, Berg-NYPL.

102 *"judgment and advice"*: RWB to HWB June 24, 1923, AP.

102 *"shove Kentucky . . . taken it myself"*: RWB to HWB, March 25, 1923, AP.

102 *"Darling, my faith . . . for you"*: RWB to HWB, und. 1923, AP.

103 *"first orders"*: Marion Tomlin to HWB, October 9, 1923, AP.

103 *"seductive picture"*: Allan Neilson to MKC, April 26, 1923, MKC-SCC.

103 *"the secret . . . social structure"*: *FF*, 26–27.

104 *"However satisfactory . . . live with the scenes!"*: DC to Rosamond Lehmann, und. RNL-KCAC.

104 *"one thing about you . . [a man's] life"*: DG to MKC, August 16, 1923, Berg-NYPL.

104 *"I do want you so much"*: DG to MKC, August 10, 1923, Berg-NYPL.

104 *The Bingham clan . . . called the Dugout*: GBB diary 1923, AP.

104 *Barry . . . once looked up . . . way down*: Sallie Bingham, *Passion and Prejudice: A Family Memoir* (New York: A. A. Knopf, 1992), 202.

104–105 *One evening the Judge . . . "particularly murderous"*: DG to MKC, August 10, 1923, Berg-NYPL.

105 *"dearest Honey, sweetest Puppin"*: DG to HWB, und. [1923], Berg-NYPL.

105 *"O darling, it was horrible . . . wits"*: Tomlin to HWB, August 27, 1923, AP.

105 *"just crazy to have a car"*: DG to Ray Garnett, und. [summer 1923], GFP-NWUL.

105 *"The whole of London"*: DG to HWB, September 6, 1923, Berg-NYPL.

105 *Henrietta assured . . . never happen"*: DG to MKC, und., Berg Collection-NYPL.

105 *He organized . . . take part*: tennis bracket, Cunard Line leaflet August 30, 1923, RWB Scrapbook 1922–1930, AP.

105–106 *tobacco growers' picnic . . . "and uncertainty"*: July 3, 1923, ibid.

106 *eighty-fifth-birthday cake*: "Colonel Bingham, 85," *Chapel Hill Weekly*, September 13, 1923, ibid.

106 *There was luncheon . . . ready to crumble*: Ellis, *RWB*, 99, and "Resting in Louisville, Briton Discusses Reparations," *NYT* [October 1923], RWB Scrapbook 1922–1930, AP.

106 *fireproof storage business for Robert*: Caron's Business Directory (Louisville), 1924.

106 *Many in Louisville . . . lovers*: Brenner, *House of Dreams*, 53; Edith Callahan, *Paris Peace Conference* (Louisville: Catholic Messenger Press, 1920).

106 *"declared herself . . . dissatisfied"*: Tomlin to DG, November 1, 1923, GFP-NWUL.

106 *"Henrietta was not congenial . . . about boys"*: Mrs. James Skinner telephone interview with Sam Thomas, September 27, 1989, STP-ULASC.

107 *she proposed opening . . . nonliterary novelties*: GBB, *Barry Bingham: A Man of His*

Word, Samuel W. Thomas, ed. (Lexington: University of Kentucky Press, 1993), 41; RWB to HWB, March 25, 1923, AP; DG to MKC, October 18 and November 2, 1923, Berg-NYPL; Tomlin to HWB, October 9, 1923, AP; DG, "London Literary Letter," *CJ*, October 12, 1924.

107 *"For me there are . . . when I am not"*: Tomlin, DG to Ray Garnett, und. [1923], GFP-NWUL.

107 *"let loose the dogs . . . vitals again"*: Tomlin to HWB, October 9, 1923, AP.

107 *"But it's no good . . . I shall remain"*: Tomlin to HWB, September 15, 1923, AP.

107 *"decoction of our tears and our Burgundy"*: DG to MKC, September 14, 1923, Berg-NYPL.

108 *"surrounded by adorers of every sex"*: Tomlin to HWB, January 1, 1924, AP.

108 *"triumphant success . . . everywhere"*: Tomlin to HWB, September 15, 1923, AP.

108 *"prestige bugger"*: RP to FM, FP-KCAC.

108 *"to be anchored . . . to you in some way"*: Tomlin to HWB, September 2, 1923, AP.

108 *"in exquisite solitude"*: Tomlin to HWB, January 1, 1924, AP.

108 *"pekon nuts"*: Tomlin to HWB, December 15, 1923, AP.

109–110 *"My Beloved . . . appreciate my development!"*: Tomlin to HWB, und. [December 1923], AP.

110 *"the person you'll . . . in your life"*: DG to MKC, August 6, 1923, Berg-NYPL.

110–111 *"Henrietta said . . . my decisions be influenced"*: January 6, 1924, MKC diary, 1918–1919, MKC-SSC.

111 *"a fair and witty girl from Kentucky"*: Franklin P. Adams, May 20, 1924, *The Diary of Our Own Samuel Pepys*, 2 vols. (New York: Simon and Schuster, 1935).

111 *"old newspaperwoman"*: Franklin P. Adams to MKC, June 24, 1924, MKC-Yale.

111 *"I can't imagine . . . amusing trip"*: DG to MKC, April 1, 1924, Berg-NYPL.

111 *a magazine . . . "mixture of other passions"*: DG to MKC, November 15, 1923, and und. [December 1923], Berg-NYPL.

111 *"no doubts what . . . shouldn't have"*: DG to HWB, January 18, 1924, AP.

7. EFFECTS OF HENRIETTA

113 *Mina the bisexual bluestocking . . . with his daughter*: MCB oral history.

113 *Judge Bingham made advances . . . for good*: Frida Laski to Benjamin Huebsch, February 24, 1933, BHP-LOC.

113 *She told a friend . . . Mina and his sister*: JH interview.

113 *"banned from the family circle"*: Ibid.

114 *"Puppin and how she is handling the judge"*: DG to MKC, March 27, 1924, AP.

114 *Garnett was not . . . "no importance"*: DG to MKC, undated [April 1924], Berg-NYPL.

114 *"find out exactly . . . business stands"*: DG to MKC, May 8, 1924, Berg-NYPL.

114 *"poor badgered"*: DG to MKC, und. [1924], Berg-NYPL.

114 *"perfectly terrible"* and *"undeniably great . . . severely criticized"*: LEK to RSK, June 5, 1924, LEK-HBS.

114 *"Henrietta is heavenly . . . almost painful"*: DG to Ray Garnett, und. [1924], GFP-NWUL.

114 *"it impossible . . . their meetings, etc."*: Ibid.

114–115 *The tobacco mission . . . Maine to Georgia*: Ellis, *RWB*, 82–86.

115 *Then came news . . . the presidency*: DG to Ray Garnett, May 27, 1924, GFP-NWUL.

115 *"much drinking . . . on all sides"*: HWB to DG, und. [summer 1924], Berg-NYPL.

115 *"Charming girl . . . love to her, Carrington"*: HWB, in RP to FM, June 23, 1924, FP-KCAC.

115 *"that bulky American"*: LS to Philip Ritchie, June 29, 1924, Strachey Papers, Add 60721, British Library.

115 *"an oasis"*: Philip Ritchie to LS, Strachey Papers Addition 60693, British Library.

115 *"only safe place . . . quiet night"*: RP to FM, June 23, 1924, FP-KCAC.

116 *"everything at sixes . . . going up, too!"*: LS in Gerzina, *Carrington*, 148–49. Carrington mentioned her diary in DC to GB, February 14 and August 14, 1924, GBP-HRC. Apparently, it was lost or destroyed.

116 *"no one knew of but us"*: DC to GB, June 13, 1924, GBP-HRC.

116 *"ecstasy . . . shame afterwards"*: DC to GB, July 21, 1925, GBP-HRC.

116 *"We are the most . . . uninteresting inside"*: DC to GB, June 13, 1924, GBP-HRC.

117 *She inspired the painter . . . too late*: DC to GB, June 3, 1924, GBP-HRC.

117 *"remarkable impression of sunlight"*: Julia Strachey, in Gerzina, *Carrington*, 252.

118 *"La Bingham"*: LS to DC [1925], Levy, ed., *Letters of Lytton Strachey*, 512.

118 *"whitewashed unceasingly . . . a word"*: LS to DG, June 23, 1924, Robert Taylor Collection, Princeton University, series III, Modern Mss Corr, box 18.

118 *"Never a drop . . . a whole day"*: DC to GB, July 6, 1924, GBP-HRC.

118–119 *"far across . . . charmingly sensitive"*: DC to GB, June 23, 1924, GBP-HRC.

119 *Their conversation . . . peeping Tom"*: DC to GB, June 26, 1924, GBP-HRC.

119 *"the buggers"*: RP to FM, June 23, 1924, FP-KCAC.

119 *Soon thereafter . . . meet in Paris*: Tomlin to HWB, July 11, 15, and und. [July 1924], AP; Jason, *Sculpture of Frank Dobson*, 44.

119 *"lost half"*: GB, Diary entry, August 23, 1925, Notebook 2, GBP-HRC.

120 *"charming and intimate friend"*: GB to DC, June 12, 1924, GBP-HRC.

120 *"I think . . . oneself"*: DC to Rosamond Lehmann, und., RNL-KCAC.

120 *"carried away . . . princesses"*: DC to GB, June 23, 1924, in DG, *Carrington*, 295.

120 *"furious with . . . come near her"*: RP to FM, June 23, 1924, FP-KCAC.

120 *"large American boys . . . there with me"*: DC to GB, July 7, 1924, GBP-HRC.

120 *"engrossed in his domains"*: Duncan Grant to MKC, November 18, 1924, Berg-NYPL.

121 *"obstacle to our . . . was Henrietta"*: DG to MKC, und. [1970s], Berg-NYPL.

121 *"when he took . . . over her body"*: Henrietta Garnett interview, October 2008, AP.

121 *"runner-up"*: Franklin P. Adams to MKC, June 22, 1924, MKC-Yale.

121 *"annual self-torture"*: Benjamin Huebsch to MKC, August 16, 1924, BHP-LOC.

121 *"permanently adolescent . . . arts"*: OPL, 12; *"delightful, talented sculptor"*: MKC, "Slices of Life," courtesy Lynne Robbins Knox.

121 *took tea with* . . . Man in the Zoo: Edward Garnett to MKC, February 4 and July 16, 1924, Berg-NYPL.

121 *"hairraising"*: Duncan Grant to MKC, September 16, 1924, Berg-NYPL; *"history"*: Duncan Grant to MKC, August 31, 1924, Berg-NYPL.

121 *"hazy memory"*: MKC to Clive Bell, und. [1924], Charleston-KCAC.

122 *"Minna's . . . best in America"*: RP to FM, July 1924, FP-KCAC.

122 *"in a state . . . dinner jacket"*: Clive Bell to MKC, June 30, 1924, Berg-NYPL.

122 *"one must expect . . . head in consequence"*: EJ to MKC, October 21, 1924, EJP-LOC.

123 *"effects of H[enrietta]"*: GB, notebook 2, GBP-HRC.

123 *"killed my desires . . . completely"*: DC to GB, July 25, 1924, in Holroyd, *Lytton Strachey*, 542–43.

123 *"I am impossible" and "Henrietta repays . . . I do yours"*: DC to GB, July 25, 1924, in DG, *Carrington*, 296.

123 *"nobody loves her . . . 'darling Henrietta'"*: RP to FM, June 23, 1924, FP-KCAC.

123 *"most Exquisite and charming character"*: DC to GB, July 21, 1924, GBP-HRC.

123 *"physical gestures"*: DC to GB, August 20, 1924, GBP-HRC.

123 *"of certain sensations . . . to repeat them"*: DC to GB, August 20, 1924, GBP-HRC.

123 *"excelerator"*: Ibid.

123 *"her as I knew her"*: DC to GB, August 6, 1924, GBP-HRC.

123 *"I fear I love her"*: DC to GB, August 11, 1924, GBP-HRC.

125 *"happier . . . a co-religionist"*: LK, *Mosaic*, 65–66.

125 *"dreadful father and brothers"*: DC to GB, August 18, 1924, GBP-HRC.

125 *In early August . . . set off for Scotland*: DC to GB, August 6, 1924, GBP-HRC.

8. AN' I WISH I WAS HAPPY AGAIN

126 *"General frightful . . . Binghamesque scenes"*: EJ to Katherine Jones, August 17, 1924, EJP-BPAS.

127 *Despite his best efforts . . . a fortune*: *The Producer's Program*, 36–39.

127 *"Bobbie . . . rich old widow"*: William J. Fields, *CJ* [1924], RWB-ADD-FHS2.

127–128 *Leopold and Loeb . . . grossest sin*: Todd C. Riniolo, *Freud and Fame: Lessons in Psychology's Fascinating History* (Amazon Digital Services, 2012); Paula Fass, "Making and Remaking an Event: The Leopold and Loeb Case in American Culture," *Journal of American History* 80 (December 1993), 919–51.

128 *"Does an incessant rain . . . in your company"*: Tomlin to HWB, August 13, 1924, AP.

128 *"to spite Henrietta . . . coldness to him"*: James Strachey to Alix Strachey, September 27, 1924, Strachey Papers, Add. 60713, British Library.

128 *David Garnett's wedding gift . . . knife*: DG to RWB, September 10, 1924, RWB-LOC.

128 *The announcement took Louisville . . . as well*: Nora Isiagi Bullitt to Amy Gore Walker Iasigi, August 15, 1924, BFP-FHS; Carrie Gaulbert Cox to Margaret Muldoon Norton, August 25, 1924, courtesy J. Walker Stites III.

129 *"belleship . . . society man"*: Aleen Muldoon scrapbook; background for Aleen's biography, "Michael McDonald Muldoon 1836–1911 and His Family: A Biographical Scrapbook for His Greatgrandchildren [*sic*] from His Granddaughter Dorothy Lithgow Norton Clay," compiled by Samuel W. Thomas, 1986, both courtesy J. Walker Stites III.

129 *a prenuptial agreement . . . Bingham property*: "Agreement between RWB and Aleen M. Hilliard," August 18, 1924, RWB-ADD-FHS.

129 *"They all got drunk"*: RP to FM, und. [August 1924], FP-KCAC.

129 *No image accompanied . . . "Bobby Franks"*: CJ, August 21, 1924.

130 *"anxious to hear . . . attendant Furies"*: Tomlin to DG, und. [August 1924], GFP-NWUL.

130 *"must be leading . . . these days"*: EJ to MKC, August 30, 1924, EJP-LOC.

130 *"dread"* and *"rebuff and desertion"*: EJ, "Early Development of Female Sexuality," *International Journal of Psycho-Analysis* 8 (October 1927), 471.

130 *"American . . . a girl with lovely red hair"*: DC to GB, August 28, 1924, GBP-HRC.

130 *"Down with the Americans! Abasso gli Americani!"*: RP to FM, 1924, FP-KCAC.

130 *"furious and pleading"*: RP to FM, September 14, 1924, FP-KCAC.

130 *"You must wait, if you can"*: DC, in Gerzina, *Carrington*, 210.

131 *"make a deep . . . weight of guilt"*: EJ to MKC, December 12, 1924, EJP-LOC.

131 *"semi-deliberate cruelty"*: FM, in Gerzina, *Carrington*, 209.

131 *"undignified"*: RP to FM, September 14, 1924, FP-KCAC.

131 *"moral degradation," "always wanted to be a man"*: Lydia Lopokova to John Maynard Keynes, October 13, 1924, in Polly Hill and Richard Keynes, eds., *Lydia and Maynard: The Letters of John Maynard Keynes and Lydia Lopokova* (New York: Scribner, 1990), 235.

131 *"curiosity . . . to know this creature better"*: DC to GB, October 6, 1924, GBP-HRC.

131 *"her voice of course . . . feelings against her"*: DC to GB, September 26, 1924, GBP-HRC.

132 *"I feel now regrets . . . for various females"*: DC to Alix Strachey, May 11, 1925, in Holroyd, *Lytton Strachey*, 535.

132 *depression*: RP to FM, September 19, 1924, FP-KCAC, and James Strachey to Alix Strachey, November 26, 1924, Strachey Papers, British Library, Add 60713.

132 *"incredibly beautiful . . . Autumn of despairs"*: Tomlin to DC, incomplete, und. [October 1924], FP-KCAC.

132 *"completely given over to the ladies"*: RP to FM, und. [1924–1925], FP-KCAC.

132 *"like a mob of starlings . . . choking me"*: Tomlin to HWB, October 24, 1924, AP.

132 *cast of Henrietta's head*: Tomlin to DC, October 15, 1924, FP-KCAC.

133 *"I really can't write out . . . relieved thereby"*: EJ to MKC, October 21, 1924, EJP-LOC.

133 *"home for Bob"*: Carrie Gaulbert Cox to Margaret Muldoon Norton, August 25, 1924, courtesy J. Walker Stites III.

133 *Jones thought it auspicious . . . Kentucky with her*: EJ to MKC, November 12, 1924, EJP-LOC.

133 *"lacerated and sore"*: MKC to EJ, December 27, 1924, EJP-BPAS.

133 *The same fall . . . yellow Stutz Bearcat*: MKC, "Slices of Life," 20–23, courtesy Lynne Robbins Knox.

133 *"myself or my golf balls . . . greater golf ball"*: HTC to Mr. [S. Merrell] Clement [Jr.], June 7, 1922, MKC-Yale.

133–134 *"English club-man," "very male Henrietta"*: MKC to EJ, December 27, 1924, EJP-BPAS.

134 *"for a man-hater . . . my poor sex!"*: EJ to MKC, December 12, 1924, EJP-LOC.

134 *"beautiful consumptive"*: Chilton to EJ, December 8, 1924, EJP-BPAS.

134 *Jones told Mina . . . ambivalence about men in general*: EJ to MKC, December 12, 1924, EJP-LOC.

134 *"lewd and lascivious co-habitation"*: MKC, "Winter Letters," MKC-SSC.

134 *"balm it has been . . . intellectual and physical"*: MKC to EJ, December 27, 1924, EJP-BPAS.

135 *"belle et brilliante Mademoiselle"* and *"friend with the Giottesque . . . Sapphistical complications"*: Clive Bell to MKC, December 25, 1924, Berg-NYPL.

135 *"American female bitches"*: DC to Alix Strachey, February 4, 1925, Strachey Papers, Add 60701, British Library.

135 *"sitting round . . . mouths open"*: Tomlin to HWB, December 3, 1924, AP.

135 *"If they only knew . . . wish I had done so"*: Tomlin to HWB, November 24, 1924, AP.

135 *Among the "bitches" . . . Henrietta's other admirers*: MCB oral history; Sallie Bingham interview, December 13, 2005, AP; EJ to MKC, October 21, 1924, EJP-LOC; Jeannette Young to RWB, October 12, 1926, RWB-ADD-FHS2.

135 *moved to London . . . local banking*: Albert interview.

135 *Sophie accepted . . . as well as dangerous*: Ibid.

136 *"my father . . . and my lover"*: MKC to EJ, December 27, 1924, EJP-BPAS. Mina credited her psychoanalysis, interview with MKC, *Smith Alumnae Quarterly*, April 1977.

136 *"perfunctory letters," "corseted little lines"*: MKC to EJ, December 27, 1924, EJP-BPAS.

136 *"untroubled by hope," "that is her method . . . strain on them"*: Tomlin to MKC, January 1, 1925, AP.

136 *"appallingly jealous . . . I suppose all"*: EJ to MKC, November 12, 1925, EJP-LOC.

136 *"pure homosexual and very narcissistic"*: EJ to MKC, September 30, 1924, EJP-LOC.

136 *"homosexuality and masculinity"*: EJ to MKC, October 21, 1924, EJP-LOC.

136–137 *"I adore Oxford . . . each other like this"*: EJ to MKC, October 21, 1924, EJP-LOC.

137 *As for Henrietta . . . Mina versus the Judge*: EJ to MKC, September 30, 1924, EJP-LOC.

137 *"backed by every cousin . . . suspect that she is still h-l [homosexual]"*: EJ to MKC, November 24, 1924, EJP-LOC.

137 *"brute"*: RP to FM, und. [1924], FP-KCAC.

137–138 *"Henrietta can at least . . . what I cabled"*: EJ to MKC, December 12, 1924, EJP-LOC.

138 *The week before . . . furious and miserable*: James Strachey to Alix Strachey, December 23, 1924, Strachey Papers, Add 6071, British Library, and Tomlin to MKC, January 1, 1925, AP.

138 *"an old fashioned . . . bed and nowhere else"*: DG to Tomlin, December 15, 1924, Berg-NYPL.

138 *Very Marlene Dietrich . . . was coming of age*: Albert interview and W. K. Martin, *Marlene Dietrich* (New York: Chelsea House Publishers, 1995), 35–42.

138 *"My darling," "For Heaven's sake . . . soon"*: Tomlin to HWB, January 2, 1925, AP.

138 *"They that desire . . . Pestilence"*: Tomlin to MKC, January 1, 1925, AP.

138 *"breaking hearts"*: Tomlin to HWB, January 2, 1925, AP.

138 *"loveliest thing in the world"*: Tomlin to HWB, December 3, 1924, AP.

139 *"Will you please . . . marry me"*: Tomlin to HWB, January 2, 1925, AP.

139–140 *"the bigness of it . . . homosexuality to build on"*: EJ to MKC, January 27, 1925, EJP-LOC.

140 *"premature sexual experiences"*: Sigmund Freud, "An Aetiology of Hysteria" (1896), in *Standard Edition*, vol. 3, 203.

140 *What if Henrietta . . . sexual contact with Robert Worth Bingham?*: For most of the twentieth century, patients who carried memories or dreams of early sexual experiences with family members were told that these were imagined or, if contact had happened, that it was a projection of their unconscious desires. By the 1980s, a bitter debate over the pervasiveness of child sexual abuse and incest divided the psychoanalytic profession, with feminists and victims accusing practitioners of re-traumatizing patients and shielding criminal adults. Herman, *Father-Daughter Incest*; Janet Malcolm, *In the Freud Archives* (New York: A. A. Knopf, 1984).

141 *nonphysical, covert . . . deserve consideration*: Judith Lewis Herman, *Father-Daughter Incest* (Cambridge: Harvard University Press, 1981); Louise Armstrong, *Kiss Daddy Goodnight: A Speak-Out on Incest* (New York: Hawthorne Books, 1978); Kenneth M. Adams, *Silently Seduced: When Parents Make Their Children Partners*, rev. ed. (Deerfield Beach, FL: Health Communications, 2011).

141–143 *"made more fundamental . . . directly or indirectly"*: EJ to MKC, April 7, 1925, EJP-LOC.

143 *"that the real reason . . . wasn't a virgin"* and *"complete Oedipus complex"*: James to Alix Strachey, May 7, 1925, in *Bloomsbury/Freud*, 259, and Minutes of the British Psycho-Analytical Society, May 18, 1925, BPAS.

143 *"done with homosexuality"*: EJ to MKC, January 27, 1925, EJP-LOC.

143 *"You needn't tell me . . . benefit of it"*: EJ to MKC, May 7, 1925, EJP-LOC.

144 *"ravishing"*: Tomlin to DG, April 16, 1925, GFP-NWUL.
144 *Lytton took her . . . farewell gift*: LS to DC, und. [March 1925], in Levy, *Letters of Lytton Strachey*, 512.
144 *"I dream of her . . . tear them up continually"*: DC to Alix Strachey, May 11, 1925, in Holroyd, *Lytton Strachey*, 535.
144 *"temps perdu," "American invasion"*: DC to GB, April 14, 1926, GBP-HRC.
144 *elaborate cardboard coffin . . . "RIP DC"*: DC to GB, March 1, 1925, GBP-HRC.
144 *in one dream . . . retribution*: GB diary, March 15, 1925, Notebook 1, GBP-HRC.
144–145 *"Oh, and what do you think" . . . "she never would"*: GB to DC, May 18, 1925, GBP-HRC.
145 *" 'intimate' relations with anyone"*: DC to GB, September 25, 1925, GBP-HRC.
145 *"An' I wish I was happy again"*: Tomlin to HWB, September 15, 1923, AP.

9. JUG BAND ORDERED

146 *"She must . . . all there is to it," "So I am sending her home"*: EJ to MKC, May 7, 1925, EJP-LOC.
146 *appendectomy*: Ellis, *RWB*, 104.
147 *This highly regarded magazine . . . African-American performers*: "Theatre Arts Monthly," *Oxford Critical and Cultural History of Modernist Magazines* (New York: Oxford University Press, 2012), vol. 2, 379–82; Edith Isaacs, *Notable American Women*, vol. 4, 370; Alain Locke, "The Negro and the American Stage," *Theatre Arts Monthly* 10 (February 1926), 703.
147 *"little child"*: JH to HWB, March 26, 1926, AP.
147 *"Dear Judge Bingham . . . Yours, Henrietta Bingham"*: HWB to RWB, March 24, 1926, RWB-LOC.
147 *"gradually coming . . . her father"*: EJ to MKC, September 30, 1925, EJP-LOC.
147 *"smell of easy money in the air"*: JH, "Run-Through," JHP-UCLA.
147 *"oil and motors . . . extravagant and alcoholic"*: Ibid.
148 *"Ain't got nobody . . . troubles on the shelf"*: Langston Hughes, "Weary Blues," in *Weary Blues* (New York: A. A. Knopf, 1926).
148 *"Take your time . . . your lard away"*: miscellaneous HWB material, AP; Dixieland Jug Blowers, "Mama Don't Give Your Lard Away," http://www.juneberry 78s.com/sounds/LV540-02.mp3, accessed July 22, 2014. The song was recorded in Chicago in 1926.
149 *"pure callousness"*: JH to Bea Howe, November 10, 1925, AP.
149–150 *"Twelve and a half hours" . . . chitlins and greens*: JH, "Run-Through," JHP-UCLA.
150 *"latest on wax"*: "Langston Hughes's Collection of Rent Party Advertisements," http://www.slate.com/blogs/the_vault/2013/03/14/rent_parties_langston _hughes_collection_of_rent_party_cards.html, accessed July 22, 2014.
150 *An edgier crowd . . . cafeteria style"*: David Levering Lewis, *When Harlem Was in Vogue* (New York: Oxford University Press, 1989), 108.
150 *"pure affection . . . infinitely grateful"*: JH to Bea Howe, November 10, 1925, AP.

150 *"excessively feminine . . . smooth-muscled boy"*: JH, "Run-Through," JHP-UCLA.
150 *"probably the only . . . ever really in love"*: JH to GBB, und. [1972], GBB-FHS.
150 *"danced like an angel"*: JH, "Run-Through," JHP-UCLA.
150 *"Southern Poetess . . . damp with tears"*: Ibid.
150–151 *"speakeasies and . . . Bourbon and mirrors"*: Ibid.
151 *"Lacking security . . . merchant prince"*: RT, 16, 19, 25–26.
151–152 *Having worked the wheat harvest . . . could not fully explain*: Ibid, 50–51.
152 *"lunatic Louisville troop"*: JH, "Run-Through," JHP-UCLA.
152 *"from the very depths," "M. Boulevard"*: Alan [Nathaniel Steyne?] to HWB, und. [c. December 1925], AP.
152 *"dilute her h-l [homosexual] whirlpool"*: EJ to MKC, September 30, 1925, EJP-LOC.
152 *"There were people . . . asked me to kiss her"*: JH, "Run-Through," JHP-UCLA.
152–153 *Provincetown Players' production . . . Delmonico's or Voisin's*: Ibid.
153 *preoccupied with his inexperience*: Ibid.
153 *"JUG BAND ORDERED" . . . holiday with his family*: Ibid.
153 *"far away . . . perfect paradise"*: "Anything Is Nice If It Comes from Dixieland" (1919), Leo Feist, Inc.
153 *"pillared mansion . . . blouses for Christmas"*: JH to Bea Howe, December 26, 1925, AP.
153–154 *dining table set . . . "start out again"*: JH, "Run-Through," JHP-UCLA.
154 *The festivities . . . to her mouth*: JH to HWB, February 8, 1926, AP.
154 *"young man she had brought home . . . firm of Jewish grain-merchants"*: JH, "Run-Through," JHP-UCLA. The couple was Louise Todd and Seymour Parker Gilbert, Jr., who were married on September 19, 1924, clipping, papers of Margaret Norton Davidson (Henrietta's cousin by marriage), courtesy J. Walker Stites III.
154 *"completely happy . . . inherent bourgeoisie and vulgarity"*: JH to Bea Howe, December 26, 1925, AP.
155 *"past deserted houseboats . . . heavy with hate"*: JH, "Run-Through," JHP-UCLA. Henrietta assembled a group that may have included Rufus "Whistler" Threlkeld, who had his roots in Louisville's rural outskirts and had been entertaining since her teenage years. He recorded as Whistler's Jug Band in 1924 and 1925; then in his early thirties, he was hustling for a living and struggled with a cocaine habit. *The Jug Bands of Louisville* (Essex, England: Storyville Publications, 1993), 32.
156 *"voluptuous excitement"*: JH to Bea Howe, December 26, 1925, AP.
156 *"bowels to water . . . delicious weeping"*: JH, *Front and Center*, 109.
156 *"terribly troubled, always"*: JH interview.
156 *"fantastically gifted writer"*: Ibid.
156 *"deep and violent," "ran a stream . . . your eyes"*: JH, "Run-Through," JHP-UCLA.
156 *"spent money . . . massively and deliberately"*: Ibid.
156 *"If she agreed . . . The Courier Journal"*: Ibid.
157 *"at the last moment . . . father's side"*: Ibid.
157 *"hideous gloom"*: JH to HWB, October 31, 1925, AP.

157 *"she could save her soul"*: Tomlin to DC, December 27, 1925, FP-KCAC.
158 *"emotional maze . . . around her"*: JH, "Run-Through," JHP-UCLA.
158 *"in a dream . . . into my mouth"*: Ibid.

10. A RED DAMASK SUITE

159 *"secret treaty"*: JH, "Run-Through," JHP-UCLA.
159 *couples celebrated . . . Whiteman Orchestra*: JH to HWB, December 28, 1926; *"funniest woman in the world"*: Coward, *Life* (May 15, 1964); *"Beatrice Lilly"*: Anthony Slide, *Encyclopedia of Vaudeville* (Oxford: University Press of Mississippi, 2012), 316.
160 *standing in the snow . . . shepherd dog*: Chapelbrook photo album, MKC-SSC.
160 *Harry imparted . . . "greatest of these"*: HTC to HWB, January 21 [1926], AP.
160 *In early 1926 . . . putting deals together*: *RT*, 56.
160 *"indifferent," "repressed . . . for you to marry"*: JH to HWB, February 22, 1926, AP.
160 *"perfect courtesy"* and *"stretched tight . . . jealousy and suspicion"*: JH, "Run-Through," JHP-UCLA.
160–161 *"I am a very dynamo," "vitality"*: JH to HWB, February 5, 1926, AP.
161 *"we will be successful . . . flamboyantly so"*: JH to HWB, February 1, 1926, AP.
161 *He directed her . . . as he sent them"*: JH to HWB, March 1, 1926, AP.
161 The New Statesman . . . *short fiction*: "Ghoul," *The New Statesman*, November 7, 1925, was listed in *The Best British Short Stories of 1926, with an Irish Supplement*, Edward J. O'Brien, ed. (New York: Dodd and Mead, 1926), 338.
161 *"of that kind"* and *"to marry . . . Do you mind?"*: JH to HWB, May 10, 1926, AP.
161 *"culture in our . . . your hands"*: JH to HWB, May 10, 1926, AP.
161 *He talked of spending . . . far from Kentucky*: JH to HWB, September 7, 1926, AP.
161 *"sullen and repressed"*: JH to HWB, February 8, 1926, AP.
161–162 *"If you are to find . . . and fresh too"*: HTC to HWB, February 9, 1926, AP.
162 *"Go slow . . . blow you both up"*: HTC to HWB, und. [early 1926], AP.
162 *"sounding him out . . . through his fear"*: Ibid.
162 *"shyness in the flesh"* and *"idleness in ink"*: JH to HWB, May 14, 1926, AP.
162 *At the end of February . . . and martial law*: Passaic strike, JH to HWB, May 1, 1926, AP; Philip S. Foner, *History of the Labor Movement in the United States. Volume 10: The TUEL, 1925–1929* (New York: International Publishers, 1994), 143; Izaak Walton Club, http://www.keyshistory.org/longkey.html, accessed July 22, 2014.
162 *"Amuse yourself in Florida, darling"*: JH to HWB, March 22, 1926, AP.
163 *"what arrangement . . . him in London"*: JH, "Run-Through," JHP-UCLA.
163 *"storms of fury . . . paternal breast"*: JH to HWB, February 28, 1926, AP.
163 *"your damned . . . your new steps"*: JH to HWB, April 30, 1926, AP.
163 *"terribly afraid of the future"*: JH to HWB, April 28, 1926, AP.
163 *"poor John Mason Brown"*: JH to HWB, und. [c. April 1926], AP.
163 *"with a leer . . . Mina Kirstein"*: JH to HWB, May 20, 1926, AP.

163 *Stephen Tomlin's heavy iron . . . coming and going*: Tomlin to RWB, January 1 and February 17, 1926, and RWB to Tomlin, March 6, 1926, AP.

164 *"I think I shall never . . . whole Henrietta"*: JH to HWB, April 26, 1926, AP.

164 *"sucked up [her] personality"*: JH to HWB, March 16, 1926, AP.

164 *"at the bootlegger's . . . propriety"*: JH to HWB, May 3, 1926, AP.

164 *"grave dangers," "pure"*: JH to HWB, May 10, 1926, AP.

164 *"God bless her . . . loving each other"*: JH to HWB, March 7, 1926, AP.

164 *"horrible half-meetings . . . furtive caresses," "for the many . . . gave you"*: JH to HWB, April 22, 1926, AP.

164 *"spiritual and physical . . . beyond all hope"*: JH to HWB, September 2, 1926, AP.

165 *"I have often . . . right level for me"*: JH to HWB, April 26, 1926, AP.

165 *"Those who accompany . . . inside my mouth"*: JH, "Run-Through," JHP-UCLA.

165 *spiriting the newlywed . . . around the countryside*: JH to HWB, September 3, 1926, AP.

166 *Henrietta left behind . . . gramophone for weeks*: DG to MKC, July 14, 1926, Berg-NYPL.

166 *The doctor was less hopeful . . . two children*: Chilton to EJ, November 11, 1925, EJP-BPAS, and EJ to MKC, July 4, 1927, EJP-LOC.

166 *Harry took his bride . . . girl she loved*: MKC, "Winter Letters," MKC-SSC, and MKC to JH, March 14, 1947 (copy), MKC-SSC.

166 *The Judge . . . with the Kirsteins*: RWB to Sadie Bingham Grinnan, July 1, 1926, RWB-LOC.

166 *Mina's brother Lincoln . . . "awfully merry"*: LK diary, March 29, 1927, box 1, folder 10, LKP-NYPL; LK, *Mosaic*, 59.

166–167 *With so much travel . . . at the edges*: GBB and HWB, *Shadows*, AP.

167 *"born with an artistic . . . along at school"*: Ibid.

167–168 *"Thank God . . . of life"* and *"How empty . . . your mother died"*: Ibid.

168 *"sour and ugly . . . and I hate it"*: Ibid.

168 *"But some day . . . lose my ambition"*: Ibid.

168 *"a woman so independent . . . be called ambition"*: Ibid.

168 *"most of the ambition for all three of us . . . breaking of old ties"*: Ibid.

169 *"very strong personality . . . old calm reasonable self"*: Ibid.

169 *"former youth and warmth . . . lonely all the time"*: Ibid.

169 *"spinach-green"*: JH to HWB, September 2, 1926, AP.

169–170 *Taking the fifty-five-room . . . nine servants*: Walker, Fraser, and Steele Estate Agents to RWB, February 12, 1926; RWB to Walker, Fraser, et al., March 3, 1926; Ivan D. Guthrie to RWB, March 29, 1926, all RWB-ADD-FHS2.

170 *"One of your most nefarious . . . too exciting"*: JH to HWB, September 3, 1926, AP.

170–171 *"teacher and counselor . . . suitor"*: JH, "Run-Through," JHP-UCLA.

171 *"delivered her relentless . . . on my part"*: Ibid.

171 *"promiscuous dramatization"*: JH to HWB, November 29, 1926, AP.

171 *"love you more . . . than before"*: JH to HWB, August 30, 1926, AP.

172 *"soft voice . . . wants me ever so badly"*: JH to HWB, September 14 and 22, 1926, AP.

172 *"lose your oddities"*: JH to HWB, March 12, 1926, AP.

172 *"in the matter . . . constant muffled conflicts"*: Ibid.

172 *"You believe . . . don't you?"*: JH to HWB, September 14, 1926, AP.

172 *Her expensive . . . over the lease*: Jeannette Young to RWB, October 12, 1926, RWB-FHS, and JH to HWB, September 3, 1926, AP.

172 *"lessons"*: JH to HWB, October 27, 1926, AP.

172–173 *"family turmoil and bitterness . . . another weakness"*: JH to HWB, November 20, 1926, AP.

173 *"ridiculous that you should be in want"*: JH to HWB, December 13, 1926, AP.

173 *"painful as hell"*: HWB in JH, "Run-Through," JHP-UCLA.

173 *By the new year . . , Robert Worth Bingham, too*: Emily Overman to HWB, December 31, 1926, RWB-LOC, and JH to HWB, January 20, 1927, AP.

173 *"dog to live with"*: JH, "Run-Through," JHP-UCLA.

174 *"disgraced herself with Kentucky"*: DC to LS, November 29, 1926, Strachey Papers, Add 62894, British Library.

174 *"dog, her slave, etc."*: DG to MKC, January 11, 1927, Berg-NYPL.

174 *"It isn't good . . . everyone unhappy"*: GBB and HWB, *Shadows*, AP.

174 *"Down South . . . to be better"*: Beverley Nichols, "Celebrities in Undress XLVII—Florence Mills," *The Sketch*, February 16, 1927, FMP-HAJTC.

174 *"'Blackbird party'"*: DG to MKC, May 30, 1927, Berg-NYPL.

174 *"I used to nearly perish . . . over their supper"*: HWB to GBB, April 6, 1943, MCB-FHS.

175 *"It was a sort of indoctrination . . . our virginity"*: JH interview.

175 *At the grand redbrick . . . miserable delight*: Ibid. and *RT*, 56.

175 *"his sex—which is something"*: DG to MKC, May 30, 1927, Berg-NYPL.

175 *She immersed herself . . . to a tree*: JH to HWB, June 20, 1927, AP.

176 *"And so he's an American . . . fond of you"*: DG to MKC, May 18, 1927, Berg-NYPL.

176 *But Henrietta and Jack were quarrelling . . . in public*: JH to HWB, June 15, 1927, AP.

176 *"first rate emotions," "rotten lover"*: JH to HWB, June 20, 1927, AP.

176 *"luscious great silver fox fur"*: GBB to MCB, May 15, 1927, MCB-FHS.

177 *"My darling . . . than passing compliments"*: JH to HWB, June 9, 1927, AP.

177 *He enumerated his demons . . . "embittered my desires"*: JH to HWB, June 22, 1927, AP.

178 *"There you are . . . what you're missing"*: JH to HWB, und. [June 1927], AP.

11. HUNTING

181 *Mina and Harry decided . . . "miracle" enough*: MKC to EJ, August 6, 1927, EJP-BPAS.

181 *Mina had her students . . . Charles Lindbergh*: Susan Hertog, *Anne Morrow Lindbergh: Her Life* (New York: Nan A. Talese, 1999), 61–62.

181 *"try the cold world . . . used to"*: EJ to MKC, July 4, 1927, EJP-LOC.

182 *"a free person" and "the financial issue"*: MKC to EJ, August 6, 1927, EJP-BPAS.

182 *"no matter what . . . by the sea"*: Ibid.

182 *Ivor Churchill . . . interest in modern art*: Consuela Vanderbilt Balsan, *The Glitter and the Gold* (New York: Harper Brothers, 1952), 80, 233, 296–97; James Brough, *Consuelo: Portrait of an American Heiress* (New York: Coward, McCann & Geoghegan, 1979), 175, 243. Lord Ivor Spencer-Churchill served on the committees that managed the British Pavilion at both the 1928 and 1930 Venice Biennales, http://venicebiennale.britishcouncil.org/timeline/1928, accessed July 22, 2014.

182 *"sought after"* and *"to achieve Harry"*: MKC to EJ, August 6, 1927, EJP-BPAS.

182 *"clever and original"* and *"virile young man"*: Ibid.

183 *"Boys don't"* . . . *accept his homosexuality*: Franz Schulz, *Philip Johnson: Life and Work* (New York: A. A. Knopf, 1994), 35, 186.

183 *"perpetual letters . . . comparatively normal one"*: MKC to EJ, August 6, 1927, JP-BPAS; Beatrix Lehmann to John Lehmann, June 1, 1927, Lehmann Family Papers, Manuscript Division, Princeton University Library; JH, *Front and Center*, 109.

183–184 *Robert had fallen for . . . Edinburgh*: Robert married Phyllis Clark; JH to HWB, October 27, 1926, AP; menu card, August 9, 1927, RWB scrapbook, 1922–30, AP.

184 *"a more depressing . . . mutual mistrust"*: GBB to MCB, und. [September 1927], MCB-FHS.

184 *"comic devilry"*: Adrian Wright, *John Lehmann: A Pagan Adventure* (London: Duckworth, 1998), 17.

184 *disguised herself as a boy . . . Scout activities*: John Lehmann, *In My Own Time: Memoirs of a Literary Life* (Boston: Atlantic Monthly Press, 1969), 52.

185 *"nerve storms . . . to learn"*: Beatrix Lehmann to Rosamond Lehmann, May 1926, RNL-KCAC.

185 *"Tallulah must . . . all the time"*: Anders, "Sir Patrick Hastings, Tallulah Bankhead, and Beatrix Lehmann," http://elvirabarney.wordpress.com/2012/01/07/sir-patrick-hastingstallulah-bankhead-and-beatrix-lehmann/, accessed June 27, 2014.

185 *American sales were strong . . . at Chapelbrook*: Selina Hastings, *Rosamond Lehmann: A Life* (London: Vintage Books, 2003), 105–108.

185 *"very much in love"*: JH interview.

185 *The* Glasgow Bulletin *. . . high stone butt*: RWB scrapbook, und. photograph 1922–1930, AP. Rosamond was in the midst of a thorny divorce, perhaps explaining why Wogan Phillips, her lover at the time, pulled down his hat to hide his face from the photographer.

185 *"rather a formal person"*: Dorothy Norton Clay in Thomas, "Michael McDonald Muldoon," 90, courtesy J. Walker Stites III.

186 *"Ma was thrilled"*: Alice Hilliard to [?], und. [1927], courtesy J. Walker Stites III.

186 *"no go"*: EJ to MKC, October 8, 1927, EJP-LOC.

186 *November brought . . . Harlem had ever seen*: *NYT*, November 27, 1927.

186 *The darkness intensified . . . oxygen tent*: MKC, "Slices of Life," 3, courtesy Lynne Robbins Knox.

186 *"just what marriage . . . broken"*: Rosamond Lehmann to MKC, January 30, 1928, Berg-NYPL.

187 *"All I wanted . . . futile"*: MKC to EJ, September 26, 1928, EJP-BPAS.

187 *"absurd little cottage with roses and arbours"*: DC to LS, [November 1, 1928], in DG, *Carrington*, 503.

188 *"almost invariably . . . 'bullet biting'"*: Hastings, *Rosamond Lehmann*, 197.

188 *"one sees to it . . . begins"*: Rosamond Lehmann, *A Note in Music* (1930; London: John Lehmann, 1948), 57.

188 *The novelist . . . homosexual crowd*: Anthony Powell, *Messengers of Day* (New York: Holt, Rinehart, and Winston, 1978), 32–35, 53, 95–96.

189 *"a splendid . . . political world," "Do you . . . want the vote"*: HWB, on Lady Astor, December 1, 1928, in RWB scrapbook 1922–30, AP.

189 *"make a living"*: HWB, "Noted Soldier Is Making Hats," *CJ*, December 16, 1928.

189–190 *"Upon Matters . . . 6 each morning"*: HWB, "Lady Oxford a Decorator at Five Guineas a Visit," *CJ*, April 14, 1929. On Anthony Asquith, see Stephen Bourne, *Brief Encounters: Lesbians and Gays in British Cinema, 1930–1971* (London: Cassell, 1996).

190 *In 1928–1929 . . . the same period*: accounts for Robert, Henrietta, Barry, 1928–1929, RWB Papers, AP.

190–191 *Henrietta then turned . . . penal colonies*: "How Europe Handles Crime and Criminals," *CJ*, August 11 and 25 and September 1, 1929.

191 *Psychiatric medicine . . . "prison commissioner"*: *Oxford History of the Prison*, ed. Norval Morris and David J. Rothman (New York: Oxford University Press, 1995), 178–79, and HHJ diary February 16, 1936.

191 *"celebrate . . . you have done for me"*: HWB to EJ, November 30, 1928, EJP-BPAS.

191 *"five cases . . . to a far stage"*: EJ, "The Early Development of Female Sexuality," *International Journal of Psycho-Analysis* 8 (October 1927), 459.

191 *"I have very little . . . 'in the know'"*: EJ to Freud, June 19, 1910, *CC*, 61.

191 *However, by the late 1920s . . . penis envy*: MKC to EJ, August 6, 1927, EJP-BPAS; EJ to Freud, May 16, 1927, and Freud to EJ, May 31, 1927, *CC*, 617–19.

191 *Psychoanalysis was breaking . . . basis for his propositions*: Frank Cioffi, "Freud and the Idea of a Pseudo-Science," in Cioffi and Robert Borger, eds., *Explanation in the Behavioral Sciences* (London: Cambridge University Press, 1970), 471–99, and Maddox, *Freud's Wizard*, 85–86.

192 *"Faced with aphanisis . . . sex or their incest"*: EJ, "The Early Development of Female Sexuality," 466, emphasis in original.

192 *"gratification . . . incorporated into themselves"*: Ibid., 468.

192 *"'disapproval' and 'desertion'"*: Ibid., 471.

192 *One family member . . . coffee came from*: MCB oral history.

192 *"revolutionary"*: Chilton to EJ, November 8, 1927, EJP-BPAS.

192 *Whether or not . . . such as it was*: HWB to EJ, November 30, 1928, EJP-BPAS.

193 *The title character . . . more popular book today*: Esther Newton, "The Mythic Mannish Lesbian: Radclyffe Hall and the New Woman," in Martin Duberman, Martha Vicinus, and George Chauncey, Jr., eds., *Hidden from History: Reclaiming the Gay and Lesbian Past* (New York: New American Library, 1989), 281–83.

193 *"punishing treatments"*: Ibid., 292.

193–194 *An international legal . . . "except as pornography"*: Leslie A. Taylor, "I Made Up My Mind to Get It": The American Trial of *The Well of Loneliness*, New York City, 1928–29," *Journal of the History of Sexuality* 10 (April 2001), 253, 256.

194 *Covici-Friede . . . "American Court"*: Ibid., 266–67, 280, 283.

194 *an image of lesbians . . . without drawing attention*: George Chauncey, Jr., "From Sexual Inversion to Homosexuality," *Salmagundi* 58/59 (Fall 1982–Winter 1983), 118–19.

194 *"marquee vamp"*: Julia Strachey to DC, und. [c. 1927], Berg-NYPL.

195 *"maimed and ugly"*: Radclyffe Hall, *The Well of Loneliness* (1928; New York: Anchor Books, 1990), 204.

195 *"It nearly broke . . . always a skirt"*: Albert interview.

12. SPEED SIX

196 *"a lot of good"*: Emily Overman to HWB (copy), October 4, 1929, RWB-ADD-FHS2.

197 *"Father has gotten . . . Rhine wine"*: GBB to MCB, June 18, 1930, MCB-FHS.

197 *"the chloroform . . . complete unconsciousness"*: GBB to MCB, May 26, 1931, MCB-FHS.

197 *"sever[ing] . . . in the morning"*: GBB to MCB, May 29, 1930, MCB-FHS.

197 *Barry amused her . . . Jack Turner*: GBB, "Baby Eyes" (Louisville: WHAS, *The Courier-Journal* and *Louisville Times*, 1930).

197 *All this fun . . . mourning Harry*: MKC, ed., *Olive, Cypress, and Palm: An Anthology of Love and Death* (New York: Harcourt, Brace, and Co., 1930), inscribed "H.W.B—M.K.C. May 8, 1930," AP.

198 *"Henrietta . . . on the lips"*: Sarah McNeal Few to author, as told by her mother, Jane Aley (1909–1963).

198 *Barry and Edie . . . the pair*: GBB to MCB, May 29, 1930, MCB-FHS.

198 *"but she has . . . about it"*: RWB to Mrs. R. T. (Sadie) Grinnan, June 20, 1930, RWB-ADD-FHS2.

198 *On July 13 . . . Le Mans road race*: http://www.sportscarmarket.com/columns /profiles/english/1373-1930-bentley-6-liter-speed-six, accessed June 28, 2014.

198–199 *"the greatest fun," "peace propaganda . . . unspeakably funny!"*: Beatrix Lehmann to Rosamond Lehmann, September 10, 1930, RNL-KCAC, and Isa Partsch-Bergsohn, *Modern Dance in Germany and the United States: Cross Currents and Influences* (Switzerland: Harwood Academic Publishers, 1994), 60–62.

199 *"a lot of screaming peacocks"*: Beatrix Lehmann to Rosamond Lehmann, September 10, 1930, RNL-KCAC.

199 *"time and money"*: Beatrix Lehman to Rosamond Lehmann, September 15, 1930, RNL-KCAC.

199 *"You'd love the Judge"*: Beatrix Lehmann to Rosamond Lehmann, September 10, 1930, RNL-KCAC.

199 *"curious glamour"*: *RT*, 134.

200 *"vaguest idea . . . situation or home life"*: MCB oral history.
200 *"made up to . . . obviously not available"*: Ibid.
200 *"mysterious, fascinating creature"*: Ibid.
201 *The redheaded . . . Black Bottom*: Bricktop with James Haskins, *Bricktop* (New York: Atheneum, 1983), 116–17.
201 *"my honey boy"*: MCB oral history.
201 *"nice tacky . . . come in to broadcast"*: GBB to MCB, November 1930, in Brenner, *House of Dreams*, 61.
201 *he appealed . . . end in embarrassment*: RWB to HWB, January 11, 1931, RWB-ADD-FHS2.
201 *"never had to . . . college phase"*: GBB to MCB, December 2, 1930; Brenner, *House of Dreams*, 68.
201 *in early 1931 . . . Jeannette Young*: MCB oral history.
201 *The Courier-Journal . . . tripled to 160,000*: RWB scrapbook 1922–1930, AP.
201–202 *When the Bank . . . more than $200,000*: *Louisville Times*, December 26, 1930, RWB scrapbook 1922–1930; thank-you letters from depositors, RWB-ADD-FHS2.
202 *"stomp[ing] up the aisle," "Hunting Field . . . worry her again"*: MCB to GBB, April 28, 1931, MCB-FHS.
202 *"unsatisfactory"*: GBB to MCB, May 1, 1931, MCB-FHS.
202 *Posing on deck . . . her father's arm*: "Off to Europe, socially prominent," June 18, 1931, University of Louisville Photographic Archives, Herald Post Collection, http://digital.library.louisville.edu/cdm/singleitem/collection/heraldpost/id/1296/rec/1, accessed June 28, 2014.
202 *"very far from . . . another Harry"*: EJ to MKC, May 13, 1931, EJP-LOC.
202 *To Mary's dismay . . . his sister*: Brenner, *House of Dreams*, 138.
202 *from the Côte . . . together in September*: John Starling to RWB, August 31, 1931, RWB-ADD-FHS2.
202–203 *In Venice . . . party broke up*: MCB oral history.
204 *"a miserable . . . that kind of work"*: Ibid.
204 *"absolutely normal . . . as I love her"*: RWB to HWB (copy), April 3, 1932, RWB-ADD-FHS2.
204 *"take hold . . . nice children"*: MCB oral history.
204 *One month before . . . to the hospital*: "Confidential Information Prepared for Legal and Financial Advisors to RWB," by Estate Planning Corp., 3, AP; and Brenner, *House of Dreams*, 143–44.
204 *"My father had . . . she was brilliant"*: GBB, *Patriarch*, 87.

13. MISS AMERICA

205 *"largesse and generosity . . . all bottles"*: Beatrix Lehmann to Rosamund Lehmann, December 26, 1931, RNL-KCAC.
206 *concussion when her horse . . . paved road*: GBB to William Hall Lewis, November 1953 (copy), AP.

206 *"getting uglier . . . the compliment"*: Beatrix Lehmann to Rosamund Lehmann, August 23, 1933, RNL-KCAC.

206 *Henrietta determined . . . typing and shorthand*: RWB to HWB, April 3 and 18, 1932, AP. On women in Foreign Office, e-mail with Adam Richardson, July 22 and 23, 2013.

206 *Citing losses . . . 20 percent*: RWB to HWB, April 18, 1932, and RWB to Robert, May 24, 1932, AP.

206 *pay cuts of 10 percent*: *Patriarch*, 122.

206 *John Houseman . . . spiraling downward*: *RT*, 70–74 and 81–88.

207 *"the best hope . . . resource I have"*: RWB to FDR, September 22, 1931, Private Corr., FDR Papers, in Ellis, *RWB*, 127.

207 *This time . . . FDR-friendly publishers*: RWB to Homer Cummings, May 17, 1932, AP, and RWB to HWB, April 3, 1932, AP.

207 *"a complete change"*: Beatrix Lehmann to HWB, August 24, 1932, RNL-KCAC.

207 *The playwright . . . especially for her*: "In or of the Shifting Broadway Panorama," *NYT*, April 15, 1928.

207 *"incompatibility"*: "Divorce Confirmed by Hope Williams," *NYT*, December 8, 1928.

207 *"bantering nonchalance"*: Charleston (WV) *Daily Mail*, December 17, 1933.

207–208 *"a great deal . . . supposed to"*: Hepburn in "Hope Williams, 92, Actress Dies," *NYT*, May 4, 1990.

208 *"all the top-drawer . . . long affair"*: Ann Andrews, in Joel Lobenthal, *Tallulah! The Life and Times of a Leading Lady* (New York: Regan Books, 2004), 184.

208 *"living . . . Tallulah's best girl"*: Beatrix Lehmann to Rosamond Lehmann, und. [1932], RNL-KCAC.

208 *In the Absaroka . . . champagne*: "Packed for Pleasure," *Sports Illustrated*, August 13, 1956.

209 *"ride-'em-cowboy . . . spectacular masculinity"*: Beatrix Lehmann to HWB, August 24, 1932, RNL-KCAC.

209 *"riotously promiscuous" . . . possibility*: Diana McLellan, *The Girls: Sappho Goes to Hollywood* (New York: L.A. Weekly Books, 2000), 23.

209 *the performers took immense care . . . their tracks*: Lesley Harris, "Kit and Guth: A Lavender Marriage on Broadway," in Robert A Schanke and Kim Marra, eds., *Passing Performances: Queer Readings of Leading Players in American Theater History* (Ann Arbor: University of Michigan Press, 1998), 197–220.

209 *Hope had money . . . ahead*: Williams's husband, R. Bartow Read, died in an aviation accident in 1931, leaving a $650,000 estate to his ex-wife. Whereas the *NYT* obituary claims that this was the source of much of her wealth, a December 22, 1931, item in that paper reported that she "renounced her claim to the property in accordance with an agreement made between the couple" and that his siblings would be the beneficiaries. It is not clear where the truth lies.

209 *The script . . . fashion writer*: 1933–1934 Hope Williams clippings, AP.

209 *Eleanor Roosevelt . . . over Hoover*: RWB to HWB and GBB, September 14, 1932, RWB-ADD-FHS2.

210 "*a sad future . . . live in!*": Beatrix Lehmann to HWB, December 15, 1932, RNL-KCAC.

210 *Henrietta helped . . . before his speech*: Minutes from Associated Press board of directors, October 5, 1932, HWB miscellany, AP, and *CJ*, October 21 and 23, 1933.

210 "*hard and faithfully*": Franklin Delano Roosevelt, in *RWB*, 128.

210 "*independence*": Emanuel Levi to RWB, January 17, 1933 (copy), AP.

211 "*What do you . . . unanalysed?*": Beatrix Lehmann to HWB, December 15, 1932, RNL-KCAC.

211 *His grain . . . Saint-Exupéry*: *RT*, 81, 88–89.

211 "*an awful, bloody . . . pinned down!*": JH to HWB, und. [January-February 1933], SBP-Duke.

211 "*Daughter . . . come with me*": JH interview.

211 "*Look . . . marry me?*": Ibid.

212 "*Absolutely not*": Ibid.

212 "*a bad time . . . top girl*": Ibid.

212 *but gossip spread*: The young woman told a New York businessman, who told the writer W. E. Woodward. William E. Woodward diary, October 10, 1934, William E. and Helen Woodward papers, Special Collections Library, University of Kentucky.

212 "*anti-American attitude*": *NYT*, March 14, 1933.

213 *Then darker . . . for the appointment*: *RWB*, 130, and *BB*, 194–96, n. 31, p. 226.

213 "*slacker . . . Republican party*": Rep. Albert May, *Congressional Record*, Vol. 77, Part 1, March 4, 1933–April 3, 1933. This was reported by the *NYT* and *CJ* on March 23, 1933. May had an axe to grind, as the *CJ* had opposed his candidacy.

213 "*I was told . . . what I did*": M. L. Ravitch, M.D., to RWB, und. [1933], AP.

213 *Bingham turned to . . . Bingham's behalf*: Raymond Clapper diary entry, September 8, 1933, Raymond Clapper Papers, box 8, folder 7, Manuscript Division, Library of Congress; Young, "To Whom it May Concern," March 13, 1933, AP; William MacCallum to Hugh Young, March 14, 1933 (copy), AP; RWB, "Memorandum for Professor Raymond Moley," March 13, 1933, AP.

213 "*my favourite murderer*": William Christian Bullitt to WMB, July 30, 1946, BFP-FHS.

213 *Growing as . . . Bingham collapsed*: *RWB*, n. 37, 241, and Aleen Bingham to Margaret Norton, April 25, 1933, courtesy J. Walker Stites III.

214 *After several weeks' . . . like the sun*: "Washington Sails with Two Envoys," *NYT*, May 11, 1933; "Plymouth to Welcome Bingham," *NYT*, May 13, 1933; photo in RWB scrapbook 1933–1935, AP.

214 *Two days later . . . read the headline*: "Miss America Looking Over London," *Daily Sketch*, May 20, 1923, AP.

214 *Next came . . . widely published*: "Last Royal Court Is Most Brilliant," *NYT*, June 24, 1933, AP, and RWB scrapbook 1933–35, AP; Josephus Daniels to RWB, July 13, 1933, RWB-LOC.

215 *Hope Williams . . . Emily Brontë*: *Cinematograph Weekly*, July 16, 1933, RWB scrapbook 1933–35, AP.

215 *"chic young daughter"*: *Tatler* (London), November 29, 1933, RWB scrapbook
     1933–35, AP; also see April 1933 Louisville *Junior League Magazine* and RWB
     diary, July 4, 1933, RWB-LOC.

215 *"just keen about everything"*: Aleen Bingham to Margaret Norton, May 26 and
     June 2, 1933, courtesy J. Walker Stites III.

216 *"piddling . . . happy with me"*: HWB to Tomlin, June 22, 1933, GFP-NWUL.

216 *where she held sway in the kitchen*: HHJ to Susan Tifft, August 6, 1987, courtesy
     Alex S. Jones.

216 *"the Prince of Wales . . . in the embassy"*: MCB oral history.

216 *"soufflé Henrietta"*: menu, March 26, 1934, RWB scrapbook 1933–1935, AP.

217 *"rather shy lady . . . to live up"*: FF, 15.

217 *Aleen adored . . . interiors at Prince's Gate*: Aleen Bingham to Margaret Norton,
     May 26, 1933, and photo album, courtesy J. Walker Stites III.

217 *"would be overlooked . . . she was"*: FF, 15.

217–218 *"delightful . . . full of humble gratitude"*: Ibid.

218 *"bad time"*: Eleanor Chilton Agar to RWB, und. [September 1933], RWB-LOC.

218 *"the horizontal ambassador"*: Raymond Clapper diary entry, September 8, 1933,
     Raymond Clapper Papers, box 8, folder 7, Manuscript Division, Library of
     Congress. Roosevelt prompted bitter complaints from the British and other al-
     lies when he reversed course and rejected monetary stabilization and debt for-
     giveness after Bingham made public pronouncements in favor of debt reduction
     and loosening trade barriers. (See "World Peace and Recovery," London *Times*,
     May 31, 1933; "Empire Trade," Adelaide, Australia, *Chronicle*, August 3, 1933;
     and "Mr. Bingham's Task," *Aberdeen Evening Express*, September 21, 1933, RWB
     scrapbook 1933–1935, AP.)

218 *a private Welsh clinic*: R. S. Allison, "Ruthin Castle: A Private Hospital for the
     Investigation and Treatment of Obscure Medical Diseases (1923–1950)," http://
     www.ncbi.nlm.nih.gov/pmc/articles/PMC2385532/, 25–26, accessed July 15, 2014.

218 *On the back of her map*: Map of England and Wales, HWB trunk, AP. The song,
     "Till the Sands of the Desert Grow Cold," composed by Ernest R. Ball with
     lyrics by George Graff and published in New York by M. Whitmark and Sons in
     1911, charted at number 1 in 1912.

219 *"a small gift . . . love, H"*: HWB to RWB, und., RWB-LOC.

219 *"BABYLON . . . grown grey"*: RWB scrapbook 1933–1935, AP.

219 *Eleanor was in contact . . . country home*: EJ to Katherine Jones, August 31 and
     September 20, 1933, EJP-BPAS.

219–220 *"great competence . . . of all kinds"*: Eleanor Chilton Agar to RWB, und. [Sep-
     tember 1933], RWB-LOC.

220 *Bingham wasn't always . . . appear ineffectual*: "Unity of Britain and America,"
     London *Times*, October 26, 1933; "Wheat Price Decline," London *Times*, No-
     vember 29, 1933; "Washington's Secret Exchange Fund," London *Times*, De-
     cember 1, 1933, all RWB scrapbook 1933–1935, AP.

220 *"neurasthenic . . . help and advice"*: "Our Diplomatic Men," *Fortune*, April 1934,
     110.

220 *"most swaggery walk"*: O. O. McIntyre, "New York Day by Day" (syndicated column) from *Lansing State Journal*, December 4, 1933, AP.

220 *"icy coiffure"*: Percy Hammond "The Theaters," *NY Herald Tribune*, December 26, 1933, AP.

220 *some reviewers complained . . . emotional range*: Jack Garver, U.P. Drama Editor, "Broadway and Side Streets," in *Battle Creek* [Michigan] *Journal*, December 26, 1933; Brooks Atkinson, "Paris Where 'All Good Americans' Go," *NYT*, December 26, 1933.

221 *"social parity"*: RWB diary entry, March 26, 1934, RWB-LOC.

221 *"extraordinary effect"*: RWB diary entry, April 12, 1934, RWB-LOC.

222 *"wonderful comfort and support"*: GBB to RWB, November 8, 1936, RWB-LOC.

222 *A 1934 profile . . . "'fast friends!'"*: "American Envoy Wins Britain's Favor," und. *Birmingham News–Age Herald*, RWB scrapbook 1933–35, AP.

14. A JOYOUS AND SATISFYING LIFE

223 *"were expected to . . . the matches"*: *BTG*, 202–203.

223 *Critics saw . . . "a woman"*: Catherine Horwood, "Women's Tennis Wear in Interwar," in *The Englishness of English Dress*, ed. Christopher Breward, Becky Conekin, and Caroline Cox (Oxford: Berg, 2002), 56–57.

224 *"looked better . . . think of"*: cartoon reproduced in *BTG* at 174–75; story of shorts, *BTG*, 173–75.

224 *"plantation airs"*: London *Evening News*, July 3, 1934, RWB scrapbook 1933–1935, AP.

224 *"expected to find . . . unto themselves"*: *BTG*, 23.

225 *"rested . . . at Sunningdale"*: clipping fragment [1934], AP; tournament ticket book, AP.

225 *When she departed . . . next year*: HHJ to RWB, July 15, 1934, RWB-LOC.

226 *"Little Miss Poker Face"*: Gallico, *Farewell to Sport* (1937; Lincoln: University of Nebraska Press, 2008), 44.

226 *"Some ten thousand . . . limp"*: Ibid., 51.

226 *"acute . . . gall bladder"*: "Miss Jacobs Ignored Physician's Advice," *NYT*, August 29, 1933.

226 *"isn't keen about the boys"*: *NY World Telegraph*, July 6, 1935, clips, HHJ-ITHFM.

226 *"that foul woman . . . lady"*: HHJ diary, July 2, 1938.

226 *Henrietta's return . . . November 1934*: RWB to GBB, October 1 and 15, 1934, RWB-LOC.

226 *Henrietta brought . . . for tea*: HHJ diary, November 8, 1934

226–227 *the next day . . . in tow*: HHJ diary, November 8 and 9, 1934.

226–227 *The women were very much . . . nickname for Henrietta*: HHJ diary, November 8, 9, 10, and 16, 1934. The Binghams also called her "Nat."

227 *"guest of . . . American Ambassador"*: London *Daily Mail*, November 24, 1934, RWB scrapbook 1933–1935, AP.

227 *"seems really to enjoy me"*: HHJ diary, November 20, 1934.
227 *"he feels . . . her judgment"*: HHJ diary, April 24, 1935.
227 *"Wish A[mbassador] . . . to endure it"*: HHJ diary, November 25, 1934.
227 *"little room"*: HHJ diary, April 9, 1935.
228 *One day . . . tennis date*: HHJ diary, April 29, 1935.
228 *Aleen presented . . . American debutantes*: "Americans to Bow at British Court," *NYT,* June 20, 1935.
228 *On one occasion . . . place at the embassy*: HHJ diary, March 20, 1936, and clipping, March 20, 1936, RWB scrapbook 1933–1935, AP.
228 *purebred puppy . . . "Scrap"*: Pedigree from G. M. Reynell & Co., "Letitia of Crendon," SBP-Duke.
228 *Judge Bingham . . . Helen could train*: RWB to GBB, November 26, 1935, and HHJ diary, April 30, 1935. The Bingham presence at the house is also documented in Catharine Meek, "Madge's—Long Crendon: A Brief History," und. courtesy of the author.
228 *"a joyous and satisfying life"*: HHJ, diary, March 28, 1938.
228–229 *"apparent necessity . . . destroys so many illusions"*: HHJ diary, March 2, 1935.
229 *They went walking . . . cottages*: HHJ diary, November 10, 1934.
229 *They toured . . . royal box*: HHJ diary, November 20, 1934.
229–230 *At the British Museum . . . medical condition*: HHJ diary, January 9 and 14, 1935.
230 *"a natural"*: HHJ diary, November 17, 1934.
230 *"You didn't fall off "*: BTG, 253.
230 *Bentley to Cornwall . . . foxhunt*: HHJ diary, December 23, 24, and 27, 1934.
230 *where the most . . . had begun*: HHJ diary, January 20, 1935.
230 *Tennis season approached . . . "good hunt"*: BTG, 254–55.
230 *"A pretty nice . . . speak"*: HHJ diary, November 30, 1934.
230 *"would do . . . only love"*: HHJ diary, December 9, 1934.
230 *"After marvelous . . . lonely now"*: HHJ diary, December 2, 1934.
230 *"an aristocrat from head to toe"*: HHJ diary, November 20, 1934.
230 *Her kindness . . . anyone's*: HHJ diary, January 30, 1936.
230 *"Nat is the best . . . ever known"*: HHJ diary, January 1, 1935.
231 *"Wonderful scenes tonight"*: HHJ diary, February 10, 1935.
231 *Henrietta mixed . . . "glorious success"*: HHJ diary, January 2 and 3, 1935.
231 *A few days later . . . bagpipe playing*: HHJ diary, January 4, 5, 6, and 7, 1935, and *Wallis and Edward, Letters 1931–1937: The Intimate Correspondence of the Duke and Duchess of Windsor*, ed. Michael Bloch (Boston: G. K. Hall, 1987), 432.
231 *"German protagonist"*: RWB to FDR, December 24, 1935, *RWB*, 166. The ambassador, the royal family, and many key British political leaders regarded the romance with deep concern. His abdication the following year over Simpson was a blessing, in Bingham's view. Henrietta, Barry, and Mary once attended a party at her chic London flat, where Mrs. Simpson surprised Barry by asking him to bite in half a sugar cube for her to mix into the prince's cocktail. They

lamented that Edward attracted the "most frivolous and indeed trashy Americans." MCB oral history, *BB*, 77–78, and *RWB*, 182–83.

231 *"lair"*: Gallico, *Farewell to Sport*, 53.
231 *"If I had been . . . shoes"*: Ibid.
232 *"There you are . . . tomorrow"*: *BTG*, 261–62.
232 *"In all the history . . . by combat"*: Gallico, *Farewell to Sport*, 54.
233 *"Finals . . . the bitch"*: HHJ, diary, July 6, 1935.
233 *The family retreated . . . bloomed*: HHJ diary, July 7 and 8, 1935, and *BTG*, 264.
233 *"operation"*: *Daily Telegraph*, July 18, 1935, RWB scrapbook 1933–1935, AP.
233 *"plans to burn . . . wives and daughters"*: HHJ diary, July 22, 1935.
233 *"drunken . . . street sweeper"*: Hugh Young: *A Surgeon's Autobiography*, 505.
233 *A LORD . . . AMBASSADOR ARRIVE*: *New York Post*, August 6, 1935, HHJ-ITHFM.
234 *"glorious nights"*: HHJ diary, August 6, 1935.
234 *"Pa here—thank god"*: HHJ diary, September 9, 1935.
234 *"got a glow on sherry"*: HHJ diary, September 11, 1935.
234 *They strolled around . . . reconstruction*: photographs of Williamsburg and Charlottesville by HWB, AP.
234 *In Staunton . . . Mary Lily*: HHJ diary, September 14, 1935, and Stuart Hall trophies, AP.

15. OUR HOUSE WITH OUR HORSES

235 *Mary and Barry threw them a mint-julep party*: HHJ diary, September 22, 1935.
235 *Herbert Agar . . . their home*: HHJ diary, September 21, 1935.
235 *aced her—once*: GBB to RWB, October 22, 1935, RWB-LOC.
235 *"En-Tout-Cas"*: *BTG*, 266.
235 *"impressive and dignified . . . its woman"*: HHJ diary, September 17, 1935.
236 *"happy and proud"*: HHJ to HWB, April 20, 1941, AP.
236 *"high bluff . . . breath away"*: GBB to RWB, October 22, 1935, RWB-LOC.
237 *"I believe she has . . . job in London"*: Ibid.
237 *"has the most . . . in the world"*: Ibid.; "Story of the Bingham Farm and Grandmother Snowden," GBB-FHS.
237 *"the two great . . . behalf of peace"*: RWB in *RWB*, 165–66.
237 *"our house with our horses"*: HHJ diary, November 28, 1935.
237 *Learning the sport . . . Bill Tilden*: HHJ, unidentified clipping [1935–1936], HHJ-ITHFM.
237–238 *"Since you are fool" . . . edge off his speed*: *BTG*, 270–74.
238 *"I could have . . . a gun"*: HHJ diary, December 22, 1935.
238 *Helen was delighted . . . clothes*: HHJ diary, December 25, 1935.
238 *Henrietta "did everything . . . us all happy"*: RWB diary, December 25, 1935, RWB-LOC.
238 *"Must stop . . . (cocktails)"*: HHJ diary, December 16, 1934.
238–239 *after dinner at the Savoy . . . composure returned*: HHJ diary, June 13, 1936.
239 *"lecherous glances . . . precipitate"*: HHJ diary, December 19, 1934.

239 *"being an English lesbian"*: JH interview.

239 *"sporadically intimate"*: MKC, "Slices of Life," 45, courtesy Lynne Robbins Knox.

239 *Mina inaugurated*... Citizen Kane: *RT,* 134, 147–59.

239 *late-term abortion*: Duberman, *Worlds of Lincoln Kirstein,* 300. Stephen Pascal, editor of Leo Lerman's letters, suggested that in his memoirs Houseman glossed over his relationship with Mina both as a lover and a financial backer of his the-atrical ventures (conversation with author, May 2008).

239 *"days since... lovely spine"*: MKC to Clive Bell, und. [spring 1936], Charleston-KCAC.

240 *Nat celebrated... filled with laughter*: HHJ diary, April 15, 1936. Phyllis's husband, Arnold Wycombe Gomme, was a noted classicist at the University of Glasgow. He was often away from Long Crendon.

240 *Hoping to avoid... Harold Nicolson*: In 1935, Nicolson published a biography of Anne's father, the American statesman Dwight Morrow.

240 *"stiff and disinterested"*: HHJ diary, April 1, 1936.

240 *"unbent"*: Ibid.

240 *"She seemed... sensible girl"*: MKC, "Charles Lindbergh: A Personal Portrait," MKC-SSC.

240 *Robert Worth Bingham's... her father*: HHJ diary, May 22 and 23, 1936; Phyllis Gomme to RWB, August 2, [1937], AP; RWB to GBB, April 22, 1936, RWB-LOC.

240 *"very kind man"*: HHJ diary, April 28, 1936.

240 *"Nothing but bed... with N"*: HHJ diary, May 8, 1936.

240 *"an angel"*: HHJ diary, May 11, 1936.

240 *"home to London"*: HHJ diary, May 16, 1936.

241 *"Nuts to him"*: HHJ diary, May 10, 1936.

241 *"perfectly trained... play temperament"*: "Title Round in Wimbledon Tennis Gained by Miss Jacobs for Fifth Time," *NYT,* July 3, 1936.

241 *"She's got to win"*: HHJ diary, July 4, 1936.

241 *The day before... morals charge*: Marshall Jon Fisher, *A Terrible Splendor: Three Extraordinary Men, a World Poised for War, and the Greatest Tennis Match Ever Played* (New York: Crown, 2009), 181–82.

241 *Helen took the first... at Wimbledon*: HHJ, *Gallery of Champions* (New York: A. S. Barnes and Co., 1949), 51–53.

241 *"made one... ever know"*: W. F. Leysmith, "20,000 Hail U.S. Star as She Ends Long Quest for British Title," *NYT,* July 5, 1936.

241 *"I think... grand training"*: "Ovation Lasts Five Minutes," *NYT,* July 5, 1936.

241–242 *British papers... American ambassador*: RWB scrapbook 1935–1937, AP.

242 *"so excited"*: unidentified newspaper article, 1936 scrapbook, HHJ-ITHFM.

242 *"that she doesn't... stroke"*: Ibid.

242 *"two girls are almost inseparable"*: Ibid.

242 *Helen fought... Ambassador Bingham*: HHJ diary, March 3, 1936.

242 *She landed on the cover of* Time: "Favorite at Forest Hills," *Time,* September 14, 1936.

242 *"Can't bear... for weeks"*: HHJ diary, September 25, 1936.

242 *"in [a] state . . . uncomfortable, unkind"*: HHJ diary, October 2, 1936.
242 *"some attractive creature"*: HHJ diary, October 11, 1936.
242–243 *"a speeding black . . . in love with her"*: *RT,* 219.
243 *"rebuffed him"*: MCB oral history.
243 *The couple celebrated . . . staff*: HHJ diary, November 3, 1936.
243 *The ambassador remained . . . back quickly*: RWB to HHJ, October 6, 1936, HHJ-ITHFM.
243 HENRIETTA-HELEN: HHJ and HWB to RWB, November 8, 1936, RWB-LOC.
243 *"grave reason . . . between them"*: RWB to FDR, September 4, 1936, in *RWB,* 169.
243 *FDR asked . . . by mid-1937*: *RWB,* 180.
244 *"wonderful support and comfort"*: GBB to RWB, November 19, 1936, RWB-LOC.
244 *At the height of the crisis . . . hospital*: MCB oral history; *BB,* 81–82.
244 ISN'T IT GRAND . . . LOVE BARRY: GBB to HWB, AP.
244 *"place is there . . . me nuts"*: HHJ diary, January 27, 1937.
244 *"to keep me company . . . became the dog love"*: HHJ to Susan E. Tifft, August 6, 1986, courtesy Alex S. Jones.
244–245 *By the time . . . only briefly*: *Encyclopedia of Louisville,* 296–97.
245 *"Packing, packing . . . just like it"*: HHJ diary, March 20, 1937.
245 *A crowd of . . . high window*: HHJ diary, May 2 and 6, 1937.
245 *"people who regard . . . argument of force"*: "Victory in Arms Race Seen by American Ambassador," *NYT,* July 6, 1937. The Nazi-controlled *Deutsche Allgemeine Zeitung* denounced the remarks as "agitational," *NYT,* July 7, 1937.
245 *"my chick"*: HHJ diary, May 15, 1937.
245 *"bloody dictators"*: *RWB,* 191.
245–246 *The day the* Aquitania *. . . from the dock*: HHJ diary July 26, 1937.
246 *For months . . . medical consultations*: *Ceylon Observer,* September 17, 1937, RWB scrapbook 1935–1937, AP, and HHJ diary, May 19 and August 25, 1937.
246 *Reversing his plan . . . Courier-Journal and Times Company*: Estate Planning Corporation memorandum, May 1937, AP; *Patriarch,* 150; *RWB,* 188.
246 *"knock out the trouble"*: *RWB,* 193.
246 *It was riddled . . . weight loss*: RWB autopsy report, December 18, 1937, RWB-ADD-FHS.
247 *The news appeared . . . The New York Times*: "R. W. Bingham, Ambassador, Dies," *NYT,* December 19, 1937.
247 *"1937 Year Papa . . . talk to him"*: HHJ diary, 1937.

16. MY NERVES ARE BAD TONIGHT

248 *"My nerves are bad tonight"*: T. S. Eliot, "The Wasteland" (1922).
248 *"overfunctioning"*: *NYT,* October 28, 1935, in Faderman, *Odd Girls and Twilight Lovers,* 100.
248 *Female athletes . . . negative innuendo*: Susan K. Kahn, *Coming On Strong: Gender and Sexuality in Twentieth-Century Women's Sport* (Cambridge: Harvard University Press, 1994), 47, 164–84.

248 *New York City . . . "into hiding"*: George Chauncey, *Gay New York: Gender, Urban Culture, and the Making of the Gay Male World, 1890–1940* (New York: Basic Books, 1994), 331–54, 8–9.

249 *Many in the gay . . . of homosexuality*: Justin Spring, *Secret Historian: The Life and Times of Samuel Steward, Professor, Tattoo Artist, and Sexual Renegade* (New York: Farrar, Straus and Giroux, 2010), xi.

249 *"highly emotional"*: HHJ to Susan E. Tifft, August 24, 1987, courtesy Alex S. Jones.

249 *"the loveliest . . . gave a father"*: RWB to HWB, November 12, 1922, AP.

249 *"You have deep . . . Father's daughter"*: Ivor Churchill to HWB, December 17, 1937, SBP-Duke.

249 *"get used to his being gone"*: HHJ diary, January 16, 1938.

250 *"misery when . . . no solution"*: Ibid.

250 *"Nothing but . . . are limited"*: HHJ diary, March 23, 1938.

250 *In the spring of 1938 . . . sideboard*: Inventory of HWB possessions, August 14, 1968, SBP-Duke.

250 *Hats, gloves, and woolen . . . forgotten*: Inventory of HWB trunks, January 6, 2009, AP.

252 *Nineteen thirty-eight was not . . . to sell*: undated memorandum, L.B. [Lisle Baker] to GBB, MCB-FHS.

252 *"really stay at the house"*: GBB to MCB, March 7, 1939, MCB-FHS.

252 *He named her treasurer . . . Corporation*: "Bingham, Henrietta W.," *Carron's Directory of the City of Louisville*, 1938, 1939, 1940, 1941, 1942 (1943–45 no publication).

253 *"queer"*: HHJ diary, January 21, 1938.

253 *Aleen . . . difficult to bear*: HHJ diary, January 20 and February 3, 1938.

253 *Her braininess . . . perhaps immoral*: MCB oral history and GBB to MCB, April 19, 1943, MCB-FHS.

253 *Dull evenings . . . often drunk*: HHJ diary, February 5, 25, and 27, 1938.

253 *Its release . . . went missing*: HHJ diary, February 5, 1938.

253 *But in New York . . . Dorothy Parker*: HHJ diary, March 16, 1938.

253 *"tremendous curiosity"*: MCB oral history.

253–254 *Gossip held . . . in their district*: Jack Kersey, oral history with Cate Fosl, January 15, 2006, courtesy Cate Fosl.

254 *While riding . . . "short of scandal"*: Wade Hall, e-mail with author, March 27, 2008.

254 *"weeks and months"*: MCB oral history.

254 *"pornographic Jewish specialty"*: *NYT*, June 5, 1938.

254 *She trained . . . "fairy" ways*: Frank Deford, *Big Bill Tilden: The Triumphs and the Tragedy* (1975; Toronto: Sport Classics Books, 2004), 174–85.

254 *"Kentucky love"*: HHJ diary, May 22, 1938.

254 *"Everything is an effort"*: HHJ diary, March 30, 1938.

254 *"close friends for a number of years"*: "Helen Jacobs Discloses Her Authorship of Novel," *NYT*, April 8, 1938.

254 PLEASE REMEMBER . . . ALL LOVE: HWB to HHJ, July 2, 1938, HHJ-ITHFM.

277 *"Miss Henrietta . . . Hominy Landing Farm"*: *NYT*, September 24, 1950.
277 *The buyer . . . another embarrassment*: "Two Country Clubs Will Arise," *CJ*, April 19, 1953; "Group to Get 200 Acres Nov. 20 for Its Club," *CJ*, November 10, 1953. She received some $135,000 for property the purchaser sold for $240,000 (undated financial notes, Henrietta Bingham file, MCB-FHS).
277 *"acute toxic psychosis"*: William Hall Lewis, Jr., M.D., to GBB, March 1, 1954, MCB-FHS. He was summarizing the previous twelve months.
277 *"for the first time . . . could be obtained"*: Ibid.
277 *When Barry arrived . . . institution*: GBB to Robert, October 5, 1953, MCB-FHS.
277 *"I am goddamned . . . she can"*: MKC to DG, November 2, 1953, GFP-NWUL.
278 *"social activities in London"*: William Hall Lewis, Jr., M.D., to GBB, March 1, 1954, MCB-FHS.
278 *"tension-relieving brain operation"*: *Time*, June 30, 1947.
278 *"haunting fear . . . permanent confinement"*: William Hall Lewis, Jr., M.D., to GBB, June 23, 1964, MCB-FHS.
278 *"Henrietta's Wedding"*: Barry Bingham interview, AP.
279 *"barkeep"*: MCB oral history, AP.
279 *"head-waiter"*: MKC to DG, April 10, 1954, GFP-NWUL.
279 *"whatever his name was"*: Sallie Bingham interview, December 13, 2005, and e-mail with Sallie Bingham, November 4, 2013.
279 *fishmonger on Fulton Street*: Barry Bingham, Jr., interview, AP.
279 *"gushing like a school girl"*: MKC to DG, April 10, 1954, GFP-NWUL.
280 *reception that Katharine Cornell . . . for the couple*: Martin C. Shallenberger, Jr., conversation with author. See Lesley Ferris, "Kit and Guth: A Lavender Marriage on Broadway," in *Passing Performances: Queer Readings of Leading Players in American Theater History*, ed. Robert A. Schanke and Kim Marra (Ann Arbor: University of Michigan Press, 1998), 197–220.
280 *"Dearest Minnie . . . our experience"*: JH to MKC, May 16, 1954, MCK-SSC.
280 *"married a gay guy"*: Thelma Barrington interview, October 4, 2007, AP.
280 *McKenzie departed . . . four years later*: MKC to DG, November 25, 1954, GFP-NWUL; A. C. Franks to Dwight W. Fanton, December 27, 1954, MCB-FHS; Beth L. Love, *Fairfield and Southport in Vintage Postcards* (Charleston, S.C.: Arcadia Publishing, 2000); Judgment, *Henrietta Bingham McKenzie vs. Benjamin Franklin McKenzie*, December 3, 1958, County of Fairfield, Ct., vol. 60, p. 521.
280–281 *"unchanged . . . scene in 1923"*: DG to MKC, March 5, 1959, Berg-NYPL.
281 *"painful beyond belief," a "crashing boor"*: MKC to DG, July 26, 1955, GFP-NWUL.
281 *"back a thousand . . . think about"*: MKC to DG, August 15, 1955, GFP-NWUL.
281 *David found her . . . "where we were going"*: DG to MKC, August 11, 1955, Berg-NYPL.
281 *"goblet . . . Edward VII"*: Ibid.
282 *Ernest Jones . . . for a week*: MKC to DG, March 8, 1956, GFP-NWUL.
282 *"nihilistic"*: MCB to GBB, December 16, 1942, MCB-FHS.
282 *"apart and never . . . together again"*: MCB oral history, AP.

283 *"beautiful faces . . . to grace"*: John Fothergill, *An Innkeeper's Diary* (1931; London: Faber and Faber, 1987), 163.

283 *"in the slightest," "her voice the same rich low bellow"*: diary entry, March 22, 1959, *The Diaries of Sylvia Townsend Warner*, ed. Claire Harman (London: Virago Press, 1994), 257.

283 *"con amore"*: Ibid.

284 *"being the unwilling witness . . . own personality"*: F. Scott Fitzgerald, "Pasting It Together," *Esquire*, March 1936, reprinted in *The Crack-Up* (1945; New York: New Directions, 2009), 76.

284 *"a veritable pharmaceutical establishment"*: GBB to Bill [William Hall Lewis, Jr., M.D.], January 11, 1956, MCB-FHS.

284 *Pharmaceuticals have their own cold poetry*: for the context Henrietta's drug use, see "Medicine: What the Doctor Ordered," *Time*, August 18, 1952; "Psychology: What Tranquilizers Have Done," *Time*, April 24, 1964; Andrea Tone, *The Age of Anxiety: A History of America's Turbulent Affair with Tranquilizers* (New York: Basic Books, 2008).

284 *"at her very best . . . not completed"*: Chistine Martin to GBB December 11, 1967, MCB-FHS.

286 *An autopsy . . . gastric ulcer*: James R. Lisa, MD, to GBB, June 20, 1968, and William Hall Lewis to GBB, July 8, 1968, MCB-FHS.

286 *But each January . . . Henrietta's grave*: Patriarch, 320.

286 *A friend watched . . . a biographer*: "These past two evenings she has been tearing and burning letters from [St. Exupéry's translator] Lewis Galantière and others. Some feel of social history, but she doesn't want anyone to read them. How very odd for a biographer to do this—and how selfish." Leo Lerman journal entry, September 5, 1965, in Pascal, *Grand Surprise*, 278.

The bulk of Mina's papers went to the Sophia Smith Collection. She also donated Bloomsbury-related correspondence to the New York Public Library. This group curiously included several letters from David Garnett to Henrietta, which Mina probably obtained from Henrietta in the 1950s, when she made the gift. She placed letters from Ernest Jones with the Freud Archive at the Library of Congress and her own literary correspondence at Yale. She burned a great deal, too. Mina so thoroughly scrubbed her correspondence with her brother Lincoln that his homosexuality never arises in the letters she gave the New York Public Library for the Performing Arts. But Lincoln Kirstein's diaries reflect his sister's involvement in this aspect of his life. "Mina said that analysis was the only way out which bored me a great deal. I hate the idea and at present I have no desire to change. She said eventually I would get myself into such a mess that I would want to. I feel that if I was completely heterosexual I would lose a great deal of intensity . . . she insists that I will lose nothing and gain everything . . . she also says I'm more hideous than ever." LK diary, December 13, 1927, box 1, LKP-NYPL.

286 *the Sports Writers Guild . . . Billie Jean King*: *NYT*, September 7, 1968.

287 *By the time . . . a boom*: Jane Hill, *The Art of Dora Carrington*, 7–8.

287 *"polymorphous"*: Malcolm Lawrence, "Interview with Christopher Hampton," November 1995, http://www.towerofbabel.com/sections/film/cinemastardust /hampton.htm, accessed July 1, 2014.
288 *Barry spent a small . . . claims of others*: MEM.

POSTSCRIPT: EXTANT

289 *"the rules they live by"*: Edward R. Murrow, "This I Believe," 1951, http://www .npr.org/thisibelieve/murrow_transcript.html, accessed July 1, 2014.
289 *"cast . . . into outer darkness"*: GBB, http://thisibelieve.org/essay/16375/, accessed July 1, 2014.
290 *"generation of Americans . . . perfect freedom"*: Ibid.
290 *"ambitious, unbridled creature"*: GBB and HWB, "Shadows," AP.
290 *"Henrietta used . . . what she wanted"*: Sallie Bingham interview, December 13, 2005, AP; e-mail with Sallie Bingham, July 14, 2009.
290 *"When she was in a room . . . you knew it"*: Albert interview.
290 *"oddities"*: JH to HWB, March 12, 1926, AP; Nabokov, *Speak, Memory: An Auto-biography Revisited* (1951; New York: Vintage, 1989), 258.
291 *"was, you know, an invert"*: MCB oral history, AP.
291 *"two frankly erotic . . . unselfconscious stance"*: Hill, *The Art of Dora Carrington*, 100; Charles Whaley, "Dora Carrington: A Bloomsbury Artist in Bloom," *CJ*, June 10, 1995.
291 *"Wish I could figure my Nat out"*: HHJ diary, May 1, 1939.
291–292 *"Prudence dictated . . . as possible"*: John D'Emilio, *Sexual Politics, Sexual Communities: The Making of a Homosexual Minority in the United States, 1940–1970* (Chicago: University of Chicago Press, 1983), 20. An aspiring professor writing in 1934 of his homosexuality conceded it would be "romantic and defiant" to announce "to the world what one is . . . It is one way of solving the original difficulty—by creating thirty subsequent ones." Spring, *Secret Historian*, 28.

ACKNOWLEDGMENTS

So many people have assisted and encouraged my long pursuit of Henrietta Bingham. I couldn't have and wouldn't have started work on this book were it not for family members who shared recollections and items from the past. I am so grateful for their unstinting support and for the interest they have shown in my work. The throwaway comment of my late grandmother, Mary Bingham, about Henrietta being an invert first got me thinking about my great-aunt; this was but one of the intellectual gifts she bestowed on me. The oral history she took the trouble to share with me provided a foundation for understanding Bingham family dynamics. Eleanor Bingham Miller's meticulous preservation of Barry and Mary's possessions (photographs, books, and un-archived letters and papers) made it possible to create and illustrate this narrative. It helped immeasurably that Sallie Bingham was thoughtful enough to keep the scattering of photographs and papers that remained in Henrietta's New York City apartment when she cleaned it out in 1968, and that Edie Bingham took such care with the contents of Melcombe, for both yielded treasures too numerous to count. Joan Bingham shared correspondence and a link to Marie Brenner. Nancy Newhouse passed on items relating to Henrietta kept by Michael Iovenko. Molly Bingham made available early family movies and stills. I feel very blessed that my father was honest (even belatedly) about his upsetting experiences with his aunt. As he couldn't fully grasp why I was going down the Henrietta rabbit hole, his tip about the trunk in the attic was especially generous.

A host of professionals made it possible to access the Henrietta most of my family had not known. With her deep knowledge of the Bloomsbury Group, Sue Fox turned up rich information in England and the United States about that part of Henrietta's story. She was also a warm and thoughtful sounding board over the years. Regan Wann and Barrett Bell supplied valuable additional assistance. The constant and intelligent support of Debby Hurst and Debbie Coleman kept me afloat throughout.

Archivists on both sides of the Atlantic made my research possible and often delightful, too. I especially appreciate the sustained support from the Sophia Smith Collection. Burd Schlesinger, who processed the Papers of Mina Kirstein Curtiss, tipped me off to the ties between Mina and my family. Sherrill Redmon extended an early research grant, and both Karen Kukil and Nanci Young provided answers to scores of questions over the years. At Louisville's Filson Historical Society I benefited from Jim Holmberg's deep familiarity with the various Bingham archives and from Michael Veach and Heather Stone's frequent assistance. The University of Louisville graciously extended borrowing privileges that enabled my research, and the archivists Tom Owen and Delinda Buie were invariably helpful. I am grateful to Nicole Markham and Joanie Agler of the International Tennis Hall of Fame—if they hadn't opened Helen Jacobs's locked diaries, I might have had to break out the hairpins! Special thanks to Ken Robinson, Allie Dillon, and Joannne Halford of London's Institute of Psychoanalysis, Laura Micham of the David M. Rubenstein Rare Book and Manuscript Library at Duke University, and Patricia McGuire and Elizabeth Ennion of the King's College Archive Centre.

A host of scholars and laypeople also helped me flesh out Henrietta's life and times. I am greatly indebted to Alex S. Jones and the late Susan E. Tifft for sharing their research. Samuel W. Thomas kept everything, including copies of letters from Judge Bingham to Henrietta. (The originals were evidently discarded.) Cate Fosl, Mark Davis, David Michaelis, Walter E. Campbell, Martin Duberman, Daniel Aaron, Stephen Pascal, William E. Ellis, Gretchen Gerzina, Selina Hastings, Paul Levy, Michael Holroyd, Perry Meisel, Simon Watney, Anne Chisholm, Tony Bradshaw, Oliver Garnett, Henrietta Garnett, and Richard and Jane Garnett added to my understanding of the Henrietta puzzle. For oral history, family records, and local stories, warmest thanks to Sarah McNeal Few, Martin Shallenberger, J. Royden Peabody, Jr., J. Walker Stites, III, Charles Whaley, Lynne Robbins Knox, Jack Kersey and Thelma Barington, Sean Sweeney, Wade Hall, Betty Chilton, and Elizabeth Valentine.

A number of friends have been readers and guides since I decided, in 2008, to "do something about Henrietta Bingham": Leah Hagedorn, Keith Runyon, Martha Sherrill, Bill Powers, Heather Kleisner, Wayne Winterrowd, Joe Eck, Alice Gray Stites, and Clara Bingham. I hope each of you realizes how much it has meant to me.

How fortunate that a publisher saw Henrietta Bingham's potential. The gifted editor Thomas LeBien took a chance on this book and, following his departure, Courtney Hodell and Christopher Richards made it something artful and whole. The production editor, Delia Casa, patiently guided it on its path to publication. At many junctures, Jonathan Galassi's encouragement enabled me to press ahead.

Cason, Henrietta, and Jim have cheered me on from start to finish and given great joy along the way. There are no words for Stephen Reily's support for this production. My abiding love and the family we build together are my best thanks.

INDEX

ILLUSTRATION CREDITS

224 Helen Hull Jacobs by Dorothy Wilding, 1935 (© National Portrait Gallery)
229 Henrietta Bingham by Dorothy Wilding, circa 1935 (family collection)
232 Helen on Henrietta's hunter Stinger, with Aleen and "Pa" at Long Crendon, 1935 (family collection)
251 Henrietta Bingham with one of her broodmares at Harmony Landing Farm, Kentucky (Mina Kirstein Curtiss Papers, Sophia Smith Collection, Smith College, Northampton, Massachusetts)
252 Henrietta with her nephew Worth, on Jubilee (family collection)
262 Henrietta in American Women's Voluntary Services uniform, 1943 (family collection)
263 Henrietta plowing by mule, Harmony Landing (family collection)
272 Mina Curtiss, Chapelbrook, 1950s (Mina Kirstein Curtiss Papers, Sophia Smith Collection, Smith College, Northampton, Massachusetts)
274 Henrietta's glass painting of Dorothie Bigelow Holland (courtesy Sallie Bingham)
279 Newlyweds Benjamin Franklin McKenzie and Henrietta, with Barry, Dorothie, and an unidentified guest, 1954 (family collection)
282 Henrietta's Kodachrome of the Spread Eagle Inn, 1957 (family collection)
285 Henrietta's shopping list, 1960s (family collection)
293 Trunk, open (photo by Sarah Lyon)

9 780374 536190